Limits of Legality

Limits of Legality
The Ethics of Lawless Judging

Jeffrey Brand-Ballard

2010

Oxford University Press, Inc., publishes works that further
Oxford University's objective of excellence
in research, scholarship, and education.

Oxford   New York
Auckland   Cape Town   Dar es Salaam   Hong Kong   Karachi
Kuala Lumpur   Madrid   Melbourne   Mexico City   Nairobi
New Delhi   Shanghai   Taipei   Toronto

With offices in
Argentina   Austria   Brazil   Chile   Czech Republic   France   Greece
Guatemala   Hungary   Italy   Japan   Poland   Portugal   Singapore
South Korea   Switzerland   Thailand   Turkey   Ukraine   Vietnam

Copyright © 2010 by Oxford University Press, Inc.

Published by Oxford University Press, Inc.
198 Madison Avenue, New York, New York 10016

www.oup.com

Oxford is a registered trademark of Oxford University Press.

All rights reserved. No part of this publication may be reproduced,
stored in a retrieval system, or transmitted, in any form or by any means,
electronic, mechanical, photocopying, recording, or otherwise,
without the prior permission of Oxford University Press.

Library of Congress Cataloging-in-Publication Data
Brand-Ballard, Jeffrey.
Limits of legality: the ethics of lawless judging / Jeffrey Brand-Ballard.
   p.   cm.
ISBN 978-0-19-534229-1 (alk. paper)
1. Judicial ethics—United States. 2. Judicial corruption—United States.
3. Rule of law—United States. I. Title.
KK8779.B73   2010
174'.3—dc22   2010007430

9 8 7 6 5 4 3 2 1

Printed in the United States of America
on acid-free paper

For my magnificent parents, Gabriella and Donald
Only this lifetime, but enough love for many

Acknowledgments

This book was conceived and written during my junior years in the Department of Philosophy at George Washington University, where I have worked with many fine people. I am especially grateful to my full-time colleagues: Peter Caws, R. Paul Churchill, David DeGrazia, Michèle Friend, William Griffith, Eric Saidel, Gail Weiss, and Tadeusz Zawidzki. In one way or another each of them has supported me—in all my endeavors, at every opportunity. Several have made specific contributions to this book by attending colloquia and responding insightfully to my arguments. For these contributions I thank Paul, David, Michèle, Bill, Eric, and my former colleagues Ilya Farber and John Rudisill.

Paul, Bill, and David have served successively as chairs of the department since I joined it. I thank Paul for welcoming me into the department with open arms and for keeping them wide open ever since. Bill reached out to me before I had even arrived. For seven years he has inspired me with his intellect, sound judgment, work ethic, sense of fair play, and devotion to our calling. David's example of productivity, moral courage, and high scholarly standards would make him an intimidating colleague were he not also such a marvelous person. I doubt I could have published this book without his wisdom.

I tested arguments from part II at various professional conferences. These included three annual meetings of the American Philosophical Association: Central Division (Chicago, 2005) and Pacific Division (Pasadena, 2004; San Francisco, 2005). Other venues for these papers included the Association for Practical and Professional Ethics (Cincinnati, 2004; San Antonio, 2005), the Midwest Political Science Association (Chicago, 2004), and the Australian Society for Legal Philosophy (Melbourne, 2004). I received useful feedback at these events, particularly from Jim Evans, Jeff Goldsworthy, and David Lefkowitz. I am especially grateful to my APA commentators: Larry Alexander, Alan H. Goldman, and Kenneth Einar Himma. Ken's combination of astute observations and gushing were just what I needed to hear. His kindness gave me confidence in the project. So did Larry and Alan, both of whom I now proudly call friends. By agreeing to serve as commentators, these two senior scholars drew attention to an unknown philosopher who was criticizing their work. They gently showed me where I was wrong and graciously conceded the minor points that I had right. Despite disagreeing with me, they have encouraged my efforts ever since.

I am also grateful for several speaking invitations. I was honored to deliver some material from part I as the 2007 Constitution Day Lecture at the College of Wooster (Ohio). I thank John Rudisill for suggesting my name and for his hospitality. In 2008, I discussed role morality with the Joint Bioethics Colloquium of the National Institutes of Health. Thanks to Dr. Ezekiel Emanuel, chair of the Department of Bioethics, for inviting me to lead the session.

Also in 2008, I was invited to present a version of chapter 6 at a conference celebrating twenty years of the Brazilian constitution, held at the Federal University of Rio de Janeiro. This invitation became a speaking tour that included Fundação Getulio Vargas Law School, the School of Federal Magistrates, and Pontific Catholic University Law School (all in São Paulo), the University of São Paulo Law School, the Rio Branco Institute, and the Department of Philosophy at the University of Brasilia. Presenting my ideas to Brazilian audiences, whose language I do not speak and whose legal system I did not understand, was an unforgettable experience. I owe it all to the initiative and generosity of Noël Struchiner, who took an interest in my research, and to a U.S. Speaker and Specialist Grant from the Department of State, Bureau of International Information Programs. Thanks to Karla Carneiro, Marcos Hirata, and Carla Waehneldt for welcoming me to their cities.

The philosophy and political science faculties at Vassar College inspired my love of theory and my curiosity about public affairs but I owe anything I know about practical philosophy to my teachers at the University of Michigan. They included Allan Gibbard, Donald Regan, J. David Velleman, and especially my dissertation supervisors: Elizabeth Anderson, Stephen Darwall, and Peter Railton. Without the tutelage of these remarkable philosophers, I would not even know how to read the texts that have engaged me since leaving Ann Arbor. I also learned from many graduate students at Michigan, notably Craig Duncan, Christina Frohock, Nadeem Hussain, Tim Schoettle, Nishi Shah, Chris Roberson, and Michael Weber.

For my legal education I thank the law faculties at Michigan and Yale and the lawyers who supervised me at the scrappy Chicago firm known, when I last worked there, as Abrahamson Vorachek & Mikva.

My editor at Oxford University Press, Peter Ohlin, has always treated me like a valued author rather than a lapse in judgment. His expertise has been most useful. I am grateful to several anonymous reviewers, including two readers of the book proposal for Oxford and one reviewer of the final manuscript. Their comments greatly improved the book, although some of their criticisms were too difficult for me to answer.

The George Washington University provided research funds in the form of a University Facilitating Fellowship and a Junior Scholar Incentive Award. Section 11.7 contains material from my doctoral dissertation, completed with fellowship support from the Andrew W. Mellon Foundation and the Horace H. Rackham School of Graduate Studies. Thanks to

Acknowledgments

the Doris Ulmann Galleries of Berea College for providing access to the cover painting on affordable terms, and to Tina McCalment and Lisa Kriner for working fast. Special gratitude goes to my friends from the Department of Philosophy and Religious Studies at the University of Wisconsin—Eau Claire, including the late Richard deGrood, for their faith in me and for fond memories.

I owe the most to my family: my parents, Donald and Gabriella Brand, to whom I dedicate the book; my beloved brother and friend for life, Thomas; my stepmother, Catherine; my stepfather, Douglas Peary; and Rebecca Rosenbaum. My daughter, Maresca, entertained her little brother, Quentin, at critical times with few complaints. Quentin often agreed to sit on my lap while I typed.

My wife, Laura, reviewed several drafts under great time pressure. She has my eternal love, gratitude, and admiration—for this and for everything else.

I found a helpful and enthusiastic audience in the Department of Philosophy at the Virginia Polytechnic Institute and State University in November 2006, a few months before a tragedy occurred on that campus. A portion of the royalties from the sale of this book will be donated to the Virginia Tech Hokie Spirit Memorial Fund: http://www.vt.edu/fund/.

I, alone, am responsible for all remaining defects and errors in this book. No one else should be assumed to agree with any of it.

Contents

PART I

1. Introduction, 3
2. Practical Reasons and Judicial Use of Force, 19
3. Deviating from Legal Standards, 35
4. The Legal Duties of Judges, 56
5. The Normative Classification of Legal Results, 74
6. Reasons to Deviate, 92
7. Adherence Rules, 111
8. Obeying Adherence Rules, 123
9. The Judicial Oath, 142
10. Legal Duty and Political Obligation, 157

PART II

11. Systemic Effects, 181
12. Agent-Relative Principles, 202
13. Optimal Adherence Rules, 212
14. Guidance Rules, 233
15. Treating Like Cases Alike, 253
16. Implementation, 270
17. Theoretical Implications, 292
18. Conclusion, 308

List of Authorities, 315
Bibliography, 319
Index, 339

Part I

1

Introduction

1.1 WHEN JUDGES DISREGARD THE LAW

Mrs. Russell has a prescription from her doctor to use marijuana for medical purposes. She grows the plant for personal use in her California home. She is charged with a crime under the federal Controlled Substances Act.[1] Her case comes before a federal district judge. Because California has legalized medical marijuana, her attorney moves for dismissal of the indictment, claiming that Congress has no authority to preempt California's law.[2] However, the U.S. Supreme Court has upheld the application of the act to marijuana possession in California in a very similar case.[3] All informed lawyers are confident that the judge will deny the motion and proceed to trial: the law on this issue is settled.

The judge knows of the Supreme Court decision. He knows that as a trial judge he is expected to follow it. However, he believes that medical marijuana should be legalized. Therefore, he does something surprising: he ignores the law and dismisses the indictment.

What should we say about this judge? One thing is clear: his decision constitutes *legal error*.[4] It could be reversed on appeal.[5] Many would also insist that the judge was *wrong* to make that decision. His conduct seems unprofessional at the least, perhaps incompetent. But did he act immorally or unethically?[6] Is his decision one that he *should not* have made, all things considered? If his action is morally wrong, how wrong is it? Worse

---

1. This is a hypothetical case, facts based loosely on the unreported case appealed in *U.S. v. Alden*, 141 Fed. Appx. 562 (9th Cir. 2005). Attorney General Eric H. Holder, Jr. has since announced that the federal government will no longer raid legitimate growers of medical marijuana. David Johnston and Neil A. Lewis, "Ending Raids of Dispensers of Marijuana for Patients," *New York Times*, Mar. 19, 2009, p. A20.
2. Under the "negative Commerce Clause." U.S. Const., art. I, §8, cl. 18; *Oregon Waste Systems, Inc. v. Department of Environmental Quality*, 511 U.S. 93, 95 (1994).
3. *Gonzales v. Raich*, 545 U.S. 1 (2005).
4. On legal error see, e.g., Harry T. Edwards, "To Err Is Human, But Not Always Harmless: When Should Legal Error Be Tolerated?" *New York University Law Review* 70 (1995): 1167–1213.
5. The prosecution may appeal the dismissal of charges as opposed to an acquittal.
6. I use *unethical* and *immoral* interchangeably, as do many philosophers.

than shoplifting a magazine? Not as bad as pressuring an employee for sexual favors? Should we publicly denounce the judge for his decision? Should he regret it? If he were your son, would you be disappointed in him? These are normative questions, not descriptive or empirical ones. They are questions about *role morality*—the moral rights and duties associated with a particular social role.[7] Asking these questions about judges can teach us about our conception of the rule of law. Our answers may have implications for our practice of praising and blaming judges, and for our standards of judicial selection, oversight, and discipline.

Someone who believes that the federal ban on marijuana, medical or otherwise, serves important social purposes might readily accuse the judge in Mrs. Russell's case of unethical behavior. His decision could weaken the deterrent effect of the Controlled Substances Act and increase marijuana usage. Someone who thinks the state should ban marijuana might conclude that the judge acted unethically, regardless of whether his decision was legally correct.

Of course, many people think the federal act should be revised, as California's laws have been, to legalize medical uses of marijuana.[8] Many proponents of legalization would be tempted to praise judges who refuse to enforce the act. Some proponents would yield to the temptation. Others would resist it. If a legalization proponent accepts a strong principle of judicial fidelity to law, then even he would agree, perhaps reluctantly, that the judge was wrong to dismiss the charges against Mrs. Russell. In Anglo-American legal systems, fidelity entails that inferior courts must follow superior court rulings on matters of law. It also entails many other basic norms of adjudication: trial judges must take all admissible evidence into account; judges must apply recognized sources of law, such as constitutions, legislation, and common-law rules; judges must obey writs of mandamus; courts should pay some deference to their own precedents; et cetera. The conviction that judges are "bound by the law" is very common among lawyers, judges, legal scholars, and members of the general public. In the words of one academic lawyer, "Jurists and legal scholars often seem to regard the judicial obligation to follow statutes as too obvious to require justification."[9] One of the most severe accusations that one

---

7. See, e.g., Arthur Isak Applbaum, *Ethics for Adversaries: The Morality of Roles in Public and Professional Life* (Princeton, N.J.: Princeton University Press, 1999); Michael O. Hardimon, "Role Obligations," *Journal of Philosophy* 91 (1994): 333–63; David Luban, *Lawyers and Justice: An Ethical Study* (Princeton, N.J.: Princeton University Press, 1988), ch. 6; Alan H. Goldman, *The Moral Foundations of Professional Ethics* (Totowa, N.J.: Rowman and Littlefield, 1980).

8. Of course, many support the legalization of marijuana, full stop.

9. Steven D. Smith, "Why Should Courts Obey the Law?" *Georgetown Law Journal* 77 (1988): 113–64, p. 114. See also M. B. E. Smith, "May Judges Ever Nullify the Law?" *Notre Dame Law Review* 74 (1999): 1657–71, p. 1658 ("[The view that] judges are always legally and morally bound to follow the law is undoubtedly the conventional wisdom among legal scholars and laypeople alike").

Introduction

can make against a public official, especially a judge, is that he has not upheld the law in his official capacity. Nevertheless, judges sometimes depart from the law,[10] disregarding either admissible evidence presented or controlling sources of law such as statutes, constitutions, and precedent.[11] When a decision is reversed on appeal, for example, either the lower court or the reversing court has made some kind of legal mistake.[12]

Judges reach legally incorrect results for various reasons. Some reasons, such as negligence and incompetence, are not especially interesting. In the interesting cases judges willfully disregard the law, although they rarely admit it.[13] Corrupt judges seek to profit financially from their decisions, to reward friends or family members, or to settle personal scores. Acting for these reasons violates codes of judicial conduct.[14] It is also morally wrong and blameworthy. Judges are ethically and legally bound to decline bribes. They are bound—ethically, at least—to recuse themselves from cases presenting conflicts of interest. This book largely ignores judges who deviate from the law either inadvertently or for self-serving reasons. I address cases in which judges disapprove of the legally required results as a matter of morality or public policy.[15] They face what Robert Cover calls "moral-formal" dilemmas: conflicts between the law and their moral convictions.[16] Sometimes they decide to misrepresent or disregard the law—a practice known as *judicial nullification*.[17]

---

10. "[J]udges ... sometimes bend or break the rules for the sake of other values, such violations being in fact rather common because detection and sanctioning are difficult." Richard A. Posner, "What Do Judges and Justices Maximize? (The Same Thing Everybody Else Does)," *Supreme Court Economic Review* 3 (1993): 1–41. See also M. B. E. Smith, "Do Appellate Courts Regularly Cheat?" *Criminal Justice Ethics* 16 (1997): 11–20 (arguing that they do). Only someone who denies that the law has any determinate content could deny that judges sometimes get it wrong. See §5.5.1.

11. An analogous phenomenon in administrative law is called *nonacquiescence*—when agencies refuse to follow federal appellate courts. See Samuel Estreicher and Richard L. Revesz, "Nonacquiescence by Federal Administrative Agencies," *Yale Law Journal* 98 (1989): 679–772.

12. Unless the law has changed in the interim at the hands of the legislature, a higher court, or the reversing court itself.

13. But see examples in §3.12.

14. See chapter 4.

15. Various sources of law—public and private—figure in my examples throughout this book. Common law, statutory law, and constitutional law differ in profound ways. There is obviously a world of difference between a lawsuit for breach of contract with $500 in controversy and a constitutional challenge to the death penalty before the Supreme Court of the United States, although both are cases in courts of law. My arguments operate at a level of abstraction that encompasses both. In practice, different sources of law have different functions, so courts should treat them differently.

16. Robert M. Cover, *Justice Accused: Antislavery and the Judicial Process* (New Haven, Conn.: Yale University Press, 1975), pp. 197–225.

17. See, e.g., Smith, "May Judges Ever Nullify the Law?"; Jack B. Weinstein, Comments on Jury Nullification: Proceedings of the Fifty-Third Judicial Conference of the District of Columbia Circuit, 145 F.R.D. 149, 170 (1993) (commenting that "trial judges are, I suppose,

Politicians and commentators often accuse judges of misunderstanding or ignoring the laws they have sworn to uphold.[18] Such accusations are especially common in high-profile constitutional cases. Few are better known than the 2000 case of *Bush v. Gore*, in which the U.S. Supreme Court overruled the Florida Supreme Court and halted the presidential recount under the Equal Protection Clause of the Fourteenth Amendment.[19] Many lawyers condemn that majority opinion as lawless.[20]

Another recent example is *Newdow v. U.S. Congress*, in which the United States Court of Appeals for the Ninth Circuit ruled that inviting public school students to recite the Pledge of Allegiance violates the Establishment Clause of the First Amendment, as the Pledge contains the words "under God."[21] Senator Tom Daschle (D-S.D.) derided the decision as "just nuts,"[22] a sentiment also expressed by many of his fellow legislators.

---

nullifying the guidelines"); Smith, "Why Should Courts Obey the Law?" p. 113; Kent Greenawalt, *Conflicts of Law and Morality* (New York: Oxford University Press, 1987), pp. 367–68; Samuel Estreicher, "Judicial Nullification: Guido Calabresi's Uncommon Common Law for a Statutory Age," *New York University Law Review* 57 (1982): 1126–73. Compare *jury nullification* (jurors disregarding their instructions).

18. See, e.g., Neil S. Siegel, "Why President Bush Should Not Take the 5th; Judges Who Ignore Law are Possible Court Candidates," *Houston Chronicle*, Jun. 17, 2005, p. B11; Thomas Sowell, "Real Judicial Crisis Is Judges Who Ignore the Law," *The Post and Courier* (Charleston, S.C.), Jan. 14, 1998, p. A11; Orrin Hatch and Sam Brownback, "'Extreme' Judicial Activism," *Washington Times*, Feb. 10, 2005, p. A19 (condemning U.S. District Judge Gary Lancaster for "ignor[ing] the law in favor of [his] own agenda"); Stephen B. Bright, "Let's Try Brian Nichols Properly the First Time," *Atlanta Journal-Constitution*, Nov. 7, 2007, p. 19A ("Like it or not, agree or disagree, trial judges must follow the law"); Rachel Graves, "The Terri Schiavo Case; Schiavo Dies, but Debate Lives; DeLay Insists Judges Must 'Answer for their Behavior,'" *Houston Chronicle*, Apr. 1, 2005, p. A1 (in 1997, Rep. Tom DeLay publicly contemplated an impeachment drive against judges whose decisions "ignored existing laws").

19. *Bush v. Gore*, 531 U.S. 98 (2000).

20. See, e.g., Ward Farnsworth, "'To Do a Great Right, Do a Little Wrong': A User's Guide to Judicial Lawlessness," *Minnesota Law Review* 86 (2001): 227–66; Alan M. Dershowitz, *Supreme Injustice: How the High Court Hijacked Election 2000* (Oxford: Oxford University Press, 2001); Cass R. Sunstein and Richard A. Epstein, eds., *The Vote: Bush, Gore, and the Supreme Court* (Chicago: University of Chicago Press, 2001); Michael J. Klarman, "*Bush v. Gore* through the Lens of Constitutional History," *California Law Review* 89 (2001): 1721–65; "Symposium: *Bush v. Gore*," *University of Chicago Law Review* 68 (2001): 613–791; Bruce Ackerman, "Anatomy of a Constitutional Coup," *London Review of Books*, Feb. 8, 2001, p. 3; Ronald Dworkin, "A Badly Flawed Election," *New York Review of Books*, Feb. 8, 2001, p. 1; Jack M. Balkin, "*Bush v. Gore* and the Boundary between Law and Politics," *Yale Law Journal* 110 (2001): 1407–58.

21. *Newdow v. U.S. Congress*, 292 F.2d 597 (9th Cir. 2002), amended by *Newdow v. U.S. Congress*, 328 F.3d 466 (9th Cir. 2003), reversed by *Elk Grove Unified School District v. Newdow* 542 U.S. 1 (2004).

22. Carl Hulse, "Lawmakers Vow to Fight Judges' Ruling on the Pledge," *New York Times*, June 27, 2002, p. A20.

Introduction

In the 2005 case of *Kelo v. City of New London*, the U.S. Supreme Court upheld municipal authority to demolish private residences for the purpose of largely private redevelopment projects.[23] Legal scholar Richard A. Epstein accused the Court of "refusing to look closely at past precedent and constitutional logic."[24] Senator F. James Sensenbrenner, Jr. (R-Wis.), called the ruling "the *Dred Scott* decision of the 21st century."[25]

In addition to criticism, judges accused of disregarding the law are increasingly threatened with reprisals: requests for resignation and threats of impeachment.[26] In 1996, United States District Judge Harold Baer, Jr., suppressed the results of a vehicle search that yielded eighty pounds of cocaine and heroin. The alleged buyers had run off when approached by police officers. Supreme Court precedent at the time held that such evasive behavior generates the "reasonable suspicion" needed for a search under the Fourth Amendment.[27] However, Judge Baer asserted that running from police does *not* necessarily generate reasonable suspicion in neighborhoods where police are widely distrusted.[28] The judge was accused of either misunderstanding the law or knowingly ignoring it. Over 200 members of the U.S. House of Representatives called for his resignation.[29] The Clinton White House stated that it disagreed with Judge Baer's ruling and had not ruled out asking him to resign on account of it.[30] Senate Majority Leader Robert Dole (R-Kan.) proposed impeachment.[31] The judge reversed himself.[32]

I shall not address whether any of these court decisions was, in fact, a legal mistake. Reaching that issue would require a full legal analysis of each case. These are just examples of decisions that reasonable people might *consider* lawless. No one denies that judges sometimes fail to apply

---

23. *Kelo v. City of New London*, 545 U.S. 469 (2005).

24. Richard A. Epstein, "Blind Justices: The Scandal of Kelo v. New London," *Wall Street Journal*, July 3, 2005.

25. David Lightman, "Lawmakers Stand up to Court; Bipartisan Coalition Hopes to Dilute Impact of Eminent Domain Ruling," *Hartford Courant*, July 1, 2005, p. A1. *Dred Scott* is the notorious ruling that returned an escaped slave to his master. *Dred Scott v. Sandford*, 60 U.S. 393 (1857).

26. Elected judges may, of course, lose reelection. In recent years there have also been a handful of disciplinary proceedings against judges for departing from the law. See chapter 4.

27. *United States v. Sokolow*, 490 U.S. 1, 8–9 (1989); *Florida v. Rodriguez*, 469 U.S. 1, 6 (1984) (per curiam); *United States v. Brignoni-Ponce*, 422 U.S. 873, 885 (1975).

28. *United States v. Bayless*, 913 F. Supp. 232 (S.D.N.Y. 1996). In a subsequent case the Supreme Court confirmed that sudden flight creates reasonable suspicion even in high-crime neighborhoods. *Illinois v. Wardlow*, 528 U.S. 119 (2000). The fact that the Court even granted certiorari on this issue might, however, suggest that Judge Baer's decision was not as obviously lawless as his critics claimed.

29. Jon O. Newman, "The Judge Baer Controversy," *Judicature* 80 (1997): 156–64, p. 156.

30. Allison Mitchell, "Clinton Pressing Judge to Relent," *New York Times*, Mar. 22, 1996, p. A1.

31. Katharine Q. Seelye, "A Get-Tough Message at California's Death Row," *New York Times*, Mar. 24, 1996, p. 29.

32. *United States v. Bayless*, 921 F. Supp. 211 (S.D.N.Y. 1996).

the law correctly. My question is this: when, if ever, is it ethically permissible for judges knowingly to promote their own values and policy preferences at the expense of the law?

Many commentators consider decisions that contradict the law to be ethically impermissible by definition. For them "what the law requires" is synonymous with "how the judge ought to decide." Ronald Dworkin suggests that people do not generally accept this as a definitional truth:

> Our lawyers and citizens recognize a difference between the question what the law is and the question whether judges or any other official or citizen should enforce or obey the law. They regard these as separate questions, not only when they have in mind foreign, wicked legal systems . . . but even in considering how citizens and officials in our own communities should behave. The opinion that our judges should sometimes ignore the law and try to replace it with better law is far from a stranger to law school classrooms and even political debates.[33]

Dworkin may be correct that people see two distinct questions, as a conceptual matter, but many believe that judges are nevertheless obligated to enforce the law even when the results are morally objectionable.

1.2 CLEAR CASES AND UNCLEAR CASES

Lawyers have different opinions regarding how much latitude judges should have to avoid morally objectionable results. We must consider cases in which the law is clear as well as those in which it is unclear. Regarding cases in which the law is clear, the most restrictive position is that judges must apply the law correctly, regardless of how unjust the legally required result may be. The least restrictive position is that judges have no moral obligation to reach legally mandated results, even when the law is clear.

Regarding legally unclear cases, the most restrictive position is that judges must endeavor to apply the law correctly, even when it is not clear what the law requires. According to this position, judges must never allow *extralegal* considerations to influence their decisions, even when the law is unclear.[34] The least restrictive position always allows judges to consult extralegal considerations when deciding unclear cases.[35]

Many writers defend unrestrictive positions with respect to unclear cases. Disregarding clear legal mandates is much more controversial, but it has advocates: the natural law tradition is often cited for the principle

---

33. Ronald Dworkin, *Law's Empire* (Cambridge, Mass.: Harvard University Press, 1986), p. 109.
34. See, e.g., Stephen J. Burton, *Judging in Good Faith* (Cambridge: Cambridge University Press, 1992), pp. 243–44.
35. See, e.g., H. L. A. Hart, *The Concept of Law*, 2nd ed. (Oxford: Oxford University Press, 1994), p. 153.

Introduction

that unjust laws do not "bind in conscience."[36] A weaker version holds that courts are not morally obligated to enforce *extremely* unjust laws: those that require returning escaped slaves to their masters, stoning women for adultery, confiscating property because of the owner's religious beliefs, or executing the innocent without due process of law. Even those who reject other precepts of natural law theory might agree that judges are morally permitted to disregard such laws.

In the past century, much has been written about judges who uphold the laws of extremely unjust systems. Robert Cover's classic, *Justice Accused*, takes on nineteen-century judges whose decisions facilitated slavery in the United States.[37] Cases from that era continue to generate important scholarship.[38] David Dyzenhaus's *Hard Cases in Wicked Legal Systems* addresses judges in apartheid South Africa.[39] Equally relevant are discussions of adjudication under fascism, beginning with Gustav Radbruch's accusation that the acceptance of legal positivism by German officials encouraged them to comply blindly with the worst Nazi laws.[40] This issue was taken up by H. L. A. Hart and Lon Fuller in their famous *Harvard Law Review* debate.[41]

The aforementioned literature has drama aplenty. However, the residents of modern democratic republics could easily conclude that these debates have little relevance to their own legal systems, in which the law does not promote such horrors as genocide, slavery, racial apartheid, or religious persecution. Some will suspect that questions about the ethics of lawless judging become interesting only under conditions of extreme injustice. They may assume that under happier conditions, lawless judging is self-evidently unethical, end of story. Few commentators assert that judges are morally permitted to disregard laws that require only moderate, rather than extreme, injustices. This includes commentators who would liberate judges to disregard extremely unjust laws and to base their decisions on extralegal considerations when the law is unclear. As Dworkin notes,

---

36. This principle does not entail the further claim that unjust legislation does not even constitute genuine *law*. I need not consider whether canonical natural lawyers believed the further claim. For discussion see Mark C. Murphy, "Natural Law Jurisprudence," *Legal Theory* 9 (2003): 241–67, pp. 244–45.

37. Cover, *Justice Accused*.

38. See, e.g., Mark A. Graber, *Dred Scott and the Problem of Constitutional Evil* (Cambridge: Cambridge University Press, 2006).

39. David Dyzenhaus, *Hard Cases in Wicked Legal Systems: South African Law in the Perspective of Legal Philosophy* (Oxford: Clarendon Press, 1991).

40. Gustav Radbruch, "Gesetzliches Unrecht und übergesetzliches Recht," *Süddeutsche Juristen-Zeitung* 1 (1946): 105–8. Translated by Bonnie Litschewski Paulson and Stanley L. Paulson, "Statutory Lawlessness and Supra-Statutory Law," *Oxford Journal of Legal Studies* 26 (2006): 1–11.

41. H. L. A. Hart, "Positivism and the Separation of Law and Morals," *Harvard Law Review* 71 (1958): 593–629; Lon L. Fuller, "Positivism and Fidelity to Law: A Reply to Professor Hart," *Harvard Law Review* 71 (1958): 630–72.

We disagree about the exact force law has in certain special circumstances, when there are strong competing considerations of justice. We disagree, perhaps, about what the judges in Massachusetts who were asked to enforce the Fugitive Slave Act before the American Civil War should have done. But we share a general, unspecified opinion about the force of law when such special considerations of justice are not present, when people disagree about the justice or wisdom of legislation, for example, but no one really thinks the law wicked or its authors tyrants. Our different convictions about the force of law unite in such cases. We think the law should be obeyed and enforced . . . .[42]

I agree with Dworkin that "we" think this but I shall argue that "we" are mistaken. I think interesting questions about the ethics of lawless judging arise even in reasonably just legal systems. I shall argue that judges are sometimes ethically permitted to deviate from the law in order to avoid results that are only moderately unjust. Writers have not developed general theories of judicial lawlessness that apply to reasonably just systems.[43]

1.3 ARGUMENTS FOR FIDELITY

Consider again the conclusion that the judge acted wrongly in Mrs. Russell's marijuana possession case. This conclusion could be supported with statements such as the following:

1. The Supreme Court has already upheld the application of the Controlled Substances Act to cases like this. The justices may have been wrong to do so, but they *outrank* district judges.
2. Perhaps the act should be revised, but that *function* belongs to Congress, not to judges.
3. We have *separation of powers* in the United States. Legislators legislate, and judges adjudicate.
4. Judges are supposed to *apply* the law, not make it.
5. The judge's *job* is to follow the law. He is paid to do it.
6. The judge swore an *oath* to uphold the law whether he likes it or not.
7. Everyone *expects* the judge to follow the law. We are all counting on him.
8. A judge is supposed to act as a *professional*. The ethics of his profession—judicial ethics—require him to apply the law.

---

42. Dworkin, *Law's Empire*, p. 111. I do not mean to imply that Dworkin, himself, believes that judges should ever appeal to *extralegal* considerations.

43. There is, however, one substantial body of literature on modern judges facing laws to which they are conscientiously opposed. This literature discusses judges, notably Roman Catholics, whose religious convictions conflict with the law. Some of this literature is useful for my purposes but it focuses on when a judge should recuse himself rather than applying laws to which he has religious objections. The literature on religious judges rarely mentions departing from the law as an acceptable option. See §6.11.

9. If judges refuse to apply laws of which they disapprove, then we will have *anarchy*.
10. By failing to apply the law, the judge damages the *rule of law*—one of our basic political values.

To most readers, especially lawyers, these ten observations will seem like common sense, hardly worth stating. In this book I shall contend that the corresponding arguments are not nearly as conclusive as they are thought to be. It would be misleading, but not literally inaccurate, to state my thesis as follows: judges in courts of law are *not* ethically obligated to apply the law correctly when they decide legal issues. This statement would be misleading because it could imply that judges are ethically licensed to misapply the law as often as they wish, and for any reason whatsoever: laziness, personal profit, dislike for a party, et cetera. As stated, my thesis seems to license irresponsible or corrupt judging. It seems to advocate the destruction of the rule of law and regression to a "government of men" (*sic*) rather than laws. It appears to commend the annihilation of law itself, perhaps even a world without order.

These are not my intentions. Once the terms of my thesis are carefully defined it has none of these implications. Even properly understood, however, it remains an unorthodox thesis with some surprising lessons.

1.4 MODIFYING PRECEDENT

I hope you are reassured that my thesis will not be utterly outrageous. It is, however, unusual. It should not be confused with some commonplace claims about legal precedent. Courts often modify their own precedents and those of courts at the same level in the judiciary hierarchy—*horizontal precedents*—including doctrines of the common law and prior interpretations of statutes and constitutions.[44] Mainstream legal scholars agree that judges are legally permitted to do so.[45] Understanding the scope of my thesis requires distinguishing between the law *simpliciter* and particular legal standards. If a judge has legal authority to modify a horizontal precedent before applying it, then he does not deviate from the law *simpliciter* in so doing. Nor does modifying horizontal precedent necessarily constitute a failure of judicial craft, much less an ethical failure. In fact, such modifications are often seen as excellent judging and as ethically sound. Commentators merely disagree about the conditions under which judges should modify horizontal precedent.[46]

---

44. Lewis A. Kornhauser, "Adjudication by a Resource-Constrained Team: Hierarchy and Precedent in a Judicial System," *Southern California Law Review* 68 (1995): 1605–29, p. 1608 (distinguishing horizontal and vertical precedents).

45. See many scholars cited in Larry Alexander, "Constrained by Precedent," *Southern California Law Review* 63 (1989): 1–64.

46. A few writers believe that judges should never modify precedents. Although I disagree with them, my objective in this book is not to challenge them directly. I am addressing

This book may, incidentally, reinforce the common view that judges are morally permitted to modify horizontal precedent, but my central topic and thesis are much broader. I am interested in decisions in which courts depart from the law *simpliciter*—cases of deviation from the legally correct result as determined by *all* applicable legal standards. These are cases in which the judge either lacks legal authority to modify the applicable standards or else declines to exercise that authority, if he has it, while still departing from the law. The trial judge who dismisses the charges against Mrs. Russell contradicts appellate precedent—*vertical* precedent—without distinguishing the case.

The conventional wisdom is that such nonacquiescence is wrong, but even state courts occasionally disregard vertical precedent[47] or entertain the possibility of doing so. In 2005, Justice Tom Parker of the Alabama Supreme Court wrote an extraordinary open letter to his fellow justices.[48] He urged them to defy a recent decision of the United States Supreme Court that banned the death penalty for murderers who were younger than eighteen when they committed the crime.[49] Parker's extremely unusual choice to openly advocate defiance was condemned even by some who agreed with him about the death penalty.[50] Decisions that deviate from vertical precedent are almost universally regarded as unlawful.[51] My question is, when are they also unethical?

1.5 WHY DEFEND JUDICIAL DEVIATION FROM THE LAW?

Instead of questioning the judicial duty to follow the law, the standard response of lawyers who disapprove of a result is to argue that the judge *misunderstood* or *misapplied* the law. The language in judicial opinions often implies that the law left the judge no choice but to reach a certain result.[52] The critic claims that the law was less clear or less rigid than the judge

---

the mainstream. See, e.g., Jeremy Bentham, *A Fragment on Government*, eds. J. H. Burns and H. L. A. Hart (Cambridge: Cambridge University Press, 1988), pp. 19–20. Even some writers who believe that courts must treat precedents as rules agree that they may sometimes modify them. Alexander, "Constrained by Precedent," pp. 51–52.

47. One writer has recently urged us to notice that "[e]very so often . . . state courts actively disregard binding Supreme Court precedent," notwithstanding the conventional wisdom that such deviation is utterly inappropriate. Frederic M. Bloom, "State Courts Unbound," *Cornell Law Review* 93 (2008): 501–54, p. 503.

48. Tom Parker, "Alabama Justices Surrender to Judicial Activism," *Birmingham (Ala.) News*, Jan. 1, 2005, p. 4B.

49. Ibid. The decision criticized is *Roper v. Simmons*, 543 U.S. 551 (2005).

50. Phillip Rawls, "Parker 'Attack' Irks Fellow State Justice," *Huntsville (Ala.) Times*, Jan. 16, 2006, p. 2B.

51. Bloom, "State Courts Unbound," pp. 502–3.

52. In the words of Judge Wald, "while judges still typically write as if they were absolutely certain about the rightness and soundness of their analysis and decisions, everyone (including the judges) knows that's not necessarily the case." Patricia M. Wald, "The Rhetoric

represented it to be. She argues that in such unclear cases judges are legally and ethically permitted to invoke extralegal considerations—considerations of morality, fairness, justice, and public policy. In this case, of course, these considerations support her favored result. She insists that it was permissible, both legally and ethically, for the judge to reach that result.

Many people appear to believe that the law always, or almost always, allows the court to reach results of which they approve, either because it clearly favors those results or because it is unclear enough to permit them. They will think it unnecessary and unnecessarily difficult to defend, as I do, the moral right of judges to disregard the law. I have no quarrel with writers who take the more cautious approach, defending the permissibility of invoking extralegal considerations in legally unclear cases without insisting that judges have the right to disregard clear legal mandates. However, I choose to defend the more difficult position—that judges sometimes have the moral right, and moral reasons, to disregard clear legal mandates, and not only when the law is extremely unjust. I have several reasons for defending this unusual position. My first reason is simply that I think there is a plausible argument for my conclusion. This argument is quite interesting whether or not it serves any practical purpose.

My second reason is that the more difficult position is also the more logically fundamental. If judges have the right to disregard clear legal mandates, then it stands to reason that they also have the right to invoke extralegal considerations when the law is unclear. Defending departures from clear laws is like running a marathon. After that, defending the use of extralegal considerations in unclear cases is like running a mile.

My final reason for defending this unorthodox position is that I think the writers who want judges to avoid unjust results put themselves at a disadvantage when they accept, uncritically, the premise that judges must follow the law when it is clear. Many of the arguments for a duty to follow clear laws can be adapted to support the claim that, whenever possible, sources of legal authority should be read as containing clear mandates. By conceding a judicial duty to follow clear laws, one actually makes it harder to defend the right of judges to invoke extralegal considerations in unclear cases.

The argument goes differently if we accept the challenge of defending the moral right of judges to deviate even from the clearest of laws. If judges have this right, then we need not argue that the law is unclear in order to maintain that judges are sometimes permitted to reach results that appear to contradict the law. The law could be entirely clear and yet good results could

---

of Results and the Results of Rhetoric: Judicial Writings," *University of Chicago Law Review* 62 (1995): 1371–419, p. 1417. Justice Cardozo observes that judges who innovate tend "to disguise the innovation even from themselves, and to announce in all sincerity that it was all as it had been before." Benjamin N. Cardozo, "Jurisprudence," in *Selected Writings of Benjamin Nathan Cardozo*, ed. Margaret E. Hall (New York: Fallon, 1947), p. 37. See generally, Dan Simon, "The Double-Consciousness of Judging: The Problematic Legacy of Cardozo," *Oregon Law Review* 79 (2000): 1033–80.

still be reached. The permissibility of reaching good results would no longer be held hostage to debates about how much latitude the law affords.[53]

1.6 OVERVIEW

Part I of this book sets up a problem. I argue that judges have moral reasons—albeit defeasible ones—to deviate from the law whenever it requires them to reach results that are otherwise objectionable on moral or policy grounds. Next I ask, are judges nevertheless morally obligated to apply the law correctly in such cases and, if so, why? I consider several affirmative answers that depend upon what I call the *undermining principle*, which holds that if the law requires a public official to perform a certain action, then any moral reasons that she would otherwise have not to perform that action are undermined. I consider every argument I know for the undermining principle. Concluding that none is sound, I reject it, although I cannot refute it. Then I consider several important arguments for the conclusion that judges have moral reasons to reach legally correct results: arguments from the judicial oath and political obligation. I find that these arguments fail to support the conclusion that judges have even a defeasible moral reason to reach legally correct results in all cases.

Most readers, however, will be confident that judges are morally obligated to apply the law correctly in at least some cases in which it requires morally objectionable results. Such readers should share my motivation to find a better argument for this conclusion. In part II, I present a different argument for the principle that judges have moral reasons to apply the law correctly. In at least some cases in which the law requires objectionable results, these reasons may be strong enough to *outweigh* reasons to deviate from the law.

Although my argument in part II incorporates many familiar elements, it is unusual and likely to be controversial. It has several implications that distinguish it from the arguments rejected in part I. The rejected arguments claim that judges have *agent-relative* reasons to reach legally correct results.[54] These are reasons that apply differently to different agents. They contrast with *agent-neutral* reasons, which apply to all agents.[55] I argue that

---

53. See section 5.5.1.
54. Also known as *agent-centered* reasons. Stephen L. Darwall, "Agent-Centered Restrictions from the Inside Out," *Philosophical Studies* 50 (1986): 291–319.
55. Formally defined, an agent-relative reason is "one that cannot be fully specified without pronominal back-reference to the person for whom it is a reason," whereas an agent-neutral reason is "one that can be fully specified without such an indexical device." Philip Pettit, "Universality without Utilitarianism," *Mind* 72 (1987): 74–82, p. 75. Classic treatments of agent-relativity include Samuel Scheffler, *The Rejection of Consequentialism*, revised ed. (Oxford: Oxford University Press, 1994); Thomas Nagel, *The View from Nowhere* (Oxford: Oxford University Press, 1986); Derek Parfit, *Reasons and Persons* (Oxford: Clarendon Press, 1984). See the excellent discussion in Michael Ridge, "Reasons for Action: Agent-Neutral vs. Agent-Relative," http://plato.stanford.edu/entries/reasons-agent/.

judges have agent-neutral reasons to adhere to the law. Unlike the reasons considered in part I, these reasons apply even when the law requires objectionable results. However, I argue that these reasons can be outweighed by reasons to deviate from the law. My argument puts pressure on the popular view that judges in reasonably just legal systems have all-things-considered reasons to adhere to the law in all cases. My argument is consistent with that claim, if certain empirical conditions are satisfied, but I do not believe that they are satisfied today in realistic legal systems such as the United States. I also argue that, because judges have *only* agent-neutral reasons to adhere when the law requires objectionable results, certain factors that are universally considered irrelevant are, in fact, relevant to the overall permissibility of deviation from the law in particular cases. These factors concern, for example, the overall health of the rule of law in the system.

My study has both interpretive and revisionist dimensions. I aim to interpret accurately some central features of the practice of adjudication as it actually occurs in modern legal systems. However, I also urge substantial revision of some hoary ideas about adjudication that remain popular with lawyers and theorists alike. I conclude that deviation from the law may be justified more often than others have claimed. At the least, I hope to persuade readers that my theory has as many virtues as more traditional theories.

Those who like labels might say that my theory combines elements of legal formalism, philosophical anarchism, sophisticated consequentialism, and natural law theories of adjudication.

1.7 RELATED DISCOURSES

My project lies at the intersection of several theoretical discourses, two of which merit special mention. First is the ongoing debate concerning the "problem of political obligation." Dozens of books and articles on this topic have appeared since the early 1970s.[56] However, most focus on the citizen's duty to obey the law, often in the context of civil disobedience, conscientious objection, or political revolution. Less often have they addressed the public official's right to enforce the law, his professional duty to enforce it, or his possible right to disregard it. By contrast, authors who concentrate on adjudication have rarely examined it through the lens of political obligation.

The book also intersects with scholarship on rule-based adjudication.[57] Most of this work answers one or more of the following questions. First,

---

56. For an excellent survey see William A. Edmundson, "State of the Art: The Duty to Obey the Law," *Legal Theory* 10 (2004): 215–59.

57. See, e.g., Alan H. Goldman, *Practical Rules: When We Need Them and When We Don't* (Cambridge: Cambridge University Press, 2002); Larry Alexander and Emily Sherwin, *The Rule of Rules* (Durham, N.C.: Duke University Press, 2001); Frederick Schauer, *Playing*

how should judges interpret legal standards that are unclear or indeterminate? Second, how should judges decide cases to which no valid legal standard applies (the question of judicial discretion)? Third, under what conditions should judges overrule existing legal standards? Although my arguments have implications for each of these questions, I concentrate on a fourth: *when, if ever, may judges deviate from a legal standard without overruling it or making a legally justified exception?* More precisely, how should they decide cases in which unjust results are dictated by determinate legal standards that should *not* be overruled? Even the laws of reasonably just societies inflict injustices. As writers on equity have recognized since Aristotle, even a law that is itself just can mandate unjust results in particular cases. I ask, inter alia, if judges are morally permitted to deviate from the law in such cases, which arise in all realistic legal systems.[58]

1.8 JUDICIAL ACTIVISM AND THE POLITICS OF LEGAL REASONING

My project will strike some readers as a labyrinthine defense of judicial activism. I may seem coy in avoiding this terminology so I should explain my choice up front. If *judicial activism* means "legally unauthorized departure from the law as it is properly understood," then I do, indeed, present an ethical defense of limited judicial activism. That confession will prompt some readers to assume that this book is yet another attempt to defend politically progressive judges and disparage conservatives. However,

---

by the Rules: A Philosophical Examination of Rule-Based Decision-Making in Law and in Life (Oxford: Oxford University Press, 1991).

58. My project is also analogous to some well-known studies of legal ethics. Lawyers often justify otherwise immoral actions undertaken in the course of zealous advocacy by appealing to the "adversary system excuse." They use the excuse to defend their choice to advocate zealously as morally permissible, if not required. The excuse has been vigorously challenged by David Luban, William Simon, and others. Sitting judges, of course, do not have clients. It is the hallmark of the judicial role that the judge does not represent any party and remains impartial between them all. But one might claim that judges are obligated "zealously to represent the law," even when the law requires morally objectionable results. One could claim that, much as lawyers are permitted, perhaps even required, to take certain otherwise immoral actions that serve their clients' interests, judges are required to take certain otherwise immoral actions when the law requires it. This is a judicial version of the adversary system excuse, which we might call the "judicial system requirement." I shall not suggest that legal ethicists have watertight arguments against the adversary system excuse, but these arguments have compelled replies and remain serious contenders in the literature. This book similarly examines, and presents ethical challenges to, the judicial system requirement. See Luban, *Lawyers and Justice*; William H. Simon, *The Practice of Justice: A Theory of Lawyers' Ethics* (Cambridge, Mass.: Harvard University Press, 1998); Gerald J. Postema, "Moral Responsibility in Professional Ethics," *New York University Law Review* 55 (1980): 63–89, p. 78; Richard A. Wasserstrom, "Lawyers as Professionals: Some Moral Issues," *Human Rights* 5 (1975): 2–15.

I believe that my theses are compatible with virtually any position on substantive issues of public policy, from far left, to moderate, to far right. I advance a distinctive understanding of how judges are ethically permitted to promote sound policy objectives, whatever these may be. Later I will say more about how my claims relate to various definitions of *judicial activism*.[59]

My project speaks directly to the relationship between politics and legal reasoning. Barry Friedman offers the following observation, discussing the state of constitutional theory in 2004:

> When the ideological valence of Supreme Court decisions shifts, constitutional theorizing about judicial review tends to shift as well. Over the last century or more there have been two general positions taken about judicial review: that it is a blight in a democratic system that must be curtailed, and that it is a valued part of U.S. government essential to the protection of constitutional liberty. One is a critique, the other a justification. Progressives and conservatives have advanced both positions (in various permutations) at different times, depending upon which position seemed most apt to present circumstances, given their political views. . . . [P]rogressive and conservative positions are shifting again at this very moment. . . . Progressives at the turn of the twenty-first century are echoing criticisms offered by progressives one hundred years earlier, though progressives took a more positive position toward judicial review during the Warren Court.[60]

Friedman discusses opinions about the legitimacy of judicial review, but opinions about adjudication in general are equally susceptible to shifts based on the political composition of the judiciary. Between 1937 and 1980, federal courts rendered many decisions that pleased political progressives. Conservatives accused the courts of deviating from the law: giving insufficient weight to precedent, misreading legal sources such as statutes and constitutions, et cetera. Since then, the federal courts have started rendering more decisions that please conservatives.[61] Liberals have increasingly taken on the role of accusing the courts of deviating from the

---

59. See §3.11.
60. Barry Friedman, "The Cycles of Constitutional Theory," *Law and Contemporary Problems* 67 (2004): 149–74, pp. 149–50.
61. A few examples from the U.S. Supreme Court include *United States v. Lopez*, 514 U.S. 549 (1995) (holding that Gun-Free School Zones Act exceeds federal commerce power); *United States v. Morrison*, 529 U.S. 598 (2000) (holding that Violence Against Women Act exceeds federal commerce power); *Boy Scouts of America v. Dale*, 530 U.S. 640 (2000) (holding that prohibition on discrimination on basis of sexual orientation in New Jersey public accommodations law, as applied to Boy Scouts of America, violates right of expressive association under First Amendment); *Bush v. Gore* (holding that Florida's manual vote recount process in 2000 presidential election violated Equal Protection Clause of Fourteenth Amendment); *District of Columbia v. Heller*, 128 S. Ct. 2783 (2008) (holding that District's total ban on handgun ownership violates respondent's individual Second Amendment right to bear arms); *Gonzales v. Carhart*, 550 U.S. 124 (2007) (upholding federal Partial-Birth Abortion Ban Act).

law. Liberals and conservatives now accuse each other of using double standards—of condemning deviation only when it thwarts their politically favored ends. Politically opinionated legal scholars display great ingenuity in trying to establish that they are consistent whereas their opponents are not. Conservatives try to justify disregarding liberal constitutional precedents by claiming that those cases themselves deviated from the Constitution. Liberals construct theories of legal content and legal reasoning designed to show that these earlier decisions were, in fact, legally correct.

Scholars in these debates disagree on many issues, but the debates also presuppose a basic point of agreement. The disputants almost always agree that, whatever the law requires, judges are obligated to apply it correctly, full stop. Liberals and conservatives merely disagree about what *constitutes* correct application of the law.[62] Each faction assumes that it can prevail by demonstrating that its opponent's legal reasoning is mistaken. My thesis entails that the underlying premise itself is mistaken. Judges are not necessarily obligated to apply the law correctly.

My thesis distinguishes this book from much legal scholarship. Legal scholars often write as advocates for particular results, doctrines, and legal arguments. They attempt to convince readers that particular cases were decided correctly or incorrectly. They advocate for particular results in pending cases. This book is different. I have opinions about cases just as you do, but I rarely have occasion to mention my legal opinions in this book and I never rely upon them. I shall not try to persuade you to embrace "my" interpretations of the Due Process Clause or the Fair Labor Standards Act. You could disagree with me on every controversial legal question and still accept my arguments in this book. My conclusions could be used to support results favored by liberal Democrats or those favored by conservative Republicans. My position entails, for example, that a federal judge is not necessarily obligated to uphold a ban on late-term abortions *even if it has been proven constitutional.*[63] But my position also entails that a judge is not necessarily obligated to invalidate such a ban even if it has been proven *un*constitutional. Such a position risks offending everyone but I am prepared to take that chance.

---

62. "Strong opponents of abortion regarded *Roe v. Wade* as utterly lawless in much the same way that Justice Ginsburg and other strong proponents of abortion rights now regard *Gonzales v. Carhart* as utterly lawless." Neil S. Siegel, "The Virtue of Judicial Statesmanship," *Texas Law Review* 86 (2008): 959–1032, p. 1027.

63. By "proven constitutional," I do not just mean "held constitutional." I mean *"correctly* held constitutional."

2

Practical Reasons and Judicial Use of Force

2.1 PRIVATE REASONS, IMPARTIAL REASONS, AND ROLE REASONS

This chapter introduces the concepts needed to develop my account of judicial reasons. Practical reasons are my basic units of analysis. A practical reason is a reason to act or to refrain from action,[1] as opposed to a theoretical reason—a reason for belief.[2] Throughout this book I shall write as though practical reasons really exist.[3] They have properties that we can meaningfully discuss. They interact with one another. They explain and justify intentional action. Most contemporary philosophers in ethics, action theory, political philosophy, and legal philosophy make these assumptions. I shall not defend them.[4]

Prudential reasons are easy to understand: they are reasons pertaining to my own welfare. I have prudential reasons to eat when I am hungry, sleep when I am tired, pursue my interests, make friends, avoid contagious diseases, et cetera.[5]

---

1. Stephen J. Burton, "Law as Practical Reason," *Southern California Law Review* 62 (1989): 747–93.
2. A note on terminology: possible readers of this book include philosophers, lawyers, judges, and social scientists. Different fields use different jargon, so I sometimes explain basic terms of art. I never mean to condescend to anyone.
3. This way of writing does not, necessarily, reflect a commitment to a fundamental ontology that includes reasons. Some philosophers think any complete ontology will include reasons at the basic level. Others think that reasons supervene on other, more basic facts. Some even think that reasons will ultimately reduce to those more basic facts, without remainder. As I incline to a naturalist ontology, I think reasons supervene on natural facts, but I shall not defend that idea in this book. Most philosophers appear to believe that some progress can be made in the theory of practical reasoning without settling fundamental ontological issues. This book proceeds in that spirit.
4. But see, e.g., J. David Velleman, *The Possibility of Practical Reason* (Oxford: Oxford University Press, 2000); Christine M. Korsgaard, "Skepticism about Practical Reason," *Journal of Philosophy* 83 (1986): 5–25.
5. I like mushrooms, so I have *preferential reasons* to eat them. I dislike bananas, so I have preferential reasons not to eat them. I could have preferential reasons to eat bananas; nevertheless, as when I want to climb a mountain, my body needs energy, and I have only bananas.

It is often said that special reasons—*reasons of partiality*—apply to family members, friends, compatriots, and so forth.[6] Perhaps the fact that a girl who needs shoes is my daughter gives me a reason to buy her shoes. I cannot have this kind of reason to buy your daughter shoes. Perhaps the fact that George H. W. Bush was a U.S. citizen gave him a reason to join the U.S. Navy. He could not have had that kind of reason to join the French armed forces.[7]

Reasons of preference, prudence, and partiality collectively comprise the class of *private reasons*. I have many reasons in addition to my private reasons. When a man with a facial disfigurement passes me on the street, I have *moral reasons* not to shout an insult at him. I have moral reasons to dial the emergency line on my cell phone if I see him having a heart attack. I have *legal reasons* not to shoplift a package of gum and legal reasons to cover my icy front steps with sand. These legal and moral reasons are *impartial reasons*: they apply to anyone in my situation if they apply to me.

Public officials are usually expected to disregard private reasons when deliberating in their official capacities. A public official is supposed to act only for reasons that would apply equally to anyone who occupied her office. Some of these are reasons that apply to her in virtue of her office. These are her *role reasons*.[8] Police officers have role reasons to arrest suspects. Public defenders have role reasons to defend them. Trial judges have role reasons to preside over trials. Some of these role reasons are legal reasons; others are moral reasons.

This book is about role reasons and impartial reasons, not private reasons. My overarching question is, what happens to someone's impartial, moral reasons when she becomes a judge? Judges retain many of their moral reasons, of course: they should not shoplift or shout cruel insults, they should help strangers in distress, et cetera. I ask which moral reasons judges retain, especially when moral reasons conflict with role reasons or legal reasons not associated with the judicial role.

Some philosophers also believe that one's welfare can be affected by events that are unrelated to the satisfaction of one's desires. They say that my welfare improves with my physical health, even if an unhealthy lifestyle would satisfy more of my desires in the long run. They insist that I have prudential reasons to live healthily even if I have no preferential reasons to do so. The distinction between preferential and prudential reasons will play no role in this book, but it is worth noting. Preferential reasons are nonmoral but agent-relative. Prudential reasons are also agent-relative. They are arguably moral, if one has duties to oneself. See chapter 12 on agent-relativity.

6. See, e.g., Susan Wolf, "Morality and Partiality," *Philosophical Perspectives* 6 (1992): 243–59.

7. One might, however, have other reasons to buy shoes for someone else's daughter or to defend a foreign country.

8. See Arthur Isak Applbaum, *Ethics for Adversaries: The Morality of Roles in Public and Professional Life* (Princeton, N.J.: Princeton University Press, 1999); David Luban, *Lawyers and Justice: An Ethical Study* (Princeton, N.J.: Princeton University Press, 1988), chs. 6–7.

2.2 REASONS INTERACTING

Before beginning to answer these questions I must draw several additional distinctions within the theory of practical reason. The most important is the distinction between *pro tanto* reasons and *all-things-considered* reasons.[9] A consideration serves as a reason when it *favors* a certain action.[10] A *pro tanto* reason to perform an action favors that action but can be overridden by a stronger *pro tanto* reason. An agent has an all-things-considered reason to do whatever the balance of *pro tanto* reasons favors. If I promise to meet you for lunch at noon, then I acquire a *pro tanto* reason to meet you. But if my young daughter breaks her leg shortly before noon, then I have a stronger *pro tanto* reason to take her to the hospital and miss our lunch appointment. We would say that I have an all-things-considered reason to take my daughter to the hospital and a reason, perhaps, to apologize to you.

Morally relevant factors can interact in various ways at the ontological level. A factor can *enable* another factor to favor a certain action without itself favoring the action. It can *intensify* (or, conversely, *attenuate*) another factor, causing the latter to favor an action more (or less) strongly.[11] One reason can *override* another without depriving the latter of its force, or it can *undermine*[12] the other, depriving it of all force. At the epistemological level one reason can *exclude* another from consideration. Such an *exclusionary reason* is a reason for an agent to disregard another reason.[13]

2.3 OBJECTIVE/SUBJECTIVE AND APPRAISAL/GUIDANCE REASONS

A fact constitutes an *objective reason* for an agent if and only if it would motivate a reasonable and fully informed agent. A fact constitutes a *subjective reason* for a less than fully informed agent if and only if it would motivate a reasonable and equally informed agent.[14] It is warranted to blame an agent for failing to act on her subjective reasons but not for failing to act on objective reasons. Subjective reasons diverge from

---

9. Many have followed W. D. Ross, who called them "prima facie reasons," but "*pro tanto*" has become the preferred terminology. Shelly Kagan, *The Limits of Morality* (Oxford: Clarendon Press, 1989), p. 17; W. D. Ross, *The Right and the Good* (Oxford: Clarendon Press, 1930). All-things-considered reasons are also known as *conclusive*, *decisive*, or *dispositive* reasons.

10. I take the term from Jonathan Dancy, *Ethics without Principles* (Oxford: Oxford University Press, 2004), p. 29.

11. Ibid., pp. 41–42.

12. Dancy calls this "disabling." Ibid., p. 41.

13. Joseph Raz, *Practical Reason and Norms*, 2nd ed. (New York: Oxford University Press, 1990), pp. 35–48.

14. Peter Railton, "Alienation, Consequentialism, and the Demands of Morality," *Philosophy and Public Affairs* 13 (1984): 134–71, p. 152.

objective reasons in cases of blameless wrongdoing and blameworthy actions that happen to be morally permitted.[15] I discuss both objective and subjective reasons in this book, but I always try to specify which is which.

A fact constitutes an *appraisal reason* for an agent to attempt to Φ if and only if she has objective reason to succeed in her attempt. A fact constitutes a *guidance reason* for an agent to attempt to Φ if and only if, in attempting to Φ, she will successfully do whatever she has objective reason to do, whether or not she succeeds in Φ-ing.[16]

The following scenario illustrates both objective/subjective and appraisal/guidance distinctions. A Marine sniper has an objective, appraisal reason to kill B.G., a terrorist who is about to explode himself in a crowd. The sniper has been assured by his superiors that the man in his rifle scope is B.G. However, the sniper knows from experience that if he aims at the target's head, then he misses, whereas if he aims at the space above the target's head, then he hits. If the man in his scope is B.G., then the sniper has an objective guidance reason to fire at the space above the head of the man in his scope. Given what he believes, he has a subjective guidance reason to fire at the space above the head of the man in his rifle scope, whoever that may be. If the man is, in fact, B.G., then the sniper has an objective guidance reason to fire at the space above the head of the man in his rifle scope.

Although I shall address what judges have subjective guidance reasons to do in chapter 14, in the earlier chapters I shall mostly address their objective appraisal reasons.

2.4 NATURAL REASONS AND DUTIES

A *duty* in my lexicon is a type of reason. It can objective or subjective, *pro tanto* or all-things-considered. We have legal duties and moral duties.[17] A duty need not be owed to any identifiable person and it need not have a correlative *right*, although many duties are owed to someone who has a right that the duty be discharged.[18]

---

15. Stephen R. Perry, "Second-Order Reasons, Uncertainty, and Legal Theory," *Southern California Law Review* 62 (1989): 913–94, p. 922.

16. Similar distinctions appear in Cynthia A. Stark, "Decision Procedures, Standards of Rightness and Impartiality," *Noûs* 31 (1997): 478–95; David O. Brink, *Moral Realism and the Foundations of Ethics* (New York: Cambridge University Press, 1989), pp. 216–17; R. E. Bales, "Act Utilitarianism: Account of Right-making Characteristics or Decision-Making Procedure," *American Philosophical Quarterly* 8 (1971): 257–65.

17. Perhaps we have other types of duties, such as duties of etiquette.

18. See David Lyons, "The Correlativity of Rights and Duties," *Noûs* 4 (1970): 45–55. My arguments are consistent with the position that all moral reasons are moral duties, which precludes the possibility of supererogatory actions: those that one has a moral reason, but no

I shall now examine the rights and duties of individuals in three groups: people in a state of nature, residents of jurisdictions with established legal systems, and public officials, particularly judges. My arguments assume that all human beings have certain moral rights and reasons just by virtue of being human. These are often called natural rights and reasons[19] either because they are natural to us or because they apply even to people in a state of nature. Some natural rights and reasons are more controversial than others. Although I assume that such rights and reasons exist, I try to make minimal assumptions about exactly which natural rights and reasons we have. I try to indicate when I make an especially controversial assumption.

Individuals in a state of nature have several rights—to life and liberty, at least. They have negative duties such as the duty not to kill other people and positive duties such as the duty to care for dependent children, to keep promises, et cetera. The details are not important at this point. The duties and rights that concern me are *duties of nonmaleficence*, *samaritan rights*, and *rights of justice*. These duties and rights are elements of common morality and are recognized by most major moral theories, including deontology, contractualism, indirect consequentialism, and virtue ethics.[20]

First consider duties of nonmaleficence, preeminently the duty not to use physical force against other human beings[21] without justification. Physical force includes, inter alia, the infliction of pain, injury, physical constraint, or confinement. Also forbidden, absent justification, are using coercion, inflicting emotional distress, and depriving someone of the use of his property. One may also have a duty not to subject anyone to excessive *risks* of pain, physical injury, emotional distress, or deprivation of property.[22] One has a duty not to threaten to do any of these things, a duty not to instruct others to do any of these things, and a duty not to assist others to do any of these things.[23]

---

moral duty, to perform. But my arguments are also consistent with the possibility of supererogatory actions. See David Heyd, *Supererogation* (Cambridge: Cambridge University Press, 1982). Similarly, my arguments are consistent with the view that all legal reasons are legal duties, but also with the view that some legal reasons are not legal duties, leaving room for the possibility of "legal supererogation."

19. See, e.g., Susan Hurley, *Natural Reasons* (Oxford: Oxford University Press, 1989).

20. See, e.g., Marcia Baron, Philip Pettit, and Michael A. Slote, *Three Methods of Ethics* (Oxford: Wiley-Blackwell, 1997); T. M. Scanlon, *What We Owe to Each Other* (Cambridge: Belknap, 1998). The many theoretical disagreements concern the basis of these duties and rights, how they apply in particular cases, and how to resolve conflicts between them.

21. I believe we have duties to nonhuman animals as well, but I shall not enter that debate.

22. See §13.4.2.

23. At least when there is a nonnegligible possibility that one's instructions will be obeyed.

Individuals also have samaritan rights: rights to help strangers. We do not often think in terms of "rights" to help strangers or to refrain from harming them, but these are implied by our samaritan duties which are widely recognized. One has a right to discharge one's moral duties. If one has no moral right to rescue strangers in distress, then one has no moral duty to do so. But one has a moral duty to rescue strangers in distress when one can easily do so at negligible cost to oneself. Therefore, one has the right to protect strangers from all kinds of misfortunes, at least when these are undeserved, and provided that one does not thereby violate anyone's moral rights. One also has the right to instruct others to perform protective acts and to assist others in doing so.[24] The fact that one has duties of nonmaleficence and samaritan rights entails that others have duties not to use force or coercion to prevent one from fulfilling these duties or exercising these rights.[25]

2.5 SELF-HELP IN A STATE OF NATURE

Finally, individuals have several rights of justice. These are rights to use force or coercion to achieve certain goals of justice. Rights of justice are limited exemptions from certain general duties of nonmaleficence.[26] There is some controversy about the goals to which our rights of justice apply, so I shall begin with the least controversial claim: individuals in a state of nature are morally permitted to use reasonable force for the purpose of defending themselves or others, at least against culpable aggressors who pose imminent threats of bodily harm or substantial loss of property. The fact that force is necessary constitutes a *pro tanto* reason that overrides or undermines one's general duty of nonmaleficence.[27]

Individuals also have a natural right to use force for the purpose of obtaining compensation or restitution for wrongful injuries and losses, and for the purpose of enforcing agreements or contracts.[28] Suppose that in a state of nature Gus deliberately sprains Valerie's arm without

---

24. A *right to instruct* does not entail that anyone has a duty to obey.
25. These are Hohfeldian *claim-rights*. Leif Wenar, "The Nature of Rights," *Philosophy and Public Affairs* 33 (2005): 223–52, p. 229. Wesley Newcomb Hohfeld, *Fundamental Legal Conceptions* (New Haven, Conn.: Yale University Press, 1919).
26. Rights of justice are, at least, *single privileges*: the possessor has no duty to refrain from using force to do justice. If one has no duties of justice, then rights of justice are also *paired privileges*. Wenar, "The Nature of Rights," p. 226.
27. See, e.g., Jeff McMahan, "Self-Defense and the Problem of the Innocent Attacker," *Ethics* 104 (1994): 252–90; Judith Jarvis Thomson, "Self-Defense," *Philosophy and Public Affairs* 20 (1991): 283–310.
28. This right exists in both Lockean and Kantian traditions, although Kant also believes that individuals in a state of nature must make efforts to found a civil society. See Katrin Flikschuh, "Reason, Right, and Revolution: Kant and Locke," *Philosophy and Public Affairs* 36

justification. On any theory of corrective justice Gus owes Valerie something. Stipulate that he owes her at least fifty apples[29] in restitution for this injury. Valerie has a right of justice to take fifty apples from Gus, by force if necessary. Gus's neighbor, Jack, has no individual duty to intervene, but he has a right of justice to take fifty apples from Gus, by force if necessary, for the purpose of delivering them to Valerie. Jack also has a right to instruct others to exercise their rights of justice and to assist others in exercising the same. Similar conclusions apply regarding the enforcement of agreements.

2.6 PUNISHMENT AS A SPECIAL CASE

Many people also believe in a natural right to punish wrongdoers, what Locke calls a "natural executive right."[30] However, this belief is more controversial than the proposition that our rights of justice extend to restitution and the enforcement of agreements, so I shall treat punishment as a special case. My arguments do not depend upon a natural executive right, although they have different implications in many cases if such a right exists. Specifically, if and only if there is a natural executive right, then my arguments could support the right of judges to punish wrongdoers who have committed no crime under positive law.[31]

Suppose for now that there is a natural executive right. Gus deliberately sprains Valerie's arm without justification. How, if at all, may someone punish Gus? This may depend, of course, upon the correct theory of punishment. Let us stipulate that according to the correct theory, whatever it may be, Gus should be punished. If the correct theory is retributive, for example, then we stipulate that Gus deserves at least one month of physical confinement. If the correct theory is consequentialist, then we stipulate that better consequences result from confining Gus for one month (or from maintaining such a practice). The same holds, mutatis mutandis, for other theories of punishment. If there is a natural executive right, then Valerie has a right of justice to punish Gus by humanely confining him for one month. Gus's neighbor, Jack, has the same right, assuming

---

(2008): 375–404; Jeremy Waldron, "Kant's Legal Positivism," *Harvard Law Review* 109 (1996): 1535–66, p. 1562; Robert Nozick, *Anarchy, State, and Utopia* (New York: Basic Books, 1974), p. 10.

29. Or something of comparable value.

30. See, e.g., A. John Simmons, "Locke and the Right to Punish," *Philosophy and Public Affairs* 20 (1991): 311–49, p. 313; Daniel McDermott, "The Permissibility of Punishment," *Law and Philosophy* 20 (2001): 403–32; Daniel M. Farrell, "Punishment without the State," *Noûs* 22 (1988): 437–53; Warren Quinn, "The Right to Threaten and the Right to Punish," *Philosophy and Public Affairs* 14 (1985): 327–73; Nozick, *Anarchy, State, and Utopia*, p. 10; John Locke, *Second Treatise of Government*, para. 89.

31. See §10.8.

that no one else has already exercised it. Jack also has a right to instruct others to exercise their rights of justice and to assist others in this exercise.

2.7 SELF-HELP IN A LEGAL SYSTEM

Jack now leaves the state of nature for a jurisdiction with a functioning legal system.[32] He retains his duties of nonmaleficence and his samaritan rights from the state of nature. Others retain their duties not to use force to prevent him from fulfilling these duties or exercising these rights. He also acquires *legal* rights and duties for the first time. For the most part his legal duties are compatible with his natural duties of nonmaleficence and his samaritan rights. However, the law imposes an almost complete prohibition on nondefensive self-help. The law generally forbids individuals to use force for the purpose of carrying out private efforts to do justice, at least when the state is prepared to intervene.[33] However, the law permits defensive self-help when one is threatened with certain kinds of imminent harm and the state is not prepared to intervene.[34]

When Jack leaves the state of nature his rights of justice change accordingly. Suppose, again, that Gus sprains Valerie's arm. Jack retains his moral right to exact restitution from batterers, but this right is undermined if the state is prepared to perform this function more effectively than Jack would, as in a reasonably just and effective legal system. For various familiar reasons it is preferable that justice be done through accountable, public agencies when these are available, rather than through private self-help. Therefore, the fact that the state is prepared to take fifty apples from Gus and deliver them to Valerie *undermines* Jack's right to do so.[35] Jack's general duties of nonmaleficence then prevail, giving him an all-things-considered moral duty not to take Gus's apples.

Similarly, if the state is prepared to enforce agreements or to punish wrongdoers, then Jack has no right to use force for these purposes either. Nor does Jack retain the right to instruct other nonofficials to exercise rights of justice, or the right to assist them in exercising rights of justice. In general terms, the fact that the state is willing and able to achieve a

---

32. I shall not discuss societies that are intermediate between the state of nature and modern legal systems, in which some legal institutions exist but enforcement relies substantially upon self-help. See the discussion of "compulsory universal suretyship" in Joel Feinberg, "Collective Responsibility," in *Doing and Deserving* (Princeton, N.J.: Princeton University Press, 1970), p. 238. See also William Ian Miller, *Bloodtaking and Peacemaking: Feud, Law, and Society in Saga Iceland* (Chicago: University of Chicago Press, 1990).

33. Landlord-tenant law was one of the last areas in which self-help was permitted. Edward H. Rabin, "Symposium: The Revolution in Residential Landlord-Tenant Law: Causes and Consequences," *Cornell Law Review* 69 (1984): 517–84, p. 539.

34. See, e.g., *Model Penal Code* §3.04 (Use of Force in Self-Protection).

35. Unless Jack himself happens to be the presiding judge in Gus's case. See §2.8.

certain goal of justice undermines the rights of justice, possessed by private individuals, to use force to achieve that goal.

This reasoning even applies to defensive force. If the state is prepared to defend Jack and others from aggression, then his moral right to use defensive force is undermined. However, in practice the state is often unable to defend individuals against imminent and unexpected attacks. Jack is morally permitted to use even deadly force when necessary for defending himself or others from attack, if the state is not prepared to perform the defensive actions.[36]

2.8 JUDGES

Unlike most of us, some public officials use physical force and threats of force against persons and property in the course of performing their professional duties. Police officers forcibly enter private residences. They physically assault, subdue, restrain, transport, confine, and detain suspects, sometimes injuring or killing them in the process. Courtroom bailiffs shackle defendants and lead them to jail. County sheriffs forcibly confiscate property. Marshals escort convicts to prison. Corrections officers force inmates into cells—assaulting, injuring, and sometimes killing those who attempt escape. Executioners carry out death sentences.

It is obvious that bailiffs, corrections officers, and other "hands-on" officials use force on the job. It is less obvious but no less true that judges regularly initiate the use of force in the course of their professional duties. Of course judges engage in many professional activities that involve no obvious use of force. They appear in court and oversee legal proceedings. They maintain order in the courtroom, rule on motions, study the law, et cetera. Trial judges examine evidence presented, hear testimony, and instruct jurors. But many judicial activities, including some just mentioned, actually involve the use of force or threats of force. Judges levy fines, award monetary damages, grant injunctions, award custody, et cetera. They sentence criminals to community service, prison, or death.

The fact that judges initiate the use of force by their decisions would be obvious if judges did the "dirty work" themselves. In modern legal systems, however, the fact that judges use force is systematically obscured.[37] Judges do not use their own hands to restrain, escort, transport, assault,

---

36. George P. Fletcher, "Domination in the Theory of Justification and Excuse," *University of Pittsburgh Law Review* 57 (1996): 553–78, p. 570; Thomson, "Self-Defense," p. 289.

37. Robert Cover identifies "three related responsibility-mitigation mechanisms" that antebellum antislavery judges used to justify to themselves and others their decisions applying the law of slavery. These included "(1) Elevation of the formal stakes (sometimes combined with minimization of the moral stakes). (2) Retreat to a mechanistic formalism. (3)

injure, execute, or confiscate property. They leave these tasks to subordinate officials.[38] In Robert Cover's memorable words,

> Legal interpretation takes place in a field of pain and death.... Legal interpretive acts signal and occasion the imposition of violence upon others: A judge articulates her understanding of a text, and as a result, somebody loses his freedom, his property, his children, even his life.... When interpreters have finished their work, they frequently leave behind victims whose lives have been torn apart by these organized, social practices of violence.[39]

The fact that subordinates, rather than the judges themselves, use the force can fool one into thinking that judges are not morally responsible for its use. This is a mistake. A principal who gives instructions to an agent is morally and legally responsible for actions taken by the agent that are reasonably pursuant to his instructions.[40] A supervisor who instructs a subordinate employee to maim a competitor, for instance, is morally and legally responsible for the injury.[41]

Likewise, when a judge awards civil damages to a plaintiff or sentences a defendant to prison, his ruling includes an instruction to his subordinates to use force—a command, in fact. He foresees that his command will be obeyed, as it almost always is. Under these conditions the judge is morally responsible for any actions taken by his subordinates that are reasonably pursuant to his command, just as the supervisor is morally responsible for the actions he orders. When a bailiff or prison guard carries

---

Ascription of responsibility elsewhere." Robert M. Cover, *Justice Accused: Antislavery and the Judicial Process* (New Haven, Conn.: Yale University Press, 1975), p. 199. Markus Dirk Dubber notes that "[t]hese strategies have proved popular not only in early nineteenth century North America, but in many countries and in many ages, whenever judges were eager to deny the violence of their official function." Markus Dirk Dubber, "The Pain of Punishment," *Buffalo Law Review* 44 (1996): 545–611, p. 582. Other writers who have emphasized the fact that judges use violence include Hans Sherrer, "The Complicity of Judges in the Generation of Wrongful Convictions," *Northern Kentucky Law Review* 30 (2003): 539–83; Patricia M. Wald, "Violence under the Law: A Judge's Perspective," in *Law's Violence*, ed. Austin Sarat and Thomas R. Kearns (Ann Arbor: University of Michigan Press, 1992); Lynne Henderson, "Authoritarianism and the Rule of Law," *Indiana Law Journal* 66 (1991): 379–456, p. 405 ("judge as agent of state violence"); and John T. Noonan, Jr., *Persons and Masks of the Law: Cardozo, Holmes, Jefferson, Holmes, and Wythe as Makers of the Masks* (New York: Farrar, Straus & Giroux, 1976).

38. Raz classifies courts as "norm-applying institutions," as distinct from "norm-enforcing institutions" such as police departments, prisons, et cetera. Raz, *Practical Reason and Norms*, pp. 132–34.

39. Robert M. Cover, "Violence and the Word," *Yale Law Journal* 95 (1986): 1601–29, p. 1601. See also Sherrer, "The Complicity of Judges in the Generation of Wrongful Convictions," p. 558.

40. Melvin Aron Eisenberg, *An Introduction to Agency, Partnerships, and LLCs*, 3rd ed. (New York: Foundation Press, 2000), p. 12.

41. *Model Penal Code* §5.02 (Criminal Solicitation); Dan B. Dobbs, *The Law of Torts*, vol. 2 (St. Paul, Minn.: West, 2001), p. 905 (respondeat superior tort liability is the general rule for employers).

out a judge's orders, as the judge intended, the judge shares moral responsibility for these actions with the compliant official.[42] Hereafter, for the sake of brevity, I shall often refer to a judge's *use* of force with the understanding that the judge never actually uses her own hands.

It is rarely noticed that when a judge takes office and begins hearing cases, she steps onto a scene in which threats of force have already been made by others and new threats will be made, regardless of what she does. Even before a judge has been assigned to his case, the defendant already lives under heightened threats of force and a substantial likelihood of being subjected to additional force or threats thereof. There is a substantial possibility that the judge who ultimately decides the case, whoever that turns out to be, will rule against the defendant. Therefore, every eligible judge poses a potential threat to the defendant *ex ante*. These potential threats from all eligible judges survive even after one judge or panel has been assigned to hear the case but before a decision has been rendered. The first judge assigned does not always decide the case. Before she decides it she may resign from the bench, be removed from office, self-recuse, become incapacitated, die, or be disqualified from deciding the case. But other judges are always waiting in the wings to be assigned as replacements. So *some* judge will decide the case whether or not this judge does. This is so even if the decision amounts to a dismissal of the case pursuant to a plea bargain or civil settlement. Until a judge decides the case the possible replacement judges pose potential threats to the defendant.[43]

These background facts partly determine how the decision should be characterized. By deciding the case, regardless of how she decides it, the judge *blocks* potential threats to the defendant posed by the other judges who could have decided it. This is so in both civil and criminal cases. If the judge rules against the defendant, however, then the same action whereby she blocks potential threats to the defendant also creates a new threat to him, or we might say that she transforms a potential threat into an actual threat. The threat is usually tacit. The judge's order rarely mentions explicitly what will happen if a civil defendant refuses to pay damages or a convict tries to escape the bailiff while leaving the courtroom. But the judge is, in fact, instructing other officials to threaten the defendant with force if he does not comply with the order. An adverse ruling usually requires the defendant to perform actions that he would prefer not to perform or to refrain from actions that he would prefer to perform. If he disobeys, then the state is very likely to compel compliance by force. The defeated defendant is expected to understand this.

---

42. The judge may even be *more* responsible for these actions than is the subordinate official because the judge gave the order. However, I need not make this claim.
43. Often, of course, one cannot predict with any confidence which threats will actually be made, but that is just to say that they are all *potential* threats.

When she rules against a defendant the judge also withdraws or blocks certain existing threats from other public officials. Because of the judge's decision these officials can now punish the (criminal) defendant or use force to extract damages from the (civil) defendant, without themselves being threatened with force by *other* officials.[44] Whereas, when a judge rules for a defendant she declines to block these threats of force, which serve to protect the defendant. In criminal cases a prison or death sentence may also block threats that the defendant poses to his future victims.

So a judge can choose to refrain from subjecting the defendant to threats of force and to protect him from threats of force by other officials (including judges) who might enforce the law against him. Or she can withdraw threats of force from subordinate officials and instruct them to use force against the defendant. Whatever the judge decides, she either creates, withdraws, or blocks threats, or she does all three. *Judges are in the force business*. In the next sections I shall ask what legal and moral authority judges have to block and create threats of force.

2.9 JUDICIAL AUTHORITY

When someone becomes a judge she acquires new legal powers. The state partially withdraws its legal prohibition on her use of force, conferring upon her a limited legal power to use it.[45] She receives partial legal authorization to exercise her rights of justice. When a judge rules on a motion, decides a case at law, or sentences a convict, she initiates the use or threat of force. As the presiding judge, she has legal authorization to do so. Her decision is called *ultra vires* if it exceeds the scope of her legal authority.[46]

Individuals ordinarily need moral justification, not just legal authorization, when they use physical force or threats of force. As David Lyons observes, "[t]he judicial process obtains against a certain background, which includes the assumption that acts intended to deprive a person of liberty, other valued goods, or even life itself require justification."[47]

---

44. If a bailiff uses force without legal authorization, for example, then police officers could arrest him.

45. "[A] judge has the legal right (power) to sentence a criminal to prison, meaning that a judge has the ability to annul the criminal's privileges of free movement." Wenar, "The Nature of Rights," p. 231.

46. See, e.g., *Boumediene v. U.S.*, 128 S. Ct. 2229, 2294 (2008) (Scalia, J., dissenting) (Court acts "ultra vires" by conferring constitutional right to habeas corpus on alien enemies detained abroad); William C. Duncan, "*Goodridge* and the Rule of Law Same-Sex Marriage in Massachusetts [sic]: The Meaning and Implications of *Goodridge v. Department of Public Health*," *Boston University Public Interest Law Journal* 14 (2004): 42–55, p. 45 (Supreme Judicial Court's decision requiring same-sex marriage was "ultra vires").

47. David Lyons, "Derivability, Defensibility, and the Justification of Judicial Decisions," in *Moral Aspects of Legal Theory* (Cambridge: Cambridge University Press, 1993), p. 134. See also Grant Lamond, "The Coerciveness of Law," *Oxford Journal of Legal Studies* 20 (2000): 39–62, p. 40 (coercion is "ordinarily regarding as something which stands in need of justification").

One could take various views of the moral permissibility of the use of force by public officials. According to the *naïve view* a public official is morally permitted to perform a certain action in a certain situation only if a private party would be permitted to do so in that situation. When a functioning legal system exists, private parties are rarely morally permitted to use force, the main exception being when force is necessary to defend oneself or others from imminent, unjustified aggression.[48] Most of the standard law enforcement and penal purposes for which officials use force do not involve defending anyone from imminent aggression. Therefore, if the naïve view were correct, then public officials would be morally forbidden to use force for most of the standard purposes.

One can imagine the naïve view occurring to a child. The child understands that it is "wrong" to hit other people. She sees one man strike another with a short club. To her this looks like wrongful action. She calls the assailant a "bad guy." She wonders why no one intervenes. Assume, however, that the assailant is actually a court bailiff striking an unruly convict with a baton in order to lead him from the courtroom. In that case the girl's reaction is, indeed, naïve. As she matures she will learn that the law authorizes certain individuals—called "bailiffs," "police officers," et cetera—to use force in situations in which private parties are legally and morally forbidden to use it. She will learn that this authorization is not just legal, but moral.[49] At least in a legal system with de facto legitimacy, adults do not ordinarily become angry when public officials use legally authorized force. They do not condemn these actions or try to stop them. Although it would be wrong for a private party to use force in this (nondefensive) situation, a legally authorized official is permitted to use it. If one lives for some time under a legal system that one regards as legitimate, then one will reject the naïve view in favor of what I shall call the *habituated view* of the morality of official uses of force within the system.[50]

Normal adults accept the habituated view. We believe that judges are morally permitted to use force as authorized by law, at least in most instances. The state is morally permitted to use force in at least the circumstances in which individuals in a state of nature are permitted to use it: for defense, restitution, contract enforcement, and punishment of *mala in se* offenses.[51] Public officials are agents of the state who exercise these

---

48. See, e.g., Thomson, "Self-Defense."
49. Children do not even draw this distinction until a certain age. Lawrence Kohlberg, *Essays on Moral Development: The Philosophy of Moral Development*, vol. 1 (New York: Harper & Row, 1981).
50. See Tom R. Tyler, *Why People Obey the Law* (New Haven, Conn.: Yale University Press, 1990).
51. Remembering, again, that the natural executive right is controversial. Criminal conduct is classified as *malum in se* if such conduct would be wrongful even if it were not proscribed by law (e.g., in a state of nature). Bryan A. Garner, ed., *Black's Law Dictionary*,

prerogatives on its behalf. Even philosophical anarchists can agree that the state is morally permitted to use force to protect citizens from violence, to punish wrongdoers, et cetera. Anarchists merely deny that individuals have a moral duty to obey the law, as such, and that legitimate states are possible.[52]

Shifting from the naïve view to the habituated view is a normal part of moral development for residents of de facto legitimate legal systems. They come to believe that the law can give public officials the moral authority to perform actions that are legally and morally forbidden to the rest of us. They correctly adopt this principle:

Moral Authority
Public officials are morally permitted to perform actions that would otherwise be morally forbidden, if the law authorizes them to do so.

By authorizing officials to use force in certain cases, the law creates a limited exception to the general moral prohibition on the use of nondefensive force in civil society. If the moral authority principle is true, then Jack's moral rights change when he becomes a judge. Earlier, I claimed that Jack's residence in a substantially just and effective legal system partially undermines his natural rights of justice.[53] However, when Jack presides over Gus's trial as a judge these rights are partially restored. Two facts are necessary to this restoration. First, the jury has found Gus civilly liable for spraining Valerie's arm and has awarded Valerie monetary damages. Second, Jack is the presiding judge in Gus's case, so the state is not otherwise prepared to extract restitution from Gus if Jack does not do so. Together, these two facts partially restore Jack's natural right to do justice.[54] Jack has a *pro tanto* moral reason to extract restitution from Gus.

The partial restoration of Jack's rights of justice is significant because Jack retains his natural *pro tanto* duty of nonmaleficence not to coerce Gus. This duty persists even if Gus has received a fair trial and morally ought to have restitution taken from him. However, Judge Jack's rights of justice undermine his duty of nonmaleficence in this case. In a highly circumscribed way, Judge Jack is returned to the state of nature with respect to Gus.

8th ed. (St. Paul, Minn.: Thomson/West, 2004). Common examples of such conduct include acts of violence against the person, such as homicide, rape, physical assault, injury, and confinement. Examples might also include theft, fraud, breach of agreement, inchoate offenses such as conspiracy and attempt, et cetera.

52. See, e.g., A. John Simmons, *Moral Principles and Political Obligations* (Princeton, N.J.: Princeton University Press, 1979), pp. 192, 196.

53. See §2.5.

54. The best way to describe this state of affairs, I think, is to say that these two facts jointly undermine the reason that undermined Jack's rights of justice: his residence in a substantially just and effective legal system. Perhaps nothing turns on the accuracy of this description.

I think this is why Judge Jack should feel no remorse about coercing Gus. Jack's act is not merely excusable, it is *justified*.[55] This contrasts with another scenario. I have been assuming that Gus ought to be coerced as a moral matter. If the law under which Gus was found liable was an unjust law, then some would deny that Jack was objectively morally permitted to use force against Gus. Suppose Jack mistakenly believes that Gus deserves to be coerced and also that he (Jack) has the moral right to coerce him. In that case Jack should feel remorse when he learns the truth—that Gus did not deserve coercion. Jack should apologize to Gus even if Jack's beliefs were reasonable at the time.[56]

Now imagine a different scenario. Damien and Pearl live in a politically legitimate state. Damien negligently and unjustifiably damages Pearl's property. Under the law Pearl is entitled to an award of monetary damages. Such an award would, moreover, be entirely just. However, Pearl does not sue Damien. Lewis, a third party, proceeds to conduct his own private "trial" of Damien. Lewis "rules" for Pearl and forcibly extracts damages from Damien. Lewis is not morally permitted to do so, even if he follows the rules of civil procedure to the letter and reaches the same result that a competent court would reach. If, however, Lewis becomes the presiding judge in Pearl's case, then he is morally permitted to rule in her favor and to extract damages from Damien. I stated earlier that a legitimate legal system provides reasons that undermine the moral reasons to use force that residents would otherwise have. I now suggest that the law restores those reasons to use force when it authorizes a judge to use it in a certain case.[57] If *Judge* Lewis has legal authorization to use force against Damien, then he reacquires whatever reasons he would have had to use it in a state of nature.[58]

We should reject the naïve view in favor of the habituated view. However, I believe that many people go too far when they abandon the naïve view. They end up embracing a stronger principle:

---

55. See, e.g., Kent Greenawalt, "The Perplexing Borders of Justification and Excuse," *Columbia Law Review* 84 (1984): 1897–1927; J. L. Austin, "A Plea for Excuses," *Proceedings of the Aristotelian Society* 57 (1956–57): 1–30.

56. See Abigail Penzell, "Note: Apology in the Context of Wrongful Conviction: Why the System Should Say It's Sorry," *Cardozo Journal of Conflict Resolution* 9 (2007): 145–61; Bernard Williams, *Moral Luck* (Cambridge: Cambridge University Press, 1981), pp. 27–30.

57. I think the fact that someone becomes a judge undermines the reason that undermined his natural rights of justice when he "entered" civil society.

58. However, legal authorization does not override or undermine whatever *other* moral reasons the judge might have not to use force. I am not morally permitted to pull your hair for fun, even if the law permits me to do so.

Undermining
If the law requires a public official to use force in a given situation, then he has no moral reason not to use it.[59]

The moral authority and undermining principles are easily conflated. The latter entails the former, but not vice versa. In many cases the distinction makes no difference. The law often requires officials to use force when it is right and good for them to use it. The difference between the moral authority and undermining principles appears only when the law requires officials to use force that is all-things-considered suboptimal. The undermining principle entails that officials are morally permitted to use force in such cases. Moral authority does not.

As you matured you made the transition from the naïve to the habituated view. If, when you did so, you came to accept the undermining principle, not just moral authority, then I am going to ask you to unlearn some of what you learned during that transition. As I do this you may feel as though I am pushing you back into the naïve view—the view of a child who does not yet understand that positive law can change what is morally permitted and required. In fact, I reject the naïve view. I merely challenge the undermining principle. I shall argue that judges retain their *pro tanto* moral reasons to perform certain actions that the law forbids and to omit certain actions that the law requires.[60]

---

59. A principle even stronger than undermining states the following: if the law authorizes a public official to use force, then he has no moral reason not to use it. This principle has many implausible implications. It entails, for example, that judges never have moral reasons not to impose the maximum sentence allowed by law, even if they have discretion to impose a lower sentence. The Montana Penal Code authorizes prison terms of up to forty years for marijuana possession, but does not mandate such lengthy sentences. The stronger principle entails that a Montana judge has no moral reason not to impose forty-year sentences in such cases. For many readers, this implication of the stronger principle will suffice to discredit it. If you find it appealing, however, you can still accept my arguments. Because the stronger principle entails undermining, my arguments against undermining also reach the stronger principle, which I shall not mention again. See *Mont. Code Ann.* § 45-9-103 (2005); *Hutto v. Davis*, 454 U.S. 370 (1982) (upholding forty-year prison sentence for distributing, and possessing with intent to distribute, less than nine ounces of marijuana).

60. See chapter 6.

3

Deviating from Legal Standards

3.1 THE JUDGE

The protagonist in this book is a judge deliberating in her chambers. She is a generic character meant to represent a wide range of judges in the real world. I will not tell you much more about her.[1] I will not tell you anything that would distinguish her from most other judges. I imagine her sitting in the United States because this is the legal system that I know best.[2] She might be a state judge, a federal judge, an administrative law judge, or what have you. She might sit at the trial level, on an intermediate appellate court, or on a high court. The case on which she is deliberating could be a civil case, a criminal case, a constitutional case, a regulatory matter, or some other type of legal proceeding. These distinctions can be important in practice, but I try to make points that apply across all these categories. I also try to notice when these distinctions make a difference to my discussion.

I imagine my judge in the judicial branch, although some of my conclusions apply, mutatis mutandis, to other officials as well, including adjudicators in the executive branch. I assume that my judge sits alone on her court rather than as a judge on a multimember panel (as when federal appellate courts sit *en banc*). Collegial courts raise special issues that I cannot discuss in this book.

My judge is far from perfect. Her mental powers, knowledge, and moral judgment are all human, not superhuman. She could be deeply religious, atheistic, or spiritually uncommitted. Her political views could fall anywhere on the political spectrum represented by modern public officials and intellectuals: she could be Ann Coulter or House Speaker Nancy Pelosi, Justice Clarence Thomas or the late Justice Thurgood Marshall. She has a conscience and a set of sincerely held values upon which she is prepared to act when appropriate. She does not simply wish to use her position to accumulate money or power. She wants to be a

---

1. My hypothetical judge changes gender frequently.
2. I suspect many of my arguments apply outside the United States, but I cannot write with confidence about this.

good judge, whatever that means to her, and a good person, whatever that means to her.

3.2 JUDICIAL INCENTIVES TO PERFORM

The first question to ask about my protagonist is what reasons she has for and against performing her professional functions. Consider prudential reasons, which operate as incentives for substantially self-interested judges. Judges have incentives, often financial, to take certain actions that are forbidden to them: to accept bribes, to practice law on the side, et cetera. However, judges who take these actions engage in judicial misconduct, inviting censure, reprimand, impeachment, removal from office, disbarment, and so forth.[3] Judges wish to avoid these sanctions, so they have strong counterincentives to reject bribes, to refrain from practicing law, et cetera. Some would refrain from these actions from a sense of professionalism or personal ethics even if no sanctions were threatened.

Judges also have positive duties of office: for example, to appear in court as scheduled, to maintain order in the courtroom, to rule on motions by parties, to examine evidence presented, to hear testimony, to study the law, to decide cases, to sentence convicts. At one time or another, every judge has an incentive to shirk his duty in order to avoid hard work. Some judges dislike their work and would prefer less of it. Even judges who enjoy the job also enjoy leisure time and would like more of it. Some judges would prefer playing golf to appearing in court. However, failure to fulfill the positive duties of the office constitutes misconduct and can bring sanctions.[4] Again, the judge who wishes to simplify his job or to avoid work altogether has counterincentives.

A judge who wishes to avoid hearing a certain case can, in theory, recuse himself, but recusal is an ineffective means of reducing one's workload. Given docket backlog, a judge who recuses himself will shortly receive another case assignment. Moreover, recusing oneself can constitute misconduct if done for an improper reason.[5] A judge who occasionally recuses himself for improper reasons is unlikely to face sanctions, but

---

3. See chapter 4.
4. "The judicial duties of a judge take precedence over all other activities." *Code of Conduct of United States Judges*, Canon 3; "The judicial duties of a judge take precedence over all the judge's other activities." *Model Code of Judicial Conduct*, Canon 3 (1990).
5. "A judge shall hear and decide matters assigned to the judge except those in which disqualification is required." *Model Code of Judicial Conduct*, Canon 3B(1) (1990); "A judge should hear and decide matters assigned, unless disqualified. . . ." *Code of Conduct of United States Judges*, Canon 3A(2). See also *Model Code of Judicial Conduct*, Rule 2.7 (1990) ("A judge shall hear and decide matters assigned to the judge, except when disqualification is required by Rule 2.11 or other law."); 28 U.S.C. § 453 ("A judge has a duty to decide whatever cases come before him to the best of his ability.")

a pattern of frequent recusal could bring sanctions if it appears that the recusals are improper (e.g., he is deliberately avoiding difficult cases, using conflict of interest as a pretext).[6]

Judges also want to maintain good professional reputations. Many want to receive interesting and/or prestigious opportunities, both remunerative and nonremunerative, in the future. Many wish to be promoted to higher office, judicial or otherwise.[7] A judge who recuses himself too frequently or fails to appear in court may harm his professional reputation long before sanctions are threatened. Therefore, he has another incentive to hear his assigned cases. Insofar as a record of unwarranted recusal (or, worse, absenteeism) reduces one's attractiveness for interesting, lucrative, and prestigious opportunities, judges have an incentive to hear and decide the cases that are assigned to them.

Many judges also want other courts to cite and follow their decisions.[8] Many want to influence the development of legal doctrine.[9] Judges who fail to show up or who recuse themselves too often have fewer opportunities to exert influence.

3.3 ANSWERING LEGAL QUESTIONS

My protagonist appears on the bench. Once there, she tries to answer legal questions on a rational basis.[10] She does not decide randomly (unless,

---

6. It is worth noting, moreover, that the usual concern is under-recusal, not over-recusal. See, e.g., Debra Lyn Bassett, "Recusal and the Supreme Court," *Hastings Law Journal* 56 (2005): 657–98.

7. See Frederick Schauer, "Incentives, Reputation, and the Inglorious Determinants of Judicial Behavior," *University of Cincinnati Law Review* 68 (1999): 615–36; Thomas J. Miceli and Metin M. Cogel, "Reputation and Judicial Decision-Making," *Journal of Economic Behavior and Organization* 23 (1994): 31–51; Richard A. Posner, "What Do Judges and Justices Maximize? (The Same Thing Everybody Else Does)," *Supreme Court Economic Review* 3 (1993): 1–41; Mark A. Cohen, "The Motives of Judges: Empirical Evidence from Antitrust Sentencing," *International Review of Law and Economics* 12 (1992): 13–30.

8. William M. Landes and Richard A. Posner, "Legal Precedent: A Theoretical and Empirical Analysis," *Journal of Law and Economics* 19 (1976): 249–307, p. 273.

9. Jonathan R. Macey, "The Internal and External Costs and Benefits of Stare Decisis," *Chicago-Kent Law Review* 65 (1989): 93–112, pp. 111–12.

10. In wanting to make decisions on a rational basis, my judge does not insist that reason and emotion are fundamentally opposed. Nor does she deny that emotions can provide moral insight. See, e.g., Shaun Nichols, *Sentimental Rules: On the Natural Foundations of Moral Judgment* (Oxford: Oxford University Press, 2004); Martha C. Nussbaum, "Emotion in the Language of Judging," *St. John's Law Review* 70 (1996): 23–30; Antonio R. Damasio, *Descartes' Error: Emotion, Reason, and the Human Brain* (New York: Harper & Row, 1995); Ronald De Sousa, *The Rationality of Emotion* (Cambridge, Mass.: MIT Press, 1987). She simply recognizes that many emotions should not control judicial thinking. For example, she does not treat parties with attractive faces more (or less) favorably than average-looking ones. Nor is she influenced by the fact that the attorney arguing before her wrote an opinion editorial in the local paper with which she disagrees. Real judges do, unfortunately, sometimes allow inappropriate emotions to influence them. My judge tries to avoid this.

perhaps, she determines that it is rational to do so).[11] Nor does she simply consider the facts presented and reach what she considers to be the optimal result without regard for the law. Rather, before she reaches a decision, she determines whether there are any applicable legal standards. Legal systems contain many putative sources of law, including constitutions, treaties, executive orders, statutes, ordinances, administrative regulations, and reported judicial opinions. These sources purport to provide legal standards for decision. The judge may ultimately decide to disregard these standards, but she always wants to know what they are.

Readers who think it obvious that competent judges aim to apply the law will be surprised that I find it necessary to mention that my judge takes an interest in legal standards. I mention this stipulation because it cannot be taken for granted after the twentieth century. The past century witnessed many interrelated debates about the process of adjudication.[12] One was a factual, psychological debate about how judges decide. The American Legal Realists claimed that real judges decide cases for nonlegal reasons, such as their personal opinions about fairness or good public policy, and then construct legal arguments, adverting to sources of law, for use in their reported opinions. The most radical realist believes that legal standards never influence judges.[13]

The concurrent debate was a normative debate about how judges *ought* to decide. Again, the realists tended to support the use of nonlegal standards whereas their critics opposed it. My judge is still deciding whether and when to take legal standards into account. She is willing to be persuaded to ignore them, but she could also be persuaded to take them into account. It remains an open question for her. If you believe that judges never take legal standards into account in any way, and that they could not be persuaded to do so, then this book has little to offer you.

3.4 STANDARDS IN CONFLICT

If you are still reading, then I assume that you are prepared to accept the possibility that at least some judges, some of the time, could be persuaded to take legal standards into account, whether or not they currently do so. If you accept this possibility, then you can share my interest in cases in which valid, applicable legal standards conflict with other normative reasons, such as justice or the general welfare.

For any legal question, one can imagine a legal standard that purports to be relevant to an answer—one that *applies* to the question. Consider

---

11. See §15.4.
12. See generally, Brian Leiter, "Legal Realism and Legal Positivism Reconsidered," *Ethics* 111 (2001): 278–301.
13. See generally, William W. Fisher, III, Morton J. Horwitz, and Thomas Reed, eds., *American Legal Realism* (Oxford: Oxford University Press, 1993).

the following: "Is it legal to sell fireworks in the City of Houston, Texas?" Imagine a municipal ordinance that states, "It shall be a misdemeanor for anyone to sell fireworks in the City of Houston." This rule applies to the question posed. Compare another proposed ordinance that states, "It shall be a misdemeanor for anyone to sell alcoholic beverages in the City of Houston." This rule does not apply to the question at all. The question here is not whether either ordinance is legally valid in Houston but whether it would apply to the question posed if it were valid.

For any legal question and any legal standard or set of standards, we can refer to the *degree to which the standard regulates the question*. A question is not legally regulated at all unless at least one legal standard applies to it. At one extreme lie questions to which the specified standards dictate a unique answer. These questions are *fully regulated* by the standards.[14] At the opposite extreme lie questions to which no answer is excluded by the standards. These questions are *fully unregulated* by the standards. In between these extremes lie *partially regulated* questions, to which the standards preclude some answers but allow others. Of course, the fact that a hypothetical standard applies to a certain legal question tells us nothing about the legally correct answer to the question in the real world. Only legally valid standards dictate legally correct answers in the real world.

For any legal question that is at least partially regulated by a standard, it is possible for a judge to give an answer that departs from that standard. This is what I call *deviating* from a standard as opposed to *adhering* to it.[15] These are the central concepts of this book. The verb "to adhere" is my term of art, referring to the judicial act of correctly applying a legal standard. I use it to distinguish adherence from the generic action of *obeying* or *following* a standard. Anyone can obey a standard, but only those in law-applying roles, such as judges, can adhere to one. Likewise, deviating from a standard is distinct from the generic action of *disobeying* a standard, which anyone can do.[16]

---

14. Some writers refer to cases in which all legal questions are fully regulated as "easy cases," in contrast to "hard cases." See, e.g., David Lyons, "Derivability, Defensibility, and the Justification of Judicial Decisions," in *Moral Aspects of Legal Theory* (Cambridge: Cambridge University Press, 1993), p. 119; Frederick Schauer, "Easy Cases," *Southern California Law Review* 58 (1985): 399–440; Ronald Dworkin, "Hard Cases," in *Taking Rights Seriously* (Cambridge, Mass.: Harvard University Press, 1977). However, the process of identifying the legally correct result may be difficult, in practice, even when there is a definite correct answer. Compare complicated arithmetic problems.

15. Others use different terminology. Alexander and Sherwin call deviation "defiance." Larry Alexander and Emily Sherwin, *The Rule of Rules* (Durham, N.C.: Duke University Press, 2001), p. 47.

16. As I have defined the terms, *deviating from a legal standard* is a redundant phrase, as is *adhering to a legal standard*, but I will sometimes use these phrases, and others, such as *deviating from the law*, for stylistic reasons. In chapter 10, I shall consider the claim that judges have a legal duty to adhere to the law. If one law requires judges to adhere to another law, then adhering to the second law is, in fact, obeying the first, and deviating from the second is disobeying the first.

The cases that interest me involve conflicts between legally valid standards and other standards, legally valid or not. Consider cases in which two opposing standards or sets of standards apply to the case, the first standard or set is legally valid in the jurisdiction, and the first standard or set requires less individual judgment to apply than the second. There are three categories of cases with these characteristics. One category comprises cases in which the first standard is a valid legal rule, and the second is another type of legal standard such as a principle.[17] The rule "Do not exceed thirty-five miles per hour" requires less judgment to apply than does the standard "Do not exceed a safe speed." In the second category, the first standard is the most *locally applicable* legal standard whereas the second standard is a more *remotely applicable* legal standard.[18] In the third category, the first is an entire set of applicable, valid legal standards (rules and/or principles) whereas the second is a moral principle or set of principles that is not found in the law at all.

In each of these three categories I am interested in the conditions under which a judge is morally permitted to deviate from the first standard, or set of standards, in favor of the second. I think my arguments in this book have implications for all three categories of cases, including cases of legally authorized deviation from legal rules. However, I concentrate on cases in the third category: conflicts between legal standards and extralegal principles. To defer to extralegal principles in such cases is to deviate from the law *simpliciter*. This is my paradigm case of deviation. For any legal question that is at least partially regulated by law, it is possible to give a legally incorrect answer—to deviate from the law *simpliciter*.

In the next three sections I shall briefly examine some other types of decisions that might easily be confused with deviation from the law.

3.5 DEPARTURES FROM VALID LEGAL RULES

A decision deviates from a valid legal rule if and only if it conflicts with a rule that is legally valid when the decision is made. Therefore, we must distinguish between invalidating legal rules and deviating from valid legal rules. Judges often have legal authority to invalidate legal rules, as when appellate courts invalidate previously valid legal rules announced by lower courts. A judge also invalidates a valid legal rule when she decides that

---

17. See Ronald Dworkin, "The Model of Rules I," in *Taking Rights Seriously* (Cambridge, Mass.: Harvard University Press, 1977).
18. For the concept of *locality* in this context see Ronald Dworkin, *Law's Empire* (Cambridge, Mass.: Harvard University Press, 1986), pp. 251–54; Frederick Schauer, *Playing by the Rules: A Philosophical Examination of Rule-Based Decision-Making in Law and in Life* (Oxford: Oxford University Press, 1991), pp. 188–89.

federal law preempts a state statute, in whole or in part.[19] These powers of invalidation are universally recognized as lawful and legitimate.

Courts also invalidate rules announced in their own prior decisions—a legally accepted practice that, nevertheless, is sometimes criticized.[20] Courts invalidate statutes as unconstitutional.[21] This practice has long been accepted, although its political legitimacy and wisdom are still sometimes questioned.[22] Historically, courts also have legal authority under the doctrine of desuetude, which allows that "under some circumstances statutes may be abrogated or repealed by a long-continued failure to enforce them."[23] Some scholars would even extend to courts the legal authority to revise or invalidate statutes that have become obsolete, without finding them unconstitutional.[24] Such proposals remain highly controversial.[25]

The U.S. Supreme Court has long recognized that courts have legal authority to depart from the plain meaning of statutory text when adhering would produce "absurd" results.[26] But even this practice, when legally authorized, could be understood as modification of the rule, rather than deviation from it. If a court has legal authority to invalidate a valid rule, then it does not deviate from the rule in so doing. There is no conflict between the rule and the result at the time of application. That conflict defines what I call *deviation*.

---

19. *Bethlehem Steel Co. v. New York State Labor Relations Bd.*, 330 U.S. 767 (1947) (holding that the National Labor Relations Act preempts the New York Labor Relations Board from allowing foremen to unionize).

20. See, e.g., *Payne v. Tennessee*, 501 U.S. 808, 844–45 (1991) (Marshall, J., dissenting).

21. *Marbury v. Madison*, 5 U.S. 137 (1803); *McCulloch v. Maryland*, 17 U.S. 316 (1819).

22. See, e.g., Jeremy Waldron, "The Core of the Case against Judicial Review," *Yale Law Journal* 115 (2006): 1346–406; Larry D. Kramer, *The People Themselves: Popular Constitutionalism and Judicial Review* (Oxford: Oxford University Press, 2004); Jeremy Waldron, *Law and Disagreement* (Oxford: Oxford University Press, 1999); Mark Tushnet, *Taking the Constitution Away from the Courts* (Princeton, N.J.: Princeton University Press, 1999).

23. Arthur E. Bonfield, "The Abrogation of Penal Statutes by Nonenforcement," *Iowa Law Review* 49 (1964): 389–440, p. 394.

24. See, e.g., Douglas E. Edlin, *Judges and Unjust Laws: Common Law Constitutionalism and the Foundations of Judicial Review* (Ann Arbor: University of Michigan Press, 2008); William N. Eskridge, Jr., *Dynamic Statutory Interpretation* (Cambridge, Mass.: Harvard University Press, 1994); Guido Calabresi, *A Common Law for the Age of Statutes* (Cambridge, Mass.: Harvard University Press, 1982).

25. See, e.g., Samuel Estreicher, "Judicial Nullification: Guido Calabresi's Uncommon Common Law for a Statutory Age," *New York University Law Review* 57 (1982): 1126–73. Even the routine practice of distinguishing prior cases constitutes a kind of invalidation. Suppose prior cases have been cited for a certain doctrine. The doctrine requires a certain result in the instant case, but the court distinguishes the instant case from the prior cases, creating a doctrinal exception where none previously existed. It thereby revises or elaborates the doctrine. The revised doctrine is consistent with the prior cases, but the new exception allows a result in the instant case that the original, exceptionless doctrine would have forbidden. See further discussion in §3.10.

26. See John F. Manning, "The Absurdity Doctrine," *Harvard Law Review* 116 (2003): 2387–486.

Of course, courts do not have the authority to invalidate most rules. If a court invalidates a rule that it lacks the authority to invalidate, then it deviates from the law *simpliciter*, in addition to deviating from the rule. It is also possible for a court to deviate from a rule that it has the legal authority to change, if it fails to change the rule before rendering its decision.[27]

3.6 DEVIATIONAL DISCRETION

As I explained in the previous section, many departures from legal rules are instances of legally authorized invalidation: federal preemption of state law, reversal of prior decisions, invalidation of unconstitutional statutes, desuetude, absurdity, distinguishing of precedents, et cetera. Such departures do not satisfy my definition of *deviation*. Coauthors Mortimer and Sanford Kadish describe decisions that come closer to satisfying my definition. They suggest that judges sometimes have legal authority to deviate from legal rules.[28] They introduce the idea of "recourse roles" within the legal system: "roles that enable their agents to take actions in situations where the role's prescribed ends conflict with its prescribed means, including grants of discretion, broad or narrow."[29]

The Kadishes defend at length the idea that jurors in criminal trials play recourse roles.[30] A juror, they claim, "considers whether literal adherence to the judge's instructions will advance or impede the goals of criminal justice as well as the institutional and background ends of the society more generally."[31] Characterizing the juror's role as a recourse role allows one to conclude that jury nullification[32] can be legally justified. According to the Kadishes this is so even if the juror's decision to nullify is morally reprehensible. They use the example of "a Southern jury that acquits a white segregationist of killing a civil rights worker, on the grounds that in the public interest carpetbag troublemakers must be discouraged from venturing into their community, and that in any event the defendant's act was a political act that should not be punished as a common crime."[33]

---

27. If a court has the authority to change a certain rule (e.g., a rule announced in horizontal precedent) and it makes a decision that conflicts with that rule, then observers are likely to conclude that the court has, by that very act, changed the rule. This inference is reasonable unless the court explicitly announces its intention *not* to change the rule from which it deviates.
28. Mortimer R. Kadish and Sanford H. Kadish, *Discretion to Disobey: A Study of Lawful Departures from Legal Rules* (Stanford, Calif.: Stanford University Press, 1973), pp. 85–91.
29. Ibid., p. 35.
30. Ibid., pp. 55–68.
31. Ibid., p. 61.
32. Jury nullification is "a jury's ability to acquit a criminal defendant despite finding facts that leave no reasonable doubt about violation of a criminal statute." Darryl K. Brown, "Jury Nullification within the Rule of Law," *Minnesota Law Review* 81 (1997): 1149–200, p. 1149.
33. Kadish and Kadish, *Discretion to Disobey*, p. 68.

They characterize this acquittal as a "legitimated rule departure" and deny that this jury has acted "lawlessly," even if it is "egregiously wrong in its interpretation of the ends of its role."[34]

The Kadishes subsequently assert that the judicial role, too, is a recourse role, although they admit that they have not defended this claim.[35] The supporting data seem to be that judges sometimes depart from legal rules when they believe that applying them would contradict the "prescribed ends" of the judicial role. Characterizing the judicial role as a recourse role allows the conclusion that judicial nullification of legal rules can be legally justified. If the judge deviates from legal rules and his "judgment is conscientiously made on his view of [the] ends [of the judicial role],"[36] then his deviation is legally legitimate, according to the Kadishes.[37]

The exercise of deviational discretion, as the Kadishes describe it, comes close to satisfying my definition of deviation, but one difference remains. The Kadishes insist that judges do not act lawlessly by exercising deviational discretion—they have legal authority to deviate. The Kadishes are not concerned to defend deviation from the law *simpliciter*, but rather to argue that deviation from legal rules can be legally legitimate. They would not contest Robert Summers' claim that the rule of law requires that rule departures be legitimated, in the sense "that any exceptional power of courts or other tribunals to modify or depart from anterior law at point of application be a power that, so far as feasible, is itself explicitly specified and duly circumscribed in rules, so that this is a power the exercise of which is itself law-governed."[38]

3.7 LEGAL PRINCIPLES

When legal scholars talk about "following the law" they often have in mind the following of rules such as we find in statutes, regulations, and case law. In this book I will accept *arguendo* that rules comprise at least part of the law. However, not everyone agrees that the law consists entirely of *posited* rules—rules that "come into existence at particular times and places" by way of enactment or announcement.[39] Some natural lawyers believe that the law incorporates moral standards that have not been enacted or announced.[40] Dworkinians and inclusive positivists

---

34. Ibid.
35. Ibid., pp. 85–91.
36. Ibid., p. 69.
37. A recent defense of the thesis that Anglo-American judges have the legal authority to overturn unjust laws is Edlin, *Judges and Unjust Laws*.
38. Robert S. Summers, "The Principles of the Rule of Law," *Notre Dame Law Review* 74 (1999): 1691–712, p. 1694. Cf. Edlin, *Judges and Unjust Laws* (judges have a legal duty to "develop the law," which requires not enforcing highly unjust laws).
39. Alexander and Sherwin, *The Rule of Rules*, p. 27.
40. See, e.g., Michael Moore, "Law as a Functional Kind," in *Natural Law Theory: Contemporary Essays*, ed. Robert P. George (Oxford: Oxford University Press, 1992).

believe that the law contains, in addition to rules, other kinds of legal standards, such as principles and policies, which can legally authorize departures from legal rules.[41] In some cases the rules require a result of which the presiding judge disapproves, for some reason, but she can sometimes identify legal principles that authorize a preferable result, rules notwithstanding. This is the reconciliation strategy that Dworkin thinks the courts used to reach putatively just results, unsupported by rules, in *Riggs v. Palmer* and *Henningsen v. Bloomfield Motors*.[42]

Disputes about whether the law includes standards other than rules arise within the theories of law and legal content. I shall not attempt to resolve these disputes. This book aims for compatibility with a wide range of theories of content so I shall not assume either that legal standards other than rules exist or that they do not.[43] When I talk about "following the law" or "adhering to the law" I shall understand *the law* as broadly as possible. If principles are part of the law, then so be it.

I am interested in the conditions under which judges are morally permitted to deviate from the law *simpliciter*, however we define *law*. It is simplest, however, to discuss cases in which the applicable law consists exclusively of codified rules such as statutory provisions. My paradigm case is one in which the only controlling legal authority is a legal rule that dictates an unwelcome result. I concentrate on such cases for three reasons.

First, everyone agrees that modern legal systems contain rules, whereas it remains controversial whether principles should even be classified as a distinct type of legal standard.[44]

Second, compared to principles and other legal standards, rules require the least judgment to apply. Ceteris paribus, it is easier to ascertain whether a result conforms to a certain rule than it is to ascertain whether a legal principle supports that result.

Third, the judicial obligation to adhere to the law must apply to rules if it applies to anything. This is not to insist that judges must always adhere to rules. It is just to observe that if judges have an obligation to

---

41. See, e.g., Mark Greenberg, "How Facts Make Law," *Legal Theory* 10 (2004): 157–98; Jules Coleman, *The Practice of Principle* (Oxford: Oxford University Press, 2001); Matthew Kramer, "How Moral Principles Can Enter into the Law," *Legal Theory* 6 (2000): 83–108; Kenneth Einar Himma, "Judicial Discretion and the Concept of Law," *Oxford Journal of Legal Studies* 19 (1999): 71–82; Nicos Stavropoulos, *Objectivity in Law* (Oxford: Clarendon Press, 1996); W. J. Waluchow, *Inclusive Legal Positivism* (Oxford: Clarendon Press, 1994); Stephen R. Perry, "Second-Order Reasons, Uncertainty, and Legal Theory," *Southern California Law Review* 62 (1989): 913–94.

42. Dworkin, "The Model of Rules I"; *Riggs v. Palmer*, 115 N.Y. 506 (1889); *Henningsen v. Bloomfield Motors*, 32 N.J. 358 (1960).

43. Here I follow Schauer, *Playing by the Rules*, p. 11.

44. See, e.g., Larry Alexander and Ken Kress, "Against Legal Principles," in *Law and Interpretation: Essays in Legal Philosophy*, ed. Andrei Marmor (Oxford: Clarendon Press, 1995).

adhere to the law, then there are *some* rules to which judges must adhere. If, conversely, we conclude that judges are morally permitted to deviate from a result dictated by clear, codified rules, when these are the only controlling legal authority, then it follows easily that they are also morally permitted to deviate from a result dictated by a wider range of legal standards, such as principles and policies. If we conclude that judges are never morally obligated to adhere to legal rules, then it follows a fortiori that they are never obligated to adhere to other legal standards.[45]

3.8 LEGALLY UNAUTHORIZED DEVIATION FROM THE LAW

Judicial departures from legal rules are commonplace. If such a departure is legally authorized in a certain case, then by definition it does not constitute deviation from the law. Deviation from legal rules can be authorized by more authoritative legal standards, such as higher level rules, constitutional provisions, or (arguably) sufficiently important legal principles. I shall write that a decision deviates from the law *simpliciter* if and only if it conflicts with all applicable legal standards, whether or not these take the form of rules.[46] Of course, if it turns out that rules are the only legal standards (contra Dworkin), then the aforementioned decision is impossible because a decision that conflicts with legal rules is ipso facto inconsistent with the law. We cannot know which decisions count as deviant until we have determined the correct theory of legal content, whatever it may be, but we can explore the concept of deviation without committing ourselves to a definite theory of legal content.

A judge engages in deviation from the law *simpliciter* when she reaches a result that cannot be supported by any reasonable reading of the controlling legal authority. Deviation from the law *simpliciter* occurs when a judge deviates from a legally valid rule without *any* higher legal authority to do so. This is the limit case of deviation—as deviant as deviation can be.

So my topic differs from that of Dworkin and the Kadishes in two related respects. First, they address departures from legal rules, whereas I address deviation from the law *simpliciter*. Second, they address legally authorized departures, whereas I am interested in cases of legally unauthorized deviation. The judicial duty that occupies me in the remainder of this book is the duty to correctly apply the law *simpliciter*.

---

45. This paragraph assumes *arguendo* that principles sometimes require particular results, just as rules do. See Dworkin, "The Model of Rules I," pp. 35–36.

46. Hereafter, unless otherwise noted, I use "deviates from the law" interchangeably with "deviates from the law, *simpliciter*."

3.9 DISCRETION VERSUS DEVIATION

Various ideas have been discussed in the jurisprudential literature under the label of *judicial discretion*,[47] so I must explain the relationship between discretion as discussed in the literature and deviation as I understand it. I shall write that a judge enjoys *objective discretion* with respect to two incompatible choices that are open to her if and only if the complete set of valid legal standards permits her to make either choice.

Jurisprudential discussions of judicial discretion have focused on the question of whether judges ever enjoy objective discretion. Does the law contain gaps such that cases can arise in which there is no unique, legally correct answer to the question posed?[48] Some think so.[49] Others disagree.[50] Some believe that the law consists entirely of rules and that cases arise to which the rules do not apply. Others believe that certain "closure rules" close all such gaps.[51] Still others believe that gaps exist between rules, but that binding principles always exist to fill those gaps.[52] And still others believe that, even if judges invoke principles, cases arise in which the law (understood to include both rules and principles) remains indeterminate.[53]

If the law consists only of rules, then a judge enjoys objective discretion when valid rules do not dictate a unique result, as when a statute mandates a fine between $1,000 and $5,000 and no other rule mandates anything more specific. Again, assuming that law consists only of rules, a judge also enjoys objective discretion when a case falls within the open texture

---

47. See, e.g., Marisa Iglesias Vila, *Facing Judicial Discretion: Legal Knowledge and Right Answers Revisited* (Boston: Kluwer, 2001); Himma, "Judicial Discretion and the Concept of Law"; H. L. A. Hart, *The Concept of Law*, 2nd ed. (Oxford: Oxford University Press, 1994), pp. 141–47; Keith Hawkins, ed., *The Uses of Discretion* (Oxford: Oxford University Press, 1992); Aharon Barak, *Judicial Discretion*, trans. Yadin Kaufmann (New Haven, Conn.: Yale University Press, 1989); Dworkin, "The Model of Rules I," pp. 31–39; Ronald Dworkin, "The Model of Rules II," in *Taking Rights Seriously* (Cambridge, Mass.: Harvard University Press, 1978), pp. 68–71.

48. "There is a gap in the law when a legal question has no complete answer." Joseph Raz, "Legal Reasons, Sources, and Gaps," in *The Authority of Law: Essays in Law and Morality* (Oxford: Clarendon Press, 1979), p. 70. Do not confuse this kind of gap with the "gap" introduced in Larry Alexander, "The Gap," *Harvard Journal of Law and Public Policy* 14 (1991): 695–701, on which see §5.4.

49. See, e.g., Schauer, *Playing by the Rules*, pp. 222–26; Raz, "Legal Reasons, Sources, and Gaps."

50. See, e.g., John Gardner, "Concerning Permissive Sources and Gaps," *Oxford Journal of Legal Studies* 8 (1988): 457–61.

51. Hans Kelsen, "On the Theory of Interpretation," *Legal Studies* 10 (1990): 127–35, p. 132.

52. Neil Duxbury, "Faith in Reason: The Process Tradition in American Jurisprudence," *Cardozo Law Review* 15 (1993): 601–705, p. 614 (attributing to Roscoe Pound the view that "principles fill in the gaps where the positive law is found wanting").

53. See, e.g., Stephen J. Burton, *Judging in Good Faith* (Cambridge: Cambridge University Press, 1992), especially pp. 185–91; Andrew Altman, "Legal Realism, Critical Legal Studies, and Dworkin," *Philosophy and Public Affairs* 15 (1986): 205–35.

of applicable rules, as when an ordinance forbids *vehicles* in the park but does not specify whether a moped constitutes a *vehicle*. The law might provide the judge with guidelines in these kinds of cases, but if these are merely advisory then she still has discretion—what the Kadishes call "delegated discretion."[54] This is not the type of discretion that interests me.

Suppose, however, that the law includes principles as well as rules. In that case, if legal principles uniquely resolve the question, then the judge does not enjoy objective discretion. If legal principles do not uniquely resolve the case, then she still enjoys objective discretion. Again, this is not the type of discretion that interests me.

Whereas objective discretion exists prior to a decision, the type of discretion that occupies me exists only when a judge makes a decision. It is exercised when the full set of valid legal standards clearly apply and clearly dictate a unique result, but the judge reaches a different result for some reason. Consider a judge who faces the statute mandating a fine between $1,000 and $5,000, but who imposes a fine of $500 or $6,000. His decision is actually forbidden by the statute. He deviates from this rule.[55] If the law consists only of rules, then he deviates from the law *simpliciter*. Such cases arise even if we assume, with Dworkin, that the law includes principles. If no other legal standard, such as a principle, permits the judge to deviate from the statute, then he deviates from the law *simpliciter*.

The debates about judicial discretion are important, and my project has implications for them. However, I challenge some of the presuppositions of these debates. The most basic presupposition is that if the law dictates a unique result, then judges are morally obligated to reach that result. The greater the number of people who accept this presupposition, the more tempted some people will be, under certain conditions, to misrepresent the law. Imagine someone (a lawyer, judge, or commentator) for whom the following is true:

1. She believes (correctly or not) that her intended audience believes that, if the law dictates a unique result, then judges are morally obligated to reach that result.
2. She believes (correctly or not) that her audience believes that the law requires a particular result in a certain case.
3. She believes with great confidence that this result is unjust or bad policy.

This individual will want to persuade her audience that the law does not, in fact, require this result. She might try to show her audience the errors in their legal reasoning. But in so doing she may succumb to wishful

---

54. Kadish and Kadish, *Discretion to Disobey*, pp. 42–44.
55. *United States v. Mosley*, 965 F.2d 906, 916 (10th Cir. 1992) (holding that a sentencing judge has no authority to sentence below a statutory mandatory minimum); Alexander and Sherwin, *The Rule of Rules*, p. 47 (on "renegade officials").

perception in which the applicable law, which precludes her favored result, appears to her less determinate than it actually is. I agree with Frederick Schauer that we should resist this kind of wishful perception:

> [W]hatever we might say about well-behaved or anaesthetized dogs, they are still dogs, and thus still literally within the semantic scope of a "No dogs allowed" prohibition. It may be that in such circumstances a decision-maker, such as a judge, should then refuse to apply the rule, or should revise the rule, but the (arguable) desirability of such an approach, and the (arguable) desirability of saving the legal system from occasional absurd results, ought not to be disguised in an implausible theory of meaning.[56]

We should admit, at least to ourselves, that the law is not so indeterminate as to always permit our favored results. That goes for judges, too. The practical question is, what should judges do in such cases?

3.10 TYPES OF LEGALLY UNAUTHORIZED DEVIATION

Legally unauthorized deviation involves either *misapplying* or *disregarding* applicable sources of law. A court misapplies a legal standard when it incorrectly presents the standard as a reason to reach a result or incorrectly treats the standard as a reason to reach the result. A court disregards a legal standard when it incorrectly fails to present the standard as a reason to reach a result or incorrectly fails to treat the standard as a reason to reach a result. Such cases include misapplying or disregarding statutes[57] and misapplying or disregarding constitutional provisions.[58]

With respect to precedent, matters are more complicated. Consider the following sequence of events. While visiting Noah's residence in order to buy something that Noah has advertised, Jacob trips on a loose brick and suffers injury. He sues Noah for damages. Imagine (implausibly) that this is a case of first impression in the state. It reaches the state supreme court, which announces that a homeowner is responsible when someone on his property suffers an injury due to his negligence. The court upholds an award of tort damages to Noah.

In the same jurisdiction, Isaac, a dinner guest of Abraham, trips on a loose brick and suffers injury. Isaac sues Abraham for damages. The rule relied upon by the supreme court in Jacob's case would seem to entail an award for Isaac. But the trial court distinguishes the cases: Jacob was an *invitee* (one present for commercial reasons), Isaac a *licensee* (a social

---

56. Schauer, *Playing by the Rules*, p. 59.
57. See, e.g., Joseph P. Bauer, "Addressing the Incoherency of the Preemption Provision of the Copyright Act of 1976," *Vanderbilt Journal of Entertainment & Technology Law* 10 (2007): 1–119, p. 58 (Fourth Circuit "misreads" Act).
58. See, e.g., Frank J. Macchiarola, "Why the Decision in *Zelman* Makes So Much Sense," *N.Y.U. Annual Survey of American Law* 59 (2003): 459–67, p. 461 (U.S. Supreme Court "misreads" Establishment Clause in *Everson v. Board of Education*, 330 U.S. 1 (1947)).

guest).[59] The trial court announces that property owners owe a higher duty of care to invitees than licensees. This rule is consistent with the supreme court's opinion in Jacob's case. The trial court rules in favor of Noah. It thereby deviates from the rule of Jacob's case, but it announces and adheres to a new rule that also supports the result in Jacob's case. The trial court is legally authorized to deviate from the rule of Jacob's case.

A judge who properly distinguishes all prior cases does not deviate from the law *simpliciter*. Although the prior rule on its own does not support his result in the instant case, the judge extends the existing rule in a way that is consistent with all prior cases and with his result in the instant case. If the extended rule *had* been applied in all prior cases, then it would have upheld the results reached in those cases. To deviate is to fail to apply the law as it exists at the time of decision. Because the process of properly distinguishing specifies or elaborates the rule, effectively creating a new rule before deciding the case, proper distinguishing does not constitute true deviation.[60]

However, it is also possible to distinguish cases improperly. The court might, for example, fail to distinguish the instant case from some relevant prior cases. If the trial court had ruled in Noah's favor without drawing the invitee/licensee distinction, then it would have deviated from the rule announced by the supreme court in Isaac's case. The trial court lacks legal authority to do so. It would have deviated from the law *simpliciter*. A court engages in legally unauthorized deviation when it reaches a result that is inconsistent with precedent without adequately distinguishing the case.[61] An especially brazen lower court could even purport to "reverse" a vertical precedent.[62]

Deviating and distinguishing precedent are also distinct from reversing precedent. Courts in the United States often reverse subordinate and horizontal precedents. They are understood to have the legal authority to do so in many cases. Of course, the overruled precedent itself might have been legally correct. A federal appellate court could, for example, reverse

---

59. See William Lloyd Prosser et al., *Prosser and Keeton on the Law of Torts*, 5th ed. (St. Paul, Minn.: West., 1984) §§ 57–60. I am assuming, again, that this is a case of first impression, so let us assume that this authority has not yet been written.

60. It resembles in this respect *norm specification*. See Henry S. Richardson, "Specifying Norms as a Way to Resolve Concrete Ethical Problems," *Philosophy and Public Affairs* 19 (1990): 279–310.

61. See, e.g., Thomas E. Roberts, "Facial Takings Claims Under *Agins-Nectow*: A Procedural Loose End," *Hawaii Law Review* 24 (2002): 623–55, p. 654 ("Ninth Circuit misreads Supreme Court precedent"); Ann C. Hodges, "Protecting Unionized Employees against Discrimination: The Fourth Circuit's Misinterpretation of Supreme Court Precedent," *Employee Rights and Employment Policy Journal* 2 (1998): 123–74.

62. I have found no actual case of a lower court explicitly purporting to *reverse* a higher court, as opposed to merely disregarding vertical precedent. See *State Oil Co. v. Khan*, 118 S. Ct. 275, 284 (1997) (noting in dictum that Court of Appeals was correct to follow precedent with which it disagreed because "it is this Court's prerogative alone to overrule one of its precedents").

its own sound interpretation of the Constitution in favor of an incorrect interpretation. In such cases the reversal constitutes deviation, not because it is a reversal, but because it is incorrect—it fails properly to apply the law. Whereas if a lower court disregards vertical precedent, but in so doing correctly interprets the underlying law, then the court still deviates from the law. A federal district court that defies the law of its circuit deviates, even if everyone else agrees that the appellate court is mistaken and the Supreme Court ultimately vindicates the district court.[63]

3.11 DEVIATION AND "JUDICIAL ACTIVISM"

I mentioned earlier that I avoid the phrase *judicial activism*.[64] Now I shall explain how my concept of deviation relates to the ideas denoted by that phrase. "Judicial activism" and its cognates appear thousands of times annually in scholarship and news media.[65] I think the phrase is meaningful if carefully defined, but too often it is not.[66] Indeed, scholars spend time just differentiating definitions. *Black's Law Dictionary* defines it as "judicial decision-making whereby judges allow their personal views about public policy, among other factors, to guide their decisions."[67] My deviating judges do, indeed, "allow their personal views about public policy, among other factors, to guide their decisions." But the dictionary definition also seems to encompass decisions in which a judge allows his personal views about policy to guide his exercise of *discretion*, as when a judge imposes the minimum sentence allowed by law because he objects to the law on policy grounds. The dictionary calls this a case of judicial activism but it is not a case of deviation in my sense.

A useful recent study of usage by Keenan Kmiec identifies five core meanings of judicial activism: "(1) invalidation of the arguably constitutional actions of other branches, (2) failure to adhere to precedent, (3) judicial 'legislation,' (4) departures from accepted interpretive methodology, and (5) result-oriented judging."[68] For each of these five practices, there are at least some instances of the practice that constitute deviation as I understand it. I shall consider each practice in turn.

---

63. See Evan H. Caminker, "Why Must Inferior Courts Obey Superior Court Precedents?" *Stanford Law Review* 46 (1994): 817–73; Paul L. Colby, "Two Views of the Legitimacy of Nonacquiescence in Judicial Opinions," *Tulane Law Review* 61 (1987): 1041–69.

64. See §1.8.

65. Keenan D. Kmiec, "The Origin and Current Meanings of 'Judicial Activism,'" *California Law Review* 92 (2004): 1441–77, p. 1442 nn.5–6 (Westlaw searches).

66. "'[J]udicial activism' is defined in a number of disparate, even contradictory, ways; scholars and judges recognize this problem, yet persist in speaking about the concept without defining it. Thus, the problem continues unabated: people talk past one another, using the same language to convey very different concepts." Ibid., p. 1443.

67. Bryan A. Garner, ed., *Black's Law Dictionary*, 8th ed. (St. Paul, Minn.: Thomson/West, 2004), p. 862.

68. Kmiec, "The Origin and Current Meanings of 'Judicial Activism,'" p. 1444.

Invalidating the actions of other branches of government constitutes deviation if those actions are, in fact, constitutional. However, many actions are both arguably constitutional *and* arguably unconstitutional. Kmiec's language suggests that a court is activist if it invalidates such actions. To avoid activism, in Kmiec's terms, courts should follow a presumption of constitutionality, invalidating an action only if it is not even arguably constitutional.[69] In contrast, a court that invalidates an action that is arguably constitutional does not deviate if the action is, in fact, unconstitutional. Kmiec calls a court *activist* if it invalidates an action that is, in fact, unconstitutional, if it is arguably constitutional. The charge of *activism* is apt when there is some uncertainty about constitutionality. The charge of *deviation* is apt when there is no uncertainty.

Kmiec's second meaning of *judicial activism* involves "failure to adhere to precedent." Deviation often takes this form, but a departure from precedent constitutes deviation only if it is legally unauthorized. As discussed earlier, all departures from vertical precedent fall in this category.[70] So do departures from horizontal precedent unless the precedent is explicitly reversed. But Kmiec's definition implies that any departure from horizontal precedent constitutes activism, even if (perhaps especially if) the court reverses the precedent. So the second meaning of *activism* encompasses more than deviation.

Judicial "legislation," Kmiec's third meaning, occurs when judges change legal standards without legal authorization. Such decisions always count as deviant in my terms. For example, courts are sometimes accused of creating new constitutional rights and ignoring existing ones.[71] Of course, commentators disagree about whether a certain right is "new" or not and I shall not enter these debates. The important point is that *if* one believes that a court has created a new right or ignored an existing one, without legal authorization, then one believes that the court has deviated.

Do courts deviate when they "depart from accepted interpretive methodology" (Kmiec's fourth definition)? It depends. If, by *accepted*, Kmiec means "mandatory," then the answer is affirmative. If, however, a methodology can be accepted but not mandatory, then we must conclude that courts deviate only if they depart from methodologies that they are required to use. For example, the standard canons of statutory construction are seen as advisory, not mandatory.[72]

Finally, Kmiec's fifth definition of activism as "result-oriented judging" is perhaps the closest to my definition of *deviation*. He states that a judge

---

69. Compare James B. Thayer, "The Origin and Scope of the American Doctrine of Constitutional Law," *Harvard Law Review* 7 (1893): 129–56.

70. See §3.10.

71. See, e.g., Antonin Scalia, *A Matter of Interpretation: Federal Courts and the Law* (Princeton, N.J.: Princeton University Press, 1997), pp. 37–47.

72. *Chickasaw Nation v. United States*, 534 U.S. 84, 94 (2001) (canons of construction are not mandatory rules); *Connecticut National Bank v. Germain*, 503 U.S. 249, 253 (1992).

engages in result-oriented judging if and only if her decision "departs from some 'baseline' of correctness," and she makes the decision for an "ulterior motive."[73] If *correctness* means "legal" correctness, then it is true by definition that deviant decisions are those that depart from a baseline of correctness, so all cases of result-oriented judges are cases of deviation. If ulterior motives include the desire to avoid normatively undesirable results, then the cases of deviation that interest me are all cases of result-oriented judging. Therefore, one might describe my central topic as "the ethics of judicial activism, understood as result-oriented judging."

3.12 JUDICIAL MENTAL STATES

A judge who deviates from the law does so either purposely, knowingly, recklessly, negligently, or innocently.[74] Much deviation is merely negligent: the judge tries to adhere, but he misreads sources that a reasonable judge would have read correctly. In 1960, a magistrate was charged with a number of errors, including releasing a defendant on parole who was ineligible because of a prior felony conviction. The magistrate was not disciplined for these errors because it was determined that he had honestly misunderstood the scope of his authority (which is not to say that his misunderstanding was reasonable).[75]

Deviation is occasionally reckless. One judge dismissed the first criminal charge he heard on the bench simply because he had once "promised himself" that he would do so.[76] Others have decided cases on the basis of coin flips.[77] One judge polled the courtroom audience on whether to grant a request to file a criminal complaint.[78] Such judges decide recklessly. If they reach legally incorrect results, then they deviate recklessly.[79]

---

73. Kmiec, "The Origin and Current Meanings of 'Judicial Activism,'" p. 1476.

74. A judge deviates innocently if and only if a reasonable judge could not be expected to understand the law in question. For example, if laws are too complicated, then judges will sometimes deviate innocently. See Lon L. Fuller, *The Morality of Law*, 2nd rev. ed. (New Haven, Conn.: Yale University Press, 1969), p. 36.

75. Gerald Stern, "Is Judicial Discipline in New York State a Threat to Judicial Independence?" *Pace Law Review* 7 (1987): 291–388, p. 315. The California Supreme Court has held that mere negligence does not suffice for discipline. *Broadman v. Commission on Judicial Performance*, 959 P.2d 715, 720–21 (Cal. 1998).

76. *In re DeRose*, 1980 Annual Report 181, 183 (New York State Commission on Judicial Conduct, Nov. 13, 1979).

77. *McCartney v. Commission on Judicial Quality*, 526 P.2d 268 (Cal. 1974); *In re Daniels*, 340 So.2d 301 (La. 1976).

78. *In re Friess*, 1984 Annual Report 84 (New York State Commission on Judicial Conduct, Mar. 30, 1983).

79. Of course, using these arbitrary methods is unethical even when it happens to yield a correct decision. They are unethical even when used to make a decision within the range of the judge's legal discretion, as when a judge decided between a twenty-day and thirty-day sentence on the basis of a coin flip. Ibid.

The cases that interest me, however, involve judges who knowingly deviate in order to avoid results of which they disapprove.[80] Within that category we can distinguish between *express* and *tacit* deviation. A judge deviates expressly if and only if she admits it publicly. Otherwise she deviates tacitly.

Most judicial deviation is tacit, but express deviation occasionally occurs, making for considerable drama. A well-publicized episode arose in the California case of *Morrow v. Hood Communications, Inc.*[81] *Morrow* involved a *stipulated reversal*, in which opposing parties settle a case after a trial court has made a final ruling on the merits. The loser pays the winner to consent to have the ruling reversed by an appeals court. This practice had been endorsed by the California Supreme Court in the case of *Neary v. Regents of the University of California*.[82] In *Morrow*, Presiding Justice J. Anthony Kline of the California Court of Appeal opened his dissenting opinion as follows:

> There are rare instances in which a judge of an inferior court can properly refuse to acquiesce in the precedent established by a court of superior jurisdiction. This is, for me, such an instance.
>
> I acknowledge that the opinion of the California Supreme Court in Neary v. Regents of University of California requires that the motion before us be granted. I would deny the motion, however, because I cannot as a matter of conscience apply the rule announced in *Neary*.
>
> I do not refuse to acquiesce in *Neary* because I believe the opinion is analytically flawed and empirically unjustified, though, as I have elsewhere explained at length, that is my view. My refusal is instead based on my deeply felt opinion that the doctrine of stipulated reversal announced in *Neary*—a doctrine employed in no other jurisdiction in this nation and unanimously repudiated by the Supreme Court of the United States—is destructive of judicial institutions.[83]

Another example of express deviation, perhaps even more shocking, is that of Justice Tom Parker of the Alabama Supreme Court, whose platform

---

80. A word about *purposeful* deviation is in order. Few judges who deviate do so purposely under that description. Rarely does a judge act with the "conscious object" of deviating from the law. One exception is the traitorous judge who intends to undermine the reputation of the judiciary and who therefore makes a decision *because* it is deviant. Even corrupt judges deviate for their own benefit. But most judges who knowingly deviate do not do so for such reasons. They deviate in order to avoid objectionable results. In the cases that interest me, fulfilling this purpose requires decisions that happen to be deviant.

81. See, e.g., *Morrow v. Hood Communications, Inc.*, 69 Cal. Rptr. 2d 489, 494–95 (Cal. Ct. App. 1997) (Kline, P.J., dissenting). For discussions of the case see, e.g., Sambhav N. Sankar, "Disciplining the Professional Judge," *California Law Review* 88 (2000): 1233–80; Pamela S. Karlan, "Two Concepts of Judicial Independence," *Southern California Law Review* 72 (1999): 535–58; Stephen C. Yeazell, "Good Judging and Good Judgment," *Court Review* 35 (1998): 8–10; Howard Mintz, "Disciplinary Case against Judge Raises Legal Uproar," *San Jose Mercury News*, July 11, 1998, p. 1A.

82. *Neary v. Regents of the University of California*, 834 P.2d 119 (Cal. 1992).

83. *Morrow v. Hood Communications, Inc.* at 494–95. Note that Kline's deviation occurred only in a dissenting opinion and thus had no legal force.

during his 2006 campaign for chief justice centered on the fact that he, unlike his colleagues, was willing to ignore the U.S. Supreme Court when he believed it to be wrong.[84]

3.13 PRIVATE REASONS TO DEVIATE

In the next chapters, I shall examine various reasons that a judge might knowingly deviate from the law *simpliciter*. Before closing this chapter, I shall consider private reasons to deviate, mainly incentives.

An incentive obviously exists when someone offers the judge a bribe to deviate: he will receive the bribe if he rules in favor of a specified party, despite the fact that a dispositive legal case has been or will be made against the latter.[85] Even in the absence of a bribe, a judge might have private reasons to deviate in favor of a relative or friend who is a party to a case and is disfavored by the law. Of course, codes of judicial conduct require judges to recuse themselves in cases of conflict of interest and they face sanctions for failing to do so.[86] But a judge who can avoid such sanctions could have a private reason to hear the case and to deviate in favor of his relative.

More common than cases involving relatives or friends are those in which the judge develops a personal like or dislike for a party and a concomitant desire for her to win or lose, respectively. If the law requires the opposite result, then the judge's feelings give him a private reason to deviate.

Even when the case does not involve bribes, conflicts of interest, personal affection, or antipathy, judges can still have incentives to deviate. Identifying and applying the correct law can be difficult and time-consuming. Adhering to the law requires knowing the law and applying it to the facts of the case. A judge could simplify his job in various ways: by ignoring the law and deciding on some simpler basis, by writing a superficial opinion, or by deciding difficult cases summarily, without writing an opinion.[87] Even if the judge happens to reach the legally correct result,

---

84. David White, "Parker Says He's Willing to Defy High Court," *Birmingham (Ala.) News*, May 26, 2006, p. 1C.

85. *Bracy v. Gramley*, 520 U.S. 899, 909 (1997) (holding that petitioner, who was convicted before a judge who was himself later convicted of taking bribes, showed "good cause" for discovery on claim of actual bias).

86. *Model Code of Judicial Conduct*, Canon 3E (2007); *Code of Conduct of United States Judges*, Canon 3C.

87. He could, for example, grant a *sua sponte* motion for summary judgment. See Arthur R. Miller, "The Pretrial Rush to Judgment: Are the 'Litigation Explosion,' 'Liability Crisis,' and Efficiency Cliches Eroding Our Day in Court and Jury Trial Commitments?" *New York University Law Review* 78 (2003): 982–1134, pp. 1006, 1052, 1055–56 (widespread federal practice of judges employing Federal Rule of Civil Procedure 16, providing case management authority, to effectively implement summary judgment merits review *sua sponte*).

these shortcuts involve deviant legal reasoning—reasoning that does not aim at reaching the legally correct result.

This book contains little more about private reasons to deviate. I shall be concerned mainly with impartial, moral reasons to deviate.[88] I shall argue that judges have *pro tanto* moral reasons to deviate whenever the legally required result is unjust or otherwise objectionable as a matter of public policy. These reasons are often outweighed by stronger reasons to adhere, but that story must await part II.

---

88. Introduced in chapter 6.

4

The Legal Duties of Judges

4.1 ADHERENCE RULES

Do judges have a *legal* duty to apply the law correctly? To ask this question is not to query the tautology: does the law require judges to do what the law requires judges to do? That the law requires certain results does not logically entail that any particular individual has a legal duty to decide cases accordingly. It might seem that the concept of *judge* entails a legal duty to apply the law, but this is incorrect. Asking whether a judge has a legal duty to apply the law is like asking whether a police officer has a legal duty to knock before entering your apartment or whether a physician has a legal duty to perform an emergency tracheotomy on a fellow airline passenger. These are questions about the legal duties of particular professionals. The concept of *judge* does not entail a legal duty to apply the law any more than the concept of *doctor* entails a legal duty to perform tracheotomies. In each of these cases we can learn the answer only by studying what the law demands of these professionals.

Judges have various professional duties while they remain on the bench. These include duties to oversee court proceedings, to maintain decorum, to study the law, to rule on motions, to examine evidence presented, to answer questions from jurors, to decide cases, et cetera.[1] These duties can be expressed in *adjudication rules*—secondary rules addressed to adjudicators.[2] Some adjudication rules are codified in constitutions, statutes, codes of judicial conduct, and case law.[3] They impose various requirements: judges must appear in court when assigned;[4] they must recuse themselves

---

1. Although they are not enumerated, these are presumably some of the duties to which the Code of Conduct for federal judges refers when it states that "a judge should perform the duties of the office . . . diligently." *Code of Conduct of United States Judges*, Canon 3.

2. They contrast with primary rules addressed to ordinary legal subjects. H. L. A. Hart, *The Concept of Law*, 2nd ed. (Oxford: Oxford University Press, 1994), pp. 93–94.

3. Although some writers would not classify rules found only in case law as *codified*, the classification serves my purposes.

4. *Model Code of Judicial Conduct*, Canon 3B(1) (1990) ("A judge shall hear and decide matters assigned to the judge except those in which disqualification is required").

in cases that present conflicts of interest;[5] they must not practice law while sitting on the bench,[6] et cetera.

Are judges legally obligated to obey codified adjudication rules? Judges have many of the same legal duties as the rest of us, certainly: to pay income taxes, to testify under subpoena, to care for dependent children, to fulfill contractual obligations, and so forth. Some scholars believe that judicial duties, likewise, are legal duties.[7] My specific question is whether, as some believe, judges have a legal duty to adhere to the law *simpliciter*.[8] Justice Cardozo appears to think so: "Judges have, of course, the power, though not the right, to ignore the mandate of a statute, and render judgment in despite of it. They have the power, though not to right, to travel beyond the walls of the interstices, the bounds set to judicial innovation by precedent and custom. Nonetheless, by that abuse of power, they violate the law."[9]

A judicial duty to adhere is entailed by the legal validity of certain *adherence rules*: adjudication rules that require judges to decide cases in accordance with certain decision rules. Adherence rules are *mandatory* rules: rules that "when accepted, furnish reasons for action simply in virtue of their existence *qua* rules."[10] Adherence rules, if authoritative, provide judges with reasons to adhere to the law.[11]

---

5. Ibid., Canon 3E(1).
6. Ibid., Canon 4G.
7. Darrell L. Keith, "The Court's Charge in Texas Medical Malpractice Cases," *Baylor Law Review* 48 (1996): 675–814, p. 778 (trial judge has a "legal duty to preside over the trial"); Joseph Raz, "Law and Value in Adjudication," in *The Authority of Law* (Oxford: Clarendon Press, 1979), p. 197 (discussing judges' official duties as "legal duties").
8. Philip Hamburger, "Law and Judicial Duty," *George Washington Law Review* 72 (2003): 1–41, p. 24 ("to the extent their office was defined by law and their oaths were imposed by law, the judges could be considered legally obliged to decide in accord with law"); Stephen J. Burton, *Judging in Good Faith* (Cambridge: Cambridge University Press, 1992), p. 35 ("judges do not fulfill their legal duty if they act only on parts of the law with which they agree"). To be more precise, one should say that a judge has a conditional legal duty: *if* he chooses to decide a case, then he has a legal duty to decide it according to law, when the law provides an answer. This formulation reflects the fact that judges may be legally permitted to avoid deciding any given case. Judges are legally permitted to recuse themselves in certain cases. Moreover, they have no legal duty to remain on the bench. Judicial service is not indentured servitude. Judges are always legally permitted to resign.
9. Benjamin N. Cardozo, *The Nature of the Judicial Process* (New Haven, Conn.: Yale University Press, 1921), p. 129. Neil MacCormick states that "the judge has a *duty*" to reach the legally required result. Neil MacCormick, *Legal Reasoning and Legal Theory* (Oxford: Clarendon Press, 1978), p. 33. See also Sambhav N. Sankar, "Disciplining the Professional Judge," *California Law Review* 88 (2000): 1233–80, p. 1240 ("[T]he integrity of the legal system relies upon each individual judge's adherence to precedent, compliance with orders from superior courts, and respect for the validity of prior judgments").
10. Frederick Schauer, *Playing by the Rules: A Philosophical Examination of Rule-Based Decision-Making in Law and in Life* (Oxford: Oxford University Press, 1991), p. 5.
11. Adherence rules are entirely separate from conduct rules addressed to legal subjects who are not judges. A judge who convicts someone of income tax evasion in a bench trial does not thereby "obey" the tax code as he does when he submits his own tax return.

My arguments in this book are consistent with the view that every judge has a *pro tanto* legal duty to decide according to law every case that he chooses to decide. I shall now consider arguments that support this proposition because some important objections to my ultimate position depend upon it.[12] Three issues seem relevant to the question whether judicial duties, such as the duty to adhere, are legal duties. First, do recognized sources of law include, or incorporate by reference, any adherence rules? Second, does the law provide sanctions for judges who break the rules? Third, are sanctions imposed, in practice?

4.2 CODIFIED ADHERENCE RULES

Adherence rules are codified in the two main codes of judicial conduct in the United States: the *Model Code of Judicial Conduct* of the American Bar Association (ABA) and the *Code of Conduct for United States Judges* adopted by the Judicial Conference of the United States. The 1990 revision of the ABA *Model Code* states, "A judge shall respect and comply with the law and shall act at all times in a manner that promotes public confidence in the integrity and impartiality of the judiciary,"[13] in which *law* is defined as "court rules as well as statutes, constitutional provisions and decisional law."[14] The *Model Code* also states, "A judge shall be faithful to the law and maintain professional competence in it. A judge shall not be swayed by partisan interests, public clamor or fear of criticism."[15] The 2007 revision of the *Model Code* states, "A judge shall uphold and apply the law, and shall perform all duties of judicial office fairly and impartially."[16] The Commentary to this section reads, "Although each judge comes to the bench with a unique background and personal philosophy, a judge must interpret and apply the law without regard to whether the judge approves or disapproves of the law in question."[17]

Several provisions of the *Code of Conduct for United States Judges* also address the adherence duty. Canon 2A states, "A judge should respect and comply with the law and should act at all times in a manner that promotes public confidence in the integrity and impartiality of the judiciary."[18] Canon 3A(1) states, "A judge should be faithful to and maintain professional competence in the law, and should not be swayed by partisan

---

12. See chapter 10.
13. *Model Code of Judicial Conduct*, Canon 2A (1990). The 2007 revision of the *Model Code* states, "A judge shall comply with the law, including the Code of Judicial Conduct." *Model Code of Judicial Conduct*, Rule 1.1 (2007).
14. *Model Code of Judicial Conduct*, Definitions (1990).
15. Ibid., Canon 3B(2).
16. Ibid., Rule 2.2.
17. Ibid., Comment on Rule 2.2.
18. *Code of Conduct of United States Judges*, Canon 2A.

The Legal Duties of Judges

interests, public clamor, or fear of criticism."[19] Also noteworthy is the commentary to Canon 1:

> Deference to the judgments and rulings of courts depends upon public confidence in the integrity and independence of judges. The integrity and independence of judges depend in turn upon their acting without fear or favor. *Although judges should be independent, they should comply with the law*, as well as the provisions of this Code. Public confidence in the impartiality of the judiciary is maintained by the adherence of each judge to this responsibility. Conversely, violation of this Code diminishes public confidence in the judiciary and thereby does injury to the system of government under law.[20] (emphasis added)

The *Model Code* has been adopted, in whole or in part, in forty-nine of the fifty states,[21] usually including provisions stating that "judges shall be faithful to the law."[22] These codes have not, however, been adopted directly by state legislatures. Some have been drafted by agencies or judicial councils which themselves enjoy statutory or constitutional authorization.[23] Although state codes of judicial conduct look very much like state statutes, the former have not actually been incorporated into the latter. Rather, the high court of each state has issued an order containing a code of judicial conduct. Such an order might be sufficient to give a code legal force, absent statutory incorporation, but it might not be.

Federal judges are not bound by these state codes. Moreover, at the federal level, the Judicial Conference of the United States holds no specific statutory grant of authority to enact binding ethical rules.[24] The *Code of Conduct* states, "The Code may . . . provide standards of conduct for application in proceedings under the Judicial Councils Reform and Judicial Conduct and Disability Act of 1980. . . ." But the *Code of Conduct* cannot thereby bestow legislative authority upon itself in this area. Federal legislation provides conditions under which judges are required to disqualify themselves but it does not incorporate any other provisions of the *Code of Conduct*.[25] Therefore, one could deny that federal judges have

---

19. Ibid., Canon 3A(1).
20. Ibid., Commentary to Canon 1.
21. Leslie W. Abramson, "Appearance of Impropriety: Deciding When a Judge's Impartiality 'Might Reasonably Be Questioned,'" *Georgetown Journal of Legal Ethics* 14 (2000): 55–102, p. 55. Montana is the holdout.
22. See, e.g., *California Rules of Court*, Appendix Division II, Code of Judicial Ethics, Canon 3 (2006); *New York CLS Judicial Appendix*, Code of Judicial Conduct, Canon 100.3 (2006).
23. See, e.g., N.Y. Const., Art. VI, § 22 (2008) (establishing commission on judicial conduct).
24. See 28 U.S.C. § 331 (establishing Judicial Conference of the United States); *In re Cargill*, 66 F.3d 1256, 1267 (1st Cir. 1995) (Campbell, J., dissenting) (noting that although "the Judicial Conference of the United States, which adopted the [Code, does not] hold a specific statutory grant of authority to enact binding ethical rules," it should still be accorded "great persuasive weight"); Debra Lyn Bassett, "Judicial Disqualification in the Federal Courts," *Iowa Law Review* 87 (2002): 1213–56, p. 1230.
25. 28 U.S.C. §455 (disqualification of justice, judge, or magistrate judge).

a legal duty to obey the adherence rules contained in the *Code of Conduct*. Circuit Judicial Councils are now authorized to investigate allegations of judicial misconduct, but they have narrow disciplinary powers.[26]

In addition to codes of judicial conduct, there are some other putative sources of legal authority for a judicial adherence duty. Judicial opinions recognize that courts have a duty to apply the law or are "bound by the law."[27] One may also infer that a judge believes in a duty to adhere to the law if he claims to have adhered in a certain case despite expressing disagreement or regret over what it "requires" him to do.[28] In such cases one could argue that a duty to adhere forms part of the reasoning necessary to the decision if the judge claims to adhere to the law, despite the fact that she disagrees with the legally required result and "wishes" that she could reach a different one.

Finally, some judicial oaths could be read as implying a duty to obey adherence rules. Mississippi judges, for example, swear that they will

---

26. Steven Lubet, "Judicial Discipline and Judicial Independence," *Law and Contemporary Problems* 61 (1998): 59–74, p. 59. See also 28 U.S.C. §§ 331, 332, 372, 604.

27. See, e.g., *Maryland St. Dept. of Educ., Div. of Rehabilitation Servs. v. United States Dept. of Veterans Affairs*, 98 F.3d 165, 168 (4th Cir. 1997) ("Courts are charged with the duty to apply the law that Congress enacted"); *Bittaker v. Enomoto*, 587 F.2d 400, 402 n. 1 (9th Cir. 1978) ("It is . . . a district court's duty to apply the law of the appropriate circuit to all persons presenting claims within its jurisdiction"); *Prima Paint Corp. v. Flood & Conklin Mfg. Co.*, 388 U.S. 395, 406 (1967) ("Federal courts are bound to apply rules enacted by Congress with respect to matters . . . over which it has legislative power"); *Jackson v. Lykes Bros. S.S. Co., No. 575*, 386 U.S. 731, 737 (1967) (Stewart, J., dissenting) ("It is our duty to apply the law, not to repeal it"); *United States v. Mirsky*, 17 F.2d 275, 276 (S.D.N.Y. 1926) (court has "duty to apply the law as it is now written"); *States v. Schooner Peggy*, 1 Cranch 103, 109 (1801) ("[T]he court must decide according to existing laws"); *United States v. Callender*, 25 F. Cas. 239, 257 (C.C.D. Va. 1800) ("No position can be more clear than that all the federal judges are bound by the solemn obligation of religion, to regulate their decisions agreeably to the constitution of the United States, and that it is the standard of their determination in all cases that come before them").

28. See, e.g., Jack B. Weinstein, "Every Day Is a Good Day for a Judge to Lay Down His Professional Life for Justice," *Fordham Urban Law Journal* 32 (2004): 131–70 (praising judges who criticize the law); Charles Fried, "Scholars and Judges: Reason and Power," *Harvard Journal of Law and Public Policy* 23 (2000): 807–32, p. 811 ("The judge is also free to criticize the law as she finds it—and there are some notable examples of judges doing just that while accepting and carrying on in a course of decision they regret or even deplore"); Gerald Gunther, *Learned Hand: The Man and the Judge* (Cambridge, Mass.: Harvard University Press, 1998), p. 149 ("[B]owing to precedent did not prevent [Hand] from expressing sharp and thoughtful criticism of the prevailing law, or from suggesting a better approach"); *United States v. Shonubi*, 895 F. Supp. 460 (E.D.N.Y. 1995) (criticizing Second Circuit rule of automatic obstruction of justice enhancement under section 3C1.1 of the Sentencing Guidelines, but imposing enhancement); *United States v. Tropiano*, 898 F. Supp. 90 (E.D.N.Y. 1995) (following appellate mandate despite serious reservations); *United States v. Ekwunoh*, 888 F. Supp. 369 (E.D.N.Y. 1994) (noting that it is important to consider mens rea in drug sentencing, despite court of appeals' instruction to disregard defendant's reasonable belief); *United States v. Isgro*, 974 F.2d 1091, 1093–94 (9th Cir. 1992) (criticizing rule of U.S. Supreme Court that prosecutors have no duty to present substantial exculpatory evidence to the grand jury, as stated in *United States v. Williams*, 504 U.S. 36 (1992)); *United States v. Orjuela*, 809 F. Supp. 193, 197 (E.D.N.Y. 1992) ("Regrettably, [*Williams*] compels the conclusion that this court lacks power to remedy the government's apparent abuse of its power").

The Legal Duties of Judges

perform their duties "agreeably to the Constitution of the United States and the Constitution and laws of the State of Mississippi."[29] One could read this language as a promise to apply the law correctly, in which case one could argue that judges who take the oath acquire a moral obligation to apply the law regardless of whether they have a legal obligation to do so. But one could instead read the language as a promise to obey the law on the job, which is a different matter.

4.3 SANCTIONS

Even if Congress and state legislatures decided to codify codes of judicial conduct into statutes, someone could still insist that no judge actually has a legal duty to adhere to the law unless he is credibly threatened with *formal sanctions* for deviating. This suggestion might reflect a discredited "command model" of law according to which each legal duty must have an associated sanction.[30] At least since H. L. A. Hart, legal theorists have recognized that the law can impose genuine legal duties without sanctions, just as it can grant legal powers without any sanctions being specified.[31] Nevertheless, it is useful to determine what formal sanctions the law provides for judges who deviate. Legal duties do not logically entail sanctions, but whether sanctions are provided may still be relevant to the existence of legal duties.

Some commentators assert that encouraging adherence to the law is a legitimate reason to discipline judges,[32] but American law has a long tradition of reluctance to sanction judges for decisions made on the merits of the case. In 1872, the U.S. Supreme Court declared that "[a] judge shall be free to act upon his own convictions without apprehension of personal consequence to himself."[33] Jeffrey Shaman, a leading scholar of judicial ethics, observes that "[i]mposing discipline upon a judge for an incorrect legal ruling is an extremely sensitive issue because it comes closer than any other ground of discipline to threatening judicial independence."[34] Another eminent ethicist, Stephen Lubet, argues that "judicial independence is most gravely threatened when judges face sanctions for 'decisional

---

29. *Miss. Const. Ann.*, Art. 6, §155 (2008).
30. See John Austin, *The Province of Jurisprudence Determined*, ed. Wilfrid E. Rumble (New York: Cambridge University Press, 1995), p. 29 (first published 1832). One might also infer that the importance of the duty is proportional to the severity of the sanction, on the command model.
31. Hart, *The Concept of Law*, ch. 3.
32. "A . . . reason for imposing discipline is to enforce adherence to legal norms. . . . ," Sankar, "Disciplining the Professional Judge," p. 1239.
33. *Bradley v. Fisher*, 80 U.S. 335, 347 (1872). See also Jeffrey M. Shaman, "Judicial Ethics," *Georgetown Journal of Legal Ethics* 2 (1988): 1–20, p. 11 ("In this nation there has been a long-standing belief in judicial independence so that judges can be free to decide cases without fear of retribution or the need to curry favor").
34. Shaman, "Judicial Ethics," p. 8.

conduct,' which may be defined as discipline based on the merits of a ruling,"[35] although he concedes that even some purely decisional conduct should be punished.[36]

The mere fact that a judge knowingly deviates from the law does not subject him to civil or criminal liability. Of course, an act of deviation can constitute a criminal act or give rise to a civil cause of action for other reasons: a judge who deviates from the law in furtherance of some other crime could end up in prison. But knowingly violating codes of judicial conduct does not, per se, constitute a crime.[37]

It is also well-settled law that judges enjoy absolute immunity from civil lawsuits, "so long as the contested action was judicial in nature and was not taken in the complete absence of jurisdiction."[38] Judges are sometimes sued for their decisions, but no civil judgment can be entered against them on the basis of their decisional conduct, even when egregiously deviant.[39]

Judges are, however, subject to various formal sanctions for violating codes of judicial conduct, including reprimand, private or public censure, suspension, impeachment, and removal.[40] But even mild disciplinary sanctions are imposed only in cases involving criminal activity, intoxication on the job, judicial patronage, inappropriate courtroom demeanor, racist or sexist remarks, sexual harassment, or similar misconduct.[41] Another example is failing to disqualify oneself when required, as when the judge has had ex parte communications with one of the parties.[42]

4.4 LEGAL ERROR AS JUDICIAL MISCONDUCT

When, if ever, does deviation from the law constitute judicial misconduct? It is commonly said that "mere legal error" does not rise to that level.[43] The commentary to Rule 2.2 of the *Model Code* states, "When

    35. Lubet, "Judicial Discipline and Judicial Independence," p. 59.
    36. Ibid., p. 72.
    37. "[T]he Code is not designed or intended as a basis for civil liability or criminal prosecution." Commentary, *Code of Conduct of United States Judges*.
    38. *Stump v. Sparkman*, 435 U.S. 349, 356–57 (1978). See also *Lewis v. Green*, 629 F. Supp. 546 (DC Dist. Col. 1986) (28 U.S.C. § 453, which sets forth oath of allegiance to Constitution taken by federal judges, does not create substantive cause of action against federal judges for violating oath by acting contrary to Constitution); James J. Alfini et al., *Judicial Conduct and Ethics*, 4th ed. (Newark, N.J.: LexisNexis, 2007).
    39. But see Abimbola A. Olowofoyeku, *Suing Judges: A Study of Judicial Immunity* (Oxford: Clarendon Press, 1993).
    40. See generally, Alfini et al., *Judicial Conduct and Ethics*.
    41. Ibid.
    42. See, e.g., *In re Cooks*, 694 So.2d 892 (La. 1997) (judge engages in punishable misconduct by failing to recuse herself after extensive ex parte communications with a party).
    43. "While the courts have often said that 'mere' legal error does not amount to judicial misconduct, that does not mean that legal error can never constitute misconduct." Shaman, "Judicial Ethics," p. 8.

The Legal Duties of Judges

applying and interpreting the law, a judge sometimes may make good-faith errors of fact or law. Errors of this kind do not violate this Rule."[44] The California Supreme Court has held that "[m]ere legal error, without more, . . . is insufficient to support a finding that a judge has violated the Code of Judicial Ethics and thus should be disciplined."[45] Gerald Stern asserts that "investigations of judges are not warranted merely because the judges abused their discretion or otherwise committed judicial error,"[46] and he notes that "[f]or most of the past ten decades, arbitrary conduct in court that deprived litigants or other persons of their guaranteed rights, with few exceptions, has not been a basis for discipline."[47] Shaman writes that "[u]nder the modern judicial disciplinary system, judges may not be censured or penalized for making erroneous or unpopular decisions."[48]

The normal remedy for legal error is the appeal process.[49] Most complaints filed with state judicial conduct commissions allege errors of law or fact and are dismissed as more properly handled via appeal.[50] However, the *Model Code* and *Code of Judicial Conduct* contain some provisions that support the idea that deviation can constitute judicial misconduct.[51] So why do leading scholars insist that mere legal error does not constitute judicial misconduct?[52]

At a minimum, these commentators are asserting that innocent, non-negligent deviation does not constitute misconduct. Perhaps they are also asserting that deviation does not constitute misconduct if it is merely negligent. It is not obvious to me that this assertion is literally correct, but I shall not pursue the issue.[53] It is still less obvious that the exemption extends to reckless or knowing deviation. Several commentators assert that intentional deviation manifests unfitness for judicial office. Stern, for instance, suggests that judicial independence "was not intended to afford protection

---

44. *Model Code of Judicial Conduct*, Commentary to Rule 2.2 (1990).
45. *Oberholzer v. Commission on Judicial Performance*, 975 P.2d 663, 680 (Cal. 1999).
46. Gerald Stern, "Is Judicial Discipline in New York State a Threat to Judicial Independence?" *Pace Law Review* 7 (1987): 291–388, p. 314. Abuse of discretion could involve, for example, a trial court interpreting in an unreasonable way the facts presented.
47. Ibid., p. 322.
48. Shaman, "Judicial Ethics," p. 12.
49. Ibid., pp. 8–9; Lubet, "Judicial Discipline and Judicial Independence," p. 74 ("It is widely understood that disciplinary complaints should not be misused as an alternative to appeal by disgruntled litigants"). See also *Harrod v. Illinois Courts Commission*, 372 N.E.2d 53 (Ill. 1977); *In re Mattera*, 168 A.2d 38 (N.J. 1961); *Murtagh v. Maglio*, 9 A.D.2d 515 (N.Y. 1960).
50. Cynthia Gray, "The Line between Legal Error and Judicial Misconduct: Balancing Judicial Independence and Accountability," *Hofstra Law Review* 32 (2004): 1245–80, p. 1245.
51. See §4.2.
52. See quotations, above.
53. "In some cases it is also said that legal error can amount to misconduct if a judge should have known the law. . . ." Shaman, "Judicial Ethics," p. 9.

to judges who ignore the law. . . ."[54] According to Shaman, "[i]ntentional refusals to follow the law are . . . [a] manifestation of unfitness for judicial office."[55] I shall address intentional deviation at greater length in §4.4.2.

Some judges, and other officials assigned to discipline judges, appear to agree with Stern and Shaman to some extent. Although mere legal error does not amount to misconduct, judges have been disciplined for "obvious" legal error, "egregious legal error, legal error motivated by bad faith, or a continuing pattern of legal error. . . ."[56] Legal error, especially a pattern of it, has been held to demonstrate unfitness for judicial office.[57] Discipline has been imposed pursuant to Canons 2 and 3 of the *Model Code*.[58] For example, judges in New York have been disciplined for ignoring the weight of the evidence, for intentionally disregarding the law, and for showing bias toward certain lawyers or parties.[59] They have been censured for showing bias in favor of tenants.[60] Under law, New York judges who abuse their power or disregard fundamental rights can be removed from office.[61] A Texas judge was censured for stating that he gave less than a life sentence to a murderer because his victims had been gay men "cruising" for teenage boys.[62] A municipal judge in South Carolina was removed from office for issuing arrest warrants based solely on his own daughter's affidavit.[63]

Similarly, the California Supreme Court has held that a judge is subject to investigation for "legal error which, in addition, clearly and convincingly reflects bad faith, bias, abuse of authority, disregard for fundamental rights, intentional disregard of the law, or any purpose other than the faithful discharge of judicial duty. . . ."[64] The same high court has found that a judge engaged in willful misconduct by directing a jury to find a defendant guilty when the judge at least should have known that the law did not give him this authority.[65]

---

54. Stern, "Is Judicial Discipline in New York State a Threat to Judicial Independence?" p. 304.
55. Shaman, "Judicial Ethics," p. 9.
56. Ibid., p. 8.
57. See, e.g., *Harrod v. Illinois Courts Commission* at 65 ("[W]here the law is clear on its face, a judge who repeatedly imposes punishment not provided for by law is subject to discipline").
58. See cases cited in Shaman, "Judicial Ethics," pp. 8–9 nn. 61, 62.
59. Stern, "Is Judicial Discipline in New York State a Threat to Judicial Independence?" p. 313.
60. Ibid.
61. Ibid.
62. *Inquiry Concerning a Judge No. 52 (Hampton)* (Texas Commission on Judicial Conduct 1989).
63. *In re McKinney*, 478 S.E.2d 51 (S.C. 1996).
64. *Oberholzer v. Commission on Judicial Performance* at 680. One commentator interprets this language to imply that Justice Kline, discussed in §3.12, would have been subject to discipline had he written the majority opinion, rather than a dissent. Sankar, "Disciplining the Professional Judge," p. 1273 n. 234.
65. *McCullough v. Commission on Judicial Performance*, 776 P.2d 259, 262 (Cal. 1989).

The Legal Duties of Judges

Consider, by contrast, the case of Howard R. Broadman, a California trial judge. Judge Broadman ordered a female defendant to receive an implanted birth control device as a condition of her probation.[66] In another case, he made "not getting pregnant" a condition of a woman's five-year probation.[67] The California Commission on Judicial Performance brought "improper sentencing" charges against Judge Broadman, both of which were ultimately dismissed after lengthy hearings.[68] In a similarly lenient decision, the Supreme Court of Alaska held that a judge should not even be privately reprimanded for ordering the overnight imprisonment of a prosecuting witness in order to ensure that she would appear in court sober the next day.[69]

Finally, recall the case of Justice Kline, whose dissenting opinion announced his unwillingness to grant a stipulated reversal.[70] The California Commission on Judicial Performance charged Justice Kline with "willful misconduct in office, conduct prejudicial to the administration of justice that brings the judicial office into disrepute, improper action, and dereliction of duty." Lubet observes that Kline's case "may well be the very first time that a state judicial conduct organization has pursued disciplinary charges solely on the basis of the substance of a judge's written ruling."[71] The commission's decision was widely criticized,[72] and the charges against Justice Kline were ultimately dismissed.[73]

4.4.1 Patterns of Error

So far I have mostly cited isolated instances of deviation, rather than patterns of deviation by a single judge over time. Lubet states that

> a pattern of repeated and uncorrected legal error is obviously more serious than an isolated instance. Judges who fail to learn and apply the law fall into a distinctly different category from those who simply hold minority—or innovative—opinions. The commission of multiple errors, or unacceptable judging

---

66. *Broadman v. Commission on Judicial Performance*, 959 P.2d 715, 725 (Cal. 1998).
67. *People v. Zaring*, 10 Cal. Rptr. 2d 263, 265 (5th Dist. 1992).
68. *Broadman v. Commission on Judicial Performance*.
69. *In re Curda*, 49 P.3d 255 (Alaska 2002) (reversing recommendation of Commission on Judicial Conduct).
70. See §3.12.
71. Lubet, "Judicial Discipline and Judicial Independence," p. 66. See also Nancy McCarthy, "Judge Faces Discipline: Commission Charge Unleashes Protest in Legal Community," *California State Bar Journal*, August 1998.
72. McCarthy, "Judge Faces Discipline."
73. Two facts about Kline's case are especially interesting. First, Justice Kline was charged with misconduct for language in a dissenting opinion that, as such, had no legal force. Second, Kline advocated deviation in order to protect the judiciary, rather than a party to the case. In fact, his position would block a transaction favored by both parties to the case, whereas deviation ordinarily benefits the legally disfavored party at the expense of the other.

that continues over a period of years, may indicate that the judge has not maintained professional competence in the law.[74]

Indeed, most judges who are actually disciplined for legal errors have patterns of the same type of error:

> Judges have been sanctioned for patterns of failing to advise defendants of their rights ... during criminal proceedings; imposing sentences in excess of statutory authority; accepting guilty pleas using a form that did not comply with statutory requirements; holding trials in absentia; violating procedural requirements when conducting arraignments; disregard of and indifference to fact or law in criminal and juvenile cases; illegally incarcerating individuals in noncriminal matters to satisfy a civil fine; accepting guilty pleas without obtaining proper written plea statements; a practice of stating, for the record, that defendants had waived their rights to have speedy preliminary examination or timely trial without obtaining the defendants' personal waivers of these rights; requiring pro se defendants who requested jury trials to answer an in-court "jury trial roll call" once a week and to discuss plea bargains with the prosecutor; and failing to advise litigants in family court cases of their statutory rights to counsel, a hearing, and the assistance of counsel.[75]

4.4.2 Bad Faith

Legal errors can also bring sanctions when committed in "bad faith." Bad faith can include a "corrupt purpose" or an improper motive, such as revenge or anger, as when a Massachusetts judge set an unusually high bail for four African-American defendants and proceeded to tell a court clerk, "That's what blacks get for voting against my brother."[76] Since at least the late nineteenth century, judges in New York State have been subject to discipline for conduct that "reflects bias, malice, or intentional disregard of the law."[77]

Lubet suggests that "[a] willful refusal to follow the law, as distinct from an honest and acknowledged difference of opinion or interpretation, may manifest unfitness for judicial office."[78] Some courts have counted intentional failure to follow the law as bad faith, even when the judge acts from a benign motive. The Court of Appeals of New York (the high court of the state) sanctioned a judge who failed to set bail, as required by law, in twenty-four cases, although he did so because he believed that the

---

74. Lubet, "Judicial Discipline and Judicial Independence," p. 72. See, e.g., *Kloepfer v. Commission on Judicial Conduct*, 782 P.2d 239 (Cal. 1989).

75. Gray, "The Line between Legal Error and Judicial Misconduct," pp. 1263–65. See also Shaman, "Judicial Ethics," p. 9.

76. *In re King*, 568 N.E.2d 588, 594 (Mass. 1991). The judge's brother had fared badly in minority voting districts in his recent run for governor. Lubet, "Judicial Discipline and Judicial Independence," p. 73.

77. Stern, "Is Judicial Discipline in New York State a Threat to Judicial Independence?" p. 303.

78. Lubet, "Judicial Discipline and Judicial Independence," p. 73.

defendants (many of them homeless) preferred to remain in jail. In a different case, the same court removed a judge for knowingly disregarding the law by dismissing cases "in the interests of justice, using the guise of factual insufficiency" when he "thought it was right to do it."[79]

4.4.3 Obvious or Egregious Errors

Judges can also be sanctioned, even for an isolated legal error, when it is especially serious or "egregious."[80] Several state high courts have held that only "obviously" mistaken rulings are subject to discipline. In New York and Indiana, judges are not to be disciplined for legal error if the correctness of the decision is "sufficiently debatable."[81] The Supreme Court of Maine has stated that discipline is proper only if "a reasonably prudent and competent judge would consider [the judge's decision] obviously and seriously wrong in all the circumstances."[82] Lubet suggests that

> legal error becomes serious enough to warrant discipline when judges deny individuals their basic or fundamental procedural rights, as when a judge proceeds to adjudication without advising a defendant of the right to counsel, declines to hold a full hearing, or coerces a guilty plea. The same may occur when judges act beyond their lawful jurisdiction, as by sentencing defendants to jail when only a fine is authorized by law or sentencing defendants to incarceration for a period longer than the maximum allowed by statute.[83]

The following are some examples of legal errors in criminal cases that have been considered sufficiently serious that one or two such errors warranted discipline:

> [F]inding a defendant guilty without a guilty plea or trial, revoking a defendant's probation without the defendant's attorney being present, accepting a defendant's guilty plea without an attorney present and adjudicating a criminal matter for which there was no formal case opened, sentencing a defendant under the wrong statute, failing to follow proper procedures when a defendant failed to pay a fine, refusing to allow a self-represented defendant to cross-examine a police officer in a trial on a speeding ticket, knowingly convicting a defendant of an offense that had not been charged and was not a lesser included offense, refusing to set appeal bonds for misdemeanor defendants when clearly obligated by law to do so, issuing bench warrants for the arrests of misdemeanor defendants when their attorneys had been late even though the

---

79. *In re Duckman*, 699 N.E.2d 872, 875 (N.Y. 1998). The judge had not given the prosecution notice or allowed it an opportunity to be heard or to redraft charges. Nor had he required written motions or consent of the prosecutor, as required by law.

80. Lubet, "Judicial Discipline and Judicial Independence," p. 73; *In re Quirk*, 705 So.2d 172, 178 (La. 1997) (holding that even a single instance of serious legal error may constitute judicial misconduct, especially if it involves denial of fundamental rights).

81. *In re LaBelle*, 591 N.E.2d 1156, 1161 (N.Y. 1992); *In re Spencer*, 798 N.E.2d 175, 183 (Ind. 2003).

82. *In re Benoit*, 487 A.2d 1158, 1163 (Me. 1985).

83. Lubet, "Judicial Discipline and Judicial Independence," p. 73.

defendants themselves had been in court, forcing a defendant to enter a plea of guilty in the absence of his counsel, using the criminal process to collect a civil debt, . . . detaining a juvenile for nearly six weeks before he had the assistance of counsel and without taking any evidence, and twice convicting a defendant in the defendant's absence and without a guilty plea.[84]

4.5 IMPEACHMENT, CONVICTION, AND REMOVAL

Could a judge be impeached and removed from office in the United States solely for deviating from the law? This is a subtle question. There is no consensus on the exact scope of the congressional impeachment power,[85] so Congress could, perhaps, impeach a federal judge for deviating from the law. But Congress impeached only thirteen federal judges between 1789 and 1991,[86] just seven of whom were eventually removed from the bench.[87] None was removed because legislators disagreed with his decisions.[88]

Most state judges in the United States are elected to finite terms of office. They can, of course, lose reelection for any reason that motivates the electorate, including deviation. But that possibility does not entail that elected judges have any *legal* obligation to adhere, as opposed to a political incentive to do so. Impeachment and removal are more relevant to my question because these remedies require a legal basis. It is significant, therefore, that since 1785 no state judge has ever been impeached, convicted, and removed from office based on political or policy disagreements with the judge's decision.[89] However, since 2001, there have been several cases of state legislatures threatening impeachment of judges based solely on a decision. In a widely publicized case from 2006, the governor and legislators in Vermont called upon District Judge Edward Cashman to resign for the sixty-day sentence he handed down in a serial child molestation case.[90] Justice James Heiple of the Illinois Supreme

84. Gray, "The Line between Legal Error and Judicial Misconduct," pp. 1270–72.

85. "Although no consensus has ever developed on the exact scope of the impeachment power, its reach is illuminated by two hundred years of experience. Congress has removed judges for various forms of official and personal misconduct, but it has not done so because it disagreed with the outcome of cases." Report of the National Commission on Judicial Discipline and Removal, 152 F.R.D. 265, 282 (Aug. 1993).

86. Warren S. Grimes, "Hundred-Ton-Gun Control: Preserving Impeachment as the Exclusive Removal Mechanism for Federal Judges," *UCLA Law Review* 38 (1991): 1209–55, p. 1214 n. 32. See also Mary L. Volcansek, *Judicial Impeachment: None Called for Justice* (Urbana: University of Illinois Press, 1993), p. 89; Eleanore Bushnell, *Crimes, Follies and Misfortunes: The Federal Impeachment Trials* (Urbana: University of Illinois Press, 1992).

87. Grimes, "Hundred-Ton-Gun Control."

88. Ibid. See also Charles Gardner Geyh, "Informal Methods of Judicial Discipline," *University of Pennsylvania Law Review* 142 (1993): 243–331.

89. John O. Haley, "The Civil, Criminal and Disciplinary Liability of Judges," *American Journal of Comparative Law* 54 (2006): 281–91.

90. Wilson Ring, "Vt. Judge Criticized for Molester Sentence," *Associated Press Online*, Jan. 10, 2006. Judge Cashman subsequently accepted the prosecution's motion for reconsideration and increased the sentence.

The Legal Duties of Judges

Court was widely lambasted in the press and by politicians for ordering that "Baby Richard" be returned to his biological father, who had not consented to the adoption, despite the ties the infant had formed to his adoptive family. The Illinois House of Representatives initiated an impeachment inquiry against Judge Heiple, ostensibly for several traffic incidents and administrative matters.[91]

Recent years have seen other, less notorious, cases as well. In 2006, the legislature of New Hampshire considered removing Superior Court Justice Kenneth R. McHugh for a decision, made years earlier, in which he ruled that a petitioner's pleadings in a divorce case were frivolous. The same year the Ohio House of Representatives considered removing Judge John Connor for his sentencing of a sex offender. The Speaker of the House issued a press release saying the House was "reviewing the processes by which Judge Connor may be removed from the bench."[92] In Colorado, a bill of impeachment was introduced against Judge John W. Coughlin in 2004 for his order in a child custody case.[93]

Notice, however, that these judges were not primarily accused of deviating from the law. Judges who make unpopular decisions receive criticism from the news media, the general public, and politicians, but the critic's usual objection is that he believes the decision to be substantively unfair, unjust, or inexpedient. In some cases, of course, a critic explicitly accuses the judge of deviating from ("ignoring," "disregarding") the law. But the most despised decisions are often exercises of lawful discretion, as in the aforementioned state cases.

Therefore, we must not conflate criticism of judges with accusations of deviation. Critics who consider a result unjust or unfair often argue that the judge has deviated from the law, and present this as a reason to take adverse action against him, when they would have remained silent had the judge deviated from the law in order to reach a result of which they approve. The reasons presented by a critic for disciplining a judge may not reflect the critic's actual motivations. Nevertheless, critics do occasionally present deviation, per se, as the target of their disapprobation, whatever their actual motivations. In 2005, for example, a bill was introduced in the Tennessee Senate that would make any decision that "deviates from a rule of law" or precedent a presumptive act of judicial misconduct.[94] Similar bills have been introduced recently in other states. In 2006, the Judiciary

---

91. Lubet, "Judicial Discipline and Judicial Independence," p. 69.
92. See William E. Raftery, "The Legislatures, the Ballot Boxes, and the Courts," *Court Review* 43 (2006): 102–7.
93. Ibid.
94. The bill required the judge to "present clear and convincing evidence that, before ruling, the adjudicator competently and thoroughly researched the law on the question controlling [and] cite uncontradicted and controlling precedent . . . confirming that the question was one of first impression." The bill died in committee. S.B. 3522, 104th General Assembly, Second Session (Tenn. 2006).

Committee of the New Jersey State Assembly considered resolutions seeking the impeachment of the entire New Jersey Supreme Court for their allegedly deviant ruling on same-sex marriage.[95]

I conclude that judges could, in theory, be impeached and removed from office for deviating from the law. But this possibility has not yet materialized in the United States. As Judge Richard Posner notes, "detection and sanctioning [of judges who] bend or break the rules for the sake of other values [are] difficult."[96] For my purposes it is also significant that even the most severe sanction—impeachment and removal—is qualitatively different from typical criminal and civil penalties, which involve deprivations of property or personal liberty. The act of knowingly deviating from the law, in itself, can bring nothing worse than public censure, impeachment, and removal from the bench. The disrobed judge retains his property and personal liberties. He loses his job, but he remains employable. He may not even lose his license to practice law.

Therefore, one might wonder whether judges really have a *legal* duty to apply the law. If they have such a duty, then the legal system does not appear to take it very seriously. At least the legal system does not provide the sanctions or remedies that it provides for violations of other important legal duties.[97] I have, of course, noted that legal duties do not entail sanctions.[98] Nevertheless, I cannot conclude with complete confidence that judges have a legal obligation to apply the law, much less a stringent one, because the legal sanctions for deviating from the law are relatively weak and so rarely applied. Nor can I rule out the possibility of a legal obligation to adhere. Therefore, in the remainder of this book I shall simply assume *arguendo* that judges have such an obligation. If this assumption proves mistaken, then so much the better for my central argument.[99]

4.6 OTHER JUDICIAL INCENTIVES TO ADHERE

Despite the weakness and rare application of formal sanctions for deviating, judges have various incentives to adhere. Most judicial decisions in Anglo-American systems are subject to reversal on appeal. Most judges

---

95. A.R. 217 (Justice Albin), 212th Legislature, Second Session (N.J. 2007); A.R. 218 (Justice LaVecchia), 212th Legislature, Second Session (N.J. 2007); A.R. 219 (Justice Rivera-Soto), 212th Legislature, Second Session (N.J. 2007); A.R. 220 (Justice Wallace), 212th Legislature, Second Session (N.J. 2007); A.R. 221 (Chief Justice Poritz), 212th Legislature, Second Session (N.J. 2007); A.R. 222 (Justice Zazzali), 212th Legislature, Second Session (N.J. 2007); A.R. 223 (Justice Long), 212th Legislature, Second Session (N.J. 2007).

96. Richard A. Posner, "What Do Judges and Justices Maximize? (The Same Thing Everybody Else Does)," *Supreme Court Economic Review* 3 (1993): 1–41, p. 30.

97. Of course, this may be because the system has not, thus far, found it necessary to impose severe sanctions for deviation.

98. See §4.3.

99. When I write that I am "accepting a proposition *arguendo*" I mean that I am assuming it to be true even though my overall argument in the book is easier to make if it is false.

The Legal Duties of Judges

dislike having their decisions reversed.[100] Insofar as deviation increases one's likelihood of reversal, the desire to avoid reversal, for those who have it, constitutes an incentive to adhere. Higher courts are "less reversible" than lower courts. At the limit are decisions on questions of state law by state supreme courts and decisions by the U.S. Supreme Court. But statutory decisions of high courts are "reversible" by legislatures, and even the constitutional decisions of high courts in the United States are reversible by constitutional amendment (state or federal). In principle, every American judge can be "reversed."

Most judges also want to maintain good professional reputations.[101] In a community in which fidelity to law is valued, the perception that a judge has deviated may harm her professional reputation. Deviating increases the likelihood that others will conclude that one has deviated. Therefore, under these conditions, a judge who cares about his reputation has an incentive to adhere. There have been a few studies of the methods of "informal discipline" that judges use to police one another.[102] Neil MacCormick observes:

> It would be strange if a judge's opinion as to the normative quality of the alternative decisions confronting him in litigation were not for him a motivating factor in making up his mind what decision to give, that is, what order to make. He does after all have to state publicly in open court the reasons for which he is deciding the case as he is. Given the institutional pressures within the legal system—the opinion of the profession, the possibility of an appeal, etc.—and given the external pressures of adverse press publicity and Parliamentary comment and the like, it would be so strange as to be barely imaginable that a judge having established the justifiability of one decision by logical argument from sound legal premises and findings of fact should then issue some diametrically different order. So institutionally and psychologically it is highly unlikely that a judge will so conduct himself, but it is not impossible.[103]

Many judges also want to receive interesting and/or prestigious opportunities, both remunerative and nonremunerative, in the future. Many

---

100. Posner, "What Do Judges and Justices Maximize? (The Same Thing Everybody Else Does)," p. 14 ("Judges don't like to be reversed.... I speak from experience...."). Posner asserts, nevertheless, that "aversion to reversal does not figure largely in the judicial utility function." See also Donald R. Songer, Martha Humphries Ginn, and Tammy A. Sarver, "Do Judges Follow the Law When There Is No Fear of Reversal?" *Justice System Journal* 24 (2003): 137–61; Richard S. Higgins and Paul H. Rubin, "Judicial Discretion," *Journal of Legal Studies* 9 (1980): 129–38, p. 130 ("For reasons not completely understood, judges seem to desire to avoid being reversed").

101. See, e.g., Posner, "What Do Judges and Justices Maximize? (The Same Thing Everybody Else Does)," p. 13; Robert D. Cooter, "The Objectives of Private and Public Judges," *Public Choice* 41 (1983): 107–32, p. 129.

102. Geyh, "Informal Methods of Judicial Discipline"; Sankar, "Disciplining the Professional Judge," pp. 1254–56.

103. MacCormick, *Legal Reasoning and Legal Theory*, pp. 33–34. See also Scott J. Shapiro, "Judicial Can't," *Noûs* 35, Supp. 1 (2001): 530–57, p. 546.

wish to be promoted to higher office, judicial or otherwise. Insofar as a record of deviation reduces one's attractiveness for interesting, lucrative, and prestigious opportunities, judges have an incentive to adhere.[104] However, one early study found that reversal rates do not affect the chance of promotion for federal district judges.[105]

Some scholars have also suggested that the less faithful to the law other judges (and scholars and lawyers) perceive a certain judge to be, the less often will they cite or follow him.[106] If this empirical hypothesis is true, then judges have another prudential reason to adhere.

Judge Posner places greatest emphasis upon yet another incentive for judges to adhere: it gives them pleasure. Posner analogizes judges to citizens voting for public officials, audience members watching stage plays, and players of games. He observes that "[a] chess player would reduce rather than enhance the pleasure he received from playing a game if he violated the rules, and so would a theatergoer who refused to enter into the lives of the characters on the stage, on the ground that they were not real people; and likewise the judge who violates the rules of the judicial game."[107]

And also:

> [M]any people do not cheat at games even when they are sure they can get away with cheating. The pleasure of judging is bound up with compliance with certain self-limiting rules that define the "game" of judging. It is a source of satisfaction for a judge to vote *for* the litigant who irritates him, the lawyer who fails to exhibit proper deference to him, the side that represents a different social class from his own; for it is by doing such things that you know that you are playing the judge role, not some other role, and judges for the most part are people who want to be—judges.[108]

Finally, in many cases simply adhering to the law is the easiest and least time-consuming option. Deciding whether one has good reasons to

---

104. "[I]f judges who were most faithful to the rules were the ones most likely to be elevated to higher positions, then the hope of this reward might for many judges provide the incentive for taking rules to be reasons for action." Schauer, *Playing by the Rules*, pp. 123–24. For research findings see, e.g., Thomas J. Miceli and Metin M. Cogel, "Reputation and Judicial Decision-Making," *Journal of Economic Behavior and Organization* 23 (1994): 31–51; Erin O'Hara, "Social Constraint or Implicit Collusion? Toward a Game Theoretic Analysis of Stare Decisis," *Seton Hall Law Review* 24 (1993): 736–78; Mark A. Cohen, "The Motives of Judges: Empirical Evidence from Antitrust Sentencing," *International Review of Law and Economics* 12 (1992): 13–30.

105. Higgins and Rubin, "Judicial Discretion."

106. See, e.g., Lewis A. Kornhauser, "Modeling Collegial Courts I: Path Dependence," *International Review of Law and Economics* 12 (1992): 169–85; Lewis A. Kornhauser, "Modeling Collegial Courts II: Legal Doctrine," *Journal of Law, Economics, and Organization* 8 (1992): 441–70; Richard A. Posner, *Economic Analysis of Law*, 4th ed. (Boston: Little, Brown, 1992), pp. 534–36, 541–42.

107. Posner, "What Do Judges and Justices Maximize? (The Same Thing Everybody Else Does)," p. 26.

108. Ibid., p. 28.

deviate often requires one to consider a wider range of factors than would blind adherence to the law. Insofar as judges value their leisure[109] and are "cognitively lazy,"[110] they have another incentive to adhere in such cases. Of course, these incentives should not be confused with a legal or moral duty to adhere.

---

109. Ibid., p. 11.
110. Karl E. Weick, *Sensemaking in Organizations* (Thousand Oaks, Calif.: Sage, 1995), pp. 61–62.

5

The Normative Classification of Legal Results

5.1 OPTIMAL VERSUS SUBOPTIMAL RESULTS

In this chapter, I shall discuss the evaluation of court decisions in normative terms that go beyond the law. In addition to forming an opinion about the legal correctness of a court's ruling, one can form an opinion that characterizes it as more or less just, more or less fair, more or less conducive to the general welfare, et cetera. Judicial decisions always have effects on someone. Most obviously, a criminal conviction has negative effects on the convict. It also has negative effects on his family members, friends, employer, employees, and so forth. An acquittal may have negative effects on the general public, on future victims, and on victims of the crime itself.

In civil cases, a decision has negative effects on the losing litigant. A losing defendant is typically made worse off than he was before the judgment (although he may be left no worse off than he was before he committed the delict). A losing plaintiff is typically not made worse off than he was before the judgment, although he may be left worse off than he was before the delict against him.

In theory, if all values were taken into account, each result in a court case could be classified into one of two moral categories: *optimal* or *suboptimal*. These could be further broken down into four subcategories. Some results are not just morally optimal, but morally *mandatory*, meaning that it is morally wrong, all things considered, for a court to reach any other result in that case. Other results are optimal but not mandatory, meaning that a court is morally permitted but not morally required to reach that result.

The worst subcategory of suboptimal results comprises those that are *impermissible*, meaning that it is morally wrong, all things considered, for a court to reach such a result. All other suboptimal results are morally permissible for a court to reach, but still suboptimal because a morally superior result exists.

At this point some readers will be impatient for concrete illustrations, which I shall provide shortly. However, in this book I stay as neutral as possible regarding which results are optimal. For me the distinctions between optimal, indifferent, and suboptimal results are conceptual

The Normative Classification of Legal Results

distinctions, like the philosopher's distinction between *justice* and *injustice*. To evaluate my arguments you need only distinguish for yourself between optimal and suboptimal results. You and I need not agree regarding the proper classification of any particular result. Our opinions will be influenced by our beliefs about empirical matters and by our probably divergent theories of corrective justice, distributive justice, criminalization, and punishment.

In the rest of this book some readers will find themselves repeatedly plagued by questions such as the following: how can a judge know that she is *correct* when she determines that a certain result is morally suboptimal? What if she is *wrong*? Are there even "correct" answers to difficult moral questions? Some readers may be unable to get past these questions. I may appear to be making some naïve assumptions: that determining whether a result is suboptimal is always an easy, mechanical process; that judges possess perfect moral insight; that judges generally agree on normative issues. These are unrealistic assumptions. My arguments are designed to succeed without them, although you will have to decide if they do. I am simply trying to respect what John Rawls calls "the fact of reasonable pluralism."[1] However, I cannot permanently ignore the fact that judges will disagree with one another on many moral questions. I shall address the fact of moral disagreement in chapter 14.[2] I beg your patience until then.

Again, my objective is not to persuade you to adopt my general normative views or my opinions on particular policy issues. For my purposes the following definitions suffice:

- In any court case to be decided, a possible result, r_1, is normatively *superior* to another possible result, r_2, if and only if it is true that the judge *would* have a stronger reason to reach r_1 than r_2 if the law permitted him to reach either.
- A result is normatively *optimal* if and only if no other result is superior to it.
- A result is normatively *suboptimal* if and only if it is not optimal.[3]

Notice that my definition of *superior* does not specify whether the law in the actual world requires the judge to reach either r_1 or r_2. It defines *superior* in terms of the reasons the judge *would* have in a specific possible

---

1. See John Rawls, "The Idea of Public Reason Revisited," *University of Chicago Law Review* 64 (1997): 765–807, pp. 765–66 ("[A] basic feature of democracy is the fact of reasonable pluralism—the fact that a plurality of conflicting reasonable comprehensive doctrines, religious, philosophical, and moral, is the normal result of its culture of free institutions"). See generally John Rawls, *Political Liberalism* (New York: Columbia University Press, 1993).
2. See §14.8.
3. Frederick Schauer, *Playing by the Rules: A Philosophical Examination of Rule-Based Decision-Making in Law and in Life* (Oxford: Oxford University Press, 1991), p. 204.

world: one that is exactly similar to the actual world except that the law permits the judge to reach either result (which the law in the actual world might or might not permit). Consider the straightforward example of a judge presiding over the bench trial of a defendant charged with criminal battery for maiming someone without justification. Which result is optimal: conviction or acquittal? On my definition of *optimal* the answer depends on what the judge would have an all-things-considered reason to do if the law gave him unguided discretion to convict or acquit on this evidence. In this trivial case, reasonable people will agree that the judge would have an all-things-considered reason to convict if the law permitted him to do so: conviction is an optimal result. Other cases, of course, will invite moral controversy.

Maiming is an offense *malum in se*.[4] Having used this example I must forestall a potential misunderstanding that could arise in connection with any *malum prohibitum* offense: one that is "not inherently immoral, but becomes so because its commission is expressly forbidden by positive law."[5] Examples include failing to file tax returns, counterfeiting, running stop signs when it is safe to do so, et cetera. Because these actions are not inherently immoral, one might jump to the conclusion that a judge would have an all-things-considered reason to impose no penalty whatsoever for them if the law permitted her to do so, which would entail that a conviction for a *malum prohibitum* offense is always a suboptimal result on my definition. I shall explain why this is not so.

Imagine a world, otherwise like ours, with one difference in the law: although counterfeiting is a crime, the law gives a certain judge unguided discretion in bench trials either to convict or to acquit defendants accused of counterfeiting.[6] This judge has an all-things-considered reason to convict counterfeiters, despite the fact that she is not legally required to do so. Whatever reasons one accepts for convicting counterfeiters in the real world apply with the same force in this hypothetical. Circulating counterfeit bills still debases the national currency, so the hypothetical society should still discourage counterfeiting. One could also argue that counterfeiting currency is immoral in the hypothetical society. Knowingly circulating counterfeit currency is fraudulent, so it is still morally wrong. Insofar as counterfeiting currency facilitates its circulation, one could argue that counterfeiting is wrong for that reason. Counterfeiting also violates the fair play principle if most people obey the law.[7] Therefore, the hypothetical judge has most of the same reasons as a real-world judge to

---

4. "[I]nherently and essentially evil, that is immoral in its nature and injurious in its consequences, without any regard to the fact of its being noticed or punished by the law of the state." Bryan A. Garner, ed., *Black's Law Dictionary*, 8th ed. (St. Paul, Minn.: Thomson/West, 2004).
5. Ibid.
6. Obviously, this is bad policy.
7. Richard Dagger, "Playing Fair with Punishment," *Ethics* 103 (1993): 473–88.

convict a counterfeiter. Conviction is the optimal result. Similar analyses apply to other *mala prohibita* offenses.

5.2 THE NORMATIVE CLASSIFICATION OF REGULATED CASES IN TERMS OF LEGALLY DICTATED RESULTS

Legally regulated cases divide into four categories corresponding to the four normative categories of results: required; optimal-but-not-required; suboptimal-but-permissible; and impermissible. I shall refer to required-result and optimal-but-not-required-result cases, collectively, as *optimal-result cases*. Suboptimal-but-permissible-result and impermissible-result cases, collectively, are *suboptimal-result cases*. An optimal-result case is one in which the law authorizes the judge to reach a result that would otherwise be morally optimal, all things considered, absent the law. All other cases are suboptimal-result cases: those in which the law requires the judge to reach a result that would otherwise be morally suboptimal, all things considered, absent the law. In such a case the law requires her to rule in favor of a certain party although she would otherwise have an all-things-considered moral reason to rule against that party, ceteris paribus. In other words, a case is a suboptimal-result case if and only if the law either (1) requires the judge to reach a result that she would have all-things-considered reason to avoid, if the law allowed her to avoid it, or (2) forbids her to reach a result that she would have all-things-considered reason to reach, if the law allowed her to reach it. By the definition of *suboptimal-result case*, it is possible for a judge who makes no legal or factual errors to reach a suboptimal result in such a case.

It is important to remember that the adjective *suboptimal* in the phrase *suboptimal-result case* modifies the result *required by the law*, not the result *actually reached* by a court. A suboptimal-result case is not one in which some court reached a suboptimal result. It is one in which the law, properly understood, requires (or required) the court to reach a suboptimal result, whatever the court actually does (or did). The same holds for the other three categories, mutatis mutandis.

Here are some examples of cases in the four categories mentioned above:

1. Criminal defendant has a moral right to be acquitted. He is morally or factually innocent. The law also requires the judge to acquit. We have natural duties not to punish morally innocent people, so the judge has a moral duty to acquit. The law requires the judge to commit or omit actions that he has a natural duty to commit or omit, respectively. This is a *required-result* case.
2. Neither party to a certain civil matter has a moral right to a favorable judgment, but a judgment for plaintiff would benefit plaintiff very greatly and harm defendant, at most, only minimally

(and no other individuals will be affected more than negligibly by either result). Therefore, the judge has a natural moral reason to rule for plaintiff, but no natural moral duty to do so. If the law requires the judge to rule for plaintiff, then the judge has a legal duty to rule for plaintiff. The judge has a judicial duty to commit or omit actions that he has natural reasons, but no natural duty, to commit or omit, respectively. This is an *optimal-but-not-required-result* case.

3. Neither party has a moral right to a favorable judgment, but a judgment for plaintiff would benefit plaintiff very greatly and harm defendant, at most, only minimally (and no other individuals will be much disadvantaged by either result). The law requires the judge to rule for defendant. The judge has no moral duty to rule for plaintiff, but he has a natural moral reason to do so. The judge has a judicial duty to commit or omit actions that he has natural reasons, but no natural duty, to omit or commit, respectively. This is a *suboptimal-but-permissible-result* case.

4. Criminal defendant has a moral right to be acquitted. He is morally or factually innocent, but the law requires the judge to convict and sentence him. The judge has a judicial duty to commit or omit actions that he has a natural duty to omit or commit, respectively. This is an *impermissible-result* case.

5.3 SUBOPTIMAL-RESULT CASES

I shall further illustrate the concept of a suboptimal-result case using a hypothetical scenario—a standard case of economic hardship.[8] Yasmin is an impoverished widow who is renting an apartment from Rafael, a wealthy landowner who inherited the property and has never worked a day in his life. Yasmin has missed several rent payments, and Rafael has filed an eviction petition before Judge Lucas. I stipulate that Yasmin is morally innocent. She is too old and frail to work, and her pension does not cover her rent. Neither retributive justice nor corrective justice requires a judgment against Yasmin. She has done nothing to deserve eviction as a moral matter (although legally, she is delinquent). Nor does Judge Lucas violate anyone's moral rights if he rules for Yasmin. That decision violates Rafael's legal rights, but Rafael was not morally entitled to Yasmin's rent in the first place, absent the law. The property rights regime in place, let us suppose, is distributively unjust, because it provides an inadequate social safety net for people in Yasmin's situation. Nor

---

8. This case is adapted from one discussed in Richard A. Wasserstrom, *The Judicial Decision: Toward a Theory of Legal Justification* (Stanford, Calif.: Stanford University Press, 1961), p. 141; and in Alan H. Goldman, *Practical Rules: When We Need Them and When We Don't* (Cambridge: Cambridge University Press, 2002), p. 43.

The Normative Classification of Legal Results

will Yasmin's eviction maximize the combined utility of Yasmin and Rafael, because Yasmin needs her apartment more than Rafael needs her money. If the law did not require eviction, then Judge Lucas would have an all-things-considered moral reason to deny Rafael's petition. However, the regulating statute requires him to grant the petition, thereby evicting Yasmin.

This is my example of a suboptimal-result case, but I offer it merely for the sake of being concrete. My point is not to persuade you that evicting Yasmin is a suboptimal result. That conclusion depends on certain theories of distributive justice that I shall not ask you to accept. If you are glad to see Yasmin evicted, then you can imagine some other case, one in which the law requires a result that *you* consider to be suboptimal. Below is a list of results, inspired by actual cases and chosen to stimulate your imagination. The fact of reasonable pluralism entails that for most of these results, you should find it easy to imagine an intelligent, informed person who considers the result to be suboptimal, whether or not you agree:

1. A court orders the deportation of an undocumented immigrant who has worked hard and contributed a great deal to his community.
2. A court forbids a student from attending a public school outside his own district, despite the fact that his own school system offers an inadequate and inferior learning environment.[9]
3. Under mandatory minimum sentencing laws, a court imposes a life sentence on someone who was convicted of one assault with a deadly weapon and two subsequent, nonviolent felonies.[10]
4. A court upholds a jury's decision to execute a defendant who received a fair trial.
5. A court orders the forfeiture of assets from a convict's innocent family members.[11]
6. A court excludes illegally obtained evidence that is necessary for conviction of a defendant accused of serial child molestation.
7. A court sentences to prison an animal rights activist who has been convicted of stealing animals from a research laboratory in order to liberate them.[12]
8. A court sentences a seventeen-year-old male to a prison term of ten years for receiving consensual fellatio from his fifteen-year-old girlfriend.[13]

---

9. *San Antonio v. Rodriguez*, 411 U.S. 1 (1973) (upholding local funding scheme for public schools despite substantial inter-district disparities in school expenditures).
10. *Lockyer v. Andrade*, 538 U.S. 63 (2003).
11. *Bennis v. Michigan*, 116 S. Ct. 994 (1996).
12. *State v. Troen*, 786 P.2d 751 (Or. Ct. App. 1990).
13. *Wilson v. State*, 279 Ga. App. 459 (Ga. Ct. App. 2006). The girl in this case was not, in fact, the defendant's girlfriend, but this makes no legal difference.

9. A court dismisses the First Amendment free speech and free exercise claims of a student who wishes to lead his fellow students in a Christian prayer at an event sponsored by a public school.[14]
10. A court dismisses criminal charges brought against a doctor for performing a previability abortion.[15]
11. A court upholds the criminal conviction of a doctor who performed an abortion via intact dilation and evacuation (a "partial-birth abortion") when the doctor believed this procedure to be necessary in order to protect the health of the pregnant woman.[16]
12. A court upholds the federal possession conviction of a defendant who grows marijuana for medical purposes.[17]
13. A court dismisses a case against a defendant who has trafficked in "virtual" child pornography—computer-generated material produced without using actual children as subjects.[18]
14. A court imposes a long sentence on a battered woman who has killed her partner in his sleep.
15. A federal court orders a public official to remove a monument of the Ten Commandments from a public building.[19]
16. A federal court overturns a ban on handgun ownership in the District of Columbia.[20]

Many commentators, regardless of their political views, believe that the United States Supreme Court under Chief Justice Earl Warren repeatedly deviated from the law—that some of the Court's opinions cannot be reconciled with any legally correct reading of the Constitution. Political conservatives who take this position condemn the decisions as unjustified instances of deviation.[21] Many liberals deny that the Warren Court deviated from the law at all, although they often admit that the justices deviated from certain *rules* of law. These liberals deny that the law actually required suboptimal results in the controversial cases. Fashioning a theory of law that is consistent with that position is one of the challenges faced by these liberal lawyers.[22] Conservative lawyers are, needless

---

14. *Santa Fe Independent School District v. Doe*, 530 U.S. 290 (2000).
15. *Planned Parenthood v. Casey*, 505 U.S. 833 (1992).
16. *Gonzales v. Carhart*, 550 U.S. 124 (2007) (upholding Partial-Birth Abortion Ban Act of 2003).
17. *Gonzales v. Raich*, 545 U.S. 1 (2005).
18. *Ashcroft v. Free Speech Coalition*, 535 U.S. 234 (2002).
19. *Glassroth v. Moore*, 335 F.3d 1282 (11th Cir. 2003).
20. *District of Columbia v. Heller*, 128 S. Ct. 2783 (2008).
21. See, e.g., Robert H. Bork, *The Tempting of America* (New York: Simon & Schuster, 1990), ch. 3; Raoul Berger, *Government by Judiciary: The Transformation of the Fourteenth Amendment* (Cambridge, Mass.: Harvard University Press, 1977), p. 265.
22. See, e.g., David A. Strauss, "The Common Law Genius of the Warren Court," *William & Mary Law Review* 49 (2007): 845–79.

The Normative Classification of Legal Results

to say, unpersuaded by their efforts. Nor is there much consensus among liberal lawyers regarding how to justify the Warren-era decisions in legal terms.[23]

My point, however, is that many liberal lawyers reluctantly agree that the Warren Court sometimes deviated from the law of its day. They see the cases in question as suboptimal-result cases in which the Court deviated—perhaps fortunately, perhaps even heroically.[24] As Brian Tamanaha explains, even *Brown v. Board of Education*[25] invites this reaction:

> The *Brown* decision arguably was not supported by legal principles or reasoned elaboration or neutral principle. Hence the decision could not be reconciled comfortably with pre-existing Constitutional law and understandings. Yet it was undoubtedly correct from a moral standpoint, at least in the view of many in the mainstream of legal academia. Other progressive Warren Court decisions raised the same dilemma: morally correct in content, as far as mainstream legal academics were concerned, but nigh impossible to justify in purely legal terms. These decisions, evidently a product of the political views of the justices, were the antithesis of the rule of law, according to infuriated critics, one more indication of its breakdown.[26]

The liberal law professors to whom Tamanaha refers were, and are, divided among themselves. Some believe that the Court's putative deviation in *Brown* was ethically justified, albeit unlawful.[27] Other liberals conclude, often with regret, that the justices acted unethically, despite reaching just results. Just results could have been reached by the political branches and, on this view, should not have been reached by the judiciary.[28]

---

23. Bruce Ackerman, *We the People: Foundations* (Cambridge, Mass.: Belknap, 1991), ch. 6; J. M. Balkin and Bruce A. Ackerman, eds., *What* Brown v. Board of Education *Should Have Said* (New York: New York University Press, 2001); J. M. Balkin, ed., *What* Roe v. Wade *Should Have Said* (New York: New York University Press, 2005). Warren Burger was Chief Justice when *Roe v. Wade* was decided.

24. Learned Hand and Herbert Wechsler were antisegregation liberals who famously declared *Brown v. Board of Education* deviant. Learned Hand, *The Bill of Rights* (Cambridge, Mass.: Harvard University Press, 1958), p. 55; Herbert Wechsler, "Toward Neutral Principles of Constitutional Law," *Harvard Law Review* 73 (1959): 1–35. The liberal John Hart Ely reached the same judgment about *Roe v. Wade* in John Hart Ely, "The Wages of Crying Wolf: A Comment on *Roe v. Wade*," *Yale Law Journal* 82 (1973): 920–49.

25. *Brown v. Board of Education*, 347 U.S. 483 (1954) (racial segregation in public schools violates Equal Protection Clause).

26. Brian Z. Tamanaha, *On the Rule of Law: History, Politics, Theory* (Cambridge: Cambridge University Press, 2004), p. 80.

27. "*Brown* . . . had serious, thoughtful critics among people who were opposed to segregation. Some of those critics . . . said that *Brown* was a lawless act. . . ." David A. Strauss, "Little Rock and the Legacy of Brown," *Saint Louis University Law Journal* 52 (2008): 1065–86, p. 1066. See also William H. Simon, "Should Lawyers Obey the Law?" *William & Mary Law Review* 38 (1996): 217–53, p. 222 ("The balance of burden and benefit in the legal order of the day was not fairly struck for African-Americans; the . . . arguably lawless [*Brown*] decision inarguably pushed the balance toward greater fairness").

28. See, e.g., Wechsler, "Toward Neutral Principles of Constitutional Law"; Hand, *The Bill of Rights*, p. 55.

Judges themselves lament conflicts between their moral convictions and the law as they understand it. Justice Blackmun firmly opposed the death penalty on moral grounds, but dissented in *Furman v. Georgia*, which forbade states to give sentencing juries "unguided discretion" in capital cases. This effectively ended capital punishment in the United States until 1976. Blackmun wrote, "Although personally I may rejoice at the Court's result, I find it difficult to accept or to justify as a matter of history, of law, or of constitutional pronouncement. I fear the Court has overstepped. It has sought and has achieved an end."[29]

Conservatives also face hard choices between swallowing politically unpalatable outcomes and supporting judicial deviation from the law. Scott Shapiro claims that

> [e]ven the most vociferous conservative critics of the regulatory state do not advocate that judges should ignore duly enacted law. Their claim is that the regulatory state must be dismantled through the proper legislative channels, by repealing certain law[s], passing others and shifting jurisdiction from larger entities, such as the federal government, to smaller more accountable ones, such as states and municipalities. In the meantime, however, "the law's the law."[30]

Of course, the fact that conservatives often condemn deviation does not entail that conservative judges never deviate.

5.4 CLASSIFYING SUBOPTIMAL-RESULT CASES

In this section, I use the previously introduced classifications to divide the universe of cases into four categories: optimal rule/optimal result; suboptimal rule/suboptimal result; suboptimal rule/optimal result; and optimal rule/suboptimal result. I call these categories *positive closure, negative closure, positive gap*,[31] and *negative gap*, respectively.

A negative-closure case is one in which a suboptimal rule generates a suboptimal result. The laws of many states in the antebellum United States permitted the ownership of slaves. Because slavery is unjust, virtually every case in which the law supported the property rights of slave owners in their slaves was a suboptimal-result case.

A positive-gap case is one in which a suboptimal rule generates an optimal result. Although a law permitting slavery usually yields bad results, on rare occasions it will, by coincidence, permit the harsh treatment of an individual who deserves it, morally, such as a rapist who has

---

29. *Furman v. Georgia*, 408 U.S. 238, 414 (1972) (Blackmun, J., dissenting).
30. Scott J. Shapiro, "Judicial Can't," *Noûs* 35, Supp. 1 (2001): 530–57, p. 532.
31. This use of *gap* originates in Larry Alexander, "The Gap," *Harvard Journal of Law and Public Policy* 14 (1991): 695–701.

avoided arrest. These unusual cases are positive-gap cases.³² I will say little more about them.

A positive-closure case is one in which an optimal rule generates an optimal result. An example would be a case in which someone drives her automobile on the left side of a two-way street when it is very dangerous to do so and she is convicted under a law that forbids driving on the left.

Finally, here is an example of a negative-gap case. On a particular occasion, Michael drives his automobile on the left, thereby knowingly breaking the law. No one else is present, and it is safe to do so. Michael would never drive unsafely. But for the law, he would not deserve a sanction, nor would a sanction promote the good in this case, because it is not necessary to deter Michael or others from driving unsafely. An official who was legally authorized to sanction Michael would have no all-things-considered moral reason to do so if no legal rule required her to do so. Therefore, sanctioning Michael is a suboptimal result. However, the rule that Michael has violated may be an optimal rule. It might be counterproductive to try to add a textual exception for cases such as Michael's. If so, then his is a negative-gap case.³³

5.5 ASSUMPTIONS UNDERLYING THE EXISTENCE OF SUBOPTIMAL-RESULT CASES

My discussion is addressed to people who believe that suboptimal-result cases actually exist. Anyone who believes this is committed to two assumptions. First, at least some legal questions have legally correct answers. Second, the law sometimes requires judges to reach results that they would have all-things-considered reasons to avoid, if the law permitted. I discuss these assumptions in this section.

5.5.1 Partial Determinacy

Suboptimal-result cases cannot exist unless at least some legal questions have legally correct answers.³⁴ The antithesis—that no legal questions

---

32. One might also refer to them as "Gettier cases," by analogy with Edmund L. Gettier, "Is Justified True Belief Knowledge?" *Analysis* 23 (1963): 121–23.
33. It is "a platitude that justifiable rules can sometimes have morally regrettable applications." David Lyons, "Derivability, Defensibility, and the Justification of Judicial Decisions," in *Moral Aspects of Legal Theory* (Cambridge: Cambridge University Press, 1993), p. 128. See also Larry Alexander and Emily Sherwin, *The Rule of Rules* (Durham, N.C.: Duke University Press, 2001), pp. 53–61; Heidi M. Hurd, *Moral Combat* (Cambridge: Cambridge University Press, 1999), pp. 185–202; Alexander, "The Gap"; Schauer, *Playing by the Rules*, pp. 128–34; Gerald J. Postema, *Bentham and the Common Law Tradition* (Oxford: Oxford University Press, 1986), p. 407 ("[E]ven the best and most just of general rules may yield injustice in some particular cases"); Rolf Sartorius, *Individual Conduct and Social Norms* (Encino, Calif.: Dickenson, 1975), pp. 56–57. The idea dates back at least to Aristotle, *Nicomachean Ethics* V.x.5.xi.
34. See M. B. E. Smith, "Do Appellate Courts Regularly Cheat?" *Criminal Justice Ethics* 16 (1997): 11–20, p. 11.

have legally correct answers—is *radical indeterminacy*.[35] Valid, mandatory legal rules purport to give their addressees at least *pro tanto* reasons for action. However, if a rule is radically indeterminate, then it does not provide such reasons. This entails that judges have no reason to adhere to the rule because the rule does not really require anything.[36] If legal rules are all radically indeterminate, then the principle that *ought* implies *can* entails that there is no judicial duty to adhere to the law and my remaining arguments are otiose.

A commitment to radical indeterminacy is often attributed to the critical legal studies movement,[37] although I hesitate to impute the thesis to any particular author without defining it more precisely.[38] The radical indeterminacy thesis has been subjected to severe and extensive critique, along with several other interrelated claims commonly ascribed to critical legal studies.[39] This debate is complicated. Some proponents of critical legal studies, and other defenders of indeterminacy, claim that their views were misunderstood or misrepresented.[40] I shall take no position on that question. Many have observed that critical legal studies is no longer a

---

35. Also known as *strong indeterminacy*. See, e.g., Lawrence B. Solum, "Indeterminacy," in *A Companion to Philosophy of Law and Legal Theory*, ed. Dennis Patterson (Oxford: Blackwell, 1996), p. 491.

36. "If one thought that rules are maximally indeterminate—that is, it is impossible to say whether a rule applies in any individual case—there would be no point in asking . . . whether they constrain those judgments once made." Shapiro, "Judicial Can't," p. 557 n. 26.

37. See, e.g., Solum, "Indeterminacy"; Andrew Altman, *Critical Legal Studies: A Liberal Critique* (Princeton, N.J.: Princeton University Press, 1990), p. 19; Ken Kress, "Legal Indeterminacy," *California Law Review* 77 (1989): 283–337, p. 283.

38. The view has been attributed to Joseph Singer, Duncan Kennedy, Clare Dalton, Mark Tushnet, Gary Peller, and many others. See, e.g., Kress, "Legal Indeterminacy," pp. 286–87 (Singer, Kennedy); Altman, *Critical Legal Studies: A Liberal Critique*, pp. 19, 58 (Dalton, Tushnet, Peller).

39. See, e.g., W.J. Waluchow, "Indeterminacy," *Canadian Journal of Law and Jurisprudence* 9 (1996): 397–409; Christian Zapf and Eben Moglen, "Linguistic Indeterminacy and the Rule of Law: On the Perils of Misunderstanding Wittgenstein," *Georgetown Law Journal* 84 (1996): 485–520; Jules L. Coleman and Brian Leiter, "Determinacy, Objectivity, and Authority," *University of Pennsylvania Law Review* 142 (1993): 549–637; Brian Bix, *Law, Language, and Legal Determinacy* (Oxford: Clarendon Press, 1993); Stephen J. Burton, *Judging in Good Faith* (Cambridge: Cambridge University Press, 1992); Kent Greenawalt, *Law and Objectivity* (Oxford: Oxford University Press, 1992), pp. 3–89; Peter Drahos and Stephen Parker, "Rule Following, Rule Scepticism and Indeterminacy in Law: A Conventional Account," *Ratio Juris* 5 (1992): 109–19; Altman, *Critical Legal Studies: A Liberal Critique*; Scott Landers, "Wittgenstein, Realism, and CLS: Undermining Rule Scepticism," *Law and Philosophy* 9 (1990): 177–203; Kress, "Legal Indeterminacy"; Lawrence B. Solum, "On the Indeterminacy Crisis: Critiquing Critical Dogma," *University of Chicago Law Review* 54 (1987): 462–503.

40. See, e.g., Duncan Kennedy, *A Critique of Adjudication (fin de siècle)* (Cambridge, Mass.: Harvard University Press, 1997), p. 24; Anthony D'Amato, "Aspects of Deconstruction: Refuting Indeterminacy with One Bold Thought," *Northwestern University Law Review* 85 (1990): 113–27.

viable scholarly movement.[41] Its demise may be partially attributable to the critique of the indeterminacy thesis, but I shall not try to make that case. Whatever the reason for its demise, the current consensus is that most mandatory rules of law are *not* radically indeterminate and that even partially indeterminate rules can guide judges.[42] In Tamanaha's words, "the theoretical debate over legal indeterminacy expired with a consensus that a degree of indeterminacy coexists with a substantial amount of predictability."[43] Leading critical scholar Roberto Unger agrees that "[t]he radicalization of indeterminacy is . . . a mistake."[44] So I shall assume that at least some legal questions have a finite number of legally correct answers—one or more—plus some legally incorrect answers.

5.5.2 Legal Content

Although I shall assume that legal standards dictate determinate results in some cases, however they do it, I shall not assume any particular theory of legal content. My topic is what Dworkin calls the *force* of law—"the relative power of any true proposition of law to justify coercion in different sorts of exceptional circumstance"—rather than the *grounds* of law—"circumstances in which particular propositions of law should be taken to be sound or true."[45] I invite you to assume whatever theory of legal content you favor: inclusive positivist, exclusive positivist, Dworkinian, et cetera. I shall not assume, for example, that legal content can always be identified without evaluative argument, as exclusive positivists insist.[46] My arguments do not presuppose a positivist theory of legal content, much less an exclusive positivist theory, although they are compatible with these theories. They are even compatible with what Hart calls "for-

---

41. Brian Z. Tamanaha, *Law as a Means to an End: Threat to the Rule of Law* (New York: Cambridge University Press, 2006), p. 132 (critical legal studies "no longer exists"); Cass R. Sunstein, "On Academic Fads and Fashions," *Michigan Law Review* 99 (2001): 1251, p. 1251 (critical legal studies has "disappear[ed]"); Jack M. Balkin, "*Bush v. Gore* and the Boundary between Law and Politics," *Yale Law Journal* 110 (2001): 1407–58, p. 1441 (critical legal studies was "dead as a doornail" in 2000).

42. See, e.g., Burton, *Judging in Good Faith*; Coleman and Leiter, "Determinacy, Objectivity, and Authority."

43. Tamanaha, *On the Rule of Law*, p. 124. See also, Alexander and Sherwin, *The Rule of Rules*, p. 97 ("[W]e reject skepticism about the possibility of communication through language").

44. Roberto Mangabeira Unger, *What Should Legal Analysis Become?* (London: Verso, 1996), p. 121. See also Duncan Kennedy, "Freedom and Constraint in Adjudication: A Critical Phenomenology," *Journal of Legal Education* 36 (1986): 518–62, p. 527 ("[P]erhaps there are some results that you simply can't reach through correct legal reasoning").

45. Ronald Dworkin, *Law's Empire* (Cambridge, Mass.: Harvard University Press, 1986), p. 110.

46. See, e.g., Joseph Raz, *The Authority of Law* (Oxford: Clarendon Press, 1979); Scott J. Shapiro, "On Hart's Way Out," in *Hart's Postscript*, ed. Jules Coleman (Oxford: Oxford University Press, 2000).

malist theories," according to which rules alone always dictate legally correct answers.[47] I shall not assume that the law consists exclusively of rules as opposed to legal principles and other types of legal standards. My arguments are compatible with, although they do not entail, Dworkin's claim that theories of legal content "need not leave entirely open the question how judges should decide actual cases."[48]

5.5.3 Imperfection

One could agree that legal rules have determinate content while denying that suboptimal-result cases exist. Indeed, many people who reject indeterminacy still appear to believe that the law, properly applied, never actually forbids their preferred results. I affectionately call these people *Panglossians*. Panglossians may complain when judges reach what they regard as *bad* results, but they do not distinguish between *morally bad* and *legally incorrect*. They condemn certain decisions as both morally bad and legally incorrect.[49] They praise other decisions as both good and faithful to the law. Justice Antonin Scalia laments "[t]he inevitable tendency of judges to think that the law is what they would like it to be."[50]

A Panglossian position could take either a conceptual or a contingent form. Imagine a theory of legal content entailing that, by definition, a positive rule is not legally valid if it dictates a suboptimal result. According to this theory, if a court decision is suboptimal, then ipso facto it is legally incorrect. This entails that suboptimal-result cases do not exist. I am unaware of any argument for such a theory of legal content, although one might exist. Certain natural lawyers almost accept such a theory, but even they do not go this far. Michael Moore notes that Cicero, Blackstone, and other natural lawyers occasionally state that the justness of a norm is sufficient for legal validity.[51] No one now holds this view.[52] Even this view does not entail that the law always permits reaching optimal results, because even just norms dictate suboptimal results in negative-gap cases.

---

47. H. L. A. Hart, *The Concept of Law*, 2nd ed. (Oxford: Oxford University Press, 1994), ch. 7.
48. Dworkin, *Law's Empire*, p. 112.
49. See, e.g., Michael Stokes Paulsen, "Accusing Justice: Some Variations on the Themes of Robert M. Cover's *Justice Accused*," *Journal of Law and Religion* 7 (1989): 33–97, p. 35 (*Roe v. Wade* is "a lawless and immoral decision"). I am not suggesting that Paulsen is a Panglossian.
50. Antonin Scalia, "Originalism: The Lesser Evil," *University of Cincinnati Law Review* 57 (1989): 849–65, p. 864.
51. Michael Moore, "Law as a Functional Kind," in *Natural Law Theory: Contemporary Essays*, ed. Robert P. George (Oxford: Oxford University Press, 1992), p. 197.
52. Mark C. Murphy, "Natural Law Jurisprudence," *Legal Theory* 9 (2003): 241–67, p. 242 (natural law theorists reject the "stupid position . . . that a norm's status as a correct moral norm is sufficient for its being a legal norm").

The Normative Classification of Legal Results

Moore's own position comes still closer to the view that suboptimality entails legal incorrectness. In addition to endorsing Augustine's slogan, *lex iniusta non est lex*,[53] Moore asserts that "an unjust court decision is not the law of the case so decided."[54] This entails that judges are never legally or morally obligated to reach unjust results. If Moore would also classify as unjust every result that counts as suboptimal on my definition, then his position would entail that the law never requires suboptimal results. However, I suspect that Moore would not classify as unjust every result that counts as suboptimal on my definition. Recall the case of the widow, Yasmin. I stipulated that Judge Lucas would have an all-things-considered reason to rule in Yasmin's favor if, counterfactually, the law gave him discretion to reach either result. That makes evicting Yasmin a suboptimal result by definition. But does that fact entail that evicting Yasmin is unjust, given that the law actually requires Judge Lucas to evict her? I do not know what Moore's answer would be, so I cannot attribute to him the view that there are no suboptimal-result cases.

If a natural lawyer wanted to maintain that the law never requires suboptimal results, then he would have to go farther than Moore does. He would have to insist that "the law," properly understood, always reflects morality rather than positive law whenever the two conflict. However, if this claim were to gain wide currency with judges, then positive law could no longer perform the important role of guiding action in morally controversial areas. For the pro-choice judge, the law would permit abortion. For the pro-life judge, it would forbid abortion. The public could have no coherent law on topics about which judges morally disagree. So the Panglossian natural lawyer would have to assume either that judges share all moral opinions that bear on legal questions, or that having settled law never matters more than doing justice, as one sees it, to the parties. These are implausible assumptions.

Rather than defining suboptimal-result cases out of existence via one's theory of legal content, one could achieve the same goal by denying as a contingent matter that the laws of one's legal system ever require suboptimal results. This is the path of a positivist Panglossian. She believes her lawmakers to be exceptionally enlightened. Their laws require judges to reach results that happen to be precisely the ones that each judge would have had an all-things-considered reason to reach, had the law not required anything of him. This would be a happy state of affairs. There would be no suboptimal-result cases. Modern people, however, do not see their lawmakers as infallible. I cannot name any positivist Panglossians.

One scholar who could be mistaken for a Panglossian is Douglas Edlin. As do the Kadishes,[55] Edlin contends that judges are legally

---

53. "An unjust law is no law at all."
54. Moore, "Law as a Functional Kind," p. 198.
55. See §3.6.

permitted to deviate from applicable legal standards under certain conditions. But Edlin goes farther, arguing that judges have a legal *obligation* to deviate from extremely unjust laws, one that outweighs their legal obligation to apply the law.[56] Consider the Fugitive Slave Act, which required judges to return escaped slaves to their masters. Edlin argues that judges did not have an all-things-considered legal obligation to adhere to the act.[57] Therefore, Edlin's position implies that a case brought under the act was not actually a suboptimal-result case, even though the act required suboptimal results. However, his position does not entail the nonexistence of suboptimal-result cases. Edlin delineates a tiny category of cases in which judges have a legal obligation to deviate. This category constitutes a small subset of the set of cases in which positive law dictates suboptimal results. The rest of the cases in the latter set still constitute suboptimal-result cases even if Edlin is correct. Edlin places several restrictions upon deviation. I shall mention only two. First, he insists upon a stringent "epistemic threshold" for deviation.[58] He states that the judge's legal obligation to deviate overrides her legal obligation to adhere only if she is *extremely* confident that the result otherwise required by law is *extremely* unjust: "no judge can properly invoke common law review unless she is as certain as she can be that a mistake was made by a prior court or a legislature and that this mistake concerns a matter of grave social importance that violates the judge's deepest convictions."[59]

Second, Edlin insists that the moral convictions of judges cannot justify deviation unless those convictions have been incorporated into "authoritative legal sources."[60] For example, a judge may not refuse to enforce the death penalty simply because of her religious convictions. She must be able to "express the wrongness of capital punishment in terms of a concrete legal violation."[61] A judge whose conviction is not reflected in any authoritative legal source will be unable to make a legal argument for deviation based upon that conviction.

Because Edlin limits the scope of permissible deviation in these ways and others, his position does not preclude the existence of suboptimal-result cases. A judge who embraces Edlin's philosophy will still confront cases in which she has a legal obligation to reach results that she believes to be suboptimal. Edlin appears to recognize and accept this conclusion. He is no Panglossian, although he comes as close as anyone I have found.

---

56. Douglas E. Edlin, *Judges and Unjust Laws: Common Law Constitutionalism and the Foundations of Judicial Review* (Ann Arbor: University of Michigan Press, 2008), chs. 5–7.
57. Ibid., p. 133.
58. Ibid., pp. 139–43.
59. Ibid., p. 167.
60. Ibid., p. 15.
61. Ibid.

The Normative Classification of Legal Results

5.6 LEGAL PRINCIPLES

Dworkin observes that judges sometimes invoke legal principles in order to decide cases in which the rules, taken alone, require suboptimal results.[62] Inclusive positivists agree that legal principles can be authoritative.[63] One might wonder whether, on that premise, suboptimal-result cases even exist. But even Dworkin understands that they do.[64] A legal system with suboptimal principles still generates suboptimal-result cases.[65] Dworkin appears to believe that the legal systems of the United States contain no suboptimal principles, but that would be a happy contingency, and someone could reasonably disagree. One can imagine someone believing the following propositions:

1. The principles to which Dworkin appeals in his arguments about abortion, euthanasia, and affirmative action are, indeed, authoritative principles of American law.[66]
2. Dworkin applies these principles correctly.
3. The results that Dworkin defends in these cases are morally repugnant.

One who believes these three propositions could conclude that Dworkin's principles are morally defective, despite being legally authoritative. The cases mentioned are, from that individual's perspective, suboptimal-result cases. So suboptimal-result cases can arise even if the law includes principles as well as rules. Reaching an optimal result sometimes

---

62. See §3.7.

63. See, e.g., Jules Coleman, *The Practice of Principle* (Oxford: Oxford University Press, 2001); Matthew Kramer, "How Moral Principles Can Enter into the Law," *Legal Theory* 6 (2000): 83–108; W. J. Waluchow, *Inclusive Legal Positivism* (Oxford: Clarendon Press, 1994).

64. Dworkin writes the following:

> Perhaps the law of the United States, properly interpreted in deference to integrity, did include the Fugitive Slave Act enacted by Congress before the Civil War. If a judge's own sense of justice condemned that act as deeply immoral because it required citizens to help send escaped slaves back to their masters, he would have to consider whether he should actually enforce it on the demand of a slave owner, or whether he should lie and say that this was not the law after all, or whether he should resign.

Dworkin, *Law's Empire*, p. 219.

65. See, e.g., Ken Kress, "Why No Judge Should be a Dworkinian Coherentist," *Texas Law Review* 77 (1999): 1375–427; Alexander and Sherwin, *The Rule of Rules*, ch. 8.

66. See, e.g., Ronald Dworkin, *Freedom's Law: The Moral Reading of the American Constitution* (Cambridge, Mass.: Harvard University Press, 1996); Ronald Dworkin, *Life's Dominion: An Argument about Abortion, Euthanasia, and Individual Freedom* (New York: Knopf, 1993); Ronald Dworkin, *A Matter of Principle* (Cambridge, Mass.: Harvard University Press, 1985).

requires judges to deviate not just from the rules but from all applicable legal standards. This is deviation from the law *simpliciter*.

It is confusing that some authors call decisions that deviate from legal rules exercises of "judicial discretion."[67] This usage works for cases in which the judge has some kind of legal authorization to deviate from the rules. However, we should distinguish decisions in which the judge has such legal authorization from those in which he lacks it. As noted, I use *discretion* exclusively to refer to cases of legally authorized choice.[68] A judge can have discretion, in this sense, to depart from legal rules. By contrast, I use *deviation* to refer to legally unauthorized decisions—those that contradict applicable law *simpliciter*. One cannot, by definition, have legal discretion to deviate from the law *simpliciter*.

I have now reviewed and found plausible several assumptions underlying the claim that suboptimal-result cases exist. In the legal systems that interest me, the law sometimes requires the judge to reach a result that she would have an all-things-considered reason to avoid if the law permitted her to do so. In the next chapter, I shall ask whether judges have *pro tanto* moral reasons to deviate in such cases. Before turning to this question, I wish to draw another distinction between my topic and a traditional concern of jurisprudence.

5.7 HARD CASES

For over a century, lawyers have used the adjective *hard* to refer to cases that are especially problematic in various respects.[69] One might assume that *suboptimal-result case* is just a new term for hard cases. It is not. *Hard case* has various meanings. The relation between suboptimal-result cases and hard cases depends upon definitions. David Dyzenhaus, in *Hard Cases in Wicked Legal Systems*, uses *hard case* to refer to cases in which "informed lawyers disagree about the proper result."[70] This usage is common, but lawyers can disagree about different things: the legally correct result or the result that the judge should reach, all things considered. Dyzenhaus appears to intend the latter when he defines a hard case as one in which "lawyers disagree about what the judge should decide."[71] But on the same

---

67. The Kadishes call it *deviational discretion*. Mortimer R. Kadish and Sanford H. Kadish, *Discretion to Disobey: A Study of Lawful Departures from Legal Rules* (Stanford, Calif.: Stanford University Press, 1973), p. 42.

68. See §3.9.

69. See, e.g., *Henchey v. City of Chicago*, 41 Ill. 136, 141 (1866) ("Hard cases make bad law").

70. David Dyzenhaus, *Hard Cases in Wicked Legal Systems: South African Law in the Perspective of Legal Philosophy* (Oxford: Clarendon Press, 1991), p. 1, citing Kent Greenawalt, "Discretion and Judicial Decision: The Elusive Quest for the Fetters that Bind Judges," *Columbia Law Review* 75 (1975): 359–99, p. 386.

71. Dyzenhaus, *Hard Cases in Wicked Legal Systems*, p. 1.

page, he describes a case as hard if its "decision turns on contested points of law,"[72] which suggests disagreement about legal correctness.

Although lawyers often disagree about how judges should decide suboptimal-result cases, they do not always disagree. All lawyers might agree that a constitutional provision requiring people to eat their children is legally valid, but they might also agree that judges should deviate from it. All lawyers might agree that a parking ordinance dictates a slightly suboptimal result in a certain case, but they might also agree that judges should adhere to it. A case constitutes a suboptimal-result case not because lawyers disagree about the morally optimal result, or about the legally correct result, but because the law requires a suboptimal result. Some suboptimal-result cases, but not all, are also hard in the first and/or second senses.

Dyzenhaus also rejects the definition of hard cases as those in which "there is no answer at law." He thinks this definition begs the question against Dworkin and in favor of positivism.[73] Dworkin describes hard cases as those that "cannot be brought under a clear rule of law, laid down by some institution in advance,"[74] although he believes that there is a legally correct answer in such cases.[75] However, there are many cases in which the only applicable legal standards—whether rules, principles, or policies—dictate a unique result that is suboptimal. These are suboptimal-result cases.

There is, however, a more generic sense of *hard case* that encompasses most suboptimal-result cases. Suboptimal-result cases are usually *hard* insofar as they present a difficult practical dilemma for anyone who believes both that judges should adhere to the law and that judges should avoid suboptimal results. Many lawyers hold both beliefs. Some give more weight to the first, others to the second. Furthermore, many lawyers disagree about what the law requires and about which results are suboptimal. As a result, lawyers will disagree sharply about "what judges should decide" in many suboptimal-result cases. But that fact is not constitutive of a suboptimal-result case.

---

72. Ibid.
73. Ibid., p. 1 n. 2.
74. Ronald Dworkin, "Hard Cases," in *Taking Rights Seriously* (Cambridge, Mass.: Harvard University Press, 1977), p. 81.
75. Ibid.

6

Reasons to Deviate

Assuming that suboptimal-result cases exist, how should judges handle them? Dworkin acknowledges the issue:

> [T]here are of course cases in which the institutional right is clearly settled by established legal materials, like a statute, and clearly conflicts with background moral rights. In these cases the judge seeking to do what is morally right is faced with a familiar sort of conflict: the institutional right provides a genuine reason, the importance of which will vary with the general justice or wickedness of the system as a whole, for a decision one way, but certain considerations of morality present an important reason against it.[1]

A judge who faces a legally regulated question has four options:

1. Adhere to the law.
2. Deviate from the law.
3. Disqualify (recuse) herself from the case.
4. Resign from the bench.[2]

A wide range of reasons can bear on the judge's choice, depending on the question before her. In what follows I shall consider the following questions. Do judges have a legal duty to adhere to the law? What incentives do they have to adhere? What incentives, and other private reasons, do they have to deviate, self-recuse, or resign? What moral reasons do they have to adhere, deviate, self-recuse, or resign in suboptimal-result cases? Does the validity of the regulating law change the judge's reasons in these cases? Can valid law give the judge reasons to reach a result that she would otherwise have an all-things-considered reason to avoid, if the law permitted her to avoid it? How does the law perform this trick, if it does?

If a judge chooses to decide a suboptimal-result case, rather than self-recusing or resigning, then she has two options: adhere or deviate. Two related questions arise. First, is it always objectively wrong for her to

---

1. Ronald Dworkin, "A Reply to Critics," in *Taking Rights Seriously* (Cambridge, Mass.: Harvard University Press, 1978), pp. 326–27.
2. Macabre as it sounds, suicide counts as "resignation" for my purposes.

deviate, even when the law requires objectively bad results? Second, is it always subjectively wrong for her knowingly to deviate, even when she sincerely believes that the law requires bad results? In other words, is a judge who knowingly deviates always blameworthy for doing so?[3]

There are many possible answers to these questions. Affirmative answers are often suggested by the rhetoric of politicians and pundits who criticize judges for deviation.[4] According to the most restrictive principle of judicial fidelity, deviation is never morally permissible, even when the law mandates extreme violations of basic human rights. A judge who disapproves of the law may express his disapproval as forcefully as he wishes, on this view, but he must adhere.[5]

I am not sure how many critics actually believe that judges should unconditionally adhere. Critics of the bench do not always distinguish clearly between disapproval of a result on the basis of their own opinions about justice or policy, and belief that the judge has deviated. One wonders if critics would complain about judicial deviation if they were otherwise pleased with the results. Historical laws have authorized genocide, slavery, penal torture, and other horrors. Critics who insist that deviation is always wrong, all things considered, do not seem to have these laws in mind. But perhaps they believe that judges should simply resign from the bench rather than apply such laws.

In opposition to the objective absolutist position, one could claim that the ethical permissibility of deviation somehow depends on whether the result in a certain case is desirable overall, as a matter of justice and public policy. This would be to assert that a judge can have decisive moral reasons to disregard the law—reasons that trump whatever legal or moral reasons she may have to adhere to it.

In opposition to the subjective absolutist position, one might claim that the subjective ethical permissibility of knowingly deviating from the law depends on whether the judge believes (or reasonably believes) that the legally required result in a certain case is desirable overall, as a matter of justice and public policy. At the far extreme lies the view that judges are always permitted to reach optimal results, even when the law forbids it: they are always permitted to deviate in suboptimal-result cases. This is a form of legal particularism, analogous to moral particularism. Moral particularists claim that particular moral judgments can be justified without appeal to any moral rules or principles.[6] Legal particularists

---

3. See §2.3 on objective/subjective.
4. See cases mentioned in §1.1.
5. See, e.g., *Khan v. State Oil Co.*, 93 F.3d 1358, 1362–64 (7th Cir. 1996) in which Judge Richard A. Posner criticizes at length, but follows, the rule announced by the Supreme Court in *Albrecht v. Herald Co.*, 390 U.S. 145 (1968).
6. See, e.g., Jonathan Dancy, *Ethics without Principles* (Oxford: Oxford University Press, 2004). Dancy's position is criticized in Sean McKeever and Michael Ridge, *Principled Ethics: Generalism as a Regulative Ideal* (Oxford: Oxford University Press, 2006).

claim that particular legal judgments can be justified without appeal to any legal rules or principles.[7] Extreme legal particularism entails that judges are always permitted to reach optimal results, notwithstanding the law.

6.1 COGNITIVE DISSONANCE

Any judicial opinion raises four questions:
1. Does a sound legal argument for the holding exist?
2. Does the opinion advance a sound legal argument?
3. Is the holding optimal?
4. Is filing the opinion morally permissible, all things considered?

The easiest positions to understand give the same answer to all four questions.[8] Critics of a verdict often attack whatever argument the court offers for it, however sound it may be, whereas supporters of the verdict are often tempted to rally in defense of the argument, however weak. Nevertheless, even the proponents of a holding can criticize the reasoning and opponents can praise it. If someone's answer to the third question diverges from his answer to the first or second, then his answer to the fourth becomes interesting. One possible view is that a negative answer to the first question entails a negative answer to the fourth: it is morally impermissible for a court to reach a verdict for which no sound legal argument exists (even if the verdict itself is optimal). A stronger view is that a negative answer to the second question entails a negative answer to the fourth: it is morally impermissible for a court to advance a fallacious legal argument, even if a sound legal argument exists for the verdict (itself optimal).

Accepting either principle can cause cognitive dissonance. I shall illustrate using the famous 1965 case of *Griswold v. Connecticut*,[9] in which the U.S. Supreme Court held that a state statute criminalizing the use of contraceptives violated the constitutional rights of married couples. I choose *Griswold* as a case in which a reasonable person might endorse the holding but reject the argument. It combines a result that is widely thought optimal with reasoning that many legal scholars—including many who

---

7. See, e.g., Larry Alexander and Emily Sherwin, *The Rule of Rules* (Durham, N.C.: Duke University Press, 2001), p. 28 (particularistic legal decision making is reasoning directly from moral principles to particular decisions); Frederick Schauer, *Playing by the Rules: A Philosophical Examination of Rule-Based Decision-Making in Law and in Life* (Oxford: Oxford University Press, 1991), pp. 77–78.

8. A negative answer to the first question, of course, entails a negative answer to the second. If one answers the second and third questions affirmatively, then I cannot imagine why one would answer the fourth question negatively.

9. *Griswold v. Connecticut*, 381 U.S. 479 (1965).

Reasons to Deviate

support the result—find unsatisfactory.[10] I shall not ask you to agree with them that the *Griswold* argument is fallacious. Think of some other such decision if you prefer.

Assume *arguendo* that Connecticut's law was unjust. The ideal solution, then, would be to change the law: Connecticut could repeal its statute or the people of the United States could amend their Constitution explicitly to ban such legislation. But neither event had occurred as of 1965. So we turn to a second-best solution: sound constitutional arguments for invalidation. If such arguments existed in 1965, then the best possible Supreme Court opinion would have used one. However, many people believe that the majority opinion in *Griswold* contains no sound legal argument for invalidation.[11] Perhaps no such argument was even available to the Court in 1965. An individual can rationally hold one of these beliefs and also believe that Connecticut's law was unjust and should have been repealed. My question is this: assuming that such an individual is correct on all counts, was it objectively wrong, all things considered, for the Court to use a fallacious argument for invalidation? If one answers affirmatively, then one may experience cognitive dissonance: a conflict between one's opposition to banning contraceptives and one's judgment that the *Griswold* Court acted wrongly. One could relieve this dissonance by acquiring the belief that the Court was morally permitted to deviate in *Griswold*.

Of course, the fact that acquiring this belief would relieve someone's cognitive dissonance does not bear on its truth. Defending its truth would require, among other things, a substantive moral argument against banning contraceptives. That belongs in another book. My upcoming arguments in this book will support a conditional conclusion: *if* the *Griswold* result was optimal, then reaching it was not necessarily impermissible, even if no sound legal argument existed for it. Defending this conclusion does not require any premises about the justice or injustice of banning birth control.

6.2 REASONS TO DEVIATE

I have explained how judges are in the business of force.[12] They instruct other officials to use force and to create, withdraw, and block threats of force. The judge's decision will influence how force is used no matter how

---

10. Robert H. Bork, *The Tempting of America* (New York: Simon & Schuster, 1990), pp. 95–100; Raoul Berger, *Government by Judiciary: The Transformation of the Fourteenth Amendment* (Cambridge, Mass.: Harvard University Press, 1977), p. 18; Louis Henkin, "Privacy and Autonomy," *Columbia Law Review* 74 (1974): 1410–33, pp. 1421–22; Hugo L. Black, *A Constitutional Faith* (New York: Knopf, 1968), p. 9; Paul G. Kauper, "Penumbras, Peripheries, Emanations, Things Fundamental and Things Forgotten: The *Griswold* Case," *Michigan Law Review* 64 (1965): 235–58, pp. 252–53; *Griswold v. Connecticut* at 527 (Stewart, J., dissenting).
11. See authors cited above.
12. See §2.8.

she decides the case. If she rules for the defendant, then she refrains from threatening him with force and protects him from threats of force by other officials. If she rules against him, then she instructs subordinate officials to threaten him with force, and to use force if necessary, and she withdraws threats to use force against them if they do so.

In optimal-result cases, judicial reasons are straightforward. If the law permits the judge to favor the defendant, when this is a superior outcome, then the judge has *pro tanto* moral reasons to refrain from threatening him with force and to protect him from threats of force by other officials. If the law permits the judge to favor the plaintiff or prosecution, when this is a superior outcome, then the judge has *pro tanto* moral reasons to instruct subordinate officials to threaten the defendant with force. She also has *pro tanto* moral reasons to withdraw threats to use force against them if they so threaten the defendant.

In suboptimal-result cases, by definition, the judge would have an all-things-considered reason not to perform the legally required actions were they not required by law. If the law favors the plaintiff or prosecution, then the judge would have all-things-considered reason to refrain from threatening the defendant with force and to protect her from threats of force by other officials, if the law permitted him to do so. If the law favors the defendant, then the judge would have all-things-considered reason to instruct subordinate officials to threaten the defendant with force, if the law permitted him to do so. He also would have all-things-considered reason to withdraw threats of force against subordinate officials if they were so to threaten the defendant.

If the law permits a judge to avoid suboptimal results, then she has all-things-considered reasons to avoid them. What happens to these reasons in suboptimal-result cases? Compare two hypothetical cases of judges sentencing convicts to prison. Both judges are legally authorized to impose these sentences, which neither convict deserves as a moral matter. Suppose that in the first case, but not the second, the law mandates the sentence. According to the undermining principle,[13] the fact that the law in the first case requires the judge to impose the sentence undermines whatever reasons, including moral reasons, she might otherwise have to avoid this result, at least in reasonably just legal systems. The principle entails that judges in reasonably just legal systems have all-things-considered moral reasons to adhere to the law in all cases. Not everyone believes the undermining principle, but it is a popular view, perhaps the view of most lawyers, judges, law professors, and legal philosophers.

In the rest of this chapter I shall present and criticize every argument for the undermining principle of which I am aware. I conclude that none is sound. I think all-things-considered moral reasons to avoid suboptimal results are not undermined when the law requires such results, but rather

13. See §2.9.

survive as *pro tanto* reasons to deviate. It is, of course, a further question whether these reasons are overridden by stronger reasons to adhere. I shall examine that question in part II.

Although I conclude that we should reject the undermining principle, I do not know how to disprove it, nor shall I try to do so. Instead, having challenged several arguments in favor of the undermining principle, I develop in part II a theory of adjudication that is assumes it to be false.

6.3 NATURAL ROLES

Individuals can acquire new moral obligations—role obligations—when they enter institutional roles. My critic might suggest that the very concept of the judicial role entails that someone who takes into account reasons for deviation is not, by definition, a judge anymore, just as a man who marries is no longer a bachelor. This is to say that the judicial role is what Arthur Applbaum calls a "natural role," and that this role requires judges to disregard reasons to deviate. Applbaum defines a natural role "by analogy to natural law," as a role the obligations of which "follow from some truths about the kind of creatures we are," such that occupants of a role who pursue ends incompatible with the natural ends of the role make a "conceptual mistake."[14] However, Applbaum argues against natural roles in favor of "practice positivism," the view that "the concept of a practice does not impose any general content requirements or restrictions on the rules of all practices."[15] His conclusion seems correct to me, but I refer skeptical readers to his argument.[16]

Practice positivism entails that roles can change over time. Even if everyone today believes that the judicial role entails the undermining principle, this could change. There is nothing conceptually incoherent or irrational about a judge adopting for herself an alternative conception of her role, one that allows her to consider moral reasons to deviate. If enough judges begin to see their role in this way, then a new judicial role emerges. I shall argue, moreover, that we have no reason to conceive of the judicial role in accordance with the undermining principle.

Even if Applbaum is mistaken about natural roles and the judicial role is a natural role that requires ignoring reasons to deviate, that would not settle the practical question. If a judge, by definition, is someone who ignores reasons to deviate, then we must ask whether anyone should become a judge, in that sense. Perhaps there is something to be said for a different and less restrictive role.

---

14. Arthur Isak Applbaum, *Ethics for Adversaries: The Morality of Roles in Public and Professional Life* (Princeton, N.J.: Princeton University Press, 1999), p. 48.
15. Ibid., p. 51.
16. Ibid., pp. 51–58.

6.4 LEGAL POSITIVISM

This book does not plunge directly into the byzantine controversies about the nature of law that have occupied legal philosophers for decades. However, I often write as though some favorite positivist theses were true, including the separability thesis,[17] the social fact thesis,[18] the sources thesis,[19] and the thesis that law consists at least partly of rules.[20] I remain agnostic about these four theses and shall not evaluate them. For me, treating them as true is a convenient expository fiction: they make my arguments easier to understand and more interesting.[21] My ideal adversary is a positivist who also believes that judges are morally obligated to adhere in all cases, at least in reasonably just societies.[22] I have no interest in persuading him to abandon positivism, but I want him to abandon the latter principle.

My tolerance of positivism could cause confusion. Someone might suggest that positivism entails the undermining principle. This is true, but only on a particular and somewhat outdated definition of *positivism* as a theory of adjudication: the view that judges must decide cases only on the basis of posited legal norms. Dworkin calls this view "strict conventionalism."[23] It resembles what Dyzenhaus attacks as "positivism."[24] Strict conventionalism does, indeed, entail the undermining principle. My arguments will entail, inter alia, that strict conventionalism is false.

However, strict conventionalism is not what most self-described positivists today mean by *positivism*. Schauer's statement is typical:

> Nothing about positivism compels the idea that only legally pedigreed rules should guide judicial decisions. . . . Positivism is about legal validity and not about ultimate action, and nothing in positivism commits any decision-maker,

---

17. See Jules Coleman, *The Practice of Principle* (Oxford: Oxford University Press, 2001), p. 151; John Austin, *The Province of Jurisprudence Determined*, ed. Wilfrid E. Rumble (New York: Cambridge University Press, 1995), p. 157 ("The existence of law is one thing; its merit or demerit is another").
18. See, e.g., Coleman, *The Practice of Principle*, pp. 75–76. Cf. Benjamin C. Zipursky, "The Model of Social Facts," in *Hart's Postscript: Essays on the Postscript to the Concept of Law*, ed. Jules Coleman (New York: Oxford University Press, 2001).
19. Joseph Raz, "Legal Positivism and the Sources of Law," in *The Authority of Law* (Oxford: Clarendon Press, 1979), p. 47.
20. See, e.g., H. L. A. Hart, *The Concept of Law*, 2nd ed. (Oxford: Oxford University Press, 1994), ch. 7.
21. Also, positivism is so popular that even a book aimed exclusively at positivists would have a large readership.
22. This is what I call *restrictive rule* in §7.3.
23. Ronald Dworkin, *Law's Empire* (Cambridge, Mass.: Harvard University Press, 1986), p. 124.
24. David Dyzenhaus, "Positivism's Stagnant Research Programme," *Oxford Journal of Legal Studies* 20 (2000): 703–22; David Dyzenhaus, *Hard Cases in Wicked Legal Systems: South African Law in the Perspective of Legal Philosophy* (Oxford: Clarendon Press, 1991).

including a judge in a court of law, to treating positivistic norms as the exclusive input into decision-making.[25]

Modern positivists understand themselves as advancing theories of legal validity and legal content, not theories of adjudication.[26] Their position is compatible with many theories of adjudication, including mine.

6.5 ORDINARY DISCOURSE

A supporter of the undermining principle might object that she rarely hears an observer describe a judge as acting "immorally" or violating his "moral duty" by rendering a decision, provided that the observer believes that the judge has adhered to the law. If, as I claim, judges have moral reasons to deviate in suboptimal-result cases, then why do observers rarely call judges "immoral" for adhering in such cases?

I shall grant *arguendo* that one rarely hears an observer call a judge "immoral" if the observer believes the judge's decision to be required by law. Calling *decisions* immoral, however, is commonplace. Consider Tamanaha's characterization of *Brown*. That decision, he asserts, was "undoubtedly correct from a moral standpoint," but "arguably was not supported by legal principles or reasoned elaboration or neutral principle." It was "impossible to justify in purely legal terms."[27] If the Court had upheld school segregation, then Tamanaha and many others would have condemned the decision as immoral, albeit legally mandated.

A supporter of the undermining principle could respond as follows. The fact that a result upholding school segregation is immoral, all things considered, does not entail that the *judge* acts immorally, all things considered, by reaching that result if the law requires it. This may be true. However, you must remember that in part I, I am claiming only that judges have *pro tanto* moral reasons to avoid suboptimal results. I need not and shall not claim that these reasons prevail against all opposition. In part II, I shall explain why adhering in some suboptimal-result cases is not just morally permissible, but morally required.

Therefore, do not confuse my modest claim—that adhering in suboptimal-result cases is *pro tanto* immoral—with the untenably strong claim that any judge who adheres in such a case performs an all-things-considered immoral

---

25. Schauer, *Playing by the Rules*, p. 200. Similar ideas appear in Coleman, *The Practice of Principle*, pp. 167–68; Joseph Raz, *The Authority of Law* (Oxford: Clarendon Press, 1979), chs. 4, 10; David O. Brink, "Legal Positivism and Natural Law Reconsidered," *Monist* 68 (1985): 364–87.

26. See, e.g., Coleman, *The Practice of Principle*, pp. 167–68; Joseph Raz, "Law and Value in Adjudication," in *The Authority of Law* (Oxford: Clarendon Press, 1979).

27. Brian Z. Tamanaha, *On the Rule of Law: History, Politics, Theory* (Cambridge: Cambridge University Press, 2004), p. 80.

action. In ordinary discourse, to claim that someone acts "immorally" or "violates a moral duty" is to claim that his actions are morally impermissible, all things considered. So you should not be surprised if you rarely hear an observer call a judge "immoral" for adhering in what the observer believes to be a suboptimal-result case. One cannot infer from the fact that she avoids this language that she believes that the judge has no reason whatsoever to deviate. She might believe that the judge has a reason to deviate but also a stronger reason to adhere. Furthermore, although some people have a higher tolerance for unjust decisions than others, most people can imagine a decision so unjust that they would call the judge's own decisional conduct "immoral," even if they were convinced that her decision was legally mandated.

6.6 FORMAL LEGALITY

The next argument for undermining appeals to the rule of law—often called one of our preeminent political values.[28] *Rule of law* is used to represent many different ideals.[29] It denotes a concept with multiple conceptions.[30] I shall primarily concern myself with *formal legality*—the most fundamental conception. A system exhibits formal legality to the

---

28. Not everyone supports it. See, e.g., Christine Sypnowich, "Utopia and the Rule of Law," in *Recrafting the Rule of Law*, ed. David Dyzenhaus (Oxford: Hart, 1999); John Hasnas, "The Myth of the Rule of Law," *Wisconsin Law Review* 1995 (1995): 199–233; Allan C. Hutchinson, *Dwelling on the Threshold: Critical Essays on Modern Legal Thought* (Toronto: Carswell, 1988), p. 40 ("The Rule of Law is a sham; the esoteric and convoluted nature of legal doctrine is an accommodating screen to obscure its indeterminacy and the inescapable element of judicial choice"); Morton J. Horwitz, "The Rule of Law: An Unqualified Human Good?" *Yale Law Journal* 86 (1977): 561–66; Roberto Mangabeira Unger, *Law in Modern Society* (New York: Free Press, 1976), pp. 238–42. Liberals and conservatives often dismiss leftist and communitarian criticism of the rule of law as naïve. Tamanaha, *On the Rule of Law*, p. 73 ("Such severe criticism [of the rule of law] could only be produced in a country in which lengthy acquaintance with the rule of law confers intimate familiarity of its limitations, and also leads to a sense of security that encourages forgetfulness about its benefits"); Judith N. Shklar, "Political Theory and the Rule of Law," in *The Rule of Law: Ideal or Ideology*, eds. Allan C. Hutchinson and Patrick Monahan (Toronto: Carswell, 1987), p. 12 ("[D]estabilizing the existing system of civil liberties and rights, and the individualistic ethos that sustains them in the hope of building a truly fraternal order does not make sense. It shows little grasp of the fragilities of personal freedom which is the true and only province of the Rule of Law").

29. See, e.g., Richard H. Fallon, Jr., "'The Rule of Law' as a Concept in Constitutional Discourse," *Columbia Law Review* 97 (1997): 1–56. Andrei Marmor notes that "the various ideas associated with the rule of law are often conflicting and not infrequently rather confused." Andrei Marmor, "The Rule of Law and Its Limits," *Law and Philosophy* 23 (2004): 1–43, p. 1. As early as 1987, Judith Shklar could observe that "[i]t would not be very difficult to show that the phrase 'the Rule of Law' has become meaningless thanks to ideological abuse and general over-use." Shklar, "Political Theory and the Rule of Law," p. 1.

30. On the concept/conception distinction see John Rawls, *A Theory of Justice* (Cambridge, Mass.: Harvard University Press, 1971), p. 5; Ronald Dworkin, *Taking Rights Seriously* (Cambridge, Mass.: Harvard University Press, 1977), pp. 134–36. The basic division

degree that its laws are general, prospective, clear, publicized, stable, noncontradictory, correctly applied, and realistically possible for subjects to obey.[31] Each branch of government has a role to play in upholding formal legality. The legislature must take care to draft legislation that is general, prospective, clear, possible to obey, and noncontradictory. Legislators must not revise the law too often or enact contradictory provisions. The executive, similarly, must not enact or enforce laws that violate these conditions. The judiciary generally has authority to determine whether the political branches have complied with these conditions. In addition, judges sometimes act in a legislative capacity. When they do so they must meet the same conditions as formal legislators: generality, prospectivity, et cetera. Many rich debates have arisen concerning the conditions of formal legality.[32] Scholars have asked, for example, to what extent the law should consist of rules, rather than other types of legal standards.[33] These debates relate directly to the prospectivity, clarity, and obedience conditions.

The legal systems that interest me exhibit formal legality to a substantial degree. Legal subjects cannot complain that they were unaware of the legal consequences of their actions. Therefore, someone might argue that a judge has no moral reason to refrain from imposing those consequences. Imagine a law that, for the purpose of discouraging Christianity, imposes a special tax on citizens who attend church. Assume that singling out Christians in this way unjustly disadvantages them. This

---

within conceptions of the rule of law separates *formal* from *substantive* conceptions. According to Tamanaha, formal theories concern the "proper sources and form of legality," whereas substantive theories impose conditions on the content of the law. Tamanaha divides formal theories into three subcategories: rule-by-law, which refers to the government using law as an instrument of action; formal legality; and "democracy plus legality," which holds that consent determines the content of law. His substantive conceptions of the rule of law include individual rights, the right of dignity and/or justice, and social welfare. Tamanaha, *On the Rule of Law*, p. 91–92.

31. Lon L. Fuller, *The Morality of Law*, 2nd rev. ed. (New Haven: Yale University Press, 1969), pp. 32–38. Some earlier writers identify the rule of law with a subset of these conditions. Montesquieu's rule of law, for example, requires only procedural safeguards in the criminal law, for the purpose of protecting individuals from violence at the hands of the executive. Shklar, "Political Theory and the Rule of Law," p. 5. Other theorists add conditions of formal legality to Tamanaha's basic list, such as the existence of a politically independent and impartial court system; the right of every legal subject to seek legal redress and to defend himself in courts of law; the right to appellate review of court decisions; and the right to have a defense attorney provided when charged with a crime. See Robert S. Summers, "The Principles of the Rule of Law," *Notre Dame Law Review* 74 (1999): 1691–712, pp. 1694–95.

32. See, e.g., Ian Shapiro, ed., *The Rule of Law: NOMOS XXXVI* (New York: New York University Press, 1994).

33. See, e.g., Louis Kaplow, "Rules Versus Standards: An Economic Analysis," *Duke Law Journal* 42 (1992): 557–629; Kathleen M. Sullivan, "The Justices of Rules and Standards," *Harvard Law Review* 106 (1992): 22–123; Duncan Kennedy, "Form and Substance in Private Law Adjudication," *Harvard Law Review* 89 (1976): 1685–1778.

unjust disadvantage would ordinarily constitute a *pro tanto* moral reason not to confiscate the money. Likewise, the injustice of the law gives legislators moral reasons to repeal it. However, let us assume that the law also has the formal rule-of-law virtues: it is publicized in advance, intelligible, prospective, possible to obey, et cetera. Everyone has a reasonable opportunity to learn that attending church will subject him to a special tax. One could argue that this fact undermines the judge's moral reasons not to confiscate the money—that formal legality entails the undermining principle.

This argument mistakes a necessary condition for a sufficient one. It might indeed be wrong to enforce a law that lacked one or more of the formal rule-of-law virtues. But the fact that an announced rule has all of these virtues does not undermine whatever moral reasons one might have to refrain from enforcing the rule. Here is an analogy. Pedro orders Ana, his neighbor, never to attend church. He threatens to take ten dollars from her purse every time she disobeys him. His order is intelligible to her, given in advance, prospective, and possible to obey. These facts do not undermine Pedro's moral reasons to keep his hands off Ana's money after she disobeys his appalling command and attends church.

Similarly, the fact that a law, and the legal system to which it belongs, has the formal rule-of-law virtues does not undermine a judge's moral reasons to deviate in a suboptimal-result case. In the words of Joseph Raz, "[a] non-democratic legal system, based on the denial of human rights, on extensive poverty, on racial segregation, sexual inequalities, and religious persecution may, in principle, conform to the requirements of the rule of law better than any of the legal systems of the more enlightened Western democracies."[34]

I will return to the subject of the rule of law in chapter 7. Before moving on I must emphasize that this section and the rest of this chapter are directed exclusively against the undermining principle. My arguments challenge neither the idea that judges have *pro tanto* reasons for adherence nor the idea that these reasons can be decisive.

6.7 SUBMITTING TO THE STATE

Plato believes that individuals have an absolute moral duty to accept even an unjust punishment from their state.[35] In this spirit one could defend the undermining principle as follows. If individuals have an absolute moral

---

34. Joseph Raz, "The Rule of Law and Its Virtue," in *The Authority of Law* (Oxford: Clarendon Press, 1979) p. 211; See also Jeremy Waldron, "The Rule of Law in Contemporary Liberal Theory," *Ratio Juris* 2 (1989): 79–96.

35. Cf. Plato, *Crito* 51c: "[I]f you cannot persuade your country you must do whatever it orders, and patiently submit to any punishment that it imposes, whether it be flogging or imprisonment. . . ."

duty to accept the legal consequences of their behavior, then judges have no moral reason to protect them from these consequences. In politically legitimate and reasonably just legal systems, individuals have an absolute moral duty to accept legal consequences. Therefore, the argument concludes, judges in such systems have no moral reason to protect individuals from these consequences. They have no moral reason to deviate in order to avoid suboptimal results.

There are two flaws in this argument. First, the major premise is suspect. One cannot infer from the fact that one party has a duty not to resist a certain threat to the conclusion that a second party has no moral reason against imposing the threat. Nor can one infer that a third party has a reason not to protect the first party from such a threat at the hands of the second.

Second, few today (*pace* Plato) defend a categorical moral duty to accept punishment or other legal consequences in suboptimal-result cases.[36] Even the much weaker principle that individuals have a *pro tanto* moral duty to obey the law, as such, has fallen into disrepute with philosophers.[37] If there is no universal *pro tanto* duty to obey the law, then there is no universal *pro tanto* duty to accept punishment.[38] One who would defend the undermining principle on the basis of the latter duty must rebut many objections that have been raised against the duty to obey.[39] That may yet be possible, but defenders of the duty to obey presently labor under a heavy argumentative burden.

6.8 LEGAL AUTHORITY

Another argument for the undermining principle appeals to the legal authority of judges: if the law authorizes a judge to reach a certain result, then any contrary reasons are undermined and he should disregard them. Consider the following hypothetical. Bud vandalizes Lou's rosebush. Stipulate that, as a moral matter, Bud owes Lou restitution. In civil society, Lou has moral reasons not to use force against Bud's person or property,

---

36. Even those who endorse a moral obligation to submit to punishment do not extend the obligation to defendants who are factually innocent or who have been charged under unjust laws. See, e.g., Gerard V. Bradley, "Plea Bargaining and the Criminal Defendant's Obligation to Plead Guilty," *South Texas Law Review* 40 (1999): 65–82.

37. Joseph Raz, "The Obligation to Obey: Revision and Tradition," in *Ethics in the Public Domain* (Oxford: Clarendon Press, 1994); A. John Simmons, *Moral Principles and Political Obligations* (Princeton, N.J.: Princeton University Press, 1979); M. B. E. Smith, "Is There a Prima Facie Obligation to Obey the Law?" *Yale Law Journal* 82 (1973): 950–76.

38. This is not to say that wrongfully convicted defendants never have moral reasons to accept punishment. Attempting to evade punishment might, for example, express disrespect for the legal system or threaten the rule of law.

39. On these objections see William A. Edmundson, "State of the Art: The Duty to Obey the Law," *Legal Theory* 10 (2004): 215–59.

even for the purpose of extracting morally justified restitution. These reasons also apply to Lou's neighbor, Sol, and to all other private parties. Lou sues Bud for damages. Sol, who happens to be a trial judge, is assigned to the case, hears the evidence, and decides to award damages to Lou. As the assigned judge, Sol is legally authorized to do so. His legal authorization undermines some of his moral reasons not to use force against Bud—reasons he had before hearing the case. Sol now has no moral reason not to use force against Bud to the extent necessary for extracting morally justified restitution under law.

Sol hears his next case. In this case, ruling against the defendant, Jon, is a suboptimal result. Jon has done nothing to justify, in moral terms, the use of force against him. However, Sol is legally authorized to rule against Jon: Sol is the assigned judge and the applicable law, properly construed, permits him to rule against Jon. The argument concludes that, just as Sol's legal authorization to use force against Bud undermines Sol's moral reasons not to use it, so does Sol's legal authorization to use force against Jon undermine Sol's moral reasons not to use it.

The flaw in this argument is that Sol's reasons not to use force against Jon are natural reasons not to use morally unjustified force. By contrast, Sol's moral reasons not to use force against Bud were created by the legal system. They are the same reasons that Lou has not to use force against Bud in civil society, even when restitution is morally justified. Sol has these reasons, too, but they are undermined for Sol when he is assigned to Bud's case and hears the evidence. But the fact that the law undermines these reasons, which the legal system itself created, does not imply that the law can undermine natural reasons. Sol's legal authorization to use morally unjustified force against Jon does not undermine his natural reasons not to do so. At least if the law gives him discretion to rule in Jon's favor, then he should take these natural reasons into account. He should not ignore them simply because the law authorizes him to do so.

6.9 INTENTION

In this section and the next, I turn to what may be the most interesting arguments for the undermining principle. They use principles that have been heavily debated in contemporary normative ethics. The first argument claims that a judge has no objective, *pro tanto* reason to deviate in a suboptimal-result case, provided that she adheres with the proper *intentions*. This is the argument:

1. A foreseeable, harmful effect of an action, Φ, on an innocent victim does not provide an agent with an objective *pro tanto* reason to refrain from Φ-ing, if Φ-ing serves a greater good and the agent does not intend the harmful effect.

2. Adhering to the law in a suboptimal-result case has foreseeable, harmful effects on the losing party.
3. A judge who adheres to the law in a suboptimal-result case serves a greater good.
4. A judge who adheres to the law in order to uphold the rule of law does not intend to inflict harm upon the losing party.
5. Therefore, the harmful effects do not provide the judge with an objective *pro tanto* reason to deviate from the law.

This argument raises several questions. Its first premise will remind some readers of the doctrine of double effect. I shall avoid that terminology because there are too many divergent formulations of double effect in the literature. Also, the first premise is stronger than most formulations of double effect, which concern all-things-considered duties. Many scholars have rejected double effect.[40] They would surely reject the first premise as well. If they are correct, then my larger argument in this book has a stronger foundation. But double effect has defenders.[41] Rather than entering the debate, I shall temporarily assume *arguendo* that the first premise is true.

The second question is, what greater good is served by adhering in suboptimal-result cases? In such cases, adhering usually harms the legally disfavored party more than deviating would harm the legally favored party. So adhering does not contribute to any greater good if we consider only the interests of the parties. But if we look beyond the interests of the parties, then some goods are, arguably, served by adhering. Fulfilling the expectations of a litigant is good, and the adhering judge fulfills the expectations of the legally favored party, if the latter expected to win. Keeping one's promise is good, and one might argue that judges promise to adhere to the law.[42] One might also argue that obeying the law is intrinsically good and that judges obey the law when they adhere.[43] Finally, one might argue that maintaining the rule of law is good, and that adhering maintains the rule of law.[44]

These are goods, certainly, but is any a *greater* good—good enough to outweigh the harm inflicted by adhering in a suboptimal-result case? In

---

40. See, e.g., F. M. Kamm, *Intricate Ethics: Rights, Responsibilities and Permissible Harm* (New York: Oxford University Press, 2007); Alison McIntyre, "Doing Away with Double Effect," *Ethics* 111 (2001): 219–55; Sophia Reibetanz (now Moreau), "A Problem for the Doctrine of Double Effect," *Proceedings of the Aristotelian Society* 98 (1998): 217–23; Jonathan Bennett, *The Act Itself* (Oxford: Oxford University Press, 1995); Samuel Scheffler, *The Rejection of Consequentialism*, revised ed. (Oxford: Oxford University Press, 1994); Shelly Kagan, *The Limits of Morality* (Oxford: Clarendon Press, 1989).

41. See, e.g., Warren Quinn, "Actions, Intentions, and Consequences: The Doctrine of Double Effect," *Philosophy and Public Affairs* 18 (1989): 334–51; Thomas Nagel, *The View from Nowhere* (Oxford: Oxford University Press, 1986).

42. See chapter 9.
43. See chapter 10.
44. See part II.

chapters 9 and 10, I shall argue that fulfilling expectations, keeping one's word, and obeying the law do not always outweigh this harm. In fact, in suboptimal-result cases I think these considerations are undermined as reasons to adhere.

The good that remains, therefore, is the rule of law. In part II, I explain how adhering serves the rule of law. The rule of law is, arguably, a greater good—good enough to outweigh the harmful effects of adhering in a suboptimal-result case. So I shall assume for now that adhering to the law in a suboptimal-result case serves a greater good.

Let us turn, then, to the third question raised by the intention argument: does a judge who adheres to the law for moral reasons in a suboptimal-result case *intend* to inflict harm upon the legally disfavored party? The debate surrounding double effect has shown that interpreting *intent* for the purpose of applying moral principles is a notoriously complicated matter.[45] How might a judge deny that he intends to harm the legally disfavored party? First, he could plausibly deny that he bears any ill will toward the losing party. The judges who interest me are those who adhere to the law for more innocuous reasons: to protect their reputations, to do their jobs, to uphold their oaths of office, to support the rule of law, et cetera. Judges who adhere to the law in suboptimal-result cases for such reasons may feel genuine sympathy for the losing parties and regret that adhering to the law in these cases inflicts undeserved harm. If they could adhere to the law without inflicting the harm, then they would do so. These judges contrast with those who enforce laws selectively against individuals whom they dislike as individuals or as members of an ethnic group. Such judges really do *intend* to harm the losing parties.[46]

However, the contrast between antipathic judges and ordinary adherent judges should not obscure the fact that even ordinary judges intend to harm the losing parties. Intent to harm does not entail ill will. It does not entail that the harm is the agent's final end. Otherwise intent to harm would be the special province of vengeance-seekers, sadists, and few others. Even the old villain of the double effect debates, the terror bomber, seeks only to advance his just military campaign.[47] If he could do so without killing innocent civilians, then he would. He bears them no ill will, but he intends to kill them nevertheless.

Different problems arise if we accept a theory of intention that is consistent with the proposition that judges who adhere in order to uphold the rule of law do not intend but only foresee the harm that they inflict upon

---

45. For a good recent treatment see William J. Fitzpatrick, "The Intend/Foresee Distinction and the Problem of 'Closeness,'" *Philosophical Studies* 128 (2006): 585–617.
46. Recall the bigoted judge in §4.4.2.
47. The terror bomber, fighting a just war, targets civilians in order to terrorize his enemy into surrender. The strategic bomber, by contrast, bombs military targets knowing that civilian casualties will result but not intending them. See, e.g., McIntyre, "Doing Away with Double Effect," p. 219.

legally disfavored parties. Such a theory of intention allows agents who cause harm to disavow intent quite easily. Consider how such a theory of intention would allow a *deviating* judge to defend herself. If she deviates for *moral* reasons, as my judge does in suboptimal-result cases, then this theory allows her to claim that she does not intend but only foresees whatever harmful consequences her deviation may produce. The theory still treats her as intending harm if vengeance or sadism motivates her or if she deviates for the purpose of undermining the rule of law. But judges who deviate in order to avoid suboptimal results have good intentions, whatever their methods, on this theory of intention. So, on this theory, whatever harmful effects deviating might have do not count against deviating. I conclude that, whatever theory of intention we employ, the first premise can exculpate adherent judges only at the price of exculpating deviant judges, too, rendering it useless to someone trying to make the case that judges have a moral duty to adhere in suboptimal-result cases.

6.10 MEANS

Instead of appealing to judicial intentions, one could assign moral relevance to the distinction between harm caused by an agent as a means to an end and harm caused as a side effect or aspect of action:

1. A harmful effect of an action, Φ, does not provide agents with an objective *pro tanto* reason to refrain from Φ-ing, if Φ-ing serves a greater good and the harmful effect is merely a side effect or aspect of Φ-ing, rather than a means to the agent's end in Φ-ing.
2. Adhering to the law in a suboptimal-result case has harmful effects on the losing party.
3. A judge who adheres to the law in a suboptimal-result case serves a greater good.
4. When a judge adheres to the law in a suboptimal-result case, the harmful effects of his decision are not a means to his end, but merely side effects or aspects of his decision.
5. Therefore, the harmful effects do not provide the judge with an objective *pro tanto* reason to deviate from the law.

The first premise of this argument resembles F. M. Kamm's principle of permissible harm closely enough that I shall refer to it as such.[48] I am not sure that the principle is true, but I shall set aside this worry. The first thing to notice about this argument is that if harming as a means or an end is impermissible, then the argument is sound only if a judge who adheres in a suboptimal-result case for moral reasons causes harm as an effect or aspect,

---

48. F. M. Kamm, *Morality, Mortality: Rights, Duties, and Status*, vol. 2 (New York: Oxford University Press, 1996); Kamm presents her latest views in *Intricate Ethics*.

not as a means or end. This is somewhat plausible, although it is equally plausible that the judge causes the harm as her means or even as her end.

More important, the principle of permissible harm does not permit harming, even as an effect or aspect, unless the harm is an effect or aspect *of a greater good*. In the previous section I suggested that adhering to the law may, indeed, serve a greater good. I shall discuss this suggestion at length in part II. But is the harm caused by adhering itself an effect or aspect of that good or a means to it?

Suppose we adopt a theory of means according to which adhering harms the legally disfavored party only as an effect or aspect, not as a means. Judge Jack adheres to the law in a suboptimal-result case, unjustly sentencing Ivan to prison. Ivan suffers the harms of incarceration. But Jack's reason for inflicting these harms is to maintain the rule of law, not to torment Ivan. Jack can deny that he has used Ivan as a means to an end. Ivan suffers harm as a side effect or aspect of Jack's decision to adhere, not as a means to Jack's end. Jack's end of upholding the rule of law would not be compromised if Ivan were to escape, miraculously, on the way to prison.

I agree that a plausible theory of means supports the conclusion that judges who adhere for rule-of-law reasons do not use the legally disfavored parties as means. This theory is not implausible, although it is not obviously correct, either. However, this theory also allows the deviating judge to make a similar claim. She can admit that deviating damages the rule of law, but insist that it does so only as an effect or aspect, not as a means to her end. Her reason for deviating is not to damage the rule of law, but to protect the legally disfavored party from unjustified harm. This end of hers would not be compromised if the rule of law were, miraculously, to avoid damage. If anything, her argument based on the principle of permissible harm seems *stronger* than the corresponding argument of the adhering judge. Unlike litigants, the rule of law is not even a sentient being with interests and rights.[49] Therefore, although judges have moral reasons not to damage the rule of law, such reasons do not undermine their reasons not to inflict harm upon human beings. The principle of permissible harm can exculpate adhering judges only at the price of exculpating deviant judges.

6.11 RELIGIOUS OBJECTIONS

So far I have found no sound argument for the undermining principle. As David Lyons notes, "a judge can be placed in a difficult moral predicament, even in easy cases."[50] It is interesting to compare my conclusion thus far with the views of writers in some religious traditions who have

---

49. Of course human beings suffer when the rule of law is damaged.
50. David Lyons, "Derivability, Defensibility, and the Justification of Judicial Decisions," in *Moral Aspects of Legal Theory* (Cambridge: Cambridge University Press, 1993), p. 120.

also addressed the plight of the judge whose personal convictions condemn laws that he is asked to enforce, or actions that are lawful in his jurisdiction. Although my position is rooted in secular ethical theory, these studies are informative and some concur with me on the basic point that judges have nonundermined, *pro tanto* moral reasons to avoid being the agent of suboptimal results. Consider a devout Roman Catholic judge facing one of the following decisions:

1. Whether to dismiss the case against a defendant who is being prosecuted for sodomy under a law that has been invalidated on constitutional grounds by the U.S. Supreme Court.
2. Whether to dismiss a criminal homicide case against a physician who has lawfully assisted a suicide (e.g., in the State of Oregon).
3. Whether to uphold a sentence for criminal battery against a nurse who forced life-sustaining treatment on a competent adult patient, against his will and the law.
4. Whether to uphold a death sentence imposed by a lower court.
5. Whether to grant a waiver of parental consent to an abortion when the petitioner, a minor child, is legally entitled to such a waiver.
6. Whether to grant a properly filed divorce petition.

Sodomy, abortion, assisting suicide, failing to preserve the life of a patient in one's care, executing people, and getting divorced are evil actions, according to the Catholic Church. There is a literature on Catholics and other religiously observant judges facing such cases.[51] Catholic judges and scholars hold that a judge who applies positive law in these cases assists the evil actor, thereby engaging in "material cooperation." But material cooperation can be permissible in Catholic ethics. Relevant factors include (1) whether there is a good reason for cooperating, such as avoiding a worse harm; (2) whether the cooperation is remote,

---

51. See, e.g., William H. Pryor, Jr., "The Religious Faith and Judicial Duty of an American Catholic Judge," *Yale Law and Policy Review* 24 (2006): 347–62; Rebekah L. Osborn, "Beliefs on the Bench: Recusal for Religious Reasons and the Model Code of Judicial Conduct," *Georgetown Journal of Legal Ethics* 19 (2006): 895–905; Mark C. Modak-Truran, "Reenchanting the Law: The Religious Dimension of Judicial Decision Making," *Catholic University Law Review* 53 (2004): 709–816; Wendell L. Griffen, "The Case for Religious Values in Judicial Decision-Making," *Marquette Law Review* 81 (1998): 513–21; Daniel O. Conkle, "Religiously Devout Judges: Issues of Personal Integrity and Public Benefit," *Marquette Law Review* 81 (1998): 523–32; Richard B. Saphire, "Religion and Recusal," *Marquette Law Review* 81 (1998): 351–63; John H. Garvey and Amy V. Coney, "Catholic Judges in Capital Cases," *Marquette Law Review* 81 (1998): 303–50; Scott C. Idleman, "The Role of Religious Values in Judicial Decision Making," *Indiana Law Journal* 68 (1993): 433–87; Sanford Levinson, "The Confrontation of Religious Faith and Civil Religion: Catholics Becoming Justices," *DePaul Law Review* 39 (1990): 1047–81; Lawrence B. Solum, "Faith and Justice," *DePaul Law Review* 39 (1990): 1083–106; Stephen L. Carter, "The Religiously Devout Judge," *Notre Dame Law Review* 64 (1989): 932–44.

rather than proximate; and (3) whether the cooperator avoids the danger of a *scandal*, which the catechism defines as "an attitude or behavior which leads another to do evil."[52]

Judge William Pryor, a Roman Catholic, claims that the first and second factors are present with respect to judges. First, "a judge has more than a good reason to apply the law impartially in every case, because the performance of that duty in a constitutional republic is a fundamental safeguard for the protection of human liberty. The resources of the judiciary are also scarce, so a judge is ordinarily obliged to perform his share of the work of the judiciary."[53]

Second, Pryor claims that "the performance of the judicial function is likely to be remote from the intended evil act of the party before the court; the typical scenario is where the judge determines that the law does not empower the government to interfere with a third party's choice to commit an immoral act."[54] However, Pryor recognizes that adhering to the law may constitute *scandal*, in the sense defined above.

Pryor believes that on these criteria a judge does not act immorally by granting a divorce petition, but he notes that the abortion and death penalty cases are more difficult for reasons of proximity and scandal. In some suboptimal-result cases such as these, Pryor believes that judges have at least *pro tanto* moral reasons to recuse themselves.[55] Some Catholic scholars believe that these are all-things-considered reasons.[56] I shall take up Pryor's position again in §10.8 and compare it to my own.

---

52. Pryor, "The Religious Faith and Judicial Duty of an American Catholic Judge," p. 361.
53. Ibid., pp. 360–61.
54. Ibid.
55. Ibid., p. 361.
56. "Catholic judges . . . are morally precluded from enforcing the death penalty. This means that they can neither themselves sentence criminals to death nor enforce jury recommendations of death. Whether they may affirm lower court orders of either kind is a question we have the most difficulty in resolving." Garvey and Coney, "Catholic Judges in Capital Cases," p. 305.

7

Adherence Rules

In this chapter and the next I return to the subject of adherence rules.[1] I pose five questions. First, are adherence rules serious rules or pseudo-rules (§7.1)? Second, what reasons do various adherence rules provide to judges (§7.2)? Third, what reasons do various adherence rules exclude from consideration (§7.3)? Fourth, which adherence rules, if any, do lawmakers have reasons to promulgate and why (§§7.4–7.11)? Fifth, how should judges take adherence rules (promulgated or not) into account in their decisions (chapter 8)?

The fourth and fifth questions are related. When deciding which adherence rules to promulgate, a rational lawmaker[2] considers the anticipated effects of his decision on judicial behavior. So the answer to the fourth question partly depends upon how judges, themselves, answer the fifth. In this chapter I ask what reasons lawmakers have to promulgate adherence rules, assuming that promulgation increases judicial conformity to promulgated rules.

7.1 ARE ADHERENCE RULES SERIOUS RULES?

Many writers split the universe of posited norms into two categories, calling the first *serious rules* (or *genuine rules*, or simply *rules*) and the second *pseudorules* or *mere standards*. Some writers classify a norm as a serious rule only if it contains both a prescription and a factual predicate

---

1. Introduced in §4.1.
2. I use *lawmaker* broadly, referring to anyone who creates valid legal standards. Legislative bodies are lawmakers, of course, but the executive and judicial branches also perform some lawmaking functions. Presidents and governors sign executive orders. Administrative agencies promulgate regulations. Judges create and revise the doctrines of the common law and doctrines of constitutional implementation and statutory construction. See Brian Z. Tamanaha, *On the Rule of Law: History, Politics, Theory* (Cambridge: Cambridge University Press, 2004), p. 124 ("Once any degree of indeterminacy is recognized, it follows that the claim that judges merely speak the law is implausible"). Judges also play a role in creating standards of professional conduct for the judiciary itself. See, e.g., Final Draft Report of the ABA Joint Commission to Evaluate the Model Code of Judicial Conduct, December 15, 2005 (listing members of Commission, including judges).

or hypothesis.³ On this theory, serious rules but not pseudorules can be applied without using normative judgment.⁴ It is also sometimes claimed that serious rules contain only precise and uncontroversial terms in their formulations whereas pseudorules contain vague or controversial terms.⁵ I agree with Alexander and Sherwin that the degree of seriousness that can be attributed to a rule is an epistemological matter: "a norm becomes a rule when most people understand it in a similar way."⁶ I think the fundamental issue is how controversial the required judgment is, not whether it is normative or factual. Some normative judgments are, of course, more controversial than some factual judgments. Whether a driver has swerved out of her lane will be less controversial than whether she has driven *responsibly*. But some factual judgments are more controversial than some normative judgments.⁷ Degree of controversy is what matters in classifying a norm as a serious rule or a pseudorule.

Consider a simple adherence rule that requires judges to adhere in every case. This rule is restated as follows: if adhering requires Φ-ing, then you must Φ. The predicate is as follows: adhering requires Φ-ing. The predicate of every adherence rule includes, inter alia, this proposition. Therefore, the greater the extent to which people disagree about what the law requires, the lower the degree of seriousness that we can attribute to adherence rules. Adherence rules are not serious rules unless there are at least some cases in which people agree about what the law requires.

I have assumed that the law is at least partially determinate.⁸ It precludes certain results in certain cases and there is a fact of the matter as to which results it precludes. The determinacy assumption might seem to entail that people agree, at least partially, about what the law requires. As a logical matter it does not. The determinacy assumption is metaphysical, not epistemological. Determinacy merely makes it *possible* for people to agree, correctly, about what the law requires. It does not guarantee agreement. Even complete legal determinacy would not entail that adherence rules were serious rules. Nevertheless, I shall assume that there are at least some cases in real legal systems in which sufficient agreement prevails regarding what the law requires. Adherence rules can function as serious rules in such systems.

---

3. Larry Alexander and Emily Sherwin, *The Rule of Rules* (Durham, N.C.: Duke University Press, 2001), p. 27.
4. Alan H. Goldman, *Practical Rules: When We Need Them and When We Don't* (Cambridge: Cambridge University Press, 2002), pp. 16–17, 107.
5. Alexander and Sherwin, *The Rule of Rules*, p. 29.
6. Ibid., p. 30.
7. Compare "There is life on other planets" with "Torturing people for fun is wrong."
8. See §5.5.1.

7.2 PROTECTED REASONS AND CONTENT-INDEPENDENT REASONS

Joseph Raz defines a mandatory rule as a "protected reason," which is "a systematic combination of a reason to perform the act . . . required by the rule, and an exclusionary reason not to act for certain reasons (for or against that act)."[9] Adherence rules are mandatory rules. If Raz is correct, then an adherence rule provides a protected reason to adhere—a reason to adhere plus an exclusionary reason that excludes certain competing reasons (i.e., reasons to deviate from the law, to recuse oneself, or to resign from the bench). We can understand adherence rules as what Jonathan Dancy calls *enablers*.[10] An authoritative adherence rule enables a certain fact—that the law requires a certain result—to constitute a reason for the presiding judge to reach that result when she decides the case.

According to Raz, exclusionary reasons can be cancelled, but they always prevail within their uncancelled scope. His position has been challenged—persuasively, I think.[11] My arguments in this book become easier to make if Raz is mistaken. However, my arguments are also compatible with Raz's position. For the sake of argument, I shall assume him to be correct hereafter. If he is wrong, then so much the better for my argument.

H. L. A. Hart distinguishes between *content-dependent* and *content-independent* reasons.[12] As Raz puts it, "a reason is content-independent if there is no direct connection between the reason and the action for which it is a reason."[13] A judge's reasons for adhering can be content dependent, content independent, or both. Consider a criminal defendant who is both morally and legally innocent. The fact that he does not deserve punishment, from a moral standpoint, constitutes a content-dependent, moral reason for the judge to acquit. If the law permits her to acquit and the defendant deserves acquittal, then the case is an optimal-result case. Judges have content-dependent reasons to adhere in optimal-result cases.

---

9. Joseph Raz, *Practical Reason and Norms*, 2nd ed. (New York: Oxford University Press, 1990), p. 191.

10. Jonathan Dancy, *Ethics without Principles* (Oxford: Oxford University Press, 2004), pp. 38–43.

11. Emran Mian, "The Curious Case of Exclusionary Reasons," *Canadian Journal of Law and Jurisprudence* 15 (2002): 99–124; Frederick Schauer, *Playing by the Rules: A Philosophical Examination of Rule-Based Decision-Making in Law and in Life* (Oxford: Oxford University Press, 1991), pp. 88–91; Larry Alexander, "Law and Exclusionary Reasons," *Philosophical Topics* 18 (1990): 5–22; Stephen R. Perry, "Second-Order Reasons, Uncertainty, and Legal Theory," *Southern California Law Review* 62 (1989): 913–94; Michael S. Moore, "Authority, Law, and Razian Reasons," *Southern California Law Review* 62 (1989): 827–96; Donald H. Regan, "Authority and Value: Reflections on Raz's Morality of Freedom," *Southern California Law Review* 62 (1989): 995–1095.

12. H. L. A. Hart, "Commands and Authoritative Legal Reasons," in *Essays on Bentham* (Oxford: Oxford University Press, 1982), p. 254.

13. Joseph Raz, *The Morality of Freedom* (Oxford: Clarendon Press, 1986), p. 35.

By contrast, authoritative adherence rules provide content-independent reasons for judges to adhere to the law. These reasons apply in both optimal-result and suboptimal-result cases. I shall examine arguments with the following structure:

1. If a certain adherence rule has practical authority, then it provides exclusionary reasons that exclude all reasons to deviate in suboptimal-result cases.
2. The aforementioned adherence rule has practical authority for judges (i.e., judges have all-things-considered reasons to obey it).
3. Therefore, judges have no reason to deviate in any suboptimal-result case that they choose to decide.

In order to evaluate such arguments we must examine various adherence rules, ascertaining if any has the requisite characteristics. In the next section I shall discuss the reasons that adherence rules provide to judges. Then I shall discuss judicial reasons to obey adherence rules and ask whether any adherence rule has practical authority.

7.3 REASONS PROVIDED AND EXCLUDED BY ADHERENCE RULES

Adherence rules divide into several overlapping categories based on the reasons that they supply. We can distinguish between different rules based on the range of cases in which they provide content-independent reasons to adhere. The strongest rules provide reasons to adhere in all cases. Weaker rules provide reasons to adhere in some but not all cases. Even the weakest rules provide content-independent reasons to adhere in required-result and optimal-but-not-required-result cases. Stronger adherence rules provide reasons to adhere in suboptimal-result cases as well.

We can also distinguish between adherence rules based on which reasons to deviate, if any, they exclude. *Restrictive rule* provides reasons to adhere in all cases and excludes all reasons to deviate. The excluded reasons include moral reasons, some of which are reasons derived from the negative effects that adherence has on losing parties. If restrictive rule has practical authority, then it provides reasons to adhere and excludes all reasons to deviate, even in suboptimal-result cases. In such cases, however, the justification lying behind the exclusionary reason provided by restrictive rule is inapplicable: there is a reason to deviate, and excluding it does *not* serve the purpose of the exclusionary reason. To this extent restrictive rule has characteristics that Raz's theory does not capture.

In order to capture this feature of restrictive rule we need Frederick Schauer's addendum to Raz. Schauer agrees with Raz that mandatory rules

Adherence Rules

include first-order reasons to act and exclusionary reasons not to act for certain other reasons. However, Schauer finds Raz's theory of rules incomplete because it misses the role of *entrenchment*. Rules, Schauer writes, include "second-order reasons whose generality is entrenched even in those circumstances in which the justification lying behind the second-order reason is inapplicable."[14] On his view, "[a] rule exists (for some agent . . .) insofar as an instantiation of a justification is treated (by that agent . . .) as entrenched, having the power to provide a reason for decision even when that instantiation does not serve its generating justification."[15]

The weakest adherence rule that I shall discuss is *permissive rule*, which has three features. First, it provides reasons to adhere in required-result and optimal-but-not-required-result cases, but not in suboptimal-result cases. Second, it excludes all private reasons to deviate.[16] Third, it never excludes moral reasons to deviate.[17]

In between permissive rule and restrictive rule lie various *moderate rules*. They provide reasons to adhere in some but not all suboptimal-result cases. They exclude all private reasons to deviate, plus some but not all impartial reasons to deviate.[18] A judge who obeys a moderate rule and not restrictive rule sometimes uses force when not authorized to do so by law and sometimes does not use force when required to do so by law.[19]

Restrictive rule is what Alexander and Sherwin call a *pure rule*: a posited norm that settles all practical questions that fall within its scope.[20] Permissive rule and moderate rules are instances of what they call an *impure rule*: a posited norm that settles some but not all unsettled questions that fall within its scope.

Hereafter, it will be convenient to refer to moderate and restrictive rules collectively as *nonpermissive rules*. A nonpermissive rule excludes private reasons to deviate in all cases, provides reasons to adhere in at least some suboptimal-result cases, and excludes impartial reasons to deviate in at least some suboptimal-result cases.

---

14. Schauer, *Playing by the Rules*, p. 93.
15. Ibid., p. 76. Schauer subsequently notes (pp. 190–91) that serious rules must be treated as entrenched with respect to *all* moral reasons, not just their own justifications.
16. See §3.13.
17. One could also describe permissive rule as a rule that directs judges to treat restrictive rule in the most particularistic fashion possible, rather than treating restrictive rule as a serious rule. Permissive rule resembles what Dworkin calls "legal pragmatism." Ronald Dworkin, *Law's Empire* (Cambridge, Mass.: Harvard University Press, 1986), pp. 95, 151–75.
18. One could say that moderate rules instruct judges to treat restrictive rule in a *partially* particularistic fashion.
19. See §2.9. One might say that moderate and permissive rules permit judges sometimes to use what Alec Walen calls "reasonable illegal force." Walen, contra Rawls, endorses the right of private parties in liberal societies to use it. I do not know if he would extend this right to judges. Alec Walen, "Reasonable Illegal Force: Justice and Legitimacy in a Pluralistic, Liberal Society," *Ethics* 111 (2001): 344–73.
20. Alexander and Sherwin, *The Rule of Rules*, p. 30.

7.4 ADHERENCE RULES AND FORMAL LEGALITY

In sections 7.5–7.11, I shall consider reasons for lawmakers to promulgate various adherence rules. Before doing so I wish to highlight a close connection between adherence rules and the rule of law, specifically its dimension of formal legality.[21] Many would argue that lawmakers should promulgate adherence rules in order to promote and maintain formal legality. The most important condition of formal legality for my purposes is the congruence condition, which is precisely the requirement that the law be applied "as written."[22] Responsibility for maintaining congruence falls primarily upon law enforcement officers, prosecutors, and adjudicators. Police officers, for example, may not arrest individuals whose conduct falls outside the scope of the criminal law, nor may prosecutors prosecute the latter.

Congruence also has implications for the design of adjudicative institutions. The main argument for judicial independence assumes the value of congruence. Judicial independence is prized because it prevents legislators and executives from pressuring judges to deviate from the law as might suit the political branches. Tamanaha notes that the "independent, neutral judiciary" is the "final preserve of the rule of law."[23] At the same time, he emphasizes the importance of a robust judicial commitment to fidelity. He speaks for many when he describes judicial commitment to following the law as a "crucial feature" of the rule of law.[24] He states that "[t]he *sina qua non* of the rule of law is striving to decide cases according to the law"[25] and claims that "the rule of law could not conceivably function without this group committed to the value of legality."[26] Timothy Endicott agrees that a community "lacks the rule of law to the extent that its officials ignore the law."[27]

Because formal legality demands judicial fidelity, we need canons of judicial ethics for neutralizing potential sources of deviation such as conflicts of interest, corruption, and bribery.[28] However, I shall focus on judges who are not corrupt and who hear cases in which bribes and conflicts of interest are not involved. I am primarily interested in what honest judges, without conflicts of interest, can and must do to uphold congruence and the other conditions of formal legality.

---

21. See §6.6.
22. As I have noted before, this requirement should not be understood as a requirement to apply rules instead of other legal standards. Congruence requires judges to apply the *law*, whatever that means.
23. Tamanaha, *On the Rule of Law*, p. 59.
24. Ibid., pp. 59, 125.
25. Brian Z. Tamanaha, *Law as a Means to an End: Threat to the Rule of Law* (New York: Cambridge University Press, 2006), p. 244.
26. Tamanaha, *On the Rule of Law*, p. 59.
27. Timothy A. O. Endicott, "The Impossibility of the Rule of Law," *Oxford Journal of Legal Studies* 19 (1999): 1–18, p. 7.
28. See chapter 4.

Adherence Rules

The value of congruence also has implications for the standards and procedures by which judges are chosen. Because judges are "uniquely situated to undermine the rule of law,"[29] they

> must be selected with the utmost care, not just focusing on their legal knowledge and acumen, but with at least as much attention to their commitment to fidelity to the law (not inclined to manipulate the law's latent indeterminacy), to their willingness to defer to the proper authority for the making of law (accepting legislative decisions even when the judge disagrees).[30]

I shall focus primarily on judges who have already been appointed to the bench by whatever procedure the law provides. I am interested in Tamanaha's suggestion that they "must be imbued with the sense that their special task and obligation is fidelity to the law."[31] What ideas about fidelity should lawmakers urge upon judges? What, exactly, should judges believe about it?

If one supports formal legality and believes that judicial fidelity is necessary to maintain it, then one is likely to support adherence rules and to care about which adherence rules lawmakers promulgate. Different conceptions of formal legality correspond to different adherence rules. Many writers seem to interpret codified adherence rules as expressing restrictive rule, which corresponds to a simple, intuitive conception of formal legality. Restrictive rule provides a reason to adhere in all cases and an exclusionary reason that excludes all reasons to deviate in all cases, yielding an all-things-considered reason to adhere in all cases. A judge who obeys restrictive rule never uses force when not authorized to do so by law, sometimes uses force when authorized to do so by law, and always uses force when required to do so by law.

In the rest of this chapter I shall consider a series of reasons for lawmakers to promulgate adherence rules. I draw upon arguments that several authors have made for the creation of rules generally. I conclude that lawmakers may have all-things-considered reasons to promulgate restrictive rule. In subsequent chapters, I turn to the reasons judges have to obey adherence rules. I argue that most of what are usually proposed as reasons to obey restrictive rule are not, in fact, good reasons. For example, the fact that the judge took an oath to uphold the law is not a good reason to obey restrictive rule. Other reasons I find are *pro tanto* reasons to obey restrictive rule, but they are often overridden by other moral considerations. In other words, judges have no all-things-considered duty to obey restrictive rule rather than a moderate rule. Codified adherence rules, if interpreted as expressing restrictive rule, lack practical authority for judges. In the remainder of this book I shall articulate and defend a moderate rule and

---

29. Tamanaha, *On the Rule of Law*, p. 59.
30. Ibid., p. 125.
31. Ibid., p. 59.

defend its practical authority. An alternative conception of formal legality will gradually emerge as I do so.

7.5 SETTLEMENT AND PREDICTABILITY

Individuals who intend to act morally often disagree or are uncertain about the morally correct course of action. These disagreements and uncertainties generate problems of coordination, efficiency, and expertise. Parties who disagree can end up in collisions, destructive competitions, and violent conflicts. They suffer from frustrated expectations and incur costs to avoid these frustrations. They forgo many benefits. One function of conduct rules is to reduce these problems by providing authoritative settlement of concrete moral disagreements and uncertainties.[32]

The problems of coordination, expertise, and efficiency carry over to the judiciary. Judges need authoritative rules, too. If authoritative settlement is sufficiently important, then a state of affairs in which all judges obey adherence rules is superior to one in which no judge obeys adherence rules. In other words, lawmakers have impartial *pro tanto* reasons to want their judges to obey adherence rules. These arguments rest upon empirical premises, but plausible ones in my view. I shall now examine some of these arguments in greater detail.

7.6 COORDINATION AND RELIANCE

Imagine a jurisdiction with no promulgated adherence rules. In such a jurisdiction, judges continue to adhere to the law when they have content-dependent reasons to do so. Such reasons could be moral, as when the judge believes that the legally required result is optimal, or they could be prudential, as when someone bribes the judge to adhere. But these judges lack content-independent reasons to adhere, so they often deviate when they have reasons to do so. They may deviate when they believe that the legally required result is suboptimal, when they can profit financially by deviating, et cetera.

As compared to parties in jurisdictions with adherence rules, a party to a dispute in this jurisdiction can more often successfully bribe the judge or persuade him that her (the party's) preferred result is optimal. Accordingly, subjects in this jurisdiction have less confidence that judges will adhere to the law. This lack of confidence has effects such as the following. Motorists are less likely to obey traffic laws and to be more worried about other motorists violating traffic laws. As a result, fewer

---

32. Alexander and Sherwin, *The Rule of Rules*, pp. 11–36.

people use the roadways, but the collision rate (per motorist) rises. Individuals are less likely to enter into mutually beneficial contracts. They are more likely to litigate and less likely to settle disputes out of court. Insurance rates rise. These are undesirable social consequences. Imagine similar consequences across the entire legal system and you have a dysfunctional society.

Lawmakers can control these problems by promulgating adherence rules. Judges who obey permissive rule do not deviate for reasons of partiality such as self-interest. They will, accordingly, deviate in fewer cases than if no adherence rule were promulgated, assuming that promulgation has some positive effect on the obedience rate. As legal subjects come to recognize this they will be more likely to obey traffic laws, enter contracts, settle lawsuits, et cetera. Insurance rates will fall. Therefore, lawmakers have a *pro tanto* reason to promulgate adherence rules at least as strong as permissive rule.

However, judges obeying permissive rule still deviate when they believe themselves to have impartial reasons for doing so. They deviate in what they believe to be suboptimal-result cases. Although bribes are ineffective with these judges, a party can still win by persuading her judge that her favored result is normatively optimal. By promulgating restrictive rule, instead, lawmakers can reduce the frequency of such victories, thereby further increasing the extent to which subjects obey traffic laws, enter contracts, settle lawsuits, et cetera. However, as Schauer acknowledges, reaching the optimal result is sometimes more important than fulfilling the expectations of others. Schauer concludes that "the force of the argument from reliance will vary across decision-making environments."[33] Nevertheless, in many environments lawmakers have a *pro tanto* reason to promulgate restrictive rule.

7.7 EFFICIENCY

A judge who is motivated to reach optimal results will spend more time, energy, and resources researching and deliberating if he obeys only permissive rule rather than restrictive rule. There is no limit to the range of moral factors and evidence that he might choose to consider before deciding each issue presented if he obeys permissive rule. By contrast, judges who obey restrictive rule exclude all nonlegal reasons from their decision making. This simplifies the decision process, thereby conserving decisional

---

33. Schauer, *Playing by the Rules*, p. 140. Lyons notes that, in unjust systems, "the relevant advantages flowing from factors like certainty and predictability are likely to be primarily conferred on those who profit from injustice." David Lyons, "Derivability, Defensibility, and the Justification of Judicial Decisions," in *Moral Aspects of Legal Theory* (Cambridge: Cambridge University Press, 1993), p. 132.

resources.[34] So the value of efficiency gives lawmakers another *pro tanto* reason to promulgate restrictive rule.

7.8 ERROR AND EXPERTISE

Rules in general promote coordination and efficiency at the cost of producing suboptimal results in certain cases.[35] In some environments this is desirable overall, because coordination and efficiency are more important than reaching optimal results. The same reasoning applies to adherence rules. In suboptimal-result cases, by definition, a judge who adheres to the law reaches a suboptimal result. Promulgating restrictive rule leads judges to adhere in some such cases, yielding suboptimal results that would otherwise not have occurred. Nevertheless, promulgating restrictive rule could reduce the total number of suboptimal results reached in the system. Judges who deviate do not always reach optimal results even when they try to do so. Judges who do not obey restrictive rule are prepared to take nonlegal considerations into account more often. Some of them will make moral mistakes, reaching suboptimal results in optimal-result cases. In such cases they would have reached optimal results had they simply adhered.[36]

This is the error argument for promulgating adherence rules, also known as the argument from expertise. It depends on the premise that judges make more moral mistakes than "the law" makes. If this premise holds, then lawmakers have another *pro tanto* reason to promulgate restrictive rule.

7.9 STABILITY

Schauer also presents an argument from stability: "[R]ule-based decision-making narrows the range of potential decisions, and in doing so makes changes from the *status quo*, both for better and for worse, more difficult than would be the case were decision-makers freer to depart from the categories and prescriptions of yesterday."[37] This argument applies straightforwardly to restrictive rule. A judge who obeys restrictive rule will find it more difficult to change the law than one who obeys permissive rule. Promulgating restrictive rule encourages judges to obey restrictive rule, thereby stabilizing the law. If the status quo is good, then lawmakers have another *pro tanto* reason to promulgate restrictive rule.

---

34. Schauer, *Playing by the Rules*, pp. 145–49.
35. Alexander and Sherwin, *The Rule of Rules*, pp. 34–36; Goldman, *Practical Rules*, pp. 32–33; Schauer, *Playing by the Rules*, pp. 128–34.
36. See Goldman, *Practical Rules*, pp. 4–5.
37. Schauer, *Playing by the Rules*, p. 157.

7.10 LEGITIMACY, AUTONOMY, AND RESPECT

Another class of arguments for restrictive rule invokes political legitimacy. Consider Schauer's claim that

> [t]he traditional theory of judicial authority, under which legislatures make the rules and judges apply them, is not based nearly so much on a fear that judges will make errors in the process of engaging in open-ended decision-making as it is based on the assumption that determination of questions of substantive value should be for popularly responsible and responsive institutions such as legislatures, and not for non-majoritarian institutions such as the judiciary.[38]

We should generalize this "traditional theory" so that it holds that lawmakers create the *law* (including but not limited to *rules* of law) and judges adhere to it. Now we can ask why someone might believe that a system is more politically legitimate if lawmakers (including judges in their lawmaking capacity), rather than judges in their law-applying capacity, determine "questions of substantive value." Plausible answers link legitimacy to values such as autonomy and respect. Many citizens who participate in the political process in representative democracies are attempting to exercise their autonomy. So are lawmakers, in many instances, when they make law. By adhering to the law, judges facilitate the exercise of autonomy by citizens and lawmakers. By deviating, judges interfere with this exercise. One might also argue that deviating expresses disrespect for lawmakers and citizens. Consider this argument:

1. Lawmakers have a *pro tanto* reason to discourage judges from interfering with the exercise of autonomy by lawmakers and citizens, and from disrespecting lawmakers and citizens.
2. When a judge deviates from the law, she interferes with the exercise of autonomy by lawmakers and citizens and she disrespects them.
3. Promulgating restrictive rule discourages judges from deviating.
4. Therefore, lawmakers have a *pro tanto* reason to promulgate restrictive rule.

Even if the second premise of the previous argument is false, a similar argument could be advanced, substituting the following premises:

1s. Lawmakers have a *pro tanto* reason to discourage judges from causing lawmakers or citizens to feel disappointment or disrespect.
2s. Acquiring the belief that a judge has deviated from the law may cause a lawmaker to feel disappointed that a product of his lawmaking

---

38. Ibid., p. 159.

efforts has been ignored. He may also feel that the judge has treated him disrespectfully. Citizens may have similar feelings insofar as they consider the lawmaker to represent them.

7.11 FAIRNESS

Finally, the argument from fairness or comparative justice is worth mentioning, although it is a fallacious argument. The idea is that lawmakers should promulgate restrictive rule in order to ensure that similar cases are treated similarly. The fallacy here is that restrictive rule merely ensures that *legally* similar cases are treated similarly. It does so, however, at the cost of causing some *morally* similar cases to be treated differently and some morally different cases to be treated similarly.[39] So restrictive rule does not implement the principle of comparative justice any more effectively than permissive rule does.[40] I will reintroduce the argument from comparative justice in chapter 15 as an objection to my own recommended adherence rule.[41]

My conclusion in this chapter is that lawmakers have reasons to promulgate adherence rules, possibly even restrictive rule, on the assumption that promulgation increases judicial conformity.

---

39. Ibid., pp. 135–37.
40. For a detailed refutation of the argument from formal justice, see David Lyons, "On Formal Justice," in *Moral Aspects of Legal Theory* (Cambridge: Cambridge University Press, 1993).
41. See §15.2.

8

Obeying Adherence Rules

8.1 PROMULGATION VERSUS OBEDIENCE

It is easy to imagine jurisdictions in which arguments from coordination, reliance, efficiency, error, stability, and legitimacy are collectively strong enough to support promulgating restrictive rule. In what follows I shall accept *arguendo* that modern legal systems are among these jurisdictions. I turn now to the reasons for judges to obey adherence rules. An agent *obeys* a rule if and only if she is guided by it and complies with its dictates.[1] As Schauer notes, "the way in which and the extent to which, if at all, rules become a part of the decisional process is ultimately determined by the decision-maker alone."[2] How, if at all, should judges take adherence rules into account? Are there any adherence rules that have practical authority for judges?

We can distinguish between *conduct rules* promulgated by rule makers, *guidance rules* followed by rule subjects, and *appraisal rules* used for evaluating the conduct of rule subjects. I shall also refer to *decision rules* used by public officials deciding cases.[3] The best conduct rule for lawmakers to promulgate for legal subjects may be stricter than the best guidance and appraisal rules.[4] The best conduct rule to promulgate regarding highway speed limits may be "Drive no more than sixty-five miles per hour," whereas a better rule for motorists to obey may be "Drive no more than seventy-five." Likewise, the better appraisal rule may be "Drivers who exceed seventy-five miles per hour act wrongly." The better decision rule for highway patrol officers and trial judges to use may be "Ticket/convict drivers who exceed seventy-five miles per hour."

Parallel distinctions apply to adherence rules. "Judges," Schauer writes, "must necessarily make their own decisions whether to treat the rules written in law books as the ones they will employ in reaching a decision."[5]

---

1. Frederick Schauer, *Playing by the Rules: A Philosophical Examination of Rule-Based Decision-Making in Law and in Life* (Oxford: Oxford University Press, 1991), p. 113.
2. Ibid., p. 128.
3. Confusingly, these decision rules are guidance rules for the officials in their official capacities.
4. See, e.g., Meir Dan-Cohen, "Decision Rules and Conduct Rules: On Acoustic Separation in Criminal Law," *Harvard Law Review* 97 (1984): 625–77.
5. Schauer, *Playing by the Rules*, p. 146 (paraphrasing Duncan Kennedy).

Therefore, we should keep reasons for lawmakers to promulgate adherence rules in a separate analytical category from any reasons that judges might have to obey these rules. We can distinguish between *first-order decision rules* codified and promulgated by lawmakers, *guidance rules* obeyed by judges, *appraisal rules* used by critics of the bench, and *second-order decision rules* used by decision makers (often other judges) during judicial disciplinary proceedings. The best first-order decision rules may be stricter than the best guidance rules, appraisal rules, and second-order decision rules.

Agents can take rules into account in several different ways. They can treat rules as mere *rules of thumb*. Rules of thumb lack independent practical authority. They merely direct agents to an action that is usually appropriate under the circumstances. When atypical conditions obtain—conditions not contemplated by the rules—they lose all force.[6]

Another approach to rules is *rule-sensitive particularism*. A particularist reasons directly from moral principles to particular decisions.[7] A rule-sensitive particularist also takes into account the value of having and following rules, so he will disobey less readily than a pure particularist, but he still does not regard himself as rule-bound. He does not treat rules as serious rules.

Should judges treat adherence rules as serious rules? Why not treat them, instead, as rules of thumb, or use the rule-sensitive particularist approach? The previous chapter rehearsed some reasons for lawmakers to promulgate adherence rules. Similar considerations might constitute reasons for judges to obey adherence rules, but this is not necessarily so. Schauer recognizes the difficulty of providing reasons for agents to treat rules as serious rules, as opposed to reasons for lawmakers to promulgate them:

> From the perspective of the agent deciding what to do, anything more rule-bound than rule-sensitive particularism is difficult (though I think not impossible) to defend. But from the perspective of some society or environment deciding what institutions to establish, and whom to empower to do what, stronger commitments to rules become considerably more appealing.[8]

8.2 OBEYING PERMISSIVE RULE

In this section I shall present an argument—drawing on Raz's theory of authority—that permissive rule has practical authority for some judges. The authority of a rule for an agent, according to Raz, derives from

---

6. See Ibid., pp. 104–11.
7. Larry Alexander and Emily Sherwin, *The Rule of Rules* (Durham, N.C.: Duke University Press, 2001), p. 28.
8. Schauer, *Playing by the Rules*, p. 98, n. 26.

Obeying Adherence Rules

the fact that the agent conforms more closely to his actual reasons if he complies with the rule than if he attempts to comply directly with those reasons.

Here is a Razian argument for the conclusion that permissive rule has authority for some judges. Judge Jerry is preparing to decide a case. He believes that he has *pro tanto* prudential reasons to deviate. Perhaps he has been offered a bribe or can otherwise profit financially by deviating. Perhaps he is in love with the legally disfavored party. He also perceives prudential reasons to adhere, including reasons of reputation, prestige, occupational status, remuneration, and influence. Taking into account all of these reasons, he concludes that his prudential reasons to deviate outweigh his prudential reasons to adhere. However, he might be mistaken. Deviating might be a prudential error, notwithstanding Jerry's deliberation: perhaps his misconduct will be detected and his career ruined.

If Jerry is so error-prone about when deviation is prudentially justified that he makes fewer prudential mistakes when he obeys permissive rule, then his prudential reasons to internalize permissive rule are stronger than his opposing prudential reasons. However, if Jerry is not so error-prone, then permissive rule lacks prudential authority for him. So the scope of this Razian argument is limited. Nevertheless, I shall accept *arguendo* that permissive rule has prudential authority for some judges in modern legal systems.

Judges also have moral reasons to obey permissive rule, corresponding to the reasons for system designers to promulgate adherence rules, discussed in the previous chapter. Neil MacCormick mentions several reasons that public officials have to accept the rule of recognition of their system:

1. "[I]t is good that judicial decisions be predictable and contribute to certainty of law, which they are and do when they apply known rules in accordance with commonly shared and understood criteria of recognition";
2. "[I]t is good that judges stay within their assigned place in the constitutional order, applying established law rather than inventing new law";
3. "[I]t is good that law-making be entrusted to the elected representatives of the people, not usurped by non-elected and non-removable judges";[9]
4. "[T]he existing and accepted constitutional order is a fair and just system, and accordingly the criteria of recognition of laws which it institutes are good and just criteria which ought to be observed."[10]

---

9. In the United States most state judges stand for reelection.
10. Neil MacCormick, *Legal Reasoning and Legal Theory* (Oxford: Clarendon Press, 1978), pp. 63–64.

These reasons correspond roughly to reasons identified in the previous chapter. The first reflects coordination and reliance, the second and third reflect legitimacy, and the fourth reflects error and stability. These are reasons for system designers to promulgate adherence rules. They may also be reasons for judges to obey permissive rule.

8.3 OBEYING RESTRICTIVE RULE

Along with many others, however, MacCormick appears to believe that these are reasons for judges to obey restrictive rule, not just permissive rule. In contrast to permissive rule, restrictive rule forbids judges from deviating even for moral reasons. In Schauer's terms, restrictive rule "entrenches the generality" of the exclusionary reason. Restrictive rule excludes moral reasons derived from the fact that adhering in a suboptimal-result case imposes undeserved disadvantages on the losing party. Restrictive rule provides a general reason to adhere and a general exclusionary reason not to deviate for certain reasons, even if the first-order and exclusionary reasons do not serve the instantiating justification of restrictive rule.

First, consider prudential reasons to obey restrictive rule. An agent cannot have prudential reasons to obey a rule that excludes moral reasons, as restrictive rule does. A prudential reason to obey restrictive rule can come into conflict with moral reasons to deviate. In such conflicts the moral reason typically wins. If a rule excludes moral reasons, then it has practical authority for an agent only if he has moral reasons to obey it. Prudential reasons cannot typically override or undermine moral reasons. A judge might have a conclusive *prudential* reason to obey restrictive rule, but if she also has moral reasons to deviate in suboptimal-result cases, then these moral reasons would undermine or override her prudential reason to obey restrictive rule. Restrictive rule excludes moral reasons, so restrictive rule cannot have practical authority for judges unless they have moral reasons, not just prudential reasons, to obey restrictive rule. So we cannot yet claim that judges have an all-things-considered reason to obey restrictive rule.

8.4 MORAL REASONS TO OBEY RESTRICTIVE RULE

My main question, then, is whether judges have moral reasons to obey restrictive rule. This question has received little attention in the legal and philosophical literatures. Philip Soper observed in 1984 that there was "virtually no literature on the question of the judge's obligation to apply the law."[11] The literature has not grown much in the decades

---

11. Philip Soper, *A Theory of Law* (Cambridge, Mass.: Harvard University Press, 1984), p. 41.

since.¹² Robin West wonders, "Why are lawyers and legal academics so oddly inattentive to the problem of the lawless adjudicator?"¹³ Despite this dearth of scholarship, commentators have long insisted that judges have strong moral reasons to adhere to the law in most cases, if not all. According to Steven Smith, "virtually everyone assumes that courts normally have a duty to follow duly-enacted statutes."¹⁴ Bentham appears to have agreed.¹⁵ Kent Greenawalt states, "Judicial power to nullify the substantive law has never been suggested as a desirable feature of trial before judges. . . ."¹⁶ Robert Summers writes that "the legal conclusions and any reasons for action or decision on the part of the law's addressees which . . . arise under valid law, duly interpreted or applied, generally remain peremptory for the law's addressees, including courts and other tribunals."¹⁷ Ronald Dworkin repeatedly asserts that the law binds judges: "The law we have, the actual concrete law for us, is fixed by inclusive integrity. This is law for the judge, the law he is obliged to declare and enforce."¹⁸ A judge, Dworkin insists, must not deviate from the law in order to advance her moral or political beliefs (although Dworkin's conception of "the law" is, of course, more expansive than many). For example, even if a judge favors extensive wealth redistribution, as does Dworkin,¹⁹ he

> cannot appeal to the Constitution to order Congress or state legislatures to adopt the economic and redistributive programs that equality of resources demands. Nor, given the various constraints he accepts about how far he is free

---

12. But see M. B. E. Smith, "May Judges Ever Nullify the Law?" *Notre Dame Law Review* 74 (1999): 1657–71; Evan H. Caminker, "Why Must Inferior Courts Obey Superior Court Precedents?" *Stanford Law Review* 46 (1994): 817–73; Michael Stokes Paulsen, "Accusing Justice: Some Variations on the Themes of Robert M. Cover's *Justice Accused*," *Journal of Law and Religion* 7 (1989): 33–97; Steven D. Smith, "Why Should Courts Obey the Law?" *Georgetown Law Journal* 77 (1988): 113–64.

13. Robin West, "The Lawless Adjudicator," *Cardozo Law Review* 26 (2005): 2253–61, p. 2256.

14. Smith, "Why Should Courts Obey the Law?" p. 113. Smith proceeds to defend the assumption.

15. Postema writes that Bentham's doctrine of stare decisis requires obedience to established precedent not only when, the rule being beneficial on the whole, nonetheless utility calls for an exception in a particular case, but also when the rule itself seems arbitrary or unreasonable. Gerald J. Postema, *Bentham and the Common Law Tradition* (Oxford: Oxford University Press, 1986), p. 197.

16. Kent Greenawalt, *Conflicts of Law and Morality* (New York: Oxford University Press, 1987), p. 367.

17. Robert S. Summers, "The Principles of the Rule of Law," *Notre Dame Law Review* 74 (1999): 1691–712, p. 1694.

18. Ronald Dworkin, *Law's Empire* (Cambridge, Mass.: Harvard University Press, 1986), p. 406. See also Jeremy Waldron, "Kant's Legal Positivism," *Harvard Law Review* 109 (1996): 1535–66, pp. 1538–39 ("The official's failure to implement the law because he believes that it is unjust . . . is tantamount to abandoning the very idea of law"). Waldron presents the quoted claim as Kantian and appears to endorse it.

19. Ronald Dworkin, *Sovereign Virtue: The Theory and Practice of Equality* (Cambridge, Mass.: Harvard University Press, 2000).

to read statutes to promote his view of justice, can he read into welfare and taxation schemes provisions equality of resources would approve.[20]

Although these programs would serve "[p]olitical integrity and justice," Dworkin thinks, the judge "would violate integrity himself" if he were to read existing law as favoring them. Judges

> may not read the abstract moral clauses [of the Constitution] as expressions of any particular moral judgment, no matter how much that judgment appeals to them, unless they find it consistent in principle with the structural design of the Constitution as a whole, and also with the dominant lines of past constitutional interpretation by other judges.[21]

Therefore, he continues,

> [e]ven a judge who believes that abstract justice requires economic equality cannot interpret the equal protection clause as making equality of wealth, or collective ownership of productive resources, a constitutional requirement, because that interpretation simply does not fit American history or practice, or the rest of the Constitution.[22]

The manifest consensus, restated in my terminology, is that judges have strong *pro tanto* reasons to obey restrictive rule. Is there also consensus that judges have all-things-considered reasons to obey restrictive rule? Some language used by commentators suggests this, although it is sometimes qualified with "normally," "generally," et cetera. The U.S. Supreme Court states that "a court is to apply the law in effect at the time it renders its decision, unless doing so would result in manifest injustice or there is statutory direction or legislative history to the contrary."[23] These qualifications seem to anticipate cases in which the law requires suboptimal results, but writers who make such exceptions usually limit them to cases in which the law requires an extreme injustice—what I call "extreme impermissible-result cases." Greenawalt, for example, finds it "conceivable that some convictions would be so abhorrent that judicial defiance of the law would be defensible, and this conclusion may be true even if such an action is considered to be outside the law in every sense."[24] Justice Antonin Scalia admits that he would invalidate a statute providing for public

---

20. Dworkin, *Law's Empire*, p. 404.
21. Ronald Dworkin, *Freedom's Law: The Moral Reading of the American Constitution* (Cambridge, Mass.: Harvard University Press, 1996), p. 10.
22. Ibid., p. 11. Elsewhere he asserts that "[n]either a Marxist nor a fascist would find enough present law distinctively explained by his political philosophy" to claim that his views are consistent with the law of the United States. Dworkin, *Law's Empire*, p. 408.
23. *Bradley v. Richmond School Board*, 416 U.S. 696, 711 (1974).
24. Greenawalt, *Conflicts of Law and Morality*, p. 368. Compare David Dyzenhaus, *Hard Cases in Wicked Legal Systems: South African Law in the Perspective of Legal Philosophy* (Oxford: Clarendon Press, 1991), p. 60 (South African judges were *legally* obligated to ignore or overturn racist laws).

flogging even though he believes it to be constitutional.[25] And some writers accept the so-called Radbruch formula, which denies legal validity to extremely unjust positive laws[26] in the spirit of the Augustinian-Thomistic slogan: *lex iniusta non est lex*.[27] One who endorses the Radbruch formula can accept restrictive rule while denying that judges are morally obligated to obey extremely unjust "laws."

David Lyons is the rare writer who actually emphasizes the justifiability of deviation, stating that "it seems possible for a judicial decision to be justified, *all things considered*, even when it is contrary to a decision that is required by law."[28] He even challenges what he calls "the doctrine of legalistic justification," which holds that "a judicial decision is at least 'prima facie' justified if it is required by law."[29] Lyons appeals to the fact that one who attempts to argue that the law merits respect under certain conditions has implicitly conceded that those conditions are not *necessarily* satisfied. He concludes by denying "that legal considerations . . . themselves provide any measure of justification for judicial decisions."[30]

The proposition that all judges in all legal systems have an all-things-considered reason to obey restrictive rule entails the doctrine of legalistic justification. If Lyons is correct, then it is not the case that all judges in all legal systems have all-things-considered reasons to obey restrictive rule. But consider the adjectives that Lyons uses to describe systems in which judicial decisions required by law lack "prima facie" justification: "unfair and unjust, undemocratic and oppressive, exploitative and inhumane."[31] Lyons' point appears to be that judges in very bad regimes have no reason to adhere, a point on which Greenawalt and others concur.

What about judges in reasonably just and effective legal systems? Lyons leaves open the possibility that judges in such systems have moral reasons

---

25. Antonin Scalia, "Originalism: The Lesser Evil," *University of Cincinnati Law Review* 57 (1989): 849–65, p. 864. From the context of this remark I infer that Scalia means that flogging is too inhumane for him to uphold, regardless of the fact that originalism entails that it is constitutional. I do not understand him to mean that he would invalidate a flogging statute in deference to nonoriginalist precedent that mandates invalidation.

26. Gustav Radbruch, "Gesetzliches Unrecht und übergesetzliches Recht," *Süddeutsche Juristen-Zeitung* 1 (1946): 105–8; translated by Bonnie Litschewski Paulson and Stanley L. Paulson, "Statutory Lawlessness and Supra-Statutory Law," *Oxford Journal of Legal Studies* 26 (2006): 1–11; Robert Alexy, "A Defence of Radbruch's Formula," in *Recrafting the Rule of Law: The Limits of Legal Order*, ed. David Dyzenhaus (Oxford: Hart, 1999).

27. See, e.g., Norman Kretzmann, "Lex Iniusta Non Est Lex: Laws on Trial in Aquinas' Court of Conscience," *American Journal of Jurisprudence* 33 (1988): 99–122.

28. David Lyons, "Derivability, Defensibility, and the Justification of Judicial Decisions," in *Moral Aspects of Legal Theory* (Cambridge: Cambridge University Press, 1993), p. 120 (emphasis in original). For a qualified defense of *nonacquiesence*, limited to administrative agencies, see Samuel Estreicher and Richard L. Revesz, "Nonacquiescence by Federal Administrative Agencies," *Yale Law Journal* 98 (1989): 679–772.

29. Lyons, "Derivability, Defensibility, and the Justification of Judicial Decisions," p. 120.

30. Ibid., p. 124.

31. Ibid., p. 131.

to adhere, even in suboptimal-result cases. Indeed, he agrees that "[j]udicial decisions may be justified directly, on their merits, on the merits of the laws that require them, or on the merits of the legal system as a whole."[32] To reject the doctrine of legalistic justification is simply to deny that such justifications always apply.

Despite the virtual consensus that judges have strong reasons to adhere, few deny that judges do, in fact, deviate from the law, sometimes knowingly. A judge who deviates from the law even once does not obey restrictive rule. The Kadishes observe that it is "striking . . . the extent to which courts in their judicial opinions proclaim obedience to a principle far more restrictive than the principle they employ in practice."[33] They suggest that judicial deviation from legal *rules* is now seen as a normal and expected practice:

> [J]udicial departures from the obligation to decide in accordance with the established rules has [sic] become a deeply ingrained and characteristic feature of the judicial process, a feature sustained by the milieu in which judges operate. So government officials take judicial lawmaking into account when acting in their own roles; legal analysis and argumentation rest on it; initiates into the legal system encounter the tension between analytical and result-oriented thinking as one of the central features of a process they are expected to master.[34]

Given the consensus that judges have moral reasons to obey restrictive rule, which reasons are these? Consider some of the reasons discussed in the previous section as reasons for lawmakers to promulgate restrictive rule: coordination, reliance, efficiency, stability, error reduction, and allocation of authority. One might hope that these reasons also serve as reasons for judges to obey restrictive rule. We shall see.

8.4.1 Predictability

It is better, ceteris paribus, for people to be able to predict court decisions. Predictability facilitates the honoring of legitimate expectations, enables subjects to have advance warning when sanctions may be applied, and makes available information required to coordinate actions over time.[35] Judges serve these predictability values when they obey restrictive rule. However, a particular deviant decision compromises predictability values only to a minimal extent. This is significant because in suboptimal-result cases there are opposing values, such as the value of not subjecting parties to undeserved disadvantages. In many suboptimal-result cases the damage that deviation does to predictability is less important from a moral standpoint than the

---

32. Ibid., p. 128.
33. Mortimer R. Kadish and Sanford H. Kadish, *Discretion to Disobey: A Study of Lawful Departures from Legal Rules* (Stanford, Calif.: Stanford University Press, 1973), p. 88.
34. Ibid., p. 91.
35. Alan H. Goldman, *Practical Rules: When We Need Them and When We Don't* (Cambridge: Cambridge University Press, 2002), p. 34.

undeserved disadvantages imposed by adherence. Judges who obey restrictive rule give predictability values lexical priority over all other values. They could instead treat restrictive rule as a rule of thumb, deviating whenever the disvalue of adherence outweighs the disvalue of deviation. This approach allows judges to serve the values of predictability along with other values.[36]

There are, of course, cases in which the parties have relied upon an expectation that the law would be enforced and disappointing these expectations would be bad enough to outweigh any moral reason to deviate. The judge has an all-things-considered reason to adhere in such cases, but these are not suboptimal-result cases by definition, because judges would have no all-things-considered reason to reach a different result in such cases even if the law permitted it. Therefore, the expectations of parties do not constitute reasons for judges to obey restrictive rule.

8.4.2 Efficient Use of Decisional Resources

Judges have at their disposal a finite supply of resources for making decisions—*decisional resources*. These include time, mental energy, money, assistance from judicial clerks, et cetera. Figuring out what the law requires consumes some of these resources—more of them in more complex cases. A judge consumes additional decisional resources if, having determined the legally correct result, she chooses to ascertain whether it is suboptimal and, if so, to decide whether to deviate. She conserves resources if, having determined the legally correct result, she simply reaches it. Obeying restrictive rule conserves more than any other reasonable adherence rule.[37]

Legal systems are conceivable in which judges should obey restrictive rule. Restrictive rule is optimal if, unrealistically, there are no suboptimal-result cases. It might also be optimal for the odd judge whose mere choice to ask herself whether the legally correct result is suboptimal causes her to consume excessive decisional resources. Imagine an "obsessive" judge who spends 100 hours agonizing over any moral question she asks herself. She should obey restrictive rule (if she remains on the bench), because she cannot be trusted to resolve moral questions in a reasonable amount of time.

However, few real judges are so obsessive. Most are, and know themselves to be, capable of budgeting their time and resources in reasonable ways. A reasonable judge can contemplate whether a legally correct result is suboptimal without consuming more than a small portion of decisional resources. In many cases she will quickly conclude whether or not the legally correct result is suboptimal in her opinion. Some decisions will

---

36. Goldman acknowledges that the need for predictability does not by itself justify treating restrictive rule as a serious rule. Ibid., p. 35.

37. Equally efficient rules include ones that prescribe decision by coin flip or (perversely) consistent deviation.

take longer, but when evaluating optimality is taking too long most judges are capable of cutting short deliberation and simply deciding the case, at which point adhering probably makes sense. This is a reasonable personal policy: attempt to evaluate optimality, but if the process becomes too costly, then adhere by default. This is a variation on permissive rule. Obeying restrictive rule, by contrast, gives conservation of decisional resources lexical priority over all other values. The question should be whether the total cost in extra decisional resources consumed by judges who reject restrictive rule is outweighed by the value of avoiding the undeserved disadvantages that restrictive rule would require them to inflict. Until we answer that question we cannot conclude that judges have reasons to obey restrictive rule. The fact that doing so conserves resources does not settle the matter.

8.4.3 Error/Fallibility

Next, consider the argument from error, which recalls Raz's theory of authority.[38] Raz writes that a directive has authority over someone if "the alleged subject is likely better to comply with reasons which apply to him (other than the alleged authoritative directive) if he accepts the directives of the alleged authority as authoritatively binding and tries to follow them, rather than by trying to follow the reasons which apply to him directly."[39]

Everyone has many laws the disobedience of which would directly and tangibly benefit him if he could avoid the legal consequences. In only a small fraction of these cases would disobedience be just or serve the general welfare. In all other cases, individuals will conform more closely to their actual reasons if they obey the law than if they disobey, assuming that they have strong reasons to act morally, whether or not doing so benefits them. However, individuals are tempted to disobey whenever they believe that disobedience will benefit them and that they can avoid the legal consequences. In such cases they will sometimes conclude, although usually incorrectly, that they have moral reasons to disobey. Therefore, if they often disobey whenever they believe themselves to have moral reasons to disobey, then they will disobey too often and will fail to conform to their actual reasons. However, if they exclude moral reasons to disobey, then their degree of aggregate conformity to their actual reasons will be higher (so the argument assumes). So some legal conduct rules have practical authority.

One could argue, analogously, that restrictive rule has authority for judges. This would involve claiming that judges conform more closely to their actual reasons, in the aggregate, if they obey restrictive rule than if

---

38. Schauer, *Playing by the Rules*, pp. 149–55; Joseph Raz, *The Morality of Freedom* (Oxford: Clarendon Press, 1986), chs. 2–4.
39. Raz, *The Morality of Freedom*, p. 53.

they obey moderate or permissive rules. Suppose a judge is motivated to avoid suboptimal results. However, he is often mistaken about which results are suboptimal. He is mistaken so often that he reaches fewer suboptimal results during his career if he obeys restrictive rule than if he tries, case by case, to avoid suboptimal results.[40]

I am not sure how many judges are such unreliable identifiers of suboptimal-result cases or how many would accept this fact about themselves. One's estimates would seem to depend in part on the degree of overlap between one's own moral opinions and those of the judges in question. Although most judges are prepared to agree that certain *other* judges have worse moral judgment than "the law," how many judges believe this of themselves?

I can imagine a judge who has learned from experience that his own moral judgment is less reliable than the law. He remembers many occasions when he was very confident that a legally required result was morally suboptimal, but later concluded that the law had been correct, after all. Or he might believe, on the basis of his knowledge of many other judges throughout history, that the law is morally correct more often than judges. A rational, morally motivated judge will obey restrictive rule if he believes, for whatever reason, that the law has better moral judgment than he.

Perhaps *all* judges are very bad at distinguishing suboptimal-result cases from optimal-result cases. A judge who disregards moral reasons to deviate will end up adhering in every case. Jack is such a judge. Over the course of his career he adheres in every case, including 100 suboptimal-result cases. But suppose Jack is so prone to misidentify suboptimal-result cases that a commitment to deviate in every case that he believed to be a suboptimal-result case would lead him to adhere in 50 suboptimal-result cases and to deviate in 51 optimal-result cases. In that case, ceteris paribus, Jack's overall track record would be better if he adhered consistently than if he tried to deviate in every perceived suboptimal-result case. This is a Razian argument for the authority of restrictive rule.

However, judges have plenty of reasons to believe that their own moral judgment is at least as good as that of the law. Because gap cases are inevitable, it is always possible that the case at bar is one of these.[41] Did the lawmaker really anticipate this case? Are lawmakers really more reliable than judges on moral matters? Are the salient facts of the case really more distorting than informative?[42] As long as judges on average identify suboptimal-result cases correctly more often than not, judges who deviate in these cases will conform more closely to the reasons they have than if they adhere consistently. I see no reason to anticipate that judges will do

---

40. See also Schauer, *Playing by the Rules*, p. 126.
41. See §5.4.
42. For an affirmative answer, see Adrian Vermeule, *Judging under Uncertainty: An Institutional Theory of Legal Interpretation* (Cambridge, Mass.: Harvard University Press, 2006).

better if they adhere consistently than if they deviate in every case that they believe to be a suboptimal-result case.

Judges are situated very differently from private individuals. In legal systems that effectively police judicial conflicts of interest, bribery, and cases of undue influence, judges almost never hear cases in which deviation would directly and materially benefit them. Judges do not, therefore, have material incentives to conclude that they have moral reasons to deviate when they do not. At least their incentives for self-delusion are nowhere near as strong as those of private individuals contemplating their own cases. So it is not as evident as in the case of ordinary folk that judges' degree of aggregate conformity to their actual reasons is higher if they always disregard what they see as moral reasons to deviate. I do not claim that a judge who knows himself well would be unreasonable to conclude that his own moral judgment is inferior to that of the law. But I also submit that it is not unreasonable for a judge to conclude that his moral judgment is at least as good as that of the law. In other words, I do not think there is a Razian argument, applicable to all judges, for obeying restrictive rule. As Goldman notes, "in the absence of special reasons to suspect bias, ignorance, or some other special source of fallibility, the assumption by rule makers that they know better is . . . presumptuous. . . ."[43]

More important, even a judge who accepts that he is "worse than the law" at identifying suboptimal results as a general matter will hear cases in which he is especially confident that the legally required result is suboptimal. The Razian offers no reason for him to obey restrictive rule in such cases. Only a judge who never concludes that the legally required result is suboptimal has a reason to adhere in every case. Such a judge is not actually obeying restrictive rule.

My general point is that in suboptimal-result cases adhering to the law does not serve the justifications for promulgating restrictive rule to a degree that is sufficient to justify obeying it. That is part of the definition of a suboptimal-result case. Suboptimal-result cases open a gap between the lawmaker's reasons to promulgate restrictive rule and a judge's reasons to obey it.[44] The lawmaker has all-things-considered moral reasons to promulgate it, but the judge lacks all-things-considered reasons to obey (at least when considering the reasons examined thus far).[45]

Alexander and Sherwin argue that the nature of rules entails that gaps cannot be closed by any means.[46] They argue that rulemakers cannot eliminate the moral flaws of rules by improving the content of the rules.[47] If they are correct, then lawmakers cannot close the gap that judges face

43. Goldman, *Practical Rules*, p. 35.
44. See §5.4 on gaps.
45. This is an instance of what Schauer calls the "asymmetry of authority." Schauer, *Playing by the Rules*, p. 128.
46. They consider, inter alia, rule-sensitive particularism, presumptive positivism, exclusionary reasons, sanctions, and deception. Alexander and Sherwin, *The Rule of Rules*, ch. 4.
47. Ibid., p. 35.

in suboptimal-result cases by improving either legal rules or adherence rules. There will always be cases in which an adherence rule, however ideal, mandates suboptimal results.

Alexander and Sherwin's conclusion that the gap is ineliminable seems to entail that judges have no reason to obey restrictive rule rather than permissive rule. Yet these coauthors appear to believe that judges should nonetheless obey restrictive rule.[48] This is an awkward position to maintain.[49] I shall describe in part II an adherence rule that Alexander and Sherwin do not consider. I think it superior to both strong and permissive rules.

8.4.4 Indirect Consequentialism

Readers who favor indirect consequentialism might argue that a version of this moral theory supports obeying restrictive rule. According to Brad Hooker's recent formulation of rule consequentialism, an act is wrong if and only if it is forbidden by the code of rules the internalization of which by the overwhelming majority of the population has maximum expected value.[50] Hooker's principle supports obeying restrictive rule only if every value-maximizing code of rules forbids deviating in every suboptimal-result case. Is this true?

There are, to be sure, some codes that permit deviation in some suboptimal-result cases and that do not maximize value. Consider a code that includes a subjective version of permissive rule that permits the judge to deviate in any case that she believes to be a suboptimal-result case. Such a code would probably not maximize expected value if internalized by the overwhelming majority of judges. If too many judges have bad moral judgment, then they would deviate in more optimal-result cases than the suboptimal-result cases in which the judges with better judgment deviate. But permissive rule is not the only rule that permits deviation in some suboptimal-result cases. Suppose Jack's moral judgment is good enough that if he deviates whenever he thinks the case is a suboptimal-result case, then he actually deviates in more suboptimal-result cases than optimal-result cases. If the overwhelming majority of judges were to internalize a code that included both permissive rule and Jack's particular criteria of optimality, then value would be maximized. So there is, after all, a value-maximizing code that permits Jack to deviate. Therefore, judges are permitted to obey permissive rule and not required to obey restrictive rule.

Of course, this conclusion depends on the highly unrealistic stipulation that an overwhelming majority of judges correctly identify suboptimal-result cases and deviate only in these. But Hooker's formulation warrants this

48. See, e.g., ibid., pp. 145–50; Larry Alexander, "'With Me, It's All er Nuthin': Formalism in Law and Morality," *University of Chicago Law Review* 66 (1999): 530–65.

49. Schauer differs from Alexander and Sherwin in that he seems prepared to have lawmakers inculcate irrational "rule-worship" in judges. Schauer, *Playing by the Rules*, p. 132.

50. Brad Hooker, *Ideal Code, Real World: A Rule-Consequentialist Theory of Morality* (Oxford: Oxford University Press, 2000), p. 32.

stipulation. In part II, I shall argue that a defense of a nonpermissive rule requires rejecting this stipulation and plunging even further into the realm of *nonideal theory* than Hooker ventures.[51]

8.4.5 Contractualism

An alternative to rule consequentialism that has generated great interest in recent years is the contractualism of T. M. Scanlon. I shall argue that contractualism does not support obeying restrictive rule, either. Contractualism holds that "an act is wrong if its performance under the circumstances would be disallowed by any set of principles for the general regulation of behavior that no one could reasonably reject as a basis for informed, unforced general agreement."[52] Contractualism could be applied to adjudication theory in many different ways, few of which have been examined in the literature. I explore just one possibility. A contractualist theory of adjudication might hold that a decision is wrong if reaching it under the circumstances would be disallowed by any set of adjudication rules that no one could reasonably reject as a basis for informed, unforced general agreement.

A set of adjudication rules that includes no nonpermissive rule permits deviation in every suboptimal-result case. Who could reasonably reject this set? In order to answer this question, we must determine on whom the burden of such rules falls. We must look at each individual separately and ask, what are the effects on him if all judges obey these rules?

A defeated party usually wants to reject whatever rule permitted his defeat. Whether such rejection is reasonable depends on whether an alternative rule would have given anyone as strong reason to object as the present rule gives him. So we need to determine who is burdened when judges obey permissive rule and who is burdened when they obey restrictive rule. Then we must compare these burdens.

The fact that a decision is deviant does not entail that it makes the defeated party worse off than an adherent decision would have made his adversary. It all depends on the facts of the case. Whether a set of adjudication rules containing permissive rule can be reasonably rejected depends entirely on the criteria used to identify suboptimal-result cases. Consider a sexist criterion that classifies as suboptimal any result that facilitates the ownership of real estate by women. A judge who accepts permissive rule and this criterion will deviate whenever the law awards real property to a female litigant. People (especially women!) can reasonably reject a set of adjudication rules containing permissive rule and this criterion of optimality. Therefore, according to the contractualist theory under consideration, the judge should obey restrictive rule.

---

51. Nonideal theory is discussed in chapter 11.
52. T. M. Scanlon, *What We Owe to Each Other* (Cambridge: Belknap, 1998), p. 153. I challenge the capacity of contractualism to capture conventional morality in Jeffrey Brand-Ballard, "Contractualism and Deontic Restrictions," *Ethics* 114 (2004): 269–300.

Obeying Adherence Rules

This is not, however, the right kind of argument against permissive rule. Its conclusion for judges is conditional: if your criteria for identifying suboptimal-result cases can be reasonably rejected, then you should obey a nonpermissive rule. This conclusion is not helpful to us because we are trying to give judges reasons to adhere even when they are confident that the law requires a suboptimal result. If contractualism is true and a certain result is actually suboptimal, then it cannot be reasonable to reject criteria simply because they classify that result as suboptimal. So a judge who is rational, accepts contractualism, and believes that a certain result is suboptimal will conclude that no one can reasonably reject criteria that classify that result as suboptimal.

Consider the following combination: a statute that forbids women to own real estate and a set of optimality criteria that classify as suboptimal any result that prevents women from acquiring property when a similarly situated man would receive title. According to these criteria, this statute typically requires results that make the legally disfavored party worse off than deviating makes the legally favored party. The legally favored parties are men. If judges deviate from the statute, then the losing men still enjoy other opportunities to own real estate. However, if judges adhere, then the losing women enjoy no such opportunities, on account of the statute. No one can reasonably reject criteria that classify the legally required result as suboptimal. Therefore, no one can reasonably reject a set of adjudication rules containing permissive rule and these optimality criteria. However, women can reasonably reject the package of restrictive rule plus the sexist statute. More generally, legally disfavored parties in suboptimal-result cases can reasonably reject any set of adherence rules that includes restrictive rule. A superior set of rules is always available, consisting of permissive rule and optimality criteria that cannot be reasonably rejected. If contractualism condemns any adherence rules, it appears to condemn restrictive rule.

Thus, I am still seeking all-things-considered reasons to obey restrictive rule. I have found that these would have to be reasons that one could offer to a judge who has at least as much confidence in his own moral judgment as in that of the law. What could we say to persuade him to obey restrictive rule, without asking him to doubt his own judgment? In the rest of this chapter and in the next two, I shall discuss arguments for obeying restrictive rule that do not rely on the dubious premise that the judgment of a judge who has access to both the law and the facts of the case is usually inferior to that of the law by itself.

8.5 LEGITIMACY, AUTONOMY, AND RESPECT

I have agreed that legitimacy arguments support the conclusion that lawmakers have *pro tanto* reasons to promulgate restrictive rule.[53] Someone

---

53. See §7.10.

might claim that such arguments also support the conclusion that judges have moral reasons to obey restrictive rule, even when they are confident that the legally required result is suboptimal. I shall explain why I disagree.

The first legitimacy argument appeals to *respect*:

1. Judges have a *pro tanto* reason to express respect for lawmakers and citizens.
2. A judge who obeys restrictive rule expresses respect for lawmakers and citizens.
3. Therefore, judges have a *pro tanto* reason to obey restrictive rule.

This argument represents the idea that reaching the morally correct decision is not the only goal that matters. It is also important that the right official make the decision. There are, after all, many situations in which it is important that the correct person make the decision, not just that the decision be correct.[54] The same zirconium earrings mean more when chosen by a lover than when received as a "gift" for opening a bank account or when chosen by the lover's office assistant. Part of the meaning of a gift is that it was chosen by the giver. Someone who intercedes and replaces the chosen gift with another gift expresses disrespect for the giver, even if the recipient actually prefers the replacement gift to the original. Analogously, when a judge adheres to the law, he expresses respect for lawmakers and citizens, even if the law requires a suboptimal result.

Striking a similar note, Philip Soper argues that deference to the views of others fosters a community of shared values.[55] Soper devotes only a few pages to the judicial obligation to apply the law,[56] but the argument applies to judges as well as citizens. Judges can, perhaps, express deference and foster communities of shared values by adhering in suboptimal-result cases. To this extent, they might have a reason to defer to rules that were made in a good faith attempt to promote the common good. Perhaps obeying restrictive rule expresses respect for lawmakers and citizens, as the second premise states.

I suggest, however, that adherence in suboptimal-result cases is only one of many ways in which judges can express respect for others, and it is not an especially desirable way. In the expressive realm, appearances matter. Judges can express respect by pretending to defer and by adopting deferential rhetoric without actually deferring.

Moreover, even if the second premise is true, the conclusion of the respect argument does not follow. Adhering in a suboptimal-result case expresses disrespect for the losing party at the least. In fact, adhering does

---

54. Schauer, *Playing by the Rules*, p. 159.
55. Philip Soper, *The Ethics of Deference: Learning from Law's Morals* (Cambridge: Cambridge University Press, 2002), p. 161. Soper does not ultimately appeal to this argument.
56. Ibid., pp. 89–99.

something worse to him: it infringes his moral rights, depriving him of liberty or property. It is never permissible to infringe someone's moral rights in order to avoid expressing disrespect for someone else. This principle may seem unfamiliar because ordinary people so rarely face dilemmas in which failure to infringe someone's moral rights will express disrespect for someone else. I do not believe that I have ever been in such a situation. That judges often face such dilemmas reflects the very moral uniqueness of their job that motivates this book.

Imagine a mythical state in which judges are required by law to pay periodic visits to legislators. The tradition of this state dictates that on these visits the judge should purchase and present to the legislator an expensive plaque that reads, "You make the law. I apply it. Respectfully, Judge _____." It is considered highly disrespectful for a judge to arrive at a legislator's office without plaque in hand.

Judge Jane is preparing to visit a legislator. Unfortunately, she has no money, having recently made some bad investments. She needs $1,000 to buy an acceptable plaque. What to do? She notices an impoverished bystander, net worth $10,000, who happens to be carrying $1,000 in cash. He sets it down momentarily, where Jane could easily take it.

Assume that taking the cash would otherwise be impermissible, all things considered. Given that assumption, the fact that Jane needs the cash in order to buy the plaque and show respect for the legislator does not constitute a reason for her to take it. It might be permissible to take the cash in order to protect life, limb, or liberty, but the need to avoid disrespect provides not even a *pro tanto* reason to take it.

Judges deciding suboptimal-result cases in the real world face an analogous dilemma. Deviating disrespects lawmakers and citizens, but adhering violates the losing party's moral rights. I conclude that the need to avoid disrespecting lawmakers provides no reason for judges to adhere.

Notice that I could have required Jane to choose between disrespecting the legislator and using physical force against the bystander—killing, maiming, assaulting, or physically confining him. I even left the bystander with $9,000, rather than having Jane reduce his net worth to zero. I can make my point without resorting to such extremes. Judges cannot invoke "respect for lawmakers" to justify adhering to a law that requires unjustly infringing someone's rights, even if it is a matter of only $1,000. A fortiori, such reasoning cannot support unjustly executing or incarcerating defendants under law.

The second legitimacy argument for obedience to restrictive rule appeals to *autonomy*:

1. Judges have a *pro tanto* reason to facilitate the exercise of autonomy by lawmakers and citizens.
2. When a judge obeys restrictive rule, she facilitates the exercise of autonomy by lawmakers and citizens.
3. Therefore, judges have a *pro tanto* reason to obey restrictive rule.

This argument is no stronger than the respect argument. We can revise the story of Judge Jane. Tradition now dictates that, rather than purchasing a plaque, the judge must donate $1,000 to the legislator's favorite charity or one chosen by the legislator's constituents. Jane again finds herself penniless on her way to visit the legislator. If she arrives without $1,000, then she fails to facilitate the efforts of the legislator and her constituents to advance their autonomously chosen ends. Again, this need does not provide Jane with a *pro tanto* reason to take $1,000 from the poor bystander.

Someone might object that individuals who do not wish to suffer the disadvantages of lawbreaking should simply obey the law, just or unjust. But this objection cannot bolster legitimacy arguments. After all, a lawmaker can always resign from office if he does not wish to be disrespected by judges who deviate in suboptimal-result cases. And a lawmaker who wants to avoid interference from deviating judges can find other ways to exercise his autonomy and promote his personal objectives.

It is also worth noting that judges who reject restrictive rule in favor of permissive rule still adhere to the law in all permissible-result cases. Every time they do so they express respect for lawmakers and citizens and facilitate the exercise of autonomy by lawmakers and citizens. This is so even in cases in which the judge would have reached the legally required result, had the law not required it, as when the judge punishes a defendant for committing a crime *malum in se*. Consider a judge who would sentence a certain rapist to five years in prison, if the law permitted but did not require him to do so. In fact, the law requires him to do so. Even if this judge rejects restrictive rule, he can treat this legal requirement as a reason to impose the five-year sentence. He can sentence the rapist to five years *because* the law requires him to do so. His decision in such a case is rationally overdetermined. His decision constitutes deference to prior lawmakers despite the fact that he would have made the same decision absent any legal mandate. I can give you flowers *because* it is your birthday even if I bought them for you before I knew about your birthday.

8.6 SEPARATION OF POWERS

Someone might object that a judge who deviates even once is "doing the lawmaker's job," and that doing so is always wrong, all things considered. I reject this argument. First, defining the *job* of the judge is precisely what is in dispute in this book. Second, I do not believe that a deviating judge necessarily even attempts to change the law. He simply fails, albeit knowingly, to apply the law. Judges can even make their intentions explicit by announcing that they do not intend to apply the law.[57]

---

57. See Justice Kline's dissent quoted in §3.12.

It is easy to overlook the possibility of deviating without changing the law. Judges in Anglo-American systems play both law-applying and law-making roles.[58] When a judge announces and applies a new legal rule or other standard that conflicts with preexisting law, she necessarily departs from preexisting law and plays a lawmaking role. Such decisions do not constitute deviation unless the judge lacks the legal authority to make law in this particular area. In such cases the judge does, indeed, both deviate and usurp lawmaking authority. She asserts and exercises an authority that she does not legally possess. In ordinary cases of deviation, by contrast, the judge makes no new law.

Even if we concede that deviation usurps some lawmaking authority, this fact does not necessarily provide a *pro tanto* reason to adhere. Lawmaking authority is a shared, divisible resource. Deviating in a single case usurps relatively little lawmaking authority. I can imagine an unrealistic scenario in which a single deviant decision by any given judge would have the effect of usurping all lawmaking authority in the system, leaving none for anyone else. In such a scenario each judge would, indeed, have moral reasons to obey restrictive rule. But in real legal systems a single deviant decision virtually never has such an effect.

I can, however, imagine a judge deviating in a way that really would constitute total usurpation. Imagine a judge making the following announcement:

> Hereafter, I shall treat the text of statutes and the opinions of superior courts much as I treat legal scholarship. These texts may contain good arguments and good legal standards to apply. I shall adopt these when I agree with them. But the fact that a proposition appears in a statute or in the *ratio decidendi* of a case, as opposed to appearing in a law review or a newspaper editorial, shall have no effect whatsoever on my deliberations. Moreover, I hereby assert jurisdiction over all cases.

This judge is declaring himself to be, effectively, both the legislative and judicial branches of government. There is a world of difference between this judge and one who, having rejected restrictive rule, deviates in suboptimal-result cases.[59]

In this chapter I examined several arguments for the conclusion that judges have *pro tanto* reasons to obey adherence rules. I concluded that judges have strong reasons to obey permissive rule, but I raised objections to the arguments for obeying restrictive rule. Next I shall consider two other important arguments for obeying restrictive rule: an argument from the judicial oath and an argument from political obligation. Each of these arguments requires its own chapter.

---

58. This is a thesis of Douglas E. Edlin, *Judges and Unjust Laws: Common Law Constitutionalism and the Foundations of Judicial Review* (Ann Arbor: University of Michigan Press, 2008).

59. It is, of course, unlikely that other officials will follow this judge's decrees. At some point, he will almost certainly be removed from office.

9

The Judicial Oath

Judges swear an oath to perform their official duties. These duties surely include obeying adherence rules.[1] Therefore, I must consider the content and moral significance of oaths. An oath traditionally involves a solemn appeal to a deity or to some revered person or thing, to witness one's determination to act: to speak the truth, to keep a promise, et cetera.[2] Federal law, for example, states the following:

> Each justice or judge of the United States shall take the following oath or affirmation before performing the duties of his office: "I, _____, do solemnly swear (or affirm) that I will administer justice without respect to persons, and do equal right to the poor and to the rich, and that I will faithfully and impartially discharge and perform all the duties incumbent upon me as _____ under the Constitution and laws of the United States. So help me God."[3]

All judges, state and federal, swear oaths of office. The wording varies at the state level,[4] but the federal oath is representative. How, if at all, does swearing an oath affect one's reasons for action after one becomes a judge? Does the oath-taker acquire moral obligations that others lack?

---

1. "[A]n official who seeks or consents to serve in a position of public trust has made a commitment, a voluntary undertaking, to follow the law. . . ." David Lyons, "Derivability, Defensibility, and the Justification of Judicial Decisions," in *Moral Aspects of Legal Theory* (Cambridge: Cambridge University Press, 1993), p. 137.

2. In our age of religious pluralism it can be a formally affirmed statement or promise that is accepted as an equivalent to divine appeal.

3. 28 U.S.C. § 453.

4. Some typical oaths of judicial office:

> I, _____, do solemnly swear that I will support the Constitution of this State and the Constitution of the United States, and will perform the duties of my office, faithfully, impartially and justly, to the best of my ability. So help me God. N.J. Stat. § 41:2A-6 (2009).

> I, the undersigned, who have been elected (or appointed) to the office of. . . ., but have not yet entered upon the duties thereof, do solemnly swear that I will support the constitution of the United States and the constitution of the state of Wisconsin; that I will administer justice without respect to persons and will faithfully and impartially discharge the duties of said office to the best of my ability. So help me God. Wis. Stat. § 757.02 (2008)

Unfortunately, there is virtually no philosophical literature on oaths of office.[5] There is, however, a vast literature on promissory obligation that is pertinent because judicial oaths incorporate promises. Oaths differ from ordinary promises in several respects that I shall discuss shortly. However, none of these differences diminishes the strength of the promissory obligations generated by oaths. If anything, they strengthen these obligations. So I can begin by stating a simplified version of the oath argument:

Oath Argument 1
1. If an agent promises to Φ, then he has a *pro tanto* moral duty to Φ.
2. By swearing the oath of office, judges promise to fulfill the duties of the judicial office.
3. Therefore, judges have a *pro tanto* moral duty to fulfill the duties of the judicial office.

Oath arguments raise the following questions, which I shall answer in order. To whom does a judge make promises when he swears his oath? What does he promise to do? What reasons for action does he acquire when he makes these promises?

9.1 PROMISES

When a judge swears his oath, he promises that he will fulfill his judicial duties in every case that he decides. Every federal judge swears, "I will faithfully and impartially discharge and perform all the duties incumbent upon me as a [federal judge] under the Constitution and laws of the United States." However the oath is worded, judges promise to perform the "duties incumbent" upon them. I conclude that a judge who swears the oath of office has promised to obey the adjudication rules that specify those duties. Which duties these are we have yet to determine.

I do solemnly swear (affirm) that I will support the Constitution of the United States, and the Constitution of the State of Illinois, and that I will faithfully discharge the duties of the office of . . . . to the best of my ability. *Illinois Const.*, Art. XIII, § 3 (2009)

The Arizona Constitution states that "Each justice, judge and justice of the peace shall, before entering upon the duties of his office, take and subscribe an oath that he will support the Constitution of the United States and the Constitution of the State of Arizona, and that he will faithfully and impartially discharge the duties of his office to the best of his ability." A.R.S. *Const.* Art. VI, § 26 (2008).

5. But see Daniel P. Sulmasy, "What Is an Oath and Why Should a Physician Swear One?" *Theoretical Medicine and Bioethics* 20 (1999): 329–46. T. M. Scanlon discusses oaths in *What We Owe to Each Other* (Cambridge: Belknap, 1998), pp. 323–26.

Swearing the oath gives the judge promissory duties to the general public, to his fellow judges, and to other public officials. As I shall discuss in the next section, he promises everyone that he will endeavor to do his job well for as long as he holds judicial office. However, his promise is not addressed to any particular promisee. It does not yet give him special duties to anyone as opposed to general duties to everyone in his legal system. I suggest that we understand him as making a conditional promise that enables his subsequent actions to generate special duties. When a case is assigned to him, he always has the option of requesting that it be reassigned to another judge. He can even resign from the bench before hearing the case. If he chooses to hear the case, then he voluntarily fulfills the condition of his promise with respect to the parties, thereby completing an unconditional promise to them that he will fulfill his judicial duties in their case. Only at that point does he acquire special promissory duties to them.

9.2 FIDELITY

It is widely agreed that individuals have a natural duty of fidelity or promise keeping.[6] Promises give promisors *pro tanto* moral reasons to perform. The judicial oath incorporates a promise to obey adjudication rules, so it gives judges *pro tanto* moral reasons to obey these rules. Promises are subject to familiar defeating conditions at formation, but these conditions are absent when judges swear oaths of office. There is no coercion or duress, for example. Judges always have reasonable alternative occupations.

Which adherence rule or rules does the oath obligate judges to obey? The easiest case is made for permissive rule. If the oath means anything, then it includes a promise to adhere to the law in required-result and optimal-but-not-required-result cases. So judges have a reason to adhere in such cases. They also have an exclusionary reason that excludes all reasons to deviate in required-result and optimal-but-not-required-result cases. These are private reasons because there are, by definition, no impartial reasons to deviate in required-result or optimal-but-not-required-result cases. Therefore, the oath gives permissive rule practical authority for judges. To obey permissive rule is to accept a reason to adhere in permissible-result cases and an exclusionary reason that excludes private reasons to deviate in all cases. I endorse the following:

---

6. See, e.g., Bernard Gert, *Morality: Its Nature and Justification* (New York: Oxford University Press, 1998), pp. 188–90. Some writers deny that promises as such normally generate moral obligations, but even they agree that promisors have moral obligations to do as they have promised. These writers simply deny that the obligation derives from the fact that the promisor makes the promise. See P. S. Atiyah, *Promises, Morals, and Law* (Oxford: Clarendon Press, 1981), pp. 123–29.

Oath Argument 2
1. If an agent promises to Φ, then he has a *pro tanto* moral duty to Φ.
2. Judges promise to obey permissive rule.
3. Therefore, judges have a *pro tanto* moral duty to obey permissive rule.

Matters are more complicated with respect to restrictive rule. Restrictive rule gives judges reasons to adhere in certain suboptimal-result cases, as well. It also excludes certain moral reasons, not just private reasons, to deviate. Does the oath give restrictive rule practical authority for judges?

First, we must examine more closely what judges promise to do when they take the oath. Do they promise to adhere in suboptimal-result cases? The language of the oath does not refer to such cases explicitly. I am not sure how much weight to place on this omission, but it could be significant. After all, the oath could easily have included a clause stating, "I will apply the law faithfully, no matter how unjust I may consider its demands to be." The oath contains no such language. In fact, federal judges swear that they "will administer *justice* without respect to persons," (emphasis added) although I do not think this language can be honestly read as supporting the thesis that judges are morally permitted to deviate in order to avoid unjust results.[7]

I have located no code of judicial conduct that so much as acknowledges the existence of suboptimal-result cases. The codes do not mention cases in which the law requires results that are *unjust, bad, immoral, inequitable*, or *wrong*. So there is no explicit textual support for the proposition that the judicial oath includes a promise to adhere in suboptimal-result cases. It is not unreasonable, however, to read such a promise into the judicial oath. After all, textual adjudication rules do not explicitly *exclude* suboptimal-result cases from the scope of the oath, either. The text is silent, but in the absence of an explicit textual exception it is reasonable to infer that the general promise to adhere to the law extends to suboptimal-result cases. Let us assume *arguendo* that the oath incorporates by implication a promise to adhere in suboptimal-result cases, despite the absence of explicit language in either the oath or the codes. If this assumption is mistaken, then so much the better for my main argument.

It is not surprising that the oath and other textual adjudication rules lack explicit language promising to adhere in suboptimal-result cases. I think such language would be otiose because such a promise would not, in fact, create moral reasons to adhere in suboptimal-result cases. I believe that the oath would not generate a moral reason to adhere in suboptimal-result cases, even if it contained an explicit promise to do so. This is to say

---

7. I do not read this language as contemplating cases of conflict between justice and positive law. Rather, the phrase expresses a commitment to impartial decision. "Administer justice" in this context is merely a sonorous way of saying, "render decisions under law."

that the oath does not give any nonpermissive rule practical authority for judges. The next sections explain my position.

9.3 IMMORAL PROMISES

My argument rests on two complementary premises. First, promises do not attenuate one's other moral reasons. Second, other moral reasons can undermine or override promissory obligations. These principles are widely recognized.[8] The first is reflected in the well-established legal principle that contracts to commit crimes or torts are unenforceable.[9] Others have noted that an agent cannot acquire a moral obligation to follow a rule by consenting, committing himself, or promising to follow it, if the rule requires an action that is morally wrong.[10] I shall now describe some hypothetical scenarios in which promisors promise to perform immoral actions. Common moral convictions hold that the immorality of these actions undermines promissory obligation. Then I shall examine how popular theories of promising support these principles.

Bruce gets on the radio, identifies himself, and swears a solemn oath before his fellow citizens that he will kick a squirrel in his yard on Saturday.[11] Taking this oath gives Bruce no reason whatsoever to kick a squirrel come Saturday. Nor does it attenuate his reasons to refrain from doing so. His natural duty of nonmaleficence forbids inflicting gratuitous pain on animals.[12] This duty undermines whatever reasons his oath might otherwise have given him.[13] Taking an oath does not give one a reason that overrides or attenuates one's natural duty of nonmaleficence.[14]

Juanita swears a public oath that she will *not* call the police if she ever happens to witness a kidnapping in progress. Taking this oath gives Juanita no reason whatsoever to refrain from calling the police in such an

---

8. Joseph Raz, *The Morality of Freedom* (Oxford: Clarendon Press, 1986), p. 173: "one's right to promise does not include the right to promise to perform immoral acts." See also Heidi M. Hurd, "Justifiably Punishing the Justified," *Michigan Law Review* 90 (1992): 2203–324, p. 2242; Joseph Raz, "Promises in Morality and Law," *Harvard Law Review* 95 (1982): 916–38, p. 926; Kurt Baier, "The Justification of Governmental Authority," *Journal of Philosophy* 69 (1972): 700–16, p. 712.

9. Restatement First of Contracts §§ 598–609 (1932).

10. Larry Alexander and Emily Sherwin, *The Rule of Rules* (Durham, N.C.: Duke University Press, 2001), p. 75.

11. Actually, kicking a squirrel is not as easy as Bruce thinks it is.

12. If you find squirrel kicking too trivial to trigger the duty of nonmaleficence, then substitute an act of violence that does, in your opinion, trigger that duty.

13. In 2005, two college students started a website, SaveToby.com, on which they promised to kill their adorable pet rabbit, Toby, unless they received donations totaling $50,000 before June 30. Stephen E. Sachs, "Saving Toby: Extortion, Blackmail, and the Right to Destroy," *Yale Law and Policy Review* 24 (2006): 251–61.

14. It is probably wrong for Bruce to swear such an oath in the first place, but that is not important here.

event. Natural samaritan duties require taking such steps to prevent kidnappings. Juanita's oath does not override or undermine her samaritan duties. Nor does it seem to me, intuitively, that Juanita can alienate her natural samaritan rights by taking an oath.

A point about the function of promises emerges from these hypotheticals: the function of a promise, including the promise imbedded in an oath, is to create a special obligation in the promisor. The reply, "Because I promised to do it," answers the question, "Why should I do *that*, rather than something else that I would now prefer to do?" It does not answer the question, "Why am I permitted to do *that*, which would otherwise be wrong?" Promises make morally optional actions morally obligatory. They do not make morally impermissible actions morally permissible, much less obligatory.

The preceding arguments entail that the first premise in Oath Argument 2 needs a qualification. Corrected, the argument reads as follows:

Oath Argument 3
1. If an agent promises to Φ and has no otherwise undefeated *pro tanto* moral duty not to Φ, then he has a *pro tanto* moral duty to Φ.
2. Judges promise to obey a permissive rule.
3. Judges have no otherwise undefeated *pro tanto* moral duty not to obey a permissive rule.
4. Therefore, judges have a *pro tanto* moral duty to obey a permissive rule.

However, we have also learned that substituting restrictive rule for permissive rule falsifies the third premise. Restrictive rule requires judges to adhere in suboptimal-result cases, which they have an undefeated *pro tanto* moral duty not to do. Therefore, oath arguments do not support a *pro tanto* moral duty to obey restrictive rule.

9.4 THEORIES OF PROMISING

My preceding argument rests upon the premise that a promise to Φ gives the promisor no reason to Φ if he has an otherwise undefeated, *pro tanto* moral duty not to Φ. I have defended this premise by appeal to hypotheticals, but it finds additional support in philosophical theories of promising. Each of these theories supports the principle that promises to perform otherwise immoral actions are void.

9.4.1 Deflationary and Act-Consequentialist Theories

According to a deflationary theory, promises add nothing to a promisor's reasons.[15] If this thesis applies to the incorporated promise in the judicial

---

15. See, e.g., Elinor Mason, "We Make No Promises," *Philosophical Studies* 123 (2005): 33–46.

oath, then a deflationary theory entails that the oath adds nothing to the judge's reasons to adhere. Such theories obviously cannot help defend the conclusion that judges should obey restrictive rule.

Act-consequentialist theories of promissory obligation offer little more. According to these theories, the fact that a particular practice of oath keeping promotes good consequences gives judges a *pro tanto* reason to keep their oaths. However, deviant decisions in suboptimal-result cases often promote better consequences than adherent decisions would, even accounting for damage done to the practice of judicial oath taking, the rule of law, et cetera. So act-consequentialist theories cannot help us defend the conclusion that judges can have all-things-considered reasons to obey restrictive rule.

9.4.2 Rule Consequentialism

Rule consequentialists hold that promisors have a duty to keep promises because a widespread practice of promise breaking has suboptimal consequences. However, rule consequentialists permit promise breaking under certain conditions. They hold that promisors may break a promise if and only if it would promote the good for people generally to internalize a *rule* permitting the breaking of promises in such situations.

Consider a rule that permits promisors to break promises to Φ if Φ-ing is immoral. For a rule consequentialist, Φ-ing is immoral if and only if it would promote the good for people to internalize a rule that forbids Φ-ing. So the question is, would it promote the good for people to internalize a rule that requires promisors to keep promises to Φ, if it would promote the good for people to internalize a rule that forbids Φ-ing?

If it promotes the good for people to internalize a rule that forbids Φ-ing, then Φ-ing must, in the aggregate, diminish the good. Now I need not deny that the fact that someone has promised to Φ can make the promisor's act of Φ-ing somewhat less good-diminishing. But Φ-ing is still good-diminishing, overall. At least, the combination of promising to Φ and then proceeding to Φ does not promote the good if Φ-ing is otherwise immoral. The world would contain more good if one simply did not promise to Φ in the first place. If this conclusion were false, then a bad agent could simply promise someone that he would Φ, proceed to Φ, and correctly claim thereby that he was promoting the good, no matter how immoral Φ-ing might be.

Therefore, it would *not* promote the good for people to internalize a rule that requires promisors to keep promises to Φ even if Φ-ing is otherwise immoral. Rule consequentialism supports the principle that if Φ-ing is immoral, then a promise to Φ gives the promisor no reason to Φ.

At this point, a defender of restrictive rule might interject. Suppose people internalize a rule that allows promisors to break promises to perform otherwise immoral actions. This rule does not promote the good if people too often misidentify immoral actions. Such people will break the wrong promises and keep the wrong ones, despite sincerely trying to obey the rule. A rule that requires keeping all promises, moral or immoral, might lead to fewer broken promises that should be kept than would a rule that permits breaking immoral promises. The exceptionless rule, if internalized, might better promote the good.

This objection exaggerates moral incompetence. The basic fidelity principle holds that a promise to Φ gives the promisor a *pro tanto* moral reason to Φ. The relevant population comprises individuals who are capable of internalizing this principle. By definition, these people recognize the immorality of promise breaking and act upon this moral knowledge. There is no reason to doubt their ability and motivation to identify other immoral actions and to use this knowledge pursuant to the principle that if Φ-ing is otherwise immoral, then a promise to Φ gives the promisor no *pro tanto* moral reason to Φ.

9.4.3 Free Riding

According to free-rider theories, if breaking a promise involves free riding on a just practice, as it often does, then the promisor has a *pro tanto* reason to keep the promise.[16] What do free-rider theories imply about immoral promises? If a promisor does not benefit from breaking an immoral promise, then he does not ride free on any practice. But what about immoral promises that the promisor benefits by breaking? In such cases it matters why the promise is broken. Breaking an immoral promise is still objectively permissible, although it may be blameworthy if the promisor breaks it for a private reason. Lazy Assassin promises to assassinate a senator but breaks his promise in order to watch television. Breaking this promise is objectively permissible but blameworthy. Although he does the objectively obligatory thing, he rides free on the general practice of *not breaking promises for nonmoral reasons*. This is a just practice from which he benefits.[17]

Another question is whether the practice upon which the promisor rides free is a just practice. To answer this question, we must identify the practice or practices upon which a promisor rides free when he breaks an immoral promise. Let us assume that the promisor (unlike Lazy Assassin) breaks the promise because keeping it would be immoral. There are two possibilities. First, we might conclude that he rides free on the general practice of promise keeping. That practice is just, and most promisors

---

16. John Rawls, *A Theory of Justice* (Cambridge, Mass.: Harvard University Press, 1971), pp. 344–48; H. A. Prichard, "The Obligation to Keep a Promise," in *Moral Obligation* (Oxford: Clarendon Press, 1949).

17. One might also argue that breaking a promise is blameworthy if the promisor has confidence level c that she is breaking it for a moral reason and there is a general practice, from which she benefits, of keeping promises unless one has at least confidence level d that one is breaking one's promise for a moral reason, and $c < d$.

benefit from it. If breaking an immoral promise constitutes free riding on the general practice, then promisors have a *pro tanto* reason to keep such promises.

Alternatively, we might conclude that he rides free on the practice of keeping *immoral* promises. Is there such a practice? The fact that many writers have treated as common knowledge the principle that immoral promises do not obligate suggests that there is no such practice. However, because I am not sure how many immoral promises are kept in modern societies, I shall assume *arguendo* that such a practice exists. The next question is whether the promisor benefits from the practice. Most promisors do not benefit from a *general practice* of keeping immoral promises. They benefit from the practice of keeping morally permissible promises. When one breaks an immoral promise, one violates the first practice, not the second. Furthermore, the practice of keeping immoral promises is not just. So breaking an immoral promise does not constitute free riding at all, much less free riding on a just practice. If breaking an immoral promise does not constitute free riding on the general practice of promise keeping, then promisors have no *pro tanto* reason to keep immoral promises, according to free-rider theories.

9.4.4 Nonpractice Theories and Reliance

T. M. Scanlon and others object that practice theories, including free-rider theories, fail to capture the sense in which breaking a promise wrongs the promisee—a particular individual—as opposed to society at large.[18] This objection might seem inapplicable to the judicial oath, which really *is* made to society at large. Actually, the objection still applies because the judge wrongs a particular litigant if she (the judge) violates her judicial duties to his detriment. When the judge swears her oath she makes a conditional promise to all parties who may come before her, promising each of them that she will fulfill her judicial duties in his case. When she deviates she breaks this promise to the litigant whose legal rights she thereby disregards. Practice theories fail to capture the way in which deviant decisions putatively wrong defeated litigants.

Contemporary theories of promising such as Scanlon's are designed to reflect the idea that breaking a promise wrongs the promisee. They base promissory obligation on promisees' expectations and reliance. In the process of discussing Scanlon's theory I shall also consider the principle that agents have moral reasons not to frustrate expectations that they have led others to form. This principle, if true, could provide a nonpromissory basis for the claim that judges have reasons to obey adherence rules.

Scanlon argues that promises generate reasons independently of any social practice. He defends

---

18. Scanlon, *What We Owe to Each Other*, ch. 7; Neil MacCormick, "Voluntary Obligations and Normative Powers I," *Proceedings of the Aristotelian Society* 46 (1972): 59–78.

The Judicial Oath

> Principle D: One must exercise due care not to lead others to form reasonable but false expectations about what one will do when one has good reason to believe that they would suffer significant loss as a result of relying on these expectations.[19]

and

> Principle F: If (1) A voluntarily and intentionally leads B to expect that A will do X (unless B consents to A's not doing so); (2) A knows that B wants to be assured of this; (3) A acts with the aim of providing this assurance, and has good reason to believe that he or she has done so; (4) B knows that A has the beliefs and intentions just described; (5) A intends for B to know this, and knows that B does know it; and (6) B knows that A has this knowledge and intent; then, in the absence of special justification, A must do X unless B consents to X's not being done.[20]

According to principles D and F, a promise to Φ gives the promisor a reason to Φ only if the promisor has led the promisee to form a *reasonable* expectation that the promisor will Φ. We must determine the conditions under which an expectation is reasonable. We can distinguish *epistemically reasonable* from *normatively reasonable*.[21] Relying on an expectation that an event will occur is epistemically unreasonable for someone in a specified epistemic state if a person in that state possessing theoretical rationality would not predict the event. By contrast, relying on an expectation that someone will Φ is normatively unreasonable if Φ-ing is otherwise immoral.

Suppose that every year for the past five years, Leo's father has hired a new assistant. Leo has tried to seduce each of these assistants. Each woman has rejected Leo's advances, whereupon Leo has asked his father to fire her and his father has complied. Leo's father has hired a new office assistant this year. She rejects Leo's advances. By firing the assistants in previous years, Leo's father has led Leo to expect that this assistant will be fired. Leo has an epistemically reasonable expectation that his father will fire her. However, it is not normatively reasonable for Leo to expect the assistant to be fired (sexual harassment is wrong). Even if Leo relies to his detriment on his expectation, these facts give his father no reason whatsoever to fire the assistant.

My first conclusion follows. Suppose one has led another to form an epistemically reasonable expectation that one will Φ, inducing detrimental reliance. These facts do not constitute a reason to Φ if Φ-ing is immoral. This principle holds whether or not the relying party reasonably believes Φ-ing to be immoral.

What might Scanlon's theory say about promises to act immorally? The "special justification" clause in principle F provides a hint that Scanlon

---

19. Scanlon, *What We Owe to Each Other*, p. 300.
20. Ibid., p. 304.
21. A similar distinction is drawn in David Lefkowitz, "A Contractualist Defense of Democratic Authority," *Ratio Juris* 18 (2005): 346–64.

does not believe that immoral promises generate all-things-considered obligations. But is his theory consistent with the proposition that immoral promises create *pro tanto* obligations? I suggest that a promise to Φ gives the promisor a reason to Φ only if the promisor has led the promisee to form an expectation that the promisor will Φ and the expectation is both epistemically and normatively reasonable.

Here is a case in which a promisor has no reason to keep her promise because the promisee's reliance is normatively unreasonable. Rachel promises to install a computer in her grandmother's bedroom. Her grandmother relies upon this promise, planning everything around it. It is *subjectively* epistemically reasonable for her to do so. However, Rachel overhears her grandmother's live-in boyfriend talking about how he plans to use the computer to plan a terrorist attack. Rachel's grandmother knows nothing about these plans. Neither Rachel's promise nor her grandmother's detrimental reliance gives Rachel any reason whatsoever to install the computer.[22]

If someone promises to Φ, then it may be epistemically reasonable for the promisee to expect him to Φ even if Φ-ing is immoral. However, if Φ-ing is immoral, then it is not normatively reasonable for the promisee to expect the promisor to Φ. Therefore, on Scanlon's theory, a promise to Φ does not give the promisor a *pro tanto* reason to Φ if Φ-ing is immoral. The reasoning applies whether or not the promisee reasonably believes that Φ-ing is immoral.

I have discussed two related principles: (1) that one has no reason to Φ if Φ-ing is immoral, even if one has led someone else to form an epistemically reasonable expectation that one will Φ and that person has relied to his detriment; and (2) that a promisor has no reason to keep a promise to Φ if Φ-ing is immoral. These principles are widely accepted and find support in current theories of justified reliance and promissory obligation.

These principles have implications for my discussion. I have asserted that relying upon a prediction that someone will Φ is objectively unreasonable if Φ-ing is otherwise immoral. The act of Φ-ing counts as "otherwise immoral" if and only if Φ-ing would be immoral if no one had relied upon it. I argued in chapter 6 that a decision to adhere in a suboptimal-result case is otherwise immoral in this sense. A judge who adheres to the law in a suboptimal-result case performs actions that would be immoral, all things considered, if the law did not require them. Even if the judge has led parties to believe that he will adhere in suboptimal-result cases, and they are epistemically reasonable to expect him to do so, and they rely to their detriment on their expectations, their expectations give him no *pro tanto* reason to adhere. It is objectively normatively unreasonable

---

22. However, these facts retain some practical significance. Both give Rachel a moral reason to apologize for disappointing her grandmother. Perhaps she should also offer to install the computer in her own home so her grandmother can use it when she visits. She might want to mention the boyfriend's proclivities, too.

The Judicial Oath

to rely on one's expectation that a judge will adhere in a case if it is a suboptimal-result case. Similarly, even if we interpret the judicial oath as incorporating a promise to adhere in suboptimal-result cases, it gives judges no reason to do so.

I shall illustrate by revisiting the eviction case.[23] Suppose Yasmin has missed three rent payments over the past twelve months. Rafael's lawyer tells him that he has a legal right to evict Yasmin. Therefore, it is subjectively epistemically reasonable for Rafael to predict that a judge will grant his eviction petition and for Rafael to rely upon that expectation. Unfortunately for Rafael, his lawyer misread the code. In Rafael's jurisdiction the law does not grant a right to evict until the tenant misses three *consecutive* rent payments. If she misses three nonconsecutive payments, then the law merely gives the court discretion to grant or deny an eviction petition, without specifying legal considerations for the judge to take into account. Granting Rafael's petition will inflict a substantial undeserved disadvantage on Yasmin. Denying it will inflict an undeserved disadvantage on Rafael. However, let us stipulate that the magnitude of the wrong against Yasmin is at least as great as the magnitude of the wrong against Rafael, even taking into account Rafael's reasonable reliance. Therefore, the court has an all-things-considered moral reason to rule for Yasmin. Suppose Judge Lucas grants Rafael's petition. He thereby orders the sheriff to force Yasmin from her apartment. No one, with the possible exception of Judge Lucas, has an all-things-considered moral reason to order anyone to do this to Yasmin. Indeed, everyone else has a strong *pro tanto* moral reason not to do so. Because the law does not require it, even Judge Lucas has an all-things-considered reason not to do it. I suggest that just as Bruce's oath gives him no reason that competes with his natural duty to refrain from kicking squirrels, likewise Judge Lucas's oath gives him no reason that competes with his natural duty to deny the eviction petition, notwithstanding Rafael's expectations—which are reasonable as a subjective epistemic matter.

Now imagine identical facts, except that the law grants a right to evict after three nonconsecutive missed payments, just as Rafael was told. The law requires the judge to grant Rafael's petition. This is now a suboptimal-result case. If the law did not require the judge to grant Rafael's petition, then the judge would have an all-things-considered moral reason against doing so, even taking into account Rafael's reliance. The judge's *pro tanto* reason to deviate has at least as much weight as the *pro tanto* reason to adhere generated by the reliance of parties to the case.

My point is that Rafael's reliance is no more subjectively reasonable or detrimental in the second version of the case than it was in the first. The fact that Rafael has reasonably relied upon the judge to grant his petition does not give the judge a reason to grant it that is any stronger in the

---

23. Introduced in §5.3.

second version of the case than it was in the first. Therefore, if judges are ever morally required to adhere in a suboptimal-result case, then they must have some other reason to do so, in addition to the reasonable reliance of parties.

This is not to deny that a judge who deviates in a suboptimal-result case may have certain residual reasons. She may have reason to apologize to parties whose expectations she has disappointed. But the reliance of parties gives her no reason to adhere.

I should also emphasize that my point is *not* that the judge has no reason to adhere in Rafael's case. That would be a much stronger claim that I shall not make. My point is that neither the judicial oath, as such, nor the reliance of parties, as such, generates any reason to adhere to the law in suboptimal-result cases. These facts generate reasons to adhere only in conjunction with certain enabling conditions that I shall spell out in the chapters ahead.

9.4.5 Contractual Duties

Some would say that it is the judge's *job* to adhere to the law. He is contractually obligated to do it. He is paid to do it. This might seem to give him a moral reason to adhere. Again, we must be careful not to slide from the indisputable thesis that judges are morally obligated to adhere in permissible-result cases to the stronger conclusion that they are so obligated in all cases. If an action is otherwise morally impermissible, then one's job description cannot give one a moral reason to do it. Nor can forming a contract, nor can receipt of compensation.

9.5 THE SPECIAL WEIGHT OF OATHS

One might be tempted to object as follows. My argument proceeds from a premise about ordinary promises—that promises to act immorally are void. But the judge's promise to obey adherence rules is no ordinary promise. It is a promise incorporated into an oath of office. One might plausibly suggest that such promises have exceptional weight, whereas I have treated them as though they were ordinary promises.

There are, indeed, several aspects of the promises incorporated into the judicial oath that would seem to give them more weight than ordinary promises. First, the judicial oath concerns a very important subject—the judge's professional duties—whereas some promises concern trivial subjects. Second, judges swear their oaths in public, whereas promises can be made to a single promisee in private. Third, with his oath the judge makes a general commitment to the law as a whole, for an indefinite time period, whereas promises can concern specific actions to be taken at specific times. Fourth, when a judge swears her oath, she promises to be a certain kind of person for the sake of the public, whereas a promise need not involve any such commitment to maintain a certain sort of character. Fifth, the judicial oath appeals to God, whereas ordinary promises make no such appeal. Finally, the force of the judicial oath may be seen as less likely to diminish with changed circumstances than in the case of promises.[24]

All of these seem to be good reasons to agree that a judge's promises, undertaken by oath, have greater weight than ordinary promises. However, this concession does not affect my argument. The moral reasons to deviate in a suboptimal-result case need not *outweigh* the reasons to adhere that are provided by the judge's promise. Rather, moral reasons to deviate *undermine* promissory duties categorically. It is not a matter of balancing. Recall that Bruce and Juanita do not merely make promises, they swear oaths.[25] It makes no difference.

9.6 OATH AS INUS CONDITION

I have argued that the judicial oath does not give judges a *pro tanto* moral reason to obey restrictive rule—or any nonpermissive rule, for that matter. However, I shall argue in part II that judges *have* reasons to obey a nonpermissive rule. So in one sense swearing the oath must generate a reason to obey a nonpermissive rule: in modern legal systems, after one has been appointed or elected to judicial office, taking the oath of office suffices to *transform* one into a judge. However, anyone can take the judicial oath without becoming a judge, in which case one does not acquire even a right, much less a duty, to decide cases. Sincerely uttering the words of the oath does not give one adherence reasons. Taking the oath is not conceptually necessary, either, because not all possible legal systems require judges to swear oaths of office.

In modern legal systems, however, taking the oath is a condition for becoming a judge. It is "an insufficient but nonredundant part of an unnecessary but sufficient condition"—an INUS condition.[26] Taking the oath is a performative speech act that, given the right background conditions, converts one into a judge. Taking the oath by itself is not sufficient. You can swear the judicial oath right now without becoming a judge. Nevertheless, the oath is part of a constellation of conditions that are jointly sufficient for becoming a judge. Moreover, given that these other conditions have occurred, rather than a different set of conditions that are sufficient for becoming a judge, taking the oath is necessary. One cannot become a judge *in the United States today* without taking the oath of office. My point is that the oath by itself does not give one a reason to obey

---

24. This list was adopted from Sulmasy, "What Is an Oath and Why Should a Physician Swear One?"
25. See §9.3.
26. J. L. Mackie, "Clauses and Conditions," *American Philosophical Quarterly* 2 (1965): 245–64.

a nonpermissive rule, even if the oath constitutes a promise to obey such a rule. The oath gives one a reason to obey a nonpermissive rule only insofar as the oath is an INUS condition on becoming a judge. Once one is a judge, aspects of the *judicial role* give one reasons to obey a nonpermissive rule, and these aspects of the role would do so even if one had taken no oath. The law could instead provide that becoming a judge requires shouting, "Open sesame!"[27]

It may seem unimportant to distinguish between the claim that the *oath* gives the judge a reason to obey a certain adherence rule and the claim that the *judicial role* gives him such a reason. In fact, the distinction is important. Promises give promisors exclusionary reasons. The judicial oath does not merely outweigh the judge's private reasons to deviate: it excludes them. That is what it means to say that the oath gives judges a reason to obey permissive rule. If the oath also excluded moral reasons to deviate, which I have denied in this chapter, then judges would have a reason to obey restrictive rule. If judges' reasons derive from other aspects of the judicial role, not from the oath, then it does not follow that they have any reason to obey restrictive rule. Whether they have such a reason remains an open question.

---

27. A detour into science fiction reinforces the point. Dr. Sam Beckett, hero of the television program *Quantum Leap*, finds himself suddenly and unexpectedly inhabiting the bodies of other people, seriatim, without his consent or volition. If Sam is suddenly thrust into the body of a judge who is about to hear a case, then I think he has moral reasons to obey the same adjudication rules that "real" judges do, despite having never taken the judicial oath. Of course, he can resign—which he should if he doubts his judicial competence (although viewers learn that Sam is a super-genius and legally knowledgeable). But if Sam chooses to hear cases, then he has as strong a moral reason to obey adjudication rules as a judge who swore the oath would have. *Quantum Leap* is wholesome, educational entertainment for young people.

10

Legal Duty and Political Obligation

This chapter explores another argument for the conclusion that judges have moral reasons to obey restrictive rule. The reasoning is that judges have a *legal* duty to obey restrictive rule and a moral duty to fulfill their legal duties:

1. Judges in reasonably just, legitimate states have a *pro tanto* moral duty to obey the law.
2. Obeying the law entails fulfilling one's legal duties.
3. Judges have a legal duty to obey restrictive rule.
4. Therefore, judges have a *pro tanto* moral duty to obey restrictive rule.

This argument is valid, but the first and third premises require discussion.

10.1 POLITICAL OBLIGATION AND JUDICIAL OBLIGATION

Chapter 4 considered arguments for the third premise. I concluded that a viable case, although not a conclusive one, can be made for it. If the third premise is false, then my larger argument in the book is easier to make. A reader who rejects the third premise can skip this chapter. In this chapter I shall assume *arguendo* that the third premise is true: judges have a legal duty to obey restrictive rule. The next question is whether they have a moral duty to fulfill their legal duties. For convenience, we can ask whether they have a moral duty to fulfill their judicial duties, provided we remember that we are interested in a moral duty to fulfill judicial duties *qua* legal duties.

There has been extensive debate on the general question whether individuals have a moral duty to obey the laws of the jurisdiction in which they reside. The debate during the past forty years has concentrated on the question whether we have a duty to obey the law that is content independent as well as "comprehensively applicable [and] universally borne," meaning that it obligates all residents to obey all laws of the jurisdiction.[1] Many different arguments have been offered in support of such a duty.[2] It is worth pausing to ask what logical relationship holds between this debate and my question concerning the moral duty to fulfill judicial duties.

One might assume that judges' moral duty to fulfill their legal duties stands or falls with the proposition that legal subjects have a "comprehensively applicable, universally borne, content-independent" duty to obey the law. After all, judges are legal subjects. If all legal subjects have a moral duty to obey traffic laws, then judges have a moral duty to obey traffic laws.

It would, however, be too quick to conclude that a successful defense of a general duty to obey the law is either necessary or sufficient to support the premise that judges have a moral duty to fulfill their judicial duties. Consider sufficiency. Although judges are, indeed, legal subjects, the arguments for a general duty to obey the law are aimed at conduct rules, not decision rules. Adjudication rules direct judges to apply decision rules, not conduct rules. Therefore, the soundness of an argument for a general duty to obey is not sufficient to support the conclusion that judges are morally obligated to fulfill their judicial duties.

Next consider necessity. Every prominent argument for a duty to obey defends a duty that is comprehensively applicable and universally borne. A moral duty to fulfill judicial duties, by contrast, is neither universally borne nor comprehensively applicable. Only judges have judicial duties, and these comprise only some of a judge's legal duties. Therefore, the fact that the law requires judges to fulfill their judicial duties could give them a moral reason to do so even if legal subjects have no duty to obey the law that is either universally borne or comprehensively applicable.

So the success of a defense of a general duty to obey the law is neither necessary nor sufficient to support the premise that judges have a moral duty to fulfill their judicial duties. In the next sections, I consider four arguments for the principle that judges are morally obligated to fulfill their legally imposed judicial duties. My arguments do not support

---

1. For useful overview see William A. Edmundson, "State of the Art: The Duty to Obey the Law," *Legal Theory* 10 (2004): 215–59. The language quoted here is attributed to Matthew Kramer on p. 215.

2. See, e.g., Mark C. Murphy, "Natural Law, Consent, and Political Obligation," *Social Philosophy and Policy* 18 (2001): 70–92; Christopher Heath Wellman, "Liberalism, Samaritanism, and Political Obligation," *Philosophy and Public Affairs* 25 (1996): 211–37; David Miller, *On Nationality* (Oxford: Oxford University Press, 1995); Margaret Gilbert, "Group Membership and Political Obligation," *The Monist* 76 (1993): 119–31; George Klosko, *The Principle of Fairness and Political Obligation* (Lanham, Md.: Rowman & Littlefield, 1992); A. D. M. Walker, "Political Obligation and the Argument from Gratitude," *Philosophy and Public Affairs* 17 (1988): 191–211; Ronald Dworkin, *Law's Empire* (Cambridge, Mass.: Harvard University Press, 1986), pp. 191–92; John Rawls, *A Theory of Justice* (Cambridge, Mass.: Harvard University Press, 1971), pp. 114–17, 333–55; H. L. A. Hart, "Are There Any Natural Rights?" *Philosophical Review* 64 (1955): 175–91.

a general duty to obey the law, but they adapt widely discussed arguments for such a general duty: arguments from consent, fair play, natural duty, and gratitude. If one of these arguments succeeds, then judges have at least a *pro tanto* moral duty to fulfill their judicial duties. I must emphasize that I am not committed to the claim that there are sound arguments for a general duty to obey the law. Such arguments have been subjected to powerful criticisms.[3]

In order to reflect the different reasons for which legal subjects can act as the law requires, philosophers often draw a distinction between *conforming* to the law and *obeying* the law, also known as *complying*.[4] An agent conforms to the law if and only if she acts as the law requires, regardless of her reasons for doing so. An agent obeys or complies with the law if and only if she treats the fact that the law requires conformity as a reason to conform. To obey the law is to conform for content-independent reasons. The conform/obey distinction is important because historical legal systems contain mandatory rules that make illegal much conduct that we have moral reasons to avoid anyway, independent of the law, such as assault, destruction of property, defamation of character, et cetera. Individuals have content-dependent moral reasons to conform to these laws. Individuals who conform to these laws for exclusively moral reasons do not obey.

By contrast, subjects obey the law if they conform for content-independent reasons. For example, subjects sometimes obey because they fear sanctions. They act from prudential, content-independent reasons. One might also assume that the law also provides its subjects with content-independent *moral* reasons to obey. In the twentieth century, the existence of such reasons came into question with the work of Joseph Raz, Leslie Green, A. J. Simmons, M. B. E. Smith, Robert Paul Wolff, Richard Wasserstrom, and many others.[5] These authors deny that legal subjects

---

3. See authors cited below.
4. Robert Paul Wolff, *In Defense of Anarchism* (New York: Harper and Row, 1970), p. 9; Joseph Raz, *Practical Reason and Norms*, 2nd ed. (New York: Oxford University Press, 1990), p. 178.
5. See, e.g., Meir Dan-Cohen, "In Defense of Defiance," *Philosophy and Public Affairs* 23 (1994): 24–51; Joseph Raz, "The Obligation to Obey: Revision and Tradition," in *Ethics in the Public Domain* (Oxford: Clarendon Press, 1994); Leslie Green, *The Authority of the State* (Oxford: Clarendon Press, 1988); Kent Greenawalt, *Conflicts of Law and Morality* (New York: Oxford University Press, 1987); Rolf Sartorius, "Political Authority and Political Obligation," *Virginia Law Review* 67 (1981): 3–17; A. John Simmons, *Moral Principles and Political Obligations* (Princeton, N.J.: Princeton University Press, 1979); M. B. E. Smith, "Is There a Prima Facie Obligation to Obey the Law?" *Yale Law Journal* 82 (1973): 950–76; Wolff, *In Defense of Anarchism*; Richard A. Wasserstrom, "The Obligation to Obey the Law," *UCLA Law Review* 10 (1963): 780–807. David Lyons even rejects the claim "that justification is always required for disobedience to law." David Lyons, "Derivability, Defensibility, and the Justification of Judicial Decisions," in *Moral Aspects of Legal Theory* (Cambridge: Cambridge University Press, 1993), p. 135.

have a general, content-independent, *pro tanto* moral reason to obey the law. A lively debate on "political obligation" continues.[6]

The question whether ordinary subjects have content-independent moral reasons to obey the law might be dismissed as a merely scholastic dispute. Whether or not this dismissal is warranted, the question has great urgency where judges are concerned. There is some reason to predict that at least one of the arguments for citizens' moral duty to obey the law will also support judges' moral duty to apply it. Several major writers have defended a *pro tanto* moral duty to obey at least some *unjust* laws.[7] Their arguments might be adapted to support a judge's moral duty to apply unjust laws or, more broadly, to adhere to the law in suboptimal-result cases. Let us consider these arguments.

Someone might suggest that obedience to the law is an end in itself—an intrinsic good—rather than a means to an end.[8] If so, then the fact that the law requires one to Φ provides one with a *pro tanto*, nonderivative, content-independent moral reason to Φ. If a judge is legally required to use force, then she has a *pro tanto*, nonderivative, content-independent moral reason to use it.

Is positive law an ultimate, nonderivative source of moral reasons? I have found no living writer who thinks so. Some believe that the law *simpliciter* incorporates parts of morality that are not mentioned in positive law. But they believe that morality, not positive law, provides the reasons. Some deny that citizens have a general, *pro tanto* moral duty to obey positive law,[9] a position that conflicts with the claim that positive law is an ultimate source of moral reasons. Even those who endorse such a general duty to obey do not claim that obedience to positive law is an end in itself—that positive law is the ultimate source of moral reasons. Rather, they defend a general moral duty to obey the law on the basis of other ultimate moral principles.

Even if positive law provides nonderivative, content-independent reasons, such reasons can surely be undermined. Consider a duty to carry on a family tradition. This duty could be understood as nonderivative and content-independent. If, however, the tradition involves the use of unjust force, then the duty is undermined. Similarly, I think a judge's reason to use force is undermined in suboptimal-result cases. The judge has a content-dependent reason to avoid suboptimal results that undermines any content-independent reason he might otherwise have to adhere to the law.

---

6. See Edmundson, "State of the Art: The Duty to Obey the Law."

7. See, e.g., J. L. Mackie, "Obligations to Obey the Law," *Virginia Law Review* 67 (1981): 143–58; Tony Honoré, "Must We Obey? Necessity as a Ground of Obligation," *Virginia Law Review* 67 (1981): 39–61; Rawls, *A Theory of Justice*, pp. 350–55.

8. Mackie, "Obligations to Obey the Law," p. 151. Note that Mackie advises us to "invent" the obligation to obey.

9. See works of Raz, Green, Simmons, Wolff, and others cited above.

10.2 ACTUAL CONSENT

Philosophers have long sought to base a general duty to obey the law on actual consent. This argument is famously problematic as applied to natural-born citizens, most of whom never give actual consent to the state.[10] Unlike most natural-born citizens, however, judges definitely consent to something: they swear an oath to uphold the law. As discussed in chapter 9, the judicial oath gives judges a moral reason to fulfill their judicial duties, but I concluded that it gives them no reason to obey restrictive rule. A parallel objection applies to actual-consent arguments in support of a duty to obey restrictive rule. Consenting to Φ does not give the consenting party a moral reason to Φ if Φ-ing is otherwise immoral, nor does consent attenuate his moral reasons not to Φ. Therefore, a judge's consent to obey restrictive rule does not give her a *pro tanto* moral reason to obey it, insofar as it requires her to adhere in suboptimal-result cases.

There are, however, many other theories of political obligation. Can any of these theories succeed where consent theories fail, supporting reasons for judges to adhere in suboptimal-result cases? One might jump to the conclusion that these other theories cannot possibly succeed if, as I have argued, consent theories fail. It is widely assumed that political obligation would be unproblematic if all citizens expressly consented to obey, absent fraud or duress. Consent theories fail to support political obligations for natural-born citizens precisely because *they* do *not* consent. That is the only reason that political philosophers turn to arguments from fair play, gratitude, et cetera. The latter arguments are designed to do the work of consent when consent is absent, not to do work that consent when present fails to do.

It would, however, be a mistake to conclude that these arguments cannot succeed if consent arguments fail. The question remains open as to whether a theory of political obligation based on fair play, natural duty, or gratitude can support a judicial duty to obey restrictive rule. Let us turn to these theories.

10.3 FAIR PLAY

Consider first the *fair play principle*: "[W]hen a number of persons engage in a mutually advantageous cooperative venture according to rules, and thus restrict their liberty in ways necessary to yield advantages to all, those who have submitted to these restrictions have a right to a similar

---

10. But see Murphy, "Natural Law, Consent, and Political Obligation"; Margaret Gilbert, "Reconsidering the 'Actual Contract' Theory of Political Obligation," *Ethics* 109 (1999): 236–60.

acquiescence on the part of those who have benefited from their submission."[11] Could this principle give judges a *pro tanto* moral reason to obey restrictive rule? When Jack becomes a judge, he joins the judicial enterprise that constitutes a "mutually advantageous cooperative venture." This enterprise is undertaken "according to rules"—the rules of adjudication. The other judges in Jack's system "restrict their liberty" by obeying adjudication rules. Jack benefits from their obedience in several ways.

First, the legal system itself would not exist if judges did not obey certain adjudication rules. It is very probable that Jack benefits from the legal system in his capacity as a private legal subject. Perhaps a lone survivalist in the uncharted wilderness could deny that any legal system benefits him, but judges cannot.

Second, being a judge probably benefits Jack. He is paid to do it. He holds a position of honor and esteem in his community. His work may be intrinsically fulfilling. These benefits would be unavailable to him without a legal system that, again, requires judicial obedience to adjudication rules.

Third, in addition to the general ways in which Jack benefits from the legal system, he may obtain a special kind of benefit from a general practice of judicial adherence to the law. As a judge, Jack may want to influence the development of the law. The satisfaction of that desire, if rational, benefits him. But his efforts to influence the path of the law would be much less effective, if effective at all, if his fellow judges did not obey rules such as stare decisis. So Jack benefits from general adherence in another way if he wants to influence the law.

Although the elements appear to be in place to apply a fair play theory to judicial duties, these theories are vulnerable to the "limiting argument,"[12] pressed by Robert Nozick and A. J. Simmons.[13] One cannot impose obligations on another by foisting unwanted benefits upon him.[14] In response to the limiting argument, George Klosko has rehabilitated fair play theory with the qualification that the benefits provided must be "(i) worth the recipients' effort in providing them and (ii) presumptively beneficial."[15] A presumptively beneficial good is something everyone is presumed to want. The benefits of having a legal system and of being

---

11. Rawls, *A Theory of Justice*, p. 112. Rawls endorses a similar principle in "Legal Obligation and the Duty of Fair Play," in *Law and Philosophy: A Symposium*, ed. Sidney Hook (New York: New York University Press, 1964). He follows Hart, "Are There Any Natural Rights?"

12. So called by George Klosko, "Presumptive Benefit, Fairness, and Political Obligation," in *The Duty to Obey the Law: Selected Philosophical Readings*, ed. William A. Edmundson (Lanham, Md.: Rowman & Littlefield, 1999), p. 195.

13. Robert Nozick, *Anarchy, State, and Utopia* (New York: Basic Books, 1974), pp. 90–95; Simmons, *Moral Principles and Political Obligations*, ch. 5.

14. Judges agree to take office, of course, but the consent argument was addressed in §10.2.

15. Klosko, "Presumptive Benefit, Fairness, and Political Obligation," p. 197.

Legal Duty and Political Obligation

a judge in one are certainly goods that every judge can be presumed to want. Obedience to adjudication rules is necessary for a legal system to exist, and for a judge to influence the law. If judges obeyed *no* adjudication rules, then no legal system could exist.

However, no *particular* set of adjudication rules is necessary. The advocate of fair play needs a principle stating that an agent has a fair play duty to obey an established rule if either that rule or some functional equivalent thereof is necessary for the production of benefits enjoyed by the agent. Therefore, a fair play argument cannot establish that other judges have a right to demand that Jack obey every adjudication rule that they obey. At most it establishes the right to demand that Jack obey a certain adjudication rule only if that rule, or its functional equivalent, is necessary for the existence of every legal system that would benefit Jack. We must examine individual adjudication rules in order to ascertain which ones fall in this category.

Consider adherence rules. Every legal system that would benefit Jack probably includes such rules. No legal system could be *indifferent* to judicial adherence to the law. So far I have established that a fair play argument could support Jack's duty to obey certain adjudication rules and that these will include certain adherence rules. But I have not established which ones. I shall take for granted that general obedience to restrictive rule benefits Jack. One might conclude, therefore, that the fair play principle gives Jack a *pro tanto* reason to obey restrictive rule. This is because the usual statements of the fair play principle make it appear to require individuals who benefit from general obedience to a certain rule to obey that same rule. However, I think this is an uncharitable reading of the principle. The only rational statement of the principle requires individuals to obey either the general rule *or an alternative rule that yields at least the same benefits as the general rule*. On my reading the fair play principle requires Jack to obey either restrictive rule or an alternative rule that yields at least the same benefits as restrictive rule.

One might object that codes of judicial conduct require judges to be "faithful to the law," which one might read as a statement of restrictive rule. How, in the name of fair play, could Jack justifiably disregard this rule in favor of another? Let us suppose *arguendo* that the objector reads the codes correctly as including restrictive rule. I suggest that restrictive rule still controls Jack's reasoning by setting a floor below which he must not fall. Whatever rule Jack obeys instead of restrictive rule must offer at least the benefits of restrictive rule.

The next question is whether there is a rule that yields at least the benefits of restrictive rule, but that gives judges no *pro tanto* reason to adhere in some suboptimal-result cases. One alternative is permissive rule, which forbids deviation in all optimal-result cases but permits it in all suboptimal-result cases. For the purposes of the fair play principle, permissive rule seems to offer all the benefits of restrictive rule with none of its disadvantages. So the fair play principle cannot support a rule that requires adherence in suboptimal-result cases. The more selective rule is more effective, overall. I conclude that the fair play principle does not support a duty to obey restrictive rule.

10.4 GRATITUDE

Some writers have defended a duty to obey the law as a duty of gratitude.[16] One owes such a duty when someone acts for one's sake, whether or not one requests or desires it. The state takes many actions for the sake of its citizens, including judges. I shall accept *arguendo* that a judge is obligated to do something that properly expresses his gratitude. Obeying adjudication rules might be one way to do so. But discharging this duty does not seem to require anything as specific as obeying adherence rules, particularly in suboptimal-result cases. At most, we could perhaps say that a judge has a *conditional* duty of gratitude to obey adherence rules if he does not adequately express his gratitude in any other way.

Also note that some actions are inappropriate and impermissible expressions of gratitude. Ron saves Daisy's life at great cost to himself. Daisy owes Ron a large debt of gratitude. Ron asks Daisy to shoplift something for him as an expression of her gratitude. Daisy has not even a *pro tanto* reason to do so. Similarly, adhering to the law in suboptimal-result cases seems a particularly inappropriate expression of gratitude because it involves performing actions that are otherwise *pro tanto* wrongful.

10.5 NATURAL DUTY

Rawls argues that individuals have a "fundamental natural duty . . . of justice." We are obligated

> to support and to comply with just institutions that exist and apply to us. [The duty] also constrains us to further just arrangements not yet established, at least when this can be done without too much cost to ourselves. Thus if the basic structure of society is just, or as just as it is reasonable to expect in the circumstances, everyone has a natural duty to do his part in the existing scheme.[17]

If Rawls is correct that we have a duty to comply with and to do our share in just institutions, and certain adjudication rules are part of a just institution, then judges have a natural *pro tanto* duty to obey those rules.

What might a Rawlsian say about adherence rules, specifically? Rawls himself acknowledges that unjust laws will be enacted even if the constitution and legislative process are just: "[T]here is no feasible political

---

16. Walker, "Political Obligation and the Argument from Gratitude."
17. Rawls, *A Theory of Justice*, p. 115.

process which guarantees that the laws enacted in accordance with it will be just."[18] He notes that "among the very limited number of procedures that have any chance of being accepted at all, there are none that would always decide in our favor . . . and . . . consenting to one of these procedures is surely preferable to no agreement at all."[19] Procedures such as majority rule will inevitably produce some unjust laws: "In choosing a constitution, then, and in adopting some form of majority rule, the parties accept the risks of suffering the defects of one another's knowledge and sense of justice in order to gain the advantages of an effective legislative procedure."[20] Rawls holds that, at least in a state of near justice, "there is normally a duty . . . to comply with unjust laws provided that they do not exceed certain bounds of injustice."[21] If this principle applies directly to judges and adherence rules, then we could conclude that, at least in a reasonably just system, judges have a duty to obey whatever adherence rules the lawmakers enact, provided that these do not exceed certain bounds of injustice. If the lawmakers enact restrictive rule, then judges have a moral duty to obey it, on this view.

I think Rawls's discussion of disobeying unjust laws suffers from a major limitation that is common to most discussions of the topic. His position may be defensible regarding the most common kinds of situations in which private parties face unjust laws. But his perspective on disobedience is fundamentally that of the private citizen. My question concerns the duties of public officials. Judges have moral reasons to disobey restrictive rule, yet Rawls does not reach the question of whether moral reasons to disobey can undermine moral reasons to obey. This omission on his part is understandable. Unjust laws rarely require private individuals to perform immoral acts or to omit morally obligatory acts. Most unjust laws merely require individuals either to perform certain morally permissible acts or to omit certain morally optional acts. Typical unjust laws deprive individuals of their rights. By contrast, restrictive rule requires judges to perform actions that would otherwise be immoral.[22]

I think Rawls's restriction of civil disobedience to "serious violations of justice" is, therefore, inappropriate for judges. In my view, the natural duty to obey the law does not give a judge a reason to obey an adherence rule that requires him to perform actions that are even slightly immoral. At least, if a judge is choosing between two adherence rules, one of which requires him to perform an action that is slightly more immoral than any

---

18. Ibid., p. 353.
19. Ibid., p. 354.
20. Ibid., p. 355. Rawls does not distinguish between unjust laws and just laws that dictate unjust results, or between suboptimal laws and optimal laws that dictate suboptimal results. But presumably he would acknowledge the existence of negative-gap cases, as well as suboptimal-rule cases.
21. Ibid., p. 355.
22. See further discussion in §10.7.

action that the second rule requires, then he may choose to obey the second rule. Or if the second rule requires him to perform two slightly immoral actions and the first rule requires him to perform only one such action, then he may choose to obey the first rule.

Rawls claims that parties in the original position[23] would choose a principle that requires us "to comply with and to do our share in just institutions when they exist and apply to us."[24] But he does not reach the question of whether they would understand it to entail that judges have *pro tanto* moral reasons to adhere in suboptimal-result cases. At most, his arguments show only that parties in the original position would choose principles that supply *pro tanto* moral reasons to obey the law and that these reasons are not undermined by *private* reasons. His arguments do not show that moral reasons to disobey cannot undermine moral reasons to obey. In fact, Rawls permits limited civil disobedience even in a nearly just society: even "forceful resistance may later be entertained."[25] However, Rawls permits disobedience only for "serious violations of justice."[26] He thinks we have a duty to obey laws that are only slightly unjust because "[w]ithout some recognition of this duty mutual trust and confidence are liable to break down."[27] The idea, which I accept, is that trust and confidence break down if individuals suspect one another of disobeying for private reasons. Disobeying for private reasons raises this suspicion. So individuals should not disobey for private reasons. By extension, judges must not deviate for private reasons, meaning that they must obey at least permissive rule. This conclusion extends to disobedience of laws that are only slightly unjust. The less obviously unjust a law is, the more likely it becomes that disobedience will be perceived as privately, rather than morally, motivated. So individuals should obey slightly unjust laws because disobeying will be perceived as motivated by private reasons.

A Rawlsian might try to apply this argument to judges, producing an argument in favor of obeying restrictive rule. I think such an extension fails. Rawls envisions a typical case of disobedience in which a private individual breaks the law, benefits in a tangible way from doing so, and believes that she has a good chance of evading the legal consequences. Under these conditions, given what we know of human behavior, it is reasonable to infer that she disobeys for private reasons. This inference is reasonable even if the law happens to be seriously unjust and disobedience morally justifiable.

By contrast, in a legal system that assigns cases randomly and adequately polices judges for conflicts of interest, corruption, bribery, and other forms of undue influence, everyone should have confidence that

---

23. For description of the original position see Rawls, *A Theory of Justice*, ch. 3.
24. Ibid., p. 334.
25. Ibid., p. 366.
26. Ibid., p. 363.
27. Ibid., p. 355.

Legal Duty and Political Obligation

judges who deviate do not do so for the obvious private reasons: money, sexual favors, promotion, revenge, et cetera. When a judge deviates he does not benefit in any tangible way. If Posner is correct, then the deviating judge actually suffers displeasure at not "playing the judicial game" according to the rules.[28] It is not reasonable to infer that he deviates for self-serving reasons, even if the legally required result is arguably optimal. The reasonable inference is that the judge sincerely, although perhaps mistakenly, believes the legally required result to be suboptimal. This inference is even more reasonable if the legally required result is arguably suboptimal, even if only slightly so. So judges who deviate in slightly suboptimal-result cases do not threaten mutual trust and confidence. This is not, of course, to deny that patterns of deviation can have other negative effects on the legal system. That is the subject of part II. These effects, I shall argue, give practical authority to moderate rules over permissive rule.

10.6 SAMARITANISM

Samaritan accounts of the duty to obey the law begin with the premise that each of us has the right to use force (or coercion) when necessary to rescue others.[29] Likewise, the state has the right to use force in order to rescue its residents from the perils of the state of nature. Each of us then has a duty to obey the law, lest he interfere with the state's performance of its samaritan duties.

A samaritan account of the judge's duty to adhere to the law is still simpler. Everyone has a natural samaritan duty to rescue others, at least when he can do so at little cost to himself. A judge occupies an unusually good position to rescue others from the perils of the state of nature at little cost to himself, merely by adhering to the law when he decides cases.

When a judge adheres to the law in a suboptimal-result case, however, he does not rescue the losing party from the state of nature. On the contrary, he partially returns the party to the state of nature and/or prevents others from rescuing her from a partial state of nature. When a judge enters a judgment against a defendant who deserves better, he uses unjustified coercion against her and forcibly prevents others from protecting or rescuing her.

When a judge deviates from the law in a suboptimal-result case, he does not interfere with the state's performance of its samaritan duties. Rather, he performs these duties when the state would otherwise fail to do so. Therefore, samaritan accounts of the duty to obey the law do not support the practical authority of restrictive rule.

---

28. See §4.6.
29. Wellman, "Liberalism, Samaritanism, and Political Obligation."

10.7 OBEYING UNJUST LAWS

In this chapter I conceded *arguendo* that judges have a legal duty to adhere in suboptimal-result cases, but I proceeded to deny that they have even a *pro tanto* moral duty to do so. Therefore, a reader might assume that my position presupposes that there are no legitimate states or at least that there is no *pro tanto* moral duty to obey the law—certainly reputable philosophical positions, but still controversial.[30] I cannot predict where the ongoing debates will lead, so I have actually tried to avoid assuming either philosophical anarchism or the nonexistence of a *pro tanto* duty to obey. In fact, I have shown how standard arguments for a duty to obey can be adapted to a narrower purpose. Assuming that judges have a legal duty to obey permissive rule, the standard arguments can be used to support a corresponding moral duty.

I have, however, rejected every argument so far for the conclusion that judges are morally obligated to obey a nonpermissive rule. I have found no reason to deny that judges are, at least sometimes, morally permitted to deviate. If judges have a legal duty to adhere, then my tentative conclusion is inconsistent with an all-things-considered moral duty to obey the law in every instance. But modern proponents of a duty to obey defend only a *pro tanto* duty, so they need not disagree with me on this score.

In fact, my position is compatible with a surprisingly broad all-things-considered duty to obey—one that encompasses even the majority of unjust laws that exist in the modern world. I think the following views are mutually consistent: (1) subjects have an all-things-considered moral obligation to obey most unjust laws; (2) judges are legally obligated to adhere; and (3) judges have no moral obligation to obey restrictive rule. These views are consistent because the law rarely requires ordinary subjects to use force at all, much less unjustified force. Sometimes laws require this, but only rarely, even in the most unjust legal systems the world has known. By contrast, restrictive rule requires judges to perform *pro tanto* immoral actions. Within the set of injustices perpetrated by states we can draw several distinctions. First, we can distinguish legally authorized injustices from injustices perpetrated ultra vires—without legal authority or in violation of the law. Within each of these categories we can distinguish *mandated injustices* from *nonmandated injustices*. An injustice is mandated if and only if either a law or a public official acting under color of law requires a private party either to commit a morally impermissible act or to omit a morally obligatory act.

It is easy to *imagine* mandated injustices. Laws could require individuals to molest children, torment animals, break promises, et cetera. Historically, however, only a small fraction of the injustices perpetrated by

---

30. See, e.g., William A. Edmundson, *Three Anarchical Fallacies* (Cambridge: Cambridge University Press, 1998).

states have involved laws requiring private parties to act immorally or to omit morally obligatory acts. Examples include the following: conscripting men to fight in unjust wars; requiring private parties to reveal the location of fugitive slaves or to deliver other innocent victims to malevolent authorities; requiring realtors to discriminate on the basis of race; et cetera.[31] But most unjust laws have not required private parties to act immorally. Even less often have unjust laws required them to use morally unjustified force. Consider typical examples of laws that most readers will consider highly unjust:

1. Until the mid-nineteenth century, married women had no legal right to own real property in the United States, but the law did not forbid private parties from selling land to married women; it merely gave title to their husbands.[32] This was a grave injustice, but the law did not require private parties to act immorally or to omit any morally obligatory acts.
2. The Cuban constitution protects freedom of speech and press only insofar as they "conform to the aims of socialist society."[33] Cuban law authorizes public officials to punish dissidents, but it does not require private parties to act immorally or to omit any morally obligatory acts. Assuming that no Cuban is morally obligated to engage in antisocialist speech (at least if the state has banned it), these injustices are nonmandated.
3. The Thirteenth Regulation under the Nazi Reich Citizenship Law stripped German citizenship from Jewish citizens living overseas.[34]

Other examples of extremely unjust laws that did not require private parties to use unjustified force include laws requiring public officials to protect the property rights of slave owners (e.g., by capturing fugitive slaves), antimiscegenation laws, laws segregating public facilities, most of the laws that sustained South African apartheid, and the federal laws that forcibly relocated and interned Americans of Japanese descent during World War II. In the overwhelming majority of cases in which a private party is subjected to an unjust law or unjust treatment by public officials acting ultra vires, he is himself a victim of the injustice. Rarely does the

---

31. Some injustices have involved public officials, acting ultra vires, requiring private parties to act immorally or to omit morally obligatory acts. There are reports of public officials in the People's Republic of China requiring parents to commit infanticide, although the state denies these reports. See Xiaorong Li, "License to Coerce: Violence against Women, State Responsibility, and Legal Failures in China's Family-Planning Program," *Yale Journal of Law and Feminism* 8 (1996): 145–91.

32. See Marylynn Salmon, *Women and the Law of Property in Early America* (Chapel Hill: University of North Carolina Press, 1986).

33. *Cuba Const.* (1992), art. 53.

34. See David Fraser, "'This Is Not Like Any Other Legal Question': A Brief History of Nazi Law before U.K. and U.S. Courts," *Connecticut Journal of International Law* 19 (2003): 59–125.

unjust law or treatment require *him* to act immorally or to omit morally obligatory acts. The injustice is usually nonmandated.

The thesis held by Rawls and others[35] that we have *pro tanto* reasons to obey unjust laws makes sense if we limit our attention to private parties. The typical unjust law requires private parties to act contrary to their preferences, welfare, and values. It may prevent them from realizing their goals and fulfilling their obligations (e.g., to provide for their children, to marry the mothers of their children), but it does not require them to perform immoral positive actions or to violate anyone else's rights. So they have no countervailing moral reason to undermine the putative *pro tanto* moral duty to obey the law.

Emily emigrates from a reasonably just state to another state, knowing that in the new state the (presumably unjust) laws will require her to pay poll taxes, forbid her to worship God, and forbid her to own real estate. Perhaps, although I emphasize the uncertainty, Emily thereby acquires a *pro tanto* duty to obey these laws if others are relying on her to do so. There is a question of whether that reliance is normatively reasonable, but I shall ignore this worry. I shall accept *arguendo* that with respect to most unjust laws, one who gives actual consent to an unjust law can acquire a *pro tanto* duty to obey it.

In these respects the law imposes very different demands on public officials than on private parties. In impermissible-result cases, the law requires judges either to act in ways that would otherwise be immoral or to omit acts that would otherwise be morally obligatory. These are mandated injustices. Even in suboptimal-but-permissible-result cases, judges have moral reasons to deviate from the law. Being moral reasons themselves they can undermine moral reasons to obey. Therefore, even if consenting to obey a typical unjust law generates a *pro tanto* moral reason to obey, a judge's consent to obey restrictive rule would not give him a *pro tanto* moral reason to obey it because doing so could involve using unjustified force, which he has moral reasons not to use.[36]

Most of the actions that one agent consents to perform on behalf of another, or to assist another to perform, are actions that the first agent has a right to perform. Therefore, consent gives the first agent a duty to perform or to assist in the performance of those actions. However, if one has no moral right to Φ, then one cannot acquire a right to have someone Φ on one's behalf or assist one to Φ. Moreover, the legally favored parties in suboptimal-result cases have no moral right to do what the law would allow them to do, or to receive assistance to do it, or to have it done on their behalf. Therefore, judges do not owe them adherence to the law in these cases. The legally *disfavored* parties did not necessarily consent to the law even if their judge did.

---

35. Rawls, *A Theory of Justice*, pp. 350–55; Honoré, "Must We Obey? Necessity as a Ground of Obligation."

36. Judges have *pro tanto* moral reasons not to consent to obey restrictive rule in the first place. If you ask a judge, "Will you uphold the law when you believe that it requires an unjust result?" I think her honest answer should be, "Not always." See part II.

10.8 PUNISHMENT WITHOUT LAW

So far I have found no argument for obeying restrictive rule, but now I must address an important special case. The suboptimal-result cases that I have had in mind thus far fall in two categories: (1) civil cases in which the law requires a judgment for the plaintiff; and (2) criminal cases in which the law requires a guilty verdict and/or punishment. When judges deviate in such cases, favoring defendants, no one can object that his moral rights have been violated. In a suboptimal-result case, by definition, if the law favors the plaintiff or prosecution, then the plaintiff or prosecution had no moral right to win in the first place.

When the law favors a civil or criminal defendant, by contrast, special questions arise about the moral permissibility of deviation. Deviation in such cases imposes liability without legal authorization. Furthermore, defendants in such cases face adverse judgments without having been duly notified that their actions could have such consequences. Deviation that results in a criminal conviction is especially troublesome because it violates the principle of *nullum crimen, nulla poena, sine lege*.[37] Many would also hold that deviation violates *nullum crimen* when it results in a sentence more severe than the law permits. A supporter of *nullum crimen* could conclude that judges must never deviate from laws favoring criminal defendants.

This depends, however, on what exactly *nullum crimen* forbids. At a minimum it forbids convicting a defendant for an action that is neither *malum in se* nor *malum prohibitum*. This prohibition is also entailed by *minimal retributivism*,[38] a principle that many readers will accept. Minimal retributivism holds that the state is morally forbidden to punish anyone in excess of what he deserves from a moral standpoint. No one deserves to be punished for an action that is neither *malum in se* nor *malum prohibitum*. If minimal retributivism is true, then it is never suboptimal to acquit a defendant for such an action. If the law requires acquittal, then the defendant's action is not, by definition, *malum prohibitum*. Therefore, there are no suboptimal-result cases in which the law requires

---

37. "No crime, no punishment, without law." This maxim "dates from the ancient Greeks." Jerome Hall, *General Principles of Criminal Law*, 2nd ed. (Indianapolis, Ind.: Bobbs-Merrill, 1960), p. 59. See also Joshua Dressler, *Understanding Criminal Law*, 3rd ed. (New York: Lexis, 2001), pp. 39–40; *Rogers v. Tennessee*, 532 U.S. 451, 467–68 (2001); *Sparf v. United States*, 156 U.S. 51, 88 (1895).

38. See J. L. Mackie, "Morality and the Retributive Emotions," in *Persons and Values* (Oxford: Clarendon Press, 1985). Minimal retributivism is also known as *negative retributivism*, *weak retributivism*, and *limiting retributivism*. See C. L. Ten, "Positive Retributivism," *Social Philosophy and Policy* 7 (1990): 194–208; Heidi M. Hurd, *Moral Combat* (Cambridge: Cambridge University Press, 1999), p. 1; Paul H. Robinson, "The A.L.I.'s Proposed Distributive Principle of 'Limiting Retributivism': Does It Mean in Practice Anything Other than Pure Desert?" *Buffalo Criminal Law Review* 7 (2003): 3–15. I challenge minimal retributivism elsewhere, but do not rely on those arguments here. See Jeffrey Brand-Ballard, "Innocents Lost: Proportional Sentencing and the Paradox of Collateral Damage," *Legal Theory* 15 (2009): 65–105.

acquittal and the defendant's action is not *malum in se*. So far there are no suboptimal-result cases in which deviation violates *nullum crimen*. Notice that *nullum crimen* remains a strong principle of limited government, with much work to do, even if we limit its scope to actions that are neither *malum in se* nor *malum prohibitum*.

The interesting cases involve actions *mala in se* that are not prohibited under criminal law. Taken literally, *nullum crimen* also extends to these cases. If there are any suboptimal-result cases in which the law requires acquittal, they are these. A hypothetical illustrates. Chester visits the (fictional) nation of Vortulia. Vortulian officials tell Chester that Vortulian law permits inducing minor children by fraudulent means to engage in sexual activity.[39] Relying upon their assurances, Chester fraudulently induces a nine-year-old into a sexual act. Although he has broken no law, Chester is charged with a sex crime. Is acquitting Chester a suboptimal result?

To answer this question, we must ask whether a judge would have an all-things-considered reason to convict Chester if the law actually permitted convicting him, despite the fact that Chester believed his conduct to be lawful. Imagine for the moment an alternative scenario. Lester visits the nation of Mortulia. Mortulian officials tell Lester that Mortulian law permits inducing children by fraudulent means to engage in sexual activity. However, the officials are misinformed about Mortulian law, which actually gives judges discretion whether to convict such defendants. Lester does not understand this either. Relying upon this misinformation, he fraudulently induces a nine-year-old into a sexual act. He is charged with a sex crime. Does a Mortulian judge who is legally authorized to convict and punish Lester have an all-things-considered reason to do so? One's answer to this question will depend upon one's theory of punishment, among other factors. Consider one who accepts minimal retributivism. She might accept in addition one of these three principles:

1. If someone believes his action to be lawful, then he does not deserve punishment for it.
2. If someone *reasonably* believes his action to be lawful, then he does not deserve punishment for it.
3. If someone reasonably believes his action to be lawful, then the state must not punish him for it, even if he deserves punishment.

Because Lester reasonably believes that tricking children into sex acts is lawful in Mortulia, any of these three principles entails that a Mortulian judge has no all-things-considered reason to convict Lester, assuming minimal retributivism. Assuming that Chester's and Lester's cases are otherwise identical, each principle also entails that acquitting Chester, back in

---

39. The fraud might involve telling the child that you will make her into a movie star if she performs the sex act when you have no intention of doing so.

Legal Duty and Political Obligation

Vortulia, is not a suboptimal result. Each principle entails that there are no suboptimal-result cases in which the law requires acquittal.

We can, however, imagine stricter principles of punishment that would give the Mortulian judge a reason to convict Lester. Consider the following retributive argument:

1R. If punishing a defendant for a seriously immoral action is permitted by law, then this immorality gives the state a reason to punish him.
2R. Lester's actions are seriously immoral.
3. Punishing Lester is permitted by law.
4. Therefore, Mortulia has a reason to punish Lester.

There is also an act-consequentialist argument for this conclusion:

1C. If punishing a defendant is permitted by law and promotes the good, then the fact that it promotes the good gives the state a reason to punish him.
2C. Punishing Lester promotes the good.
3. Punishing Lester is permitted by law.
4. Therefore, Mortulia has a reason to punish Lester.

If both 1R and 1C are false, then there are no suboptimal-result cases in which the law requires acquittal. If either 1R or 1C is true, then such cases might exist, although they are probably rare. If 4 is true and Mortulia has no stronger reason not to punish Lester, then Mortulia has an all-things-considered reason to punish Lester. This entails that acquitting Chester, back in Vortulia, is a suboptimal result. However, if we take *nullum crimen* literally, then it applies to Chester's case and forbids punishment. We appear to have found a case in which *nullum crimen* forbids reaching the optimal result.

Here we reach a fork in the road. One could adopt an exceptionless version of *nullum crimen* and treat cases in which the law requires a suboptimal acquittal as special cases in which judges are obligated to reach suboptimal results simply because *nullum crimen* requires it. Readers who are sufficiently committed to an exceptionless version of *nullum crimen* will take this path.

Alternatively, one could qualify *nullum crimen*, arguing as follows. If either argument for 4 is sound, then *nullum crimen* as applied to Chester's case becomes difficult to justify. This is so because the moral basis for *nullum crimen* is the idea that individuals must not be convicted or punished for actions that they reasonably believe to be lawful. However, both arguments for 4 entail that it is sometimes morally permissible to punish defendants who reasonably believe their actions to be lawful. The retributive argument entails that it is permissible in the case of seriously immoral actions. The consequentialist argument entails that it is permissible if punishing the action promotes the good. If the retributive argument is sound, then there is no moral justification for extending *nullum crimen* to seriously immoral actions. If the consequentialist argument is sound, then there is no moral justification for extending *nullum crimen* to actions the punishment of which promotes the good.

Some special remarks apply to the consequentialist argument. Premise 2C might be false. Punishing Chester for his actions promotes the good only if similar actions are regularly punished in Vortulia. Because Chester's actions are lawful in Vortulia it is unlikely that a regular practice of punishing such actions exists. So it is unlikely that punishing Chester promotes the good. Therefore, it is unlikely that acquitting Chester is a suboptimal result. If punishing Chester does, perchance, promote the good, then acquitting him is a suboptimal result, but *nullum crimen* is not properly applied to his punishment in that instance.

I should also mention two opinions of mine that bear on the *nullum crimen* issue, although my larger argument does not rely upon them. First, I do not believe that modern Western states criminalize too little.[40] Therefore, I believe that acquittal is rarely a suboptimal result when the substantive criminal law requires it. Acquittal might be suboptimal, however, when procedurally required because of a statute of limitations, police or prosecutorial misconduct, et cetera. This brings me to my second opinion: rejecting 1R. In my view the fact that someone deserves to suffer, morally speaking, is rarely (if ever) a good reason for the state to convict or punish him. This is not the dominant opinion in contemporary philosophy, but it is mine. If 1R is false, then the state is permitted to punish only for non-retributive reasons, as 1C holds. Nevertheless, there are gap cases in which it promotes the good to convict a defendant who must be acquitted under law, as when prosecutorial misconduct requires acquitting a dangerous defendant who should be incarcerated for the sake of the general welfare. The procedural rules that generate such cases may, of course, be good rules to promulgate, but I do not believe that courts should treat *nullum crimen* as an independent moral principle that extends to such cases. I do not believe that judges are morally obligated to acquit in *all* such cases, although my argument in part II entails that they are so obligated in most such cases.

Again, my larger argument does not depend upon my idiosyncratic rejection of 1R. I have argued that reaching optimal results does not violate *nullum crimen*, properly understood, whether 1R is true or false.

10.9 RECUSAL OR RESIGNATION

Part I is nearing an end. Its lesson is that judges retain *pro tanto* moral reasons not to reach suboptimal results even when they are legally required

---

40. See, e.g., Douglas Husak, *Overcriminalization: The Limits of the Criminal Law* (New York: Oxford University Press, 2008).

to do so. The law does not undermine these reasons to deviate. But are these really reasons to deviate, specifically? Judges always have another option: recusal.

Let us revisit a Catholic perspective on this issue from §6.11. As do most commentators who have addressed the topic, Judge William Pryor simply assumes that recusal is morally permissible but will rarely be necessary for a Catholic judge.[41] Pryor just wants to avoid material cooperation with specific actions designated as intrinsically evil by his church. Avoiding such cooperation rarely requires recusal—only in cases involving abortion, divorce, capital punishment, unjust warfare, et cetera. In this book, by contrast, I consider a much larger set of suboptimal-result cases. I assume that *all* uses and threats of force against other human beings demand moral justification. Even threatening to use nonlethal force to defend one's life against an imminent threat from a culpable attacker requires moral and legal justification, although adequate justifications exist in such cases.[42]

As I explained in chapter 2, judges threaten and/or use force with virtually every ruling. The judge's cooperation with these actions is proximate, not remote. The judge orders his subordinates to threaten or use force. The use of force or threats thereof is difficult to justify in suboptimal-result cases. On many theories of justice, plenty of cases are suboptimal-result cases, even in reasonably just legal systems. Therefore, whether judges are morally permitted to recuse themselves in every suboptimal-result case is a more urgent question for me than for Catholic scholars.

I begin by extending the scope of one tenet of Pryor's position. Just as he claims that judges are morally permitted to recuse themselves in order to avoid "impermissible cooperation with evil," I shall assume that judges are morally permitted to recuse themselves in order to avoid legally mandated suboptimal results, whether or not these meet the Catholic definition of evil. Again, I am not sure that judges are morally permitted to recuse themselves under these conditions, but I shall assume that they are so as to reach more important issues.

The important question is whether judges are morally *required* to recuse themselves in suboptimal-result cases. Pryor implies that they are in the cases that concern him. Church doctrine forbids adhering to the law when it conflicts too directly with Catholic teachings. Pryor does not entertain the possibility of deviating in such cases. If adhering would

---

41. William H. Pryor, Jr., "The Religious Faith and Judicial Duty of an American Catholic Judge," *Yale Law and Policy Review* 24 (2006): 347–62, pp. 359, 361.

42. Kate brandishes a knife and demands Jodie's purse. The remarkably even-tempered Jodie threatens to punch Kate in the stomach. Under the law, both Kate and Jodie could be prosecuted: Kate for assault with a deadly weapon, and Jodie for misdemeanor assault. Jodie, however, has a complete legal defense. See *Model Penal Code* § 3.04(1) (1985) (use of force in self-defense is justified when used to protect self from present threat).

conflict too directly with Catholic doctrine, then a Catholic judge has a duty to recuse himself, according to Pryor.[43]

Interestingly, some individuals who have faced this conundrum identify resignation, rather than recusal, as the only permissible alternative to adherence. Judge Thomas Gee of the Fifth Circuit expressed such a view in the course of explaining his decision to defer to the Supreme Court after it reversed the judgment of his court: "Subordinate magistrates such as I must either obey the orders of higher authority or yield up their posts to those who will. I obey, since in my view the action required of me by the Court's mandate is only to follow a mistaken course and not an evil one."[44]

Judge Lois Forer, by contrast, resigned:

> I was faced with a legal and moral dilemma. As a judge I had sworn to uphold the law, and I could find no legal grounds for violating an order of the supreme court. Yet five years' imprisonment was grossly disproportionate to the offense.... Given the choice between defying a court order or my conscience, I decided to leave the bench where I had sat for 16 years.[45]

Mahatma Gandhi seems to agree with Judges Gee and Forer that judges must either enforce the law or resign. On March 18, 1922, Gandhi was indicted and convicted at the Circuit House at Shahi Bag. Upon his indictment, he addressed the judge as follows:

> The only course open to you, the Judge, is either to resign your post and thus dissociate yourself from evil, if you feel that the law you are called upon to administer is an evil and that in reality I am innocent; or to inflict on me the severest penalty if you believe that the system and the law you are assisting to administer are good for the people of this country and that my activity is therefore injurious to the public weal.[46]

Apparently even recusal would not satisfy Gandhi. He wants his judge to dissociate himself entirely from the colonial system, which requires resignation from the bench, not just recusal. Notice also that Gandhi insists that the judge has *only* two options: resign or inflict the "severest penalty." This is not literally true: the judge could have inflicted a light sentence. He could also have deviated, overtly or covertly. He could have announced that the law required him to convict and sentence Gandhi, but that the law in this case dictated such an unjust result that he would refuse to apply it. This outcome might not have served Gandhi's political strategy of embarrassing the British Empire, but if the argument of part I is sound, then it would have been ethically permissible

---

43. Pryor, "The Religious Faith and Judicial Duty of an American Catholic Judge," p. 361.
44. *Weber v. Kaiser Aluminum & Chemical Corp.*, 611 F.2d 132, 133 (5th Cir. 1980).
45. Lois Forer, "Justice by Numbers," *Washington Monthly*, April 1992, p. 12.
46. M. K. Gandhi, *Selected Writings of Mahatma Gandhi* (Boston: Beacon Press, 1951), p. 145. Thanks to Michèle Friend.

for the judge to make such an announcement, Gandhi's claim notwithstanding.

Recusal also raises its own moral issues. Judges have *pro tanto* moral reasons against recusal—reasons to hear and decide all assigned cases. This is obvious regarding permissible-result cases. Recusal delays proceedings and imposes administrative costs on the court system. The presence of such reasons explains why judges must not recuse themselves for private reasons such as laziness. There are also fair play considerations. However, I have argued that judges have *pro tanto* moral reasons not to adhere to the law in suboptimal-result cases. One might argue that in a suboptimal-result case, the judge's reasons not to adhere to the law outweigh her reasons to hear and decide the case, yielding a moral reason to recuse herself.

Deviation is another option. By deviating, a judge respects both competing reasons: his reason not to adhere and his reason to decide the case. Ceteris paribus, deviating seems like the ideal choice, but Gandhi, Pryor, Gee, and Forer do not so much as mention the possibility. Perhaps they believe it to be morally impermissible as well, leaving recusal or resignation as the only permissible options. They could reply that the judge has moral reasons not to deviate. These putative reasons would then *combine* with his reasons not to adhere, outweighing his reasons to decide the case and yielding a reason for recusal.

The problem with this argument is that we have not yet discovered reasons against deviation that extend to suboptimal-result cases. I have examined many reasons in part I and found that they are neutralized in suboptimal-result cases. In fact, I see no arguments, even from Catholic principles, against the conclusion that judges have *pro tanto* moral reasons to deviate in suboptimal-result cases, although I am no expert in Catholic ethics.[47] The Catholic arguments for the conclusion that judges have strong moral reasons to recuse themselves seem also to support the conclusion that judges have *pro tanto* moral reasons to deviate. This is so even if Catholics also believe that these *pro tanto* reasons to deviate are usually outweighed by reasons to adhere or to recuse. Church teachings appear to entail that Catholic judges must not obey adherence rules, such as restrictive rule, that exclude as a reason against applying the law the fact that doing so constitutes impermissible material cooperation with evil as the Church understands it.

Moreover, we have reason to believe that a judge's reason to deviate in a suboptimal-result case is usually stronger than her reason to recuse herself. By recusing herself in a suboptimal-result case, the judge simply passes the buck. Not only does she delay proceedings and impose administrative costs on the judicial system, but, more important, she

---

47. There are, however, also *pro tanto* reasons to adhere in suboptimal-result cases, which I discuss in part II. Catholic ethicists could surely state their own *pro tanto* reasons to adhere.

substantially and unnecessarily increases the chance that the case will eventually be disposed of in a suboptimal way. The reason is simple. After she recuses herself, the next judge who is assigned to the case will either adhere, or deviate, or recuse himself, in turn. If he adheres to the law, then a suboptimal result occurs, just as if the original judge had adhered. If he deviates, then the suboptimal result is avoided, anyway.[48] However, if the original judge decides the case and deviates, then she reduces the chance that a suboptimal result will ultimately be reached in the case after any appeals are exhausted. I conclude that the judge has a *pro tanto* moral reason to deviate, not just a reason to self-recuse, in a suboptimal-result case. This is not to say that she has an all-things-considered reason to deviate—we have not yet reached that point. As I shall discuss in part II, reasons to deviate face competition from reasons to adhere. Therefore, the judge might or might not have an all-things-considered reason to adhere to the law in a given suboptimal-result case, depending on the relative strengths of the competing reasons for and against deviation. Such a position contradicts the claim that restrictive rule has practical authority for judges.

If judges have no all-things-considered moral reason to obey restrictive rule, then they are sometimes morally permitted to deviate in suboptimal-result cases. Permissive rules and moderate rules permit this. In part II, I shall defend moderate rules.

---

48. Notwithstanding appeals, et cetera.

Part II

Let us pause to notice where we stand in the dialectic. I have concluded that judges have *pro tanto* moral reasons to deviate in suboptimal-result cases. Therefore, suboptimal-result cases present apparent conflicts between moral reasons and the demands of the law. In these cases judges have strong, although not necessarily conclusive, moral reasons to commit or omit actions that they must omit or commit, respectively, if they are to adhere to the law. They have strong moral reasons to use force when the law forbids them to do so and strong moral reasons to refrain from using force when the law requires them to do so. Schauer observes:

> The outcome of a legal decision may make a litigant a prince or a pauper, famous or infamous, a success or a failure. And when the litigants for whom such consequences attach are standing before the legal decision-maker, the pressure to reach the correct result, rather than the substantively incorrect result generated by faithful application of the rules, is likely to be enormous.[1]

In part I, I sought objective all-things-considered moral reasons for judges to obey restrictive rule. My search was unsuccessful. If that were the end of the story, then we would be left with the conclusion that judges are objectively morally permitted to deviate in all suboptimal-result cases.

Maybe that *is* the end of the story—maybe judges *are* morally permitted to deviate in all suboptimal-result cases. If so, then we may be forced to revise our conception of the rule of law, and the contribution of this book consists exclusively in part I, which established the need for revision. But most observers of the courts seem entirely confident that judges act impermissibly if they deviate in every suboptimal-result case. In fact, some writers believe that judges are *never* morally permitted to deviate. Many others believe that judges are permitted to deviate only when necessary to avoid extreme injustices. In part II, I look for arguments to support these positions that are consistent with my findings in part I. As you will see, I find some of these arguments fairly persuasive. I conclude that deviating in every suboptimal-result case

---

1. Frederick Schauer, *Playing by the Rules: A Philosophical Examination of Rule-Based Decision-Making in Law and in Life* (Oxford: Oxford University Press, 1991), p. 202.

constitutes an impermissible practice in realistic legal systems. That should surprise no one who believes in the rule of law. But I also conclude that judges *are* morally permitted to deviate in some suboptimal-result cases. Even in reasonably just legal systems there could, in principle, be cases in which judges were morally permitted to deviate in order to avoid results that were only moderately suboptimal. This conclusion is unorthodox. So is my argument. I contend that the permissibility of deviation in a given case turns on some systemic factors that are ordinarily seen as irrelevant to adjudication.

11

Systemic Effects

This chapter introduces some new arguments for the thesis that judges have all-things-considered reasons to obey nonpermissive rules. These arguments appeal to the *systemic effects* of deviating from the law: effects on individuals other than parties to the case. Systemic-effects arguments belong to nonideal theory—the study of how to act when other agents do not act as they should.[1] In this chapter, and in the rest of part II, I shall explore the powers and limitations of systemic-effects arguments.

First, a few words about systemic effects. We can distinguish three aspects of any court decision: its content, its actual legality, and its perceived legality. A decision has different effects in virtue of different aspects. The content of a decision has direct effects on the parties, of course. Civil damage awards redistribute money from defendants to plaintiffs, sentencing decisions send convicts to prison, et cetera. Losing money and being incarcerated are disadvantageous whether or not the court's decision was legally correct and whether or not anyone perceives the court's decision as legally correct.[2]

Equally important for my purposes is whether observers classify a decision as legally correct or incorrect. This classification has effects—systemic effects—that extend beyond the parties to the case. I shall argue that the systemic effects of deviation constitute important *pro tanto* moral reasons to adhere to the law—reasons that apply in both optimal-result and suboptimal-result cases.

---

1. The term comes from John Rawls, *A Theory of Justice* (Cambridge, Mass.: Harvard University Press, 1971), pp. 8–9, 245–46, 351. It is also known as *partial-compliance theory*. See Tamar Schapiro, "Compliance, Complicity, and the Nature of Nonideal Conditions," *Journal of Philosophy* 100 (2003): 329–55; Liam B. Murphy, *Moral Demands in Nonideal Theory* (Oxford: Oxford University Press, 2000); George Sher, *Approximate Justice: Studies in Non-Ideal Theory* (Lanham, Md.: Rowman & Littlefield, 1997).

2. The content of a decision also has effects on individuals who are affiliated with the parties: friends, family members, business associates, et cetera. Again, what matters here is content, not legality or perceived legality. Losing one's father or business partner to prison is disadvantageous whether or not the decision is, or is perceived to be, legally correct. See Jeffrey Brand-Ballard, "Innocents Lost: Proportional Sentencing and the Paradox of Collateral Damage," *Legal Theory* 15 (2009): 65–105.

For your sake and mine, I wish my arguments were simple, decisive, and proceeded from widely accepted premises. Sadly, that is not the case. The arguments are complicated, unfamiliar, and far from conclusive. They employ philosophical resources and arguments that remain controversial in the literature. Persuading you to embrace these resources and arguments would require wandering into these debates and take me too far afield. I cite defenses of these positions in the literature, but these defenses are not dispositive.

In addition to resting upon controversial philosophical premises, systemic-effects arguments rely upon empirical hypotheses about complex social facts, such as the extent to which judges actually imitate the deviational tendencies of their colleagues. Reliable data supporting or challenging these hypotheses would be difficult to collect. I cite the studies I have found, but these are few, speculative, and not directly on point.[3]

I shall not try to prove the philosophical and empirical premises of systemic-effects arguments. Rather, I shall show how these premises could be used to support a nonpermissive adherence rule. I anticipate that some readers are so committed to such a rule that, in the absence of other sound arguments for it, they will come to look more favorably upon premises that can be used to support it—even premises that seem dubious at first.

The arguments needed to support a nonpermissive rule are quite different from those criticized in part I. They do not support the undermining principle. Rather, they support *pro tanto* reasons to adhere in suboptimal-result cases—reasons that compete with judges' natural reasons to avoid suboptimal results. These arguments are prospective[4] and agent-neutral, not retrospective and agent-relative. In subsequent chapters, I shall explain why these distinctions matter.

11.1 GOLDMAN ON SYSTEMIC EFFECTS

Alan Goldman presents a systemic-effects argument that, if sound, provides a reason for a judge to adhere to the law even if she correctly believes it to require a suboptimal result. It is somewhat ironic that Goldman should be the author to provide such a promising argument for obeying a

---

3. See §14.1.

4. Prospective arguments are often called *consequentialist* arguments, but this usage causes confusion, because it connotes consequentialist moral theories that hold that prospective reasons are the *only* ultimate moral reasons. Even nonconsequentialists accept prospective moral reasons: "All ethical doctrines worth our attention take consequences into account in judging rightness. One which did not would simply be irrational, crazy." Rawls, *A Theory of Justice*, p. 30.

Systemic Effects

nonpermissive rule. He is not especially enthusiastic about rules.[5] As a legal philosopher, he opposes formalism: the view that judges must obey first-order rules of law.[6] As a moral philosopher, he defends weak particularism.[7] Nevertheless, he faults strong particularists for ignoring "situations that do call for following rules even when ordinary judgment opposes them...."[8] He thinks there are special contexts in which agents should, indeed, adopt strong rules. These include cases involving "individually harmless acts that have cumulatively harmful results."[9] His paradigm is, conveniently, judges deviating in suboptimal-result cases. He refers to "the fundamental but unwritten rule of the legal system: that judges must defer to legal requirements even when they disagree morally with their implications in particular cases."[10] He states that we want judges "to accept a rule as morally binding that they will follow settled law in their decisions, even when they disagree with the outcomes."[11] I read this as claiming that judges must obey restrictive rule. In fact, as do most writers on the topic,[12] Goldman takes for granted that judges must obey restrictive rule.[13] He sets himself the task of explaining why they must, but he never entertains the possibility that they might not have this obligation at all.

First, let us consider Goldman's defense of restrictive rule, beginning with his description of a suboptimal-result case (this was my model for Yasmin's case in §5.3):

> [C]onsider the specific case of a bank seeking to foreclose on a house and evict a poor, elderly widow. The additional assets to the bank will have a negligible effect on its overall financial position, while the widow will suffer greatly if evicted. Similarly, a single court's decision on moral merits instead of law will have little effect on the stability or predictability of the legal system.

Using this case, Goldman defends restrictive rule, describing it as a "second-best" strategy:

> The problem is that the cumulative effects of many judges reasoning only on these grounds could be disastrous to the legal and financial institutions (also, in our example, to the ability of widows to obtain loans). This special fallibility, the inability in the absence of a rule to take account of overall effects in the single case, together with the fact that morally minded judges

---

5. Alan H. Goldman, *Practical Rules: When We Need Them and When We Don't* (Cambridge: Cambridge University Press, 2002), p. 36 ("[T]he adoption of rules in normal contexts represents a suspect and defeasible strategy").
6. Ibid., ch. 3.
7. "[T]he justification for and coherence of particular judgments do not require their support by universal rules." Ibid., p. 2; also ch. 4.
8. Ibid., p. 3.
9. Ibid., p. 5.
10. Ibid., p. 8.
11. Ibid., p. 42.
12. See those quoted in §8.4.
13. But see §14.3.

will be tempted to bypass law on moral grounds in such cases, justifies the imposition of a rule requiring a legal decision according to law and not unfettered moral perception.[14]

More generally:

[J]udges may correctly perceive that they could do better morally by following their own moral perceptions in particular cases in which legal norms require different decisions. But the cumulative effect of allowing such judgments would be to destroy the legal authority of legislators and of the law itself. Hence the rule that removes the authority of judges to decide cases on direct moral grounds is both itself a moral rule and a cornerstone of the legal system.[15]

I think Goldman outlines an argument with the right structure, but it moves too quickly. In the next several sections I shall unpack his argument. I introduce some intermediate steps that he omits and rebut some objections that he neglects.

First, Goldman's argument requires some philosophically controversial premises that he never states, much less defends. I shall draw out and examine these premises. I am prepared to grant them, but doing so has implications that we must eventually recognize.[16]

Second, Goldman's systemic-effects argument as presented in his book, *Practical Rules*, does not actually support the conclusion that judges must obey an adherence rule. At most it supports the conclusion that lawmakers should promulgate one. I present a supplemental argument that fills this gap, supporting the conclusion that judges must obey an adherence rule.[17] Adopting this argument, however, makes restrictive rule more difficult to defend over moderate rules.

Third, Goldman's systemic-effects argument by itself supports a non-permissive rule but not necessarily restrictive rule. It leaves various moderate rules in the running. Goldman notices this. In fact, he acknowledges that a moderate rule initially appears to be optimal.[18] Then he argues that all moderate rules are flawed, leaving restrictive rule as the only remaining option.[19] I shall challenge his arguments. I think there is a moderate rule to which his objections do not apply. Ultimately, I shall conclude that

---

14. Goldman, *Practical Rules*, p. 43.
15. Ibid.
16. See chapter 14.
17. In a subsequent paper, Goldman presents his own argument for a similar conclusion, not pertaining to judges. Alan H. Goldman, "The Rationality of Complying with Rules: Paradox Resolved," *Ethics* 116 (2006): 453–70. Goldman, however, supports a counterpart to restrictive rule that I reject. I discuss his paper in chapter 13.
18. "The optimal pattern would consist in some percentage of widows spared just below the threshold at which cumulative damage to the legal system begins to outweigh the further good to individual widows." Goldman, *Practical Rules*, p. 44.
19. Ibid., pp. 44–55.

Systemic Effects

there may be a sound systemic-effects argument for moderate rules, but not for restrictive rule.[20]

In discussing systemic effects it is important to remember that we are seeking objective reasons for a judge to adhere when she *correctly* determines that the law requires a suboptimal result. We are imagining a judge who deviates for moral reasons and advances a moral purpose as she sees it. We must argue that deviation has systemic effects that compromise other moral purposes to a greater degree and that these moral purposes also provide the judge with reasons. There is no point in trying to persuade a judge who is an avid rifle hunter to adhere to a gun-control law in the case at bar by pointing out that deviating will encourage the sport of hunting. Instead, one must argue that deviating will compromise other values to which the judge herself is committed. Ideally, the proponent of adherence would argue that deviation is somehow self-defeating for the judge *given her own values*. That is one of the ground rules of this dialectic.

In the rest of this chapter I shall examine systemic effects more closely. They fall into two categories: *adaptation effects* and *mimetic effects*. Goldman does not distinguish between these, but I shall argue that they are not interchangeable. Mimetic effects, I shall suggest, are much more useful than adaptation effects for defending the conclusion that judges must obey nonpermissive rules.

11.2 ADAPTATION

First, consider the phenomenon of adaptation. When a judge deviates, her decision can lead nonjudicial actors to adapt their behavior. Bank sues Borrower for defaulting on her small-business loan. Judge rules for Borrower. Practicing lawyers and scholars criticize this decision as legally incorrect. They believe that the controlling statute entails a judgment for Bank on the facts presented and that no higher source of law dictates otherwise. Likewise, journalists report that Judge has disregarded the law.

Bank officers at other banks also notice the decision. What effect will it have on their behavior? This will depend in part on what they believe to be Judge's reasons for ruling in Borrower's favor. If they conclude that Judge simply made a random, careless mistake in applying the law, then the effect on bank behavior will be minimal. Banks already knew that judges make mistakes. Some mistakes favor lenders, others favor borrowers. Banks have no incentive to alter their behavior provided they conclude that the mistake was random and does not portend an increase in rulings unfavorable to lenders.

Suppose, instead, that bank officers reach the following conclusions: first, that Judge's decision evidences a trend of increasing judicial deviation

20. See chapter 13.

in loan-default cases in which the law requires results that judges consider to be suboptimal; and second, that judges in their jurisdiction will often conclude that results favoring lenders, rather than small-business owners, are suboptimal. Rational bank officers who accept these premises will conclude that judges are becoming more inclined to deviate in order to reach verdicts that favor small-business owners over lenders. Accordingly, banks may begin to offer fewer small-business loans, and/or to offer them on less favorable terms.

This is a simple argument from economic incentives. It may represent a sound argument for lawmakers to promulgate a rule that requires a judgment for Bank. The argument requires some unstated normative and empirical premises, but they are fairly plausible ones. Later, however, I shall argue that adaptation effects cannot provide a general reason for a judge to obey a nonpermissive rule.[21]

11.3 MIMESIS

In this section I introduce another kind of systemic effect, distinct from adaptation. Whereas nonjudicial actors *adapt* to judicial decisions, other judges may attempt to *imitate* prior decisions. The decisions of one or more judges (*anterior judges*) can lead another judge (a *posterior judge*) to make a decision that resembles the anterior decision(s) in some respect. Consider judges who follow legal precedent. A judge applies a certain legal doctrine to a certain fact pattern. A posterior judge, at the same level or below, hears a case with a similar fact pattern and treats the anterior judge's decision as a reason to apply the same legal doctrine. Or a judge interprets a legal standard in a certain way and a posterior judge treats the anterior decision as a reason to interpret a similar standard similarly.[22]

Judges who follow precedent imitate one another at the first-order level. I am interested in second-order imitation, which I call *mimesis*.[23] Mimesis occurs when a judge imitates the way in which other judges treat not a particular legal standard, but a whole category of legal standards. For example, a judge engages in mimesis if she follows precedents more often, the higher she believes to be the rate at which other judges follow precedents.[24] Likewise, she engages in mimesis if she adheres to statutes more often, the higher she believes to be the rate at which other judges adhere to statutes.

All legal standards—not just case law—can be the object of mimesis, including constitutions, statutes, and administrative regulations. Also,

---

21. See §13.7.
22. I discuss precedent in chapter 16.
23. I apologize for the Greek, but if I called it *imitation*, then readers would assume I meant "following precedent."
24. The belief need not be conscious.

mimesis can refer to any way of treating a legal standard, not just adhering to it. Mimesis occurs when a judge adheres to *or deviates from* a certain legal standard in part because he believes that anterior judges have adhered to or deviated from other legal standards. Furthermore, on my definition of mimesis, the posterior judge need not consciously treat the anterior decisions as a reason to decide as he does. All that I require for mimesis is some kind of contributory causal link between anterior and posterior decisions.

Mimesis is socially beneficial when anterior decisions causally contribute to a posterior judge reaching an optimal result. For example, an anterior decision to adhere in an optimal-result case might encourage a posterior judge to adhere in another optimal-result case, one in which he would otherwise have deviated. This is a success story for mimesis. *Mimetic failure* occurs when optimal decisions by anterior judges make a causal contribution to an outcome in which a posterior judge reaches a suboptimal result. This happens because judges do not always agree about which results are suboptimal. Imagine a group of judges who deviate in all and only cases that Dave the Democrat considers to be suboptimal-result cases. From Dave's perspective, these are optimal judges—*Group* O. There are, however, other judges in the system who disagree with Dave about which results are suboptimal. From Dave's perspective, they are subpar judges. He might think them less enlightened, less morally perceptive, less intelligent, less careful, or less scrupulous than Group O. These subpar judges begin to notice when the members of Group O deviate. Trying to imitate Group O, they begin deviating in what *they* believe to be suboptimal-result cases, thereby reaching results that Dave considers suboptimal. Thus, although Group O always reaches results that Dave considers optimal, it causally contributes to results that he considers suboptimal.

Of course, reasonable people disagree about which results are suboptimal, so they disagree about who actually belongs to Group O. The structure of the scenario just described remains the same if we substitute Ruth the Republican for Dave the Democrat. Because I am not trying to convince you that any particular result is suboptimal, I shall simply refer to optimal and suboptimal results in the abstract. For the sake of concreteness, I shall continue using Yasmin's eviction as my proxy for a suboptimal result, without presuming to have established that it is in fact suboptimal.

If my story about Group O is realistic, then deviation, even in suboptimal-result cases, can encourage deviation in optimal-result cases. This is a significant claim. By deviating in an optimal-result case a judge performs the *same type* of *pro tanto* wrongful action, and causes the *same type* of bad effects, as when he adheres in a suboptimal-result case. A suboptimal result, such as evicting Yasmin, is just as suboptimal when the law forbids it as when the law requires it. It is no less wrongful for the judge and no less harmful to Yasmin.

I shall argue that because deviating can be just as bad as adhering, the need to prevent posterior judges from reaching suboptimal results can constitute a *pro tanto* moral reason for a judge to reach a suboptimal result in the case at bar. Mimetic failure can provide *pro tanto* reasons for judges to adhere. These are, moreover, reasons of the right kind to compete with the strong reasons that judges have to deviate in suboptimal-result cases. In some suboptimal-result cases the former reasons win, producing an all-things-considered reason to adhere. If there is any truth to the common assumption that deviation, as such, "damages the rule of law," then I think the destructive mechanism at work must involve mimetic failure. Mimetic failure also explains why even optimal judges inevitably confront negative-gap cases[25] if they inhabit jurisdictions in which more than a certain fraction of the other judges are less accurate identifiers of suboptimal results.

In the rest of this chapter and the next, I argue that the prospect of mimetic failure gives the judges in Group O reasons to obey a nonpermissive rule.

11.4 SYSTEMIC EFFECTS AS REASONS TO ADHERE

My ultimate position will be that mimetic failure provides an all-things-considered reason to adhere in some suboptimal-result cases. However, spelling out the argument will take much of part II. I begin by arguing that judges in Group O have reasons to obey a nonpermissive rule. The first obstacle to overcome is that for any given judge, the systemic effects that she actually causes by deviating do not provide her with even a *pro tanto* reason to adhere:

> **Individual Adherence Argument**
> 1. If Agent B has an objective *pro tanto* moral reason to Φ, then Agent A has an objective *pro tanto* moral reason not to act in ways that discourage B from Φ-ing.
> 2. Judges have objective *pro tanto* moral reasons to adhere in optimal-result cases.
> 3. If Judge J deviates in a suboptimal-result case, then she will discourage some other judge from adhering in some optimal-result case.
> 4. Therefore, Judge J has an objective *pro tanto* moral reason to adhere in the suboptimal-result case.

Here is a crude example of what the individual adherence argument envisions. Picture a judge who initially believes that her reasons to adhere are stronger than any reasons to deviate. Then she learns that an anterior

---

25. See §5.4 on gap cases.

judge has deviated, which leads her to revise downward her belief about the strength of her own reasons to adhere. Perhaps she was concerned that deviating would injure her professional reputation, but she is reassured by learning that the anterior judge has not suffered reputational damage. Or perhaps she previously believed that deviation was always wrong, but she trusts the moral judgment of the anterior judge enough that his decision changes her mind. Or perhaps the anterior decision influences her subliminally without her paying it any conscious attention. Whatever her mental process, the result is that she deviates in what she mistakenly believes to be a suboptimal-result case. The fact that deviating in the anterior case has this result gives the anterior judge a *pro tanto* reason to adhere, according to the individual adherence argument.

The individual adherence argument is valid, but the truth of the first and third premises depends on what it means to *discourage* someone from acting. Here is a broad understanding of *discourage*. Agent B believes that she has *pro tanto* reasons not to Φ.[26] She intends to Φ, nevertheless, because she believes that she has stronger reasons to Φ. If the actions of A cause B to stop believing that she has an all-things-considered reason to Φ, and this change in belief motivates B not to Φ, then A discourages B from Φ-ing. On this understanding of *discourage*, A need not have the goal of changing the beliefs or conduct of B, nor need A even be aware that his actions will affect B. In the rest of this chapter, I shall examine further this broad understanding of *discourage*.

11.5 MORAL-MORAL PRISONER'S DILEMMAS

The third premise of the individual adherence argument is empirically false as to most suboptimal-result cases. Judge Jack's choice to deviate in a given case does not lead any identifiable judge, who would otherwise have adhered, to deviate in a subsequent optimal-result case. Remember, our concern is not that Jack's deviation will cause other judges to decide *similar* cases similarly, as when they follow precedent. Our concern is posterior judges deviating in optimal-result cases as a result of Jack's deviation in a suboptimal-result case. One can agree that a pattern of widespread deviation in suboptimal-result cases encourages deviation in optimal-result cases and still deny that *Jack's* individual choice to deviate in a single case encourages any other identifiable judge to deviate in an optimal-result case. So the individual adherence argument does not establish that any individual judge always has objective *pro tanto* reasons to adhere.

Nevertheless, I concede the conceptual possibility of a particular judge who, by choosing to deviate in a suboptimal-result case, provokes some posterior judge to deviate in an optimal-result case. This would be the case if, for example, the posterior judge so revered the anterior judge in

---

26. These reasons could be prudential, moral, or what have you.

particular that he would attempt to imitate her, but would do so incorrectly. The anterior judge in that case would have a *pro tanto* reason to obey restrictive rule.

There is even the conceptual possibility of a "hypersensitive" legal system in which any judge who deviates provokes deviation in an optimal-result case. Imagine a posterior judge who is extremely aware of how all other judges decide, extremely inclined to engage in mimesis, and an extremely poor identifier of suboptimal results. A system with many such judges is hypersensitive. Judges in such systems would have *pro tanto* reasons to obey restrictive rule.

In realistic legal systems, however, few deviant decisions provoke deviation by other judges in optimal-result cases. This entails that, as Goldman observes, a judge assigned to decide a suboptimal-result case finds herself in a special type of collective action problem: a multiplayer *moral-moral prisoner's dilemma*.[27] Players in a standard prisoner's dilemma have reasons of self-interest to defect from the cooperative scheme, although collective defection is collectively and individually self-defeating. Similarly, each player in a moral-moral prisoner's dilemma has *pro tanto* moral reasons to defect, although collective defection produces a morally inferior outcome.

Anyone who believes that systemic effects give judges reasons to obey a nonpermissive rule must identify reasons for parties to a moral-moral prisoner's dilemma to cooperate. Some readers will find intuitive the idea that such reasons exist, just as some find intuitive the idea that parties to a standard prisoner's dilemma have reasons to cooperate.[28] Those who do not find the idea intuitive will want arguments. Several are possible. First, one could argue that an agent who defects in a moral-moral prisoner's dilemma is morally responsible for more than the direct consequences of his defection. Alternatively, one could "introduce a different notion of rationality and of moral reasons."[29] Goldman and Christopher Kutz take the first path, Christopher McMahon the second.[30] Other approaches are surely possible. In the rest of this chapter I shall offer my own version of the argument, drawing on the insights of these authors and others. My argument is designed to describe reasons to cooperate in more detail and to bolster the intuitions of readers who already believe in such reasons. My

---

27. Goldman, *Practical Rules*, pp. 13, 49–55. See related discussion in Garrett Cullity, "Moral Free Riding," *Philosophy and Public Affairs* 24 (1995): 3–34; Michael Otsuka, "The Paradox of Group Beneficence," *Philosophy and Public Affairs* 20 (1991): 132–49; George Klosko, "Parfit's Moral Arithmetic and the Obligation to Obey the Law," *Canadian Journal of Philosophy* 20 (1990): 191–214; Jean Hampton, "Free-Rider Problems in the Production of Collective Goods," *Economics and Philosophy* 3 (1987): 245–73.

28. "Intuitively, rational persons ought to be able to cooperate [in a prisoner's dilemma]." David Copp, "Introduction: Metaethics and Normative Ethics," in *Oxford Handbook of Ethical Theory*, ed. David Copp (New York: Oxford University Press, 2006), p. 17.

29. Goldman, "The Rationality of Complying with Rules: Paradox Resolved," p. 456.

30. Ibid.; Christopher Kutz, *Complicity: Ethics and Law for a Collective Age* (Cambridge: Cambridge University Press, 2000); Christopher McMahon, *Collective Rationality and Collective Reasoning* (Cambridge: Cambridge University Press, 2001).

argument might also persuade readers who do not share these intuitions, but I feel little pressure to persuade them. If there are no reasons to cooperate in moral-moral prisoner's dilemmas, and the arguments of part I are sound, then judges have no all-things-considered reason to obey a nonpermissive rule. I think even readers who find reasons to cooperate counterintuitive will find that conclusion still more counterintuitive. I think we can ultimately avoid it, but only with some effort.

11.6 COLLECTIVE REASONS

As far as I know, Goldman was the first to try to use a systemic-effects argument to solve a moral-moral prisoner's dilemma. He uses the example of citizens who contemplate rerouting their tax payments to charitable causes. He adopts the premise that a rule requiring citizens to pay taxes is justified by the value of the public goods provided by tax revenue. He also assumes that "[g]iven the negligible effect of the contribution of each on the provision of the public goods, and the amount of tax money that must pay for government bureaucracy, it is easy to claim that each could produce a morally better result by giving directly to a charity or needy person."[31] Nevertheless, Goldman claims, the group of all citizens has a "group obligation" to produce the public goods.[32] This means more than that the members of the group have individual obligations. It means that the group as such has an obligation. I am obligated to feed my dogs and my neighbor to feed hers, but we do not form a group with group obligations. By contrast, my wife, my daughter, and I could have a group obligation to feed our dogs. At least we could have such an obligation if groups as such can have obligations.

A moral obligation is a kind of moral reason, so a group obligation is a kind of group reason or (synonymously) *collective reason*. The question whether groups can have reasons is prior to the question whether groups can have obligations. Hereafter, when I refer to group reasons or group obligations I shall mean reasons or obligations of the group as such.

If Group O can have reasons, then we can modify the individual adherence argument to apply to Group O:

Group Adherence Argument
1. If Agent B has an objective *pro tanto* moral reason to Φ, then Agent A has an objective *pro tanto* moral reason not to act in ways that discourage B from Φ-ing.
2. Judges have objective *pro tanto* moral reasons to adhere in optimal-result cases.

---

31. Goldman, "The Rationality of Complying with Rules: Paradox Resolved," p. 454.
32. Ibid., p. 463.

3. By deviating in all suboptimal-result cases, Group O will discourage some other judges from adhering in some optimal-result cases.
4. Therefore, Group O has an objective *pro tanto* moral reason not to follow a policy of deviating in all suboptimal-result cases (i.e., a reason to obey a nonpermissive rule).

If Goldman is correct, then something like the group adherence argument has potential. However, he says virtually nothing about the conditions under which groups have reasons. In the next sections I shall describe these conditions in greater detail. Then we can see how Group O satisfies them.

11.7 COLLECTIVE REASONS AND SHARED INTENTIONS

A theory of collective reasons specifies conditions under which a group of human beings, as such, has reasons. There is a substantial literature on collective reasons, most of which concentrates on group obligations. For the group adherence argument to succeed, some theory of collective reasons must be correct. I expect that any of several theories could support the argument. I shall not defend the superiority of any one theory, but shall present an influential one that serves my purposes. This theory proceeds from the assumption that a group as such can have intentional states, namely intentions. Some readers will question this assumption, reasoning as follows. Two human beings can share a single intentional state only if they share a single mind. It is metaphysically impossible for two human beings to share a single mind. Therefore, two human beings cannot share a single intentional state.

The major premise of the preceding argument has been refuted by Michael Bratman, Margaret Gilbert, David Velleman, John Searle, Carol Rovane, Raimo Tuomela, and others. They advance conceptions of shared intentional states that do not presuppose the existence of any kind of metaphysically problematic group mind.[33] Bratman's theory of shared intention illustrates. Bratman takes a functional approach, asking what roles shared intentions play in our lives. He argues that shared intentions serve three main functions: they help us to coordinate our intentional activities, facilitate the coordination of further planning, and provide a

---

33. See, e.g., Carol Rovane, *The Bounds of Agency* (Princeton, N.J.: Princeton University Press, 1998); David Velleman, "How to Share an Intention," *Philosophy and Phenomenological Research* 57 (1997): 29–50; Margaret Gilbert, *Living Together: Rationality, Sociality, and Obligation* (Lanham, Md.: Rowman & Littlefield, 1996); Raimo Tuomela, *The Importance of Us* (Stanford, Calif.: Stanford University Press, 1995); Michael E. Bratman, "Shared Intention," *Ethics* 104 (1993): 97–113; John R. Searle, "Collective Intentions and Intentional Actions," in *Intentions in Communication*, eds. Philip R. Cohen, Jerry Morgan, and Martha E. Pollack (Cambridge, Mass.: MIT Press, 1990); Margaret Gilbert, *On Social Facts* (Princeton, N.J.: Princeton University Press, 1989).

background framework that structures bargaining. On Bratman's view, two individuals share an intention if and only if each has certain attitudes that are specially interrelated with those of the other.[34] A shared intention to paint the house might form in the following way. I say, "I'll paint the house with you if you'll do the same." You reply, "Then I'll do so." At this point each of us has the intention that we paint the house together. Furthermore, each of us intends that we paint the house in accordance with and because of his own intentions and those of the other. Each of us intends that the intentions of the other, along with his own, be jointly efficacious. All of this is common knowledge between us. I know that you know, you know that I know that you know, and so on.[35] Here is Bratman's full analysis of shared intention:

We intend to J if and only if
1. (a) I intend that we J and (b) you intend that we J.
2. I intend that we J together in accordance with and because of 1a, 1b, and meshing subplans of 1a and 1b; you intend that we J in accordance with and because of 1a, 1b, and meshing subplans of 1a and 1b.
3. 1 and 2 are common knowledge between us.[36]

Bratman's theory shows how the attitudes of individuals can constitute a shared intention, notwithstanding the fact that an individual seems only to be able to intend that she herself perform an action, not that anyone else do so.[37] Bratman appeals to the fact that we have the capacity not only to intend to act but also to intend that some state of affairs obtain. He proposes that we can intend a joint action just in the sense that we can intend that we perform the joint action. Bratman acknowledges, however, that such intentions are subject to an "influence condition."[38] In other words, I can intend that we jointly act only if I see myself as affecting both the fact that you play your role in our joint action and the manner in which you do so. I must believe that you will play your role in our activity in part because of and in accordance with my intention that we act. Velleman has argued that we can understand our two intentions as combining to form a single joint intention—an intentional state that motivates each of us precisely by virtue of representing itself as having this

---

34. This is not to suggest that shared intentions die with the brains of the human beings who share them, any more than an individual intention dies with the brain of the human being who has it.

35. For this sense of *common knowledge* see David Lewis, *Convention* (Cambridge, Mass.: Harvard University Press, 1969).

36. Bratman, "Shared Intention," p. 106.

37. For a different solution see Raimo Tuomela and Kaarlo Miller, "We-Intentions," *Philosophical Studies* 53 (1988): 115–37.

38. Michael E. Bratman, "I Intend that We J," in *Contemporary Action Theory*, eds. Ghita Holmström-Hintikka and Raimo Tuomela (Netherlands: Kluwer, 1997).

motivational efficacy.[39] In this way we can understand the idea of two human beings sharing a single token intention.

I find it both convenient and accurate to refer to a group as a *collective agent*[40] if its members share an intention. A collective agent is a single agent composed of two or more different human beings yet irreducible to its constituents.[41] Many have argued, and I agree, that a collective agent can have its own reasons and obligations.[42]

11.8 OPTIMIZING COLLECTIVE AGENTS

For my purposes, two judicial intentions are especially important: to adhere to the law and to avoid reaching results that one considers suboptimal. Most judges in realistic legal systems have both. Only the most incompetent or corrupt judge is indifferent either to the law or to the optimality of results. A judge could, of course, find herself with desires that conflict with these intentions. She could reconsider and/or revise either or both of these intentions. But a typical judge maintains both of these intentions throughout her career.

Some will claim that every judge is morally obligated to form these intentions before hearing her first case and to maintain and fulfill them while she remains on the bench. I think this is probably correct. Such obligations can probably be derived from natural duties, combined with the judge's decision to remain a judge and the situation in which she finds herself. However, my argument requires no defense of this position. I can limit myself to judges who actually have these intentions, whether or not they are morally obligated to form them. My argument depends only on the premise that these intentions generate reasons for action.

---

39. Velleman, "How to Share an Intention."

40. Also known as a collective subject, plural subject, group person, group agent, et cetera.

41. See, e.g., Margaret Gilbert, *Sociality and Responsibility: New Essays in Plural Subject Theory* (Lanham, Md.: Rowman & Littlefield, 2000); Rovane, *The Bounds of Agency*; Tuomela, *The Importance of Us*; Philip Pettit, *The Common Mind: An Essay on Psychology, Society, and Politics* (Oxford: Oxford University Press, 1993). The terminology of agency, although useful, can mislead. The most familiar agents are individual human beings. They possess the highest degree of moral status. They develop extremely complex psychologies as they mature. Most collective agents, by contrast, are psychologically rudimentary and possess only a low degree of moral status, if any. Consider a group that shares only a house-painting intention. It constitutes an agent only in the most minimal sense. It does not enjoy any moral rights beyond those of its individual members. When I refer to a group as an *agent* I do not mean to imply that it possesses anything approaching the psychological complexity or moral status of a typical adult.

42. See, e.g., Philip Pettit, "Responsibility Incorporated," *Ethics* 117 (2007): 171–201; Tracy Isaacs, "Collective Moral Responsibility and Collective Intention," *Midwest Studies in Philosophy* 30 (2006): 59–73; Abraham Sesshu Roth, "Shared Agency and Contralateral Commitments," *Philosophical Review* 113 (2004): 359–410; Gilbert, *Sociality and Responsibility*.

In addition to forming these individual intentions, the members of a group of judges could form shared intentions with similar content. Consider a shared intention to avoid suboptimal results. On Bratman's theory, Judges Jack and Jill share this intention if and only if:

(1)(a)(i) Jack intends that Jack and Jill avoid suboptimal results.
(1)(a)(ii) Jack intends that Jack and Jill avoid suboptimal results in accordance with and because of meshing subplans of (1)(a)(i) and (1)(b)(i).
(1)(b)(i) Jill intends that Jack and Jill avoid suboptimal results.
(1)(b)(ii) Jill intends that Jack and Jill avoid suboptimal results in accordance with and because of meshing subplans of (1)(a)(i) and (1)(b)(i).
(2) It is common knowledge between Jack and Jill that (1).

If Jack and Jill share this intention, then they constitute an *optimizing collective agent*. Notice that they cannot share it unless they intend to mesh subplans.[43] How well their subplans mesh will depend upon the extent to which they share judgments about which results are optimal. The more they disagree about which results are optimal, the more their subplans conflict. So they cannot form an optimizing collective agent unless they share many, perhaps most, optimality judgments. If they share enough optimality judgments, then they can form interlocking intentions and meshing subplans.

If Jack and Jill share both the intention to avoid suboptimal results and enough optimality judgments, then Jill encourages and helps Jack to deviate in suboptimal-result cases and to adhere in optimal-result cases, at least when she can do so without compromising more important goals. One way in which Jill encourages Jack is by deviating herself in suboptimal-result cases and adhering in optimal-result cases. She considers her effects on Jack to be, at least, welcome side effects of her decisions. Likewise for Jack, mutatis mutandis. Each sees deviation by the other in suboptimal-result cases as partial fulfillment of the shared intention of the optimizing collective agent to which they belong. Neither Jack nor Jill condemns, discourages, or disavows such deviation by the other.

In the remainder of this book I shall present arguments requiring at least one of the following premises: (1) some judges in realistic legal systems actually form optimizing collective agents; or (2) judges in realistic legal systems are morally obligated to form optimizing collective agents. I think both premises are true. Some readers will disagree. Some will reject the very idea of shared intentions. I shall not directly defend either premise or offer much more in defense of the underlying theory of collective agency. Rather, I shall advance indirect arguments. I claim that despite the arguments of part I, accepting one of these premises allows one to defend

---

43. A subplan is undertaken in order to advance another intention: a subplan to buy eggs is undertaken in order to advance the intention to make an omelet.

the widely held conviction that judges must obey a nonpermissive rule. Perhaps these premises are even necessary to the task, although I shall not argue for this stronger claim. Part I found no individual moral reasons for judges to adhere in any suboptimal-result case. Part II, by contrast, argues that an optimizing collective agent could have collective reasons to adhere in certain suboptimal-result cases. Readers who are moved by part I, but who still believe that judges have all-things-considered reasons to obey a nonpermissive rule, should be motivated to conclude either that judges actually form optimizing collective agents or that they are morally obligated to do so. That is my inspiration for part II.

In the rest of this section I shall clarify some points about optimizing collective agents. A reader who accepts the Bratman-Velleman theory of shared intention might object that judges never explicitly communicate pledges to one another that would form the constitutive, shared intentions of optimizing collective agents. But the Bratman-Velleman theory does not require explicit exchanges. Explicit promises just illustrate how shared intentions might form. In many real-life scenarios shared intentions arise without any explicit exchange of promises.[44] Judges need not make explicit pledges to form optimizing collective agents.[45]

Any realistic judiciary will contain multiple optimizing collective agents. One might wonder if a single judge could belong to more than one. After all, it is usually possible for one person to belong to multiple

---

44. When the chair of a philosophy department offers you a position, part of the meaning of her offer is, in effect, "We'll treat you as a colleague, educate students, and advance the discipline, so long as you proceed to do the same." When you accept the offer, part of what you implicitly communicate is that you will do the same, on the same conditions, mutatis mutandis. These messages constitute part of the unspoken background of the social context of academic job offers. This background is so taken for granted that none of the participants may ever consciously reflect on it. But counterfactuals immediately reveal its presence. If a member of the department begins giving trombone lessons in the middle of what is supposed to be an introductory logic class, or begins publishing only detective novels, everyone will understand him to have contravened the department's constitutive shared intentions to educate undergraduates, advance the discipline, and so forth. I suggest that this is how it happens with Group O, as well. See Lewis, *Convention*; Gilbert, *On Social Facts*.

45. For convenience, I shall refer to the members of an optimizing collective agent as *judges*, but this usage is not strictly accurate. The members of an optimizing collective agent share optimality judgments, but a judge can change her mind over time. She exits an optimizing collective agent when she ceases to share enough of its optimality judgments. Then she can join another optimizing collective agent whose judgments she comes to share. Consider a particular holding on a legal issue: that §271 of the Telecommunications Act of 1996 was not an unconstitutional bill of attainder, as applied to the Bellsouth Corporation in 1998. Judge Rhonda might believe in 2001 that this was a suboptimal result, but change her mind in 2002 without ever changing her mind about the *legally correct* result. (Perhaps she studies more economics in the interim.) The *judge-segment*, Rhonda-in-2001, is a member of a group who believes that the holding was suboptimal, whereas Rhonda-in-2002 is not a member thereof. So an optimizing collective agent is really composed of judge segments, each of which comprises a judge during a certain finite time period. A *judge* is simply a judge segment that happens to endure for an entire judicial career. Hereafter, for simplicity, I shall refer to the members of groups as *judges*, but I really mean *judge segments*.

collective agents: one woman can be an Episcopal deacon, an FBI agent, and an actor portraying Lady Macbeth. However, this is possible only because these collective agents—the Episcopal Church, the FBI, the cast of *Macbeth*—have substantially compatible, although largely nonoverlapping, subplans. By contrast, because the members of one optimizing collective agent share optimality judgments that differ from those of other optimizing collective agents, the subplans of different optimizing collective agents always clash. Therefore, it is best to think of each judge as belonging to one at a time.

Several legal philosophers have used theories of shared intention to bring greater precision to the *social fact thesis* at the heart of positivism, the thesis that "the possibility of legal authority is to be explained not in terms of substantive morality, but, rather, in terms of certain social facts."[46] Scott Shapiro, Jules Coleman, and Christopher Kutz have all adapted Bratman's theory for this purpose.[47] Matthew Noah Smith has argued, against these three, that most actual public officials do not satisfy Bratman's requirements for joint intentional activity.[48] Although I agree with Shapiro and company that public officials can share intentions, I take no position in this book on whether shared intentions are at the foundations of law. I need not claim that all judges participate in a single joint intentional activity. I plan to use shared intentions for a more limited purpose—to explain how a group of judges, as such, can have practical reasons.

11.9 GROUP O'S REASONS

We can define Group O as the optimizing collective agent whose members share what we are assuming *arguendo* to be *correct* optimality judgments. Different people will disagree about which group of judges is, in fact, Group O, but that is not important here. The intention to avoid suboptimal results gives Group O a *pro tanto* reason to deviate in all suboptimal-result cases. But Group O may also have reasons to adhere in suboptimal-result cases. If Group O is large enough and deviates in enough suboptimal-result cases (the *anterior set*), then it causes other judges to deviate in certain optimal-result cases (the *posterior set*). This causal relationship could, in theory, be expressed as a mathematical function. Begin by defining a *judicial entity* as an individual judge, a set of judges, a single

---

46. Jules Coleman, *The Practice of Principle* (Oxford: Oxford University Press, 2001), p. 75. Coleman notes that "no claim is more central to legal positivism."
47. Ibid., pp. 96–99; Christopher Kutz, "The Judicial Community," *Philosophical Issues* 11 (2001): 442–69; Scott J. Shapiro, "Law, Plans, and Practical Reason," *Legal Theory* 8 (2002): 387–441.
48. Matthew Noah Smith, "The Law as a Social Practice: Are Shared Activities at the Foundations of Law?" *Legal Theory* 12 (2006): 265–92.

court,[49] a court system,[50] a geographic region,[51] or something similar. Next, define the *deviation rate* of a judicial entity over a specified period of time as the fraction of cases in which deviation occurs relative to the total number of cases decided by the entity during that period. In realistic legal systems the function is probably monotonic: higher deviation rates in anterior suboptimal-result cases correlate with higher deviation rates in posterior optimal-result cases. If Group O deviates in all suboptimal-result cases, then posterior judges try to imitate Group O. Not being members of Group O, however, the posterior judges mistakenly deviate in some optimal-result cases.

The causal relationship just described is expressed in the third premise of the group adherence argument.[52] I think the third premise is true in realistic legal systems. However, as an empirical hypothesis it is not true in all conceivable legal systems. There is a conceivable system in which Group O deviates in all suboptimal-result cases yet no systemic damage results. Imagine systems in which a very small fraction of the cases are suboptimal-result cases, or in which judges outside Group O are few, or rarely attempt to imitate judges in Group O. In such systems no mimetic failure would occur, so mimetic failure would never give Group O even a *pro tanto* reason to adhere in suboptimal-result cases. In such "hyposensitive" systems, Group O would not be morally obligated to obey a nonpermissive rule. It could permissibly obey an adherence rule as weak as permissive rule.

If actual legal systems fit the foregoing description, then the third premise of the group adherence argument is false and my arguments in part I support the objective moral permissibility of obeying permissive rule: deviating in all suboptimal-result cases. However, I do not believe that actual legal systems have any of these attractive features. In modern legal systems there are many suboptimal-result cases. There are also many judges who are outside Group O and who are vulnerable to mimetic failure.[53]

11.10 DEVIATION DENSITY

We should also keep in mind the likelihood that the deviation rate in posterior optimal-result cases is a function of more than the anterior deviation rate. The *deviation density* of a judicial entity is defined as the

---

49. The Supreme Court of the United States, the Federal District Court for the Southern District of New York, the United States Court of Appeals for the Seventh Circuit, et cetera.
50. For example, the state courts of Ohio.
51. For example, every court in New England.
52. See §11.6.
53. Again, you and I need not agree about which results are suboptimal or which judges belong to Group O.

modal deviation rate of all its subsidiaries.[54] I think the density as well as the rate of anterior deviation matters. The reason is variable salience. Suppose one mixes a milliliter of red dye uniformly into a swimming pool. The naked eye cannot detect the dye. But that same milliliter of dye is easily visible if sealed in a tiny plastic bag in the middle of the pool. The mimetic effects of a set of deviant decisions depends on how evenly distributed they are on various dimensions that affect salience, such as time, jurisdiction, legal issues involved, et cetera. A set of deviant decisions by the same court, or issued within a short period of time, will usually receive more attention than the same set of decisions issued by different courts, or over longer periods of time. A set of deviant decisions on the same or related legal issues will usually receive more attention than a set containing the same number of equally deviant decisions on a diversity of unrelated legal issues. Therefore, I shall treat deviation density, rather than mere deviation rate, as the relevant variable in the rest of this book.

11.11 INTRANSITIVITY AND SLIPPERY SLOPES

The mimetic-failure argument will remind some readers of slippery-slope arguments. The parallel merits attention because such arguments are familiar and often used fallaciously.[55] In the words of coauthors Mario J. Rizzo and Douglas Glen Whitman, a slippery-slope argument has three components:

1. An initial, seemingly acceptable argument and decision
2. A "danger case"—a later argument and decision that are clearly unacceptable
3. A "process" or "mechanism" by which accepting the initial argument and making the initial decision raise the likelihood of accepting the later argument and making the later decision[56]

In the mimetic-failure argument, the "initial, seemingly acceptable argument" is an argument addressed to Group O that runs as follows: (a) you have all-things-considered reasons to avoid reaching suboptimal results; (b) the law requires you to reach a suboptimal result in these cases; (c) therefore, you have all-things-considered reasons to deviate in these cases.

---

54. David Lyons uses the term *density* similarly in *Forms and Limits of Utilitarianism* (Oxford: Clarendon Press, 1965), p. 72.
55. For discussion of valid and invalid uses see Eugene Volokh, "The Mechanisms of the Slippery Slope," *Harvard Law Review* 116 (2003): 1026–137; Eric Lode, "Slippery Slope Arguments and Legal Reasoning," *California Law Review* 87 (1999): 1469–543; Douglas Walton, *Slippery Slope Arguments* (Oxford: Clarendon Press, 1992); Frederick Schauer, "Slippery Slopes," *Harvard Law Review* 99 (1985): 361–83.
56. Mario J. Rizzo and Douglas Glen Whitman, "The Camel's Nose Is under the Tent: Rules, Theories, and Slippery Slopes," *UCLA Law Review* 51 (2003): 539–92, p. 544.

The "seemingly acceptable decisions" are the decisions by the members of Group O to deviate in these cases. These decisions are acceptable because ex hypothesi the cases are suboptimal-result cases.

The mimetic-failure argument also identifies a "danger case," but it does not necessarily fit Rizzo and Whitman's description. In the mimetic-failure argument the danger case involves posterior judges outside Group O deciding to deviate in optimal-result cases, but the mimetic-failure argument does not require that the judges "accept an argument" that persuades them to do so. The posterior judges need not even be consciously aware of the influence of Group O. However, as do Rizzo and Whitman, the mimetic-failure argument posits a "process" or "mechanism" by which Group O's acceptance of the initial argument raises the likelihood that posterior judges will deviate in optimal-result cases. The members of Group O deviate in all suboptimal-result cases. Their deviation is recognized by some observers (e.g., journalists, colleagues, scholars, lawyers, members of the general public), but they receive, at most, only mild public criticism. Some posterior judges who notice these developments come to believe that they could deviate under similar conditions without receiving any greater degree of criticism than Group O received. As a result they proceed to deviate in cases that they *believe* to be suboptimal-result cases and that they *believe* to be legally and factually similar to those in which Group O deviated. For the sake of the story, imagine that the first generation of posterior judges chooses to deviate in cases that happen to be genuine suboptimal-result cases. Then the pattern recurs. A second generation of posterior judges notices that the first generation deviated. The second generation concludes that they could do the same without suffering more criticism. So they proceed to deviate in cases that they believe to be suboptimal-result cases, and that they believe to be legally and factually similar to those in which the first generation deviated, and so on.

The process just described could culminate in judges deviating in optimal-result cases, even if every judge in the system is sincerely attempting to imitate either Group O or judges who have themselves attempted to imitate Group O. This can happen because the relation of similarity is *intransitive*: Case A resembles B in the relevant respects, which resembles C in the relevant respects, . . ., which resembles Y, which resembles Z, but Z does not resemble A in the relevant respects.[57] To be more concrete, imagine a series of eviction cases, beginning with Yasmin's. In each successive case the legally required result is less suboptimal than in the previous case. As we move through the series, the defendants become increasingly responsible, morally speaking, for their circumstances, whereas the plaintiffs become increasingly entitled, morally speaking, to have the corresponding defendant evicted. Any two adjacent cases are legally and factually similar to one another, but the final case in the series is legally

---

57. See Walton, *Slippery Slope Arguments*, p. 131.

and/or factually dissimilar to Yasmin's case. In the final case in the series we might find that the defendant is a lazy, middle-aged woman who could easily afford rent whereas the plaintiff is a hardworking landlord who needs the rent in order to support his own modest lifestyle. This is not a suboptimal-result case at all. But a judge could end up deviating in this case because he thinks it resembles previous suboptimal-result cases in which judges have properly deviated.

Mimetic failure occurs because each successive generation of cases chosen for deviation bears less and less resemblance to the original cases with respect to the legal and factual features that justify deviation. At some point, the danger case or "slippery-slope event" occurs: a judge deviates in a case that resembles a case that resembles a case . . . that resembles the original suboptimal-result cases, but the new case is actually an optimal-result case. Because the similarity relation between cases is intransitive, Group O's deviation in suboptimal-result cases provokes mimetic failure even if all posterior judges sincerely attempt to imitate Group O—by deviating only in cases that they consider relevantly similar to those in which Group O would deviate.

12

Agent-Relative Principles

12.1 DOES MIMETIC FAILURE GIVE GROUP O REASONS TO ADHERE?

Recall the group adherence argument:

1. If Agent B has an objective *pro tanto* moral reason to Φ, then Agent A has an objective *pro tanto* moral reason not to act in ways that discourage B from Φ-ing.
2. Judges have objective *pro tanto* moral reasons to adhere in optimal-result cases.
3. By deviating in all suboptimal-result cases, Group O will discourage some other judges from adhering in some optimal-result cases.
4. Therefore, Group O has an objective *pro tanto* moral reason not to follow a policy of deviating in all suboptimal-result cases (i.e., a reason to obey a nonpermissive rule).

One defining feature of the group adherence argument is that it assigns to Group O some degree of moral responsibility for the decisions of other judges. Applied to Group O, the first premise imputes to the group a collective intention to discourage judges outside the group from reaching suboptimal results. If Group O has this intention, then it has a *pro tanto* reason to obey a nonpermissive rule.

Given Group O's intention to avoid suboptimal results, one might readily assume that it also has the intention to discourage other judges from reaching suboptimal results. But the former intention does not logically entail the latter. Group O could take a much more limited view of its own moral responsibilities. It could regard itself as responsible for avoiding suboptimal results in its own decisions, while bearing no responsibility whatsoever for discouraging other judges from reaching suboptimal results. But the important question is not whether Group O *believes* itself to be responsible for decisions it provokes other judges to make. The question is whether Group O *really is* responsible for such decisions. Does the fact that by deviating in suboptimal-result cases, Group O encourages other judges to deviate in optimal-result

202

Agent-Relative Principles

cases give Group O *pro tanto* reasons to adhere?[1] We must answer this question in order to determine which adherence rule Group O has an all-things-considered reason to obey (i.e., how often Group O may deviate).

The answer depends on three factors: (1) the suboptimal results that Group O avoids if it deviates in all suboptimal-result cases; (2) the suboptimal results that posterior judges reach if Group O deviates in all suboptimal-result cases; and (3) the normative principle used to compare these two sets of results.

First, consider an additive principle for comparing the results. To apply it, assign to each result in the first set of cases a number expressing its degree of suboptimality. Total these numbers. Then do the same for the second set. The additive principle entails that if the first total exceeds the second, then Group O has a stronger reason to deviate than to adhere in all suboptimal-result cases, so it has an all-things-considered reason to deviate in such cases. However, if the second total exceeds the first, then Group O has a stronger reason to adhere than to deviate in all suboptimal-result cases and thus an all-things-considered reason to adhere.

The additive principle is agent-neutral. It reflects the controversial idea that, ceteris paribus, an agent is no less responsible for leading someone else to cause harm or to act wrongfully than for himself causing harm or acting wrongfully. The additive principle contrasts with agent-relative principles, four of which I shall discuss in this chapter. Any of these four principles in its strongest form entails that Group O's reason to deviate in suboptimal-result cases is always stronger than its reason to adhere. This is because of the following contrast. When judges adhere in suboptimal-result cases they cause negative effects in a direct way. However, when they deviate, resulting in systemic effects, they cause these effects indirectly. According to the agent-relative principles that I shall discuss, only the effects of adherence—the relatively direct effects—provide judges with reasons. Systemic effects do not. It is therefore necessary to determine whether any of these agent-relative principles is true.

Consider how systemic effects such as mimetic failure are related to anterior deviant decisions. These relations have four noteworthy features:

1. By deviating in suboptimal-result cases, Group O does not *intend* to encourage other judges to deviate in optimal-result cases. At most, it *foresees* that deviating will have this result.
2. Group O does not use the parties who suffer, in cases of mimetic failure, as means to its end. The harm inflicted by posterior judges

---

1. For the purposes of this chapter, I am assuming as sound the mimetic-failure argument of the previous chapter.

who deviate in optimal-result cases is merely a *side effect* or *aspect* of anterior deviation by Group O.
3. Mimetic-failure effects are spatiotemporally *remote* from the original deviant decisions. Judges who deviate in optimal-result cases do so at later times and in different places than the decisions of Group O.
4. Mimetic-failure effects are *mediated* by voluntary interventions subsequent to the anterior deviant decisions. Group O does not coerce, bribe, command, or threaten posterior judges. Posterior judges decide autonomously to deviate.

For each of these features there is an agent-relative principle with serious defenders that assigns moral significance to the feature in question. Most contemporary deontologists accept one or more of the following principles, or variants thereof:

1. Unintended effects provide weaker reasons than intended effects.
2. Harm caused as a side effect or aspect of action provides weaker reasons than harm caused as a means to an end.
3. Remote effects provide weaker reasons than local effects.
4. Effects mediated by subsequent voluntary interventions provide weaker reasons than unmediated effects.

Many deontologists today accept only threshold versions of these principles,[2] not absolute versions, but I have formulated them as absolute principles for now. As absolute principles they have the following implications. One is not permitted to cause harm intentionally in order to prevent foreseeable harm, however great the quantity of harm that one could prevent. One is not permitted to cause harm in order to avoid causing harm, however great the quantity, as a side effect or aspect of one's action. One is not permitted to cause local harm in order to prevent remote harm, however great the quantity. Finally, one is not permitted to cause unmediated harm in order to prevent mediated harm, however great the quantity.

None of the aforementioned relations holds between adherent decisions in suboptimal-result cases and the effects of those decisions on the legally disfavored parties. Compare the effects of adherence in a

---

2. See Leo Katz, "Incommensurable Choices and the Problem of Moral Ignorance," *University of Pennsylvania Law Review* 146 (1998): 1465–85, p. 1483 ("[M]ost people are threshold deontologists"). Threshold deontologists include Michael S. Moore, *Placing Blame* (Oxford: Clarendon Press, 1997), p. 723; Thomas Nagel, "War and Massacre," in *Mortal Questions* (Cambridge: Cambridge University Press, 1979), p. 53; Robert Nozick, *Anarchy, State, and Utopia* (New York: Basic Books, 1974), p. 30. For critical discussion see Larry Alexander, "Deontology at the Threshold," *San Diego Law Review* 37 (2000): 893–912; Russell L. Christopher, "Deterring Retributivism: The Injustice of 'Just' Punishment," *Northwestern University Law Review* 96 (2002): 843–976, pp. 877 n. 185, 878 n. 188, 879–80.

suboptimal-result case to the effects of deviation. When a judge deviates, the negative effects on the losing party are not mediated by subsequent voluntary interventions. The effects are spatiotemporally local, not remote. In some cases these effects are also intended, not just foreseen. In some cases they are means or ends, not just effects or aspects.[3]

Therefore, if any of the absolute agent-relative principles is true, then Group O's reason to adhere is never stronger than its reason to deviate in suboptimal-result cases. Accordingly, the systemic effects of deviation do not provide Group O with reasons to adhere that are strong enough to override countervailing reasons to deviate. If any of these absolute agent-relative principles is true, then deviating in suboptimal-result cases is morally preferable to adhering for Group O, which means that permissive rule is vindicated. I conclude that anyone who supports obeying a nonpermissive rule must reject or qualify these absolute agent-relative principles. I shall now examine them in more detail.

12.2 INTENTION

If Group O obeys a nonpermissive rule, then it *intentionally* reaches suboptimal results in some suboptimal-result cases, whereas if Group O deviates in all suboptimal-result cases, then it does not intentionally reach any suboptimal result. It merely provokes other judges to deviate in optimal-result cases. These judges intentionally reach results that are actually suboptimal, but Group O does not. Group O provokes these bad decisions, but it does not intend them, nor does it intend to provoke other judges to make them.

Recall our earlier discussion of the moral significance of intention.[4] Again, I shall not claim to represent the doctrine of double effect, but shall entertain the simpler precept that the intended effects of an action supply stronger reasons than do the merely foreseen effects. If this intention principle is true, then the suboptimal results reached by other judges in optimal-result cases provide relatively weak reasons for Group O to adhere in suboptimal-result cases. This is so despite the fact that Group O, by deviating in suboptimal-result cases, provokes the other judges to reach suboptimal results. However, the suboptimal results reached when Group O adheres in suboptimal-result cases provide Group O with relatively strong reasons to deviate in these cases. If the intention principle is true, then Group O has a stronger reason to deviate than to adhere in suboptimal-result cases.

---

3. Remember also that adhering in a suboptimal-result case inflicts greater undeserved disadvantages on the legally disfavored party than deviating would inflict on the legally favored party.

4. See §6.9.

12.3 MEANS

If Group O obeys a nonpermissive rule in order to support the rule of law, then it reaches suboptimal results in some suboptimal-result cases as a means to that end. In those cases it uses unjustified force and inflicts undeserved harm upon legally disfavored parties in order to avoid encouraging other judges to deviate in optimal-result cases. Contrast the scenario in which Group O deviates in all suboptimal-result cases and provokes other judges to deviate in optimal-result cases. These others use unjustified force and inflict undeserved harm, but Group O does not use this force or harm as a means to its end. Its end is simply to avoid *itself* using unjustified force and inflicting undeserved harm upon the legally disfavored parties in suboptimal-result cases. Group O provokes this unfortunate deviation by other judges, but merely as a side effect or aspect of its own deviation.

F. M. Kamm and others argue that the effects of actions taken as means or ends supply stronger reasons than do effects that are *mere* effects or aspects of the action. This view is expressed in Kamm's principle of permissible harm.[5] If this principle is true, then Group O has a stronger *pro tanto* reason to deviate in suboptimal-result cases than to adhere, no matter how much suboptimal deviation by other judges it encourages.

12.4 PROXIMITY

The proximity principle holds that the effects of an action supply stronger reasons, the greater their spatiotemporal proximity to the action.[6] Systemic effects are spatiotemporally remote from the original deviant decision. Therefore, if the proximity principle is true, then Group O does not have an especially strong reason to avoid provoking other judges to deviate in optimal-result cases.

More important, the spatiotemporal distance between an act of deviation in a suboptimal-result case and its mimetic effects is greater than

---

5. See §6.10; F. M. Kamm, *Morality, Mortality: Rights, Duties, and Status*, vol. 2 (New York: Oxford University Press, 1996), p. 172.

6. See, e.g., F. M. Kamm, *Intricate Ethics: Rights, Responsibilities and Permissible Harm* (New York: Oxford University Press, 2007), chs. 11–12. Kamm believes that proximity may affect the duty to aid, but not the duty not to harm. Ibid., p. 386. Most of the literature on the moral significance of proximity concerns duties to aid distant, needy strangers. See, e.g., Francesco Orsi, "Obligations of Nearness," *Journal of Value Inquiry* 42 (2008): 1–21; Richard W. Miller, "Beneficence, Duty and Distance," *Philosophy and Public Affairs* 32 (2004): 357–83; Jeremy Waldron, "Who Is My Neighbor? Humanity and Proximity," *Monist* 86 (2003): 333–54; Violetta Igneski, "Distance, Determinacy and the Duty to Aid: A Reply to Kamm," *Law and Philosophy* 20 (2001): 605–16; David Schmidtz, "Islands in a Sea of Obligation: Limits of the Duty to Rescue," *Law and Philosophy* 19 (2000): 683–705; Peter Singer, "Famine, Affluence, and Morality," *Philosophy and Public Affairs* 1 (1972): 229–43.

the distance between an act of adherence in a suboptimal-result case and its negative effects on parties to the case. Therefore, if the proximity principle is true, then ceteris paribus the negative effects of adherence provide stronger reasons to deviate in suboptimal-result cases than mimetic failure provides to adhere.

12.5 MEDIATED CAUSATION

The fourth and final agent-relative principle holds that subsequent voluntary interventions by other agents attenuate or eliminate an agent's moral responsibility for the foreseeable effects of his actions. At law the principle is known as *novus actus interveniens*.[7] I shall use this phrase to refer also to the moral version of the principle.

There are exceptions to *novus actus*. If A causes B to Φ, but B's Φ-ing is less than fully voluntary, then A retains at least partial responsibility for B's Φ-ing. This includes cases in which B acts from mental incapacity or reflex and those in which A coerces, commands, or instructs B to Φ. In these cases, A retains full responsibility for the Φ-ing. However, none of these exceptions applies to mimetic failure. Group O does not coerce, command, or instruct other judges to deviate. Nor does a judge who is provoked by the deviation of Group O deviate due to mental incapacity or reflex. He deviates because of poor judgment or misinformation (factual, legal, or moral) that leads him to conclude erroneously that the legally required result in the case at bar is suboptimal. Mimetic failure occurs when deviation by Group O provokes another judge to deviate in an optimal-result case. But for the latter judge's reaction, the group's deviation would not have had this negative effect. The judge's decision is a subsequent voluntary intervention.

Therefore, if *novus actus* is true, then the negative effects of mimetic failure provide Group O with only weak reasons to adhere, if they provide any reasons at all. By contrast, the negative effects on the disadvantaged parties are not mediated by subsequent voluntary interventions. According to *novus actus*, the negative effects of adherence in a suboptimal-result case give Group O a reason to deviate that is stronger than the reason to adhere generated by the mimetic effects of deviation.

---

7. The locus classicus is H. L. A. Hart and Tony Honoré, *Causation in the Law* (Oxford: Clarendon Press, 1959). See also Michael E. Bratman, "What Is the Accordion Effect?" *Journal of Ethics* 10 (2006): 5–19; Michael S. Moore, "The Metaphysics of Causal Intervention," *California Law Review* 88 (2000): 827–77; Michael J. Zimmerman, "Intervening Agents and Moral Responsibility," *Philosophical Quarterly* 35 (1985): 347–58; Joel Feinberg, "Causing Voluntary Actions," in *Metaphysics and Explanation*, eds. W. H. Capitan and D. D. Merrill (Pittsburgh: University of Pittsburgh Press, 1966).

12.6 AGENT-RELATIVE PRINCIPLES AND THE MORAL SIGNIFICANCE OF SYSTEMIC EFFECTS

If we wish to maintain that systemic effects provide Group O with all-things-considered reasons to obey a nonpermissive rule, then we must hold that an agent can have reasons to inflict local, intended, unmediated harm as a means to prevent comparable harms that are remote, unintended, mediated, and merely effects or aspects. In the previous sections I described four popular agent-relative principles: the intention principle, the principle of permissible harm, the proximity principle, and *novus actus interveniens*. If any of these constitutes a true, absolute moral principle, then systemic effects never provide Group O with an all-things-considered reason to adhere in suboptimal-result cases.

I conclude that if we wish to preserve the possibility that systemic effects provide strong reasons to obey a nonpermissive rule, then we must reject absolute versions of the four agent-relative principles. However, if my arguments from part I are sound, then Group O has no *other* reasons to obey a nonpermissive rule. Therefore, the price of absolute, agent-relative principles is the conclusion that no nonpermissive rule has moral authority for Group O.

If we wish to maintain that systemic effects generate all-things-considered reasons to obey a nonpermissive rule, then we must take one of two paths. First, we could reject the four agent-relative principles altogether, at least for the purpose of adjudication theory, and embrace agent-neutral principles such as the additive principle.[8] Alternatively, we could qualify agent-relative principles with thresholds. A threshold principle forbids a certain kind of harm unless it is necessary to prevent consequences that are not just worse, but much worse. A threshold version of the intention principle, for example, forbids intending harm[9] unless it is necessary to prevent much greater quantities of foreseeable harm. Threshold versions of the other agent-relative principles are similar, mutatis mutandis.

I shall consider both options in §12.8. Before doing so I shall examine another way in which comparison principles differ from one another.

12.7 COMPARATIVE HARM FUNCTIONS

Different comparison principles incorporate different comparative harm functions. Here are some possible comparison principles. I formulate them initially in their harm-minimizing versions:

---

8. See §12.1.
9. More precisely: harm to innocent, nonconsenting, nonthreatening parties.

Agent-Relative Principles

> *Pareto*: adhering in the anterior set of cases is justified if and only if deviating in the posterior set produces at least one result that is more suboptimal than any result produced by adhering in the anterior set.
>
> *Aggregative*: adhering in the anterior set of cases is justified if and only if the aggregate results of deviating in the posterior set are worse than the aggregate results produced by adhering in the anterior set.[10]

Suppose we have empirical evidence that by deviating in all suboptimal-result cases, Group O causes posterior judges to reach at least one result that is more suboptimal than any result that it thereby avoids reaching. The Pareto principle entails that under this condition deviating in all suboptimal-result cases is not justifiable. The aggregative principle does not entail this.

Alternatively, suppose we have empirical evidence that by deviating in all suboptimal-result cases, Group O causes posterior judges to reach results that are more suboptimal in the aggregate than the results that Group O thereby avoids reaching. The aggregative principle entails that under this condition deviating in all suboptimal-result cases is not justifiable. The Pareto principle does not entail this.

The comparison principles can also be reformulated as *threshold* principles:

> *Pareto/threshold*: adhering in the anterior set is justified if and only if deviating in the posterior set produces at least one result that is *much* more suboptimal than any result produced by adhering in the anterior set.
>
> *Aggregative/threshold*: adhering in the anterior set is justified if and only if the aggregate results of deviating in the posterior set are *much* worse than the aggregate results produced by adhering in the anterior set.

Suppose we have empirical evidence that by deviating in all suboptimal-result cases, Group O causes via mimetic failure at least one result that is much more suboptimal than any result that it thereby avoids reaching. The Pareto/threshold principle entails that under this condition deviating in all suboptimal-result cases is not justifiable. The aggregative/threshold principle does not entail this.

Suppose we have empirical evidence that by deviating in all suboptimal-result cases, Group O causes posterior judges to reach results that are much worse in the aggregate than the results that Group O thereby avoids reaching. The aggregative/threshold principle entails that under this condition deviating in all suboptimal-result cases is not justifiable. The Pareto/threshold principle does not entail this.

Any of these four principles, combined with the right empirical evidence, supports the conclusion that Group O has an all-things-considered reason to obey a nonpermissive rule. Notice that the case is easier to make under aggregative principles than under Pareto principles. It is also easier to make under harm-minimizing principles than under threshold

---

10. The additive principle from §12.1 is a version of this.

principles. The easiest case for obeying a nonpermissive rule is made under an aggregative/harm-minimizing principle. The hardest case is made under a Pareto/threshold principle.

12.8 THRESHOLD PRINCIPLES

Threshold principles also raise their own problems.[11] I confess that I am skeptical about treating them as ultimate moral principles. I see no reason to set the threshold at any particular point. Perhaps others have more confidently held intuitions than I do about the number of lives that would have to be at risk in order to justify incinerating an innocent patient infected with a contagious disease or torturing a single innocent person to death (e.g., at the behest of a terrorist with a ticking bomb). "One hundred," people say. Or one thousand. Or 10^4, 10^5, 10^6.... Intuitions vary widely. It is not simply that we cannot agree on a precise figure (25,444 yes, 25,443 no). It is not, as some think, a vagueness problem. The problem is that we cannot even achieve rough consensus on an order of magnitude. We are reduced to mumbling that infringing agent-relative restrictions is permissible in "extreme" cases without specifying the extension of "extreme," even vaguely.

Instead of trying to intuit our way to thresholds, we could base our theory of adjudication on agent-neutral principles. These, in contrast to agent-relative principles, assign no ultimate moral significance to the relations between an action and its effects. This shift does not entail abandoning agent-relative principles altogether. We could simply *demote* them from foundational to derivative status. Agent-relative principles would survive, but only as derivative principles, presumably with thresholds specified by the foundational, agent-neutral principles. Agent-relative principles make very useful heuristics.[12] No one should object to them in that capacity.

Debates about agent-relative principles are among the most central and contentious in normative ethics. Different philosophers try to ground agent-relative principles in different moral theories, including contractualism, consequentialism, Kantianism, virtue theories, et cetera.[13] Some argue that agent-relative principles have enough intuitive support that they need no theoretical defense. Meanwhile, disagreement persists about

---

11. See Alexander, "Deontology at the Threshold"; Christopher, "Deterring Retributivism: The Injustice of 'Just' Punishment"; Anthony Ellis, "Deontology, Incommensurability and the Arbitrary," *Philosophy and Phenomenological Research* 52 (1992): 855–75.

12. See, e.g., Cass R. Sunstein, "Moral Heuristics," *Behavioral and Brain Sciences* 28 (2005): 531–73.

13. See, e.g., Paul Hurley, "Agent-Centered Restrictions: Clearing the Air of Paradox," *Ethics* 108 (1997): 120–46; Philip Pettit, "The Consequentialist Can Recognise Rights," *Philosophical Quarterly* 38 (1988): 42–55; Stephen L. Darwall, "Agent-Centered Restrictions from the Inside Out," *Philosophical Studies* 50 (1986): 291–319.

where the thresholds lie.[14] I believe that agent-relative principles are true only insofar as they can be derived from agent-neutral first principles and that the only principles that can be so derived have relatively low thresholds.[15] However, this book is the wrong place for me to defend these positions. You can accept the rest of my arguments even if you disagree with me about agent-relative principles, perhaps preferring to treat them as foundational although qualified with thresholds. I shall not offer any direct, global critique of principles that are both foundational and agent-relative. But my arguments call into question the applicability of such principles to adjudication theory, however applicable they may be to interpersonal ethics or anything else. At least, I question the applicability of these principles to adjudication theory for anyone who believes that judges are ever morally obligated to adhere to the law in a suboptimal-result case. If my arguments are sound, then anyone who would support foundational, agent-relative principles in interpersonal ethics, for example, must explain why these ostensibly foundational principles cease applying to judges when they enter the courtroom and being applying to them again when they leave, at the close of business, to resume their lives as private individuals.

Notice, also, that stronger adherence rules require *lower* thresholds. The lower we set the threshold, the closer our overall theory becomes to one with no agent-relative restrictions whatsoever—one that simply permits agents to minimize harm. As we approach that limit, treating agent-relative principles as foundational appears increasingly ad hoc and implausible. In these respects my arguments converge with those of writers outside adjudication theory who conclude that agent-relative principles do not bind states, however important they may be in interpersonal ethics.[16]

---

14. As discussed in Samantha Brennan, "Thresholds for Rights," *Southern Journal of Philosophy* 33 (1995): 143–68.

15. See Jeffrey Brand-Ballard, "Contractualism and Deontic Restrictions," *Ethics* 114 (2004): 269–300.

16. See David Enoch, "Intending, Foreseeing, and the State," *Legal Theory* 13 (2007): 69–99; Cass R. Sunstein and Adrian Vermeule, "Deterring Murder: A Reply," *Stanford Law Review* 58 (2006): 847–57, pp. 849–52; Louis Kaplow and Steven Shavell, *Fairness versus Welfare* (Cambridge, Mass.: Harvard University Press, 2001); Robert E. Goodin, *Utilitarianism as a Public Philosophy* (New York: Cambridge University Press, 1995), pp. 51–57.

13

Optimal Adherence Rules

So far in part II, I have argued that Group O has an all-things-considered reason to obey a rule that sometimes requires adherence in suboptimal-result cases—a nonpermissive rule. My argument has many controversial premises: certain empirical assumptions about mimetic failure, a theory of collective practical reason, and a normative ethics for adjudication that includes either no agent-relative principles whatsoever, or else principles with relatively low thresholds.

After all this, we still do not know *which* adherence rule Group O has reason to obey: restrictive rule or a moderate rule. Each adherence rule maps onto a set of *decision patterns* that are consistent with Group O obeying that rule. The optimal adherence rules are the ones associated with the optimal decision patterns. The more often Group O adheres, the greater is the quantity of *pro tanto* unjustified harm that it inflicts upon legally disfavored parties in suboptimal-result cases. The more often Group O deviates, the more *pro tanto* unjustified harm it encourages other judges to inflict upon legally favored parties in optimal-result cases, via mimetic failure. So Group O has *pro tanto* reasons to adhere and *pro tanto* reasons to deviate. The relative strength of those two sets of reasons dictates what Group O has an all-things-considered reason to do. The optimal decision patterns are those with the highest possible deviation rate in suboptimal-result cases that conform to whichever harm-comparison principle we accept. Group O has an all-things-considered reason to obey a certain adherence rule if and only if doing so brings the system as close as possible to the optimal decision pattern.

Goldman recognizes the idea of an optimal decision pattern when discussing his taxpayer hypothetical. He appears to assume what I called, in chapter 12, an *aggregative/minimization* principle: "[G]iven that the effect of each individual's deviation on the overall desired outcome . . . is minimal or negligible, there will be an optimal level of deviation just below the threshold at which collective harm begins to set in and outweigh further individual benefits."[1] For any given harm-comparison principle, there

---

1. Alan H. Goldman, "The Rationality of Complying with Rules: Paradox Resolved," *Ethics* 116 (2006): 453–70, p. 455.

Optimal Adherence Rules

is a level of deviation density that produces a rate of deviation in optimal-result cases that the principle classifies as "too high," given the associated rate of deviation in suboptimal-result cases.[2] This is the *deviation density threshold*, or *threshold*. An optimal decision pattern is one that approaches threshold without exceeding it. Group O achieves the optimal pattern if it successfully conforms to *group restriction*: do not deviate so often as to cross the deviation density threshold.

The higher the thresholds specified for the agent-relative principles mentioned in chapter 12, the more deviation group restriction permits. The lower these thresholds, the less deviation group restriction permits. The poles are absolute deontology and harm minimization. Absolute deontology permits deviation in all suboptimal-result cases. Harm minimization permits only as much deviation as minimizes suboptimal results. Threshold deontology permits less than absolute deontology but more than harm minimization.

Obeying group restriction is, of course, impossible without some idea where threshold falls in realistic legal systems. This question has a large empirical component. The answer partly depends on how mimetic failure varies with deviation density. Consider two judges who disagree with one another about which results are suboptimal. The first judge makes a decision that the second judge believes to be deviant. To what extent, if any, does this belief increase the probability that the second judge will deviate in cases in which the first judge would adhere (i.e., provoke mimetic failure)? This is an empirical question to which I have no good empirical answer. The closest thing we have is evidence that judges engage in first-order imitation: they sometimes announce that they are following precedents with which they disagree. We can infer from such an announcement that the judge engages in first-order imitation.

We can also infer that judges engage in second-order imitation (mimesis), although the evidence is less conspicuous. When judges follow precedent they do not ordinarily assert that they are following precedent "because others have done so." However, courts regularly cite authority for the doctrine of stare decisis, which warrants the same inference. The same is true of adhering to statutes, constitutions, and other legal standards.

If adhering encourages other judges to adhere, then perhaps deviating encourages others to deviate. This is harder to establish because judges rarely admit when they deviate. In fact, they usually pretend to adhere in such cases.[3] I cannot find any empirical research on the tendency of judges to imitate the deviational tendencies of others. This is not surprising. Nevertheless, we can fall back on our general understanding of how social norms function. Common sense tells me that judges adhere in perceived

---

2. Assuming we are not discussing hyposensitive systems. See §11.9.
3. See §16.1 on "surreptitious deviation."

suboptimal-result cases in part because of a social norm to do so. Consider a judge with the following attributes: he wants to deviate in perceived suboptimal-result cases, and he adheres in such cases in part because of a social norm to do so. If other judges deviate at an increasing rate, then at some point he will notice and become more likely to deviate himself.

So common sense tells me that judges engage in mimesis, but it tells me little about the shape or endpoints of the curve representing the relationship between deviation density and mimetic failure. Common sense does not tell me how far along the curve my legal system falls or how close it is to its threshold. It would be helpful for social scientists to develop mathematical models of the relationship between deviation density and mimetic failure and to test them in the field. I believe that progress in the prescriptive theory of adjudication requires such models. While we await these models, however, it is not unreasonable to believe that judges could sometimes deviate without pushing a realistic legal system past its threshold. If so, then group restriction permits more deviation than restrictive rule in realistic legal systems. I shall grant *arguendo* that it permits less than permissive rule: consistent deviation in suboptimal-result cases would eventually push a realistic system past its threshold. In other words, I think group restriction supports a moderate rule.

Group O has an all-things-considered reason to obey group restriction. Remember that this group reason is an objective appraisal reason. Recall the distinctions among the following:

1. The best rule to which an agent's decisions could conform
2. The best rule that a rule maker could promulgate for the agent
3. The best rule that a rule enforcer could enforce against the agent
4. The best rule for an agent to obey as a subjective, conscious matter—to use as a guide for conduct[4]

Group restriction fits the first description. It answers the question, what is the rule to which the decisions of Group O should conform, given the tendencies of judges outside of Group O? This rule is not necessarily the same as the rule that Group O should try to obey as a subjective, conscious matter. Conscious efforts to obey group restriction could be counterproductive for Group O.

Group O obeys group restriction if and only if its members collectively deviate at a rate that keeps their system below threshold. One way to maintain acceptable deviation density is for every member to deviate at the same rate—the optimal collective rate. But there are thousands of other patterns that also maintain optimal density. For example, half the members could deviate at 10 percent above the optimal collective rate and half at 10 percent below. Only the average rate matters for the purpose of maintaining optimal deviation density.

---

4. See §8.1.

13.1 GENERAL COMPLIANCE AND FREE RIDING

The next question is, which adherence rules do the individual members of Group O have objective reasons to obey? This is now a question about the individual judge rather than the group, but it is still a question about the best rule to which the agent's decisions could conform. It is not yet a question about which rule a judge should subjectively try to obey.

Goldman claims that if a group has an obligation to perform a task, then each individual member has an obligation to contribute her fair share to the enterprise.[5] The most familiar forms of free riding involve tangible benefits and disadvantages such as collective goods and unpleasant labor, respectively. But the structure of free riding applies to any benefit or disadvantage whatsoever. Someone who desires to act morally benefits when she satisfies this rational desire. Conversely, she suffers when she performs a *pro tanto* impermissible action. Performing an action that is *pro tanto* impermissible is worse for her than performing an action that is not *pro tanto* impermissible, even if the former action is all-things-considered permissible. When *pro tanto* impermissible actions must be performed, there is a *pro tanto* reason to distribute them evenly across agents who are disadvantaged by performing them, just as with any other unpleasant task that must be done.

Recall the citizen who reroutes her tax payment to charity. She treats unfairly those who pay. Goldman states that "other complying members of the group justifiably would resent defection."[6] He concludes that each citizen has an obligation to pay taxes rather than rerouting the funds to charity, even if rerouting would do more good. Note that the consumers of public goods are not the people who are wronged when a citizen reroutes his taxes to charity. Those consumers have no greater moral claim on the citizen's resources than do the beneficiaries of his chosen charity. Rather, the citizen who reroutes his taxes wrongs those who pay their taxes. They, too, could have rerouted their funds to charities, thereby doing more good. But they did not. They bore their fair share of a collective burden. The citizen who reroutes his taxes makes an unjustified exception of himself. That is why his free riding is wrong. He violates the duty of fair play. This reasoning applies to judges, too:

Fair Share Argument
1. If, by Φ-ing, a group acts on its group reasons, then each member has an individual *pro tanto* reason to contribute his fair share to the group effort to Φ.
2. Group O has an all-things-considered group reason to obey group restriction (by the group adherence argument).
3. Group O obeys group restriction.

---

5. Goldman, "The Rationality of Complying with Rules: Paradox Resolved," pp. 462–63.
6. Ibid., p. 465.

4. Therefore, each member of Group O has an individual *pro tanto* reason to contribute his fair share to the group effort to obey group restriction.
5. A member of a group that obeys group restriction contributes his fair share to the group effort if and only if he adheres to the law at the optimal average rate or higher.
6. Therefore, every member of Group O has an individual *pro tanto* reason to adhere to the law at the optimal average rate or higher.

The conclusion of the fair share argument is that every member of Group O has an individual *pro tanto* reason to obey the following:

First Individual Restriction
If Group O deviates as often as group restriction permits, but no more often, then deviate at no higher than the optimal average deviation rate.

If most judges adhere in suboptimal-result cases, then they inflict unjustified disadvantages. If a judge deviates while others adhere, then she rides free on them. By refusing to reach a suboptimal result, she wipes her hands clean, but she wipes them on the hands of her fellow judges. "What is so special about her?" her peers might ask. "Why must we adhere while she deviates?" We could make this same point by reintroducing Scanlonian contractualism, which now has some real work to do. Rather than focusing on potential litigants,[7] we now ask what adherence rules *judges* could reasonably reject. That is another way of highlighting the partiality of deviating when others obey.

Christopher McMahon offers yet another path to this conclusion. His principle of collective rationality states in part, "One has sufficient reason to contribute as provided to a cooperative scheme that produces something that one regards as good if the value to one of the outcome of the scheme, when one's contribution is added to the others that will actually be made, exceeds the value to one of the noncooperative outcome."[8]

Let us stipulate that in the judicial case the cooperative outcome is all members of Group O adhering in all suboptimal-result cases, whereas the noncooperative outcome is all members deviating. Given that stipulation, each member prefers the cooperative to the noncooperative outcome, so the principle of collective rationality entails that each has a *pro tanto* reason to adhere.

13.2 AVERAGE DEVIATION RATE IS OPTIMAL OR BELOW

If Group O's average deviation rate is optimal, according to group restriction, then Judge Jack is permitted to deviate at the optimal average rate as

---

7. As in §8.4.5.
8. Christopher McMahon, *Collective Rationality and Collective Reasoning* (Cambridge: Cambridge University Press, 2001), pp. 21–22.

Optimal Adherence Rules

well. This inflicts *pro tanto* unjustified harm on legally disfavored parties in suboptimal-result cases, but it is justifiable, all things considered, because necessary to avoid free riding. Jack must not deviate above the optimal average rate. Otherwise he rides free on his fellow judges who properly limit their deviation.

In realistic legal systems, however, Group O does not conform to group restriction. What reasons does a member have under these nonideal conditions? It depends where the system stands in relation to threshold. First, consider a scenario in which the system is below the optimum. The analogous scenario for Goldman's taxpayers is one in which so many citizens pay their taxes that more good would be done if some of them were to reroute. Goldman's position appears to be that each citizen still has an all-things-considered reason to pay his taxes under these conditions.

Goldman is correct if his position is that the rerouters ride free on the taxpayers. But this just gives each rerouter a *pro tanto* reason to pay. He also has a *pro tanto* reason to reroute based on impartial considerations: he can do more good by rerouting. A rerouter rides free on every taxpayer, so he has a *pro tanto* reason to pay. But a taxpayer fails to benefit all those who would have benefited from his diversion, so he has a *pro tanto* reason to reroute. Therefore, we cannot conclude that he has an all-things-considered reason to pay taxes unless we can show that the former reason is stronger than the latter. Goldman does not show this, so he offers an inconclusive argument for the conclusion that citizens are obligated to cooperate when they could do more good by rerouting their funds.

Goldman reaches a similar conclusion about judges: they must adhere in suboptimal-result cases, with no exception for scenarios in which all other judges adhere.[9] But Goldman's fairness argument is even less persuasive as applied to judges. Someone who pays his taxes rather than rerouting his payment to charity does not infringe anyone's rights. He does not use force against the beneficiaries of the charity. He withholds from them a benefit, but it is one to which they had no moral right as against him.

By contrast, if Judge Juan adheres to the law in a suboptimal-result case, then he infringes the moral rights of the losing party. He uses or threatens *pro tanto* unjustified force against *someone*. Although he is unfair to judges who adhere when he deviates, he neither uses nor threatens any force against them. So his reason to deviate may be stronger than his fairness reasons to adhere. Therefore, Juan may be permitted to deviate at the optimal average rate even if the other members of Group O deviate less often.

Juan may even be permitted to deviate *above* the optimal average rate under these conditions. The system has "room" for additional deviation by Juan. Consider a thought experiment. Ned lives on an island inhabited by

---

9. Alan H. Goldman, *Practical Rules: When We Need Them and When We Don't* (Cambridge: Cambridge University Press, 2002), pp. 104, 125–26, 137–39, 145–48.

four other individuals, A, B, C, and D. Ned cannot communicate with the others, but he knows that there are four and that they all, himself included, have plenty to eat. In addition to the ample food supply, delicious wild berries grow on the island. Shortly after they ripen they fall from the bush and spoil. Each inhabitant has a natural claim to an equal share of the berries. Every day Ned picks some berries. He would gladly use all the berries himself, but he knows that he is only entitled to one fifth of the crop, so he limits his daily harvest so that by summer's end he will have taken only his share. However, he notices that only one of the other inhabitants—D—is taking anything. The other three take nothing at all. Finally, after watching the unclaimed shares rot for several weeks in a row, Ned decides to take twice his share. This continues for several weeks. Ned thinks maybe D will likewise begin to take more than his share, but D never does. So Ned proceeds to take three times his share. Again he waits, but the final share continues to go unclaimed. By summer's end Ned's daily harvest amounts to four times his share.

Of course, a better solution would be for Ned to consult with the other four at some point, to confirm that none wants the shares to which A, B, and C are entitled. But I have ruled out communication. Under these conditions, Ned may not be blameworthy for exceeding his entitlement. I do not think that Ned is morally obligated to limit himself to his fair share no matter how clear it becomes that berries are going to waste. Whether his actions are objectively wrong depends on whether the others actually wanted the berries that Ned takes beyond his entitlement. We could also argue about how confident Ned must be that the berries are unwanted before he begins taking them. But there must be a level of confidence that allows Ned blamelessly to take the extra berries.

Let us now modify the facts of the hypothetical. Suppose Ned has been taking only his fair share and observes that the others are doing likewise for several weeks. One day Ned greedily takes more than his share. He is blameworthy for doing so because his maxim is something like "I will take as many berries as I want." However, his actions may not be objectively wrong. If, by coincidence, the others had no plans to harvest the extra berries that Ned takes, then his greedy behavior is objectively permissible (although still as blameworthy as ever).

Apply these lessons to the situation of the judge. First, consider the objective permissibility of a judge deviating in every suboptimal-result case he hears. Suppose Judge Juan's system is below its threshold and few other judges have any interest in deviating. They would not deviate even if Juan himself adhered consistently. Nor will Juan push the system over threshold if he deviates in every suboptimal-result case. Under such conditions, Juan is objectively permitted to deviate in every suboptimal-result case. His situation parallels Ned's when the other islanders have no interest in the berries.

The question of whether Juan is blameworthy is more difficult. It depends on his maxim of action, not just his behavior. Juan is blameworthy if his maxim is permissive rule ("I will deviate in every suboptimal-result case"), just as Ned was blameworthy for using the maxim, "I will take as many berries as I want." But suppose Juan's maxim is "I will deviate in every suboptimal-result case unless my system is close to its deviation density threshold." This maxim is a moderate rule. Using this maxim, Juan is not blameworthy even if he deviates in every suboptimal-result case. He is not blameworthy because his maxim responds appropriately to the behavior of his fellow judges. He is like Ned in the first hypothetical, when he has adequate reason to conclude that his fellow islanders have no plans to harvest their shares. We might say that Juan is "consuming opportunities to deviate" that would otherwise be "wasted." He takes more than his fair share, but doing so is neither blameworthy nor objectively impermissible under the conditions described.

If Juan wants to stay on the safe side, of course, he can deviate less frequently than the aforementioned moderate rule permits, obeying a more restrictive moderate rule, or even restrictive rule. Any judge who maintains a deviation rate higher than the optimal average is playing a risky game. His fellow judges will always be able to claim that they wanted to deviate more often than they did but refrained because of judges such as him. To this Juan could reply that the others should have made their desires clearer to him, but he may find it difficult to persuade others that his maxim is, indeed, sufficiently responsive to facts about the proximity of his system to its threshold. A more restrictive rule is safer for the judge who wants to avoid blame.

Deviating above the optimal average rate constitutes free riding and is *pro tanto* wrong, but it may be all-things-considered permissible if the system is below threshold, for the following reason: if Juan deviates less often, then he inflicts *pro tanto* unjustified harm on legally disfavored parties in suboptimal-result cases. Infringing moral rights is usually *worse* than free riding. However, the further Juan goes above the optimal average rate, the more of his fellow judges he "passes" with his deviation rate. His fair play reasons to adhere strengthen commensurately the further he goes. So there is still a limit to how often he is permitted to deviate, although he is not limited to the optimal average rate. I suggest the following rule:

> **Second Individual Restriction**
> Where n is the maximum number of cases in which group restriction permits deviating during a certain time period and m is the number of cases in which Group O actually deviates during that period, if $m < n$ during that period, then do not deviate in more than $n - m$ cases during that period.

Remember, I am not claiming that the best *guidance rule* for judges directs them to estimate how close their system is to threshold. That might prove impractical. I am still addressing the level of appraisal rules.

13.3 GENERAL DEFECTION

Now consider a legal system that is far above its threshold. In this system, every member of Group O deviates in more suboptimal-result cases than first individual restriction permits. Every member is above the optimal average rate. Other judges attempt to imitate Group O, but they misidentify suboptimal-result cases and end up deviating unknowingly in too many optimal-result cases, based on the stipulated threshold. In other words, the deviation of Group O causes too much mimetic failure.

Group O still has an all-things-considered reason to obey group restriction—a stronger rule than its members actually obey. But does any individual member have a reason to obey first individual restriction when no one else obeys it? Goldman's taxpayer argument does not support the unconditional conclusion that taxpayers have a reason to pay their taxes. It supports, at most, the conditional conclusion that each citizen has a reason to pay her taxes *if enough other citizens pay theirs*. Consider the citizen who reroutes her tax payment to charity while all other citizens do the same. She rides free on no one, so she has no reason of fairness to pay. Moreover, the public goods are not provided whatever she does. Her act makes no perceptible difference. Does she still have a reason to pay? Goldman does not distinguish between general cooperation and general defection or entertain the possibility that citizens' obligations differ across these states of affairs. But his argument does not support the conclusion that all citizens have unconditional reasons to pay their taxes.

Similarly, the fair share argument establishes only that judges have reasons to obey first individual restriction if the other members of Group O obey it. In order to cover the neglected case of general defection, we must supplement the argument. We must hold each deviating judge responsible for the cumulative effects of patterns of general deviation in which he participates, even if his own decisions have no perceptible effect and he rides free on no one.

Of course, a pattern in which *every* member of Group O deviates more often than first individual restriction permits is not realistic. In a more realistic pattern, some members deviate more often than first individual restriction permits, others conform to first individual restriction, and the overall rate is too high. The greater the number of conformists, the stronger the judge's fairness reasons to adhere. But these reasons still may not be strong enough to outweigh his reasons to deviate, even if the system is above threshold. Indeed, as the system rises beyond threshold, the number of conformists falls, commensurately weakening fairness reasons to adhere.

There are, however, additional arguments for adherence that are based not on fairness but more directly on systemic effects. I turn to these arguments in the next sections.

13.4 IMPERCEPTIBLE EFFECTS

How might systemic effects provide a member of Group O with a reason to adhere in a suboptimal-result case, given that a single choice to deviate makes no perceptible difference? Such a reason might exist if what I shall call the *causal limitation* is false. This limitation holds that only the perceptible effects of an action constitute objective reasons for or against performing it. Act consequentialists accept the causal limitation, holding that an act is wrong, all things considered, if and only if it causes less agent-neutral value to be produced than would an alternative act. Act consequentialism combines the causal limitation with agent neutrality. It is important to keep these elements separate as we proceed. One could, for example, hold that an agent acts wrongly if and only if her actions *amuse* someone who maximizes agent-neutral value. This preposterous principle is agent-neutral because it ultimately defines the right in agent-neutral terms. But it is noncausal because it does not define right action in terms of how much value it actually promotes. In this chapter and the next, I shall argue that anyone who believes that judges must obey a nonpermissive rule should embrace foundational agent-neutral principles but reject the causal limitation. This seems like a coherent position to me, although maybe not the only coherent position on the subject.

The fact that a deviant decision typically has no perceptible systemic effects is especially significant because the immediate adverse effects of adherence are typically very perceptible. A judge who adheres to the law in a suboptimal-result case disadvantages particular, identified individuals, notably the losing party. Of course, adherence also benefits the winner, but in suboptimal-result cases the winner does not receive enough deserved benefits to outweigh the loser's undeserved losses. So the objection from the imperceptibility of systemic effects has great urgency for anyone who believes that judges should obey a nonpermissive rule. We still have not identified a *pro tanto* reason to adhere that is strong enough to override the *pro tanto* moral reason to deviate in suboptimal-result cases.

If we wish to advance a systemic-effects argument for the conclusion that judges have *pro tanto* reasons to adhere in suboptimal-result cases, then we must maintain that a judge who deviates acts *pro tanto* wrongly, despite the fact that her deviation makes no perceptible causal contribution to harming the legal system. Many philosophers believe that an action that causes no perceptible harm to anyone can still be *pro tanto* wrong. Some consider it intrinsically *pro tanto* wrong for a soldier to tell his fallen comrade's grieving mother, falsely, that her son died painlessly. I myself do not. But deviating as such does not require deception, so I can drop the issue.[10]

---

10. A judge who deviates might decide, in addition, to misrepresent his decision as conforming to the law. He might have a *pro tanto* moral reason not to do so under conditions that will foreseeably mislead others.

More analogous is one's decision to break a promise, made to a dying woman, to deliver a pointlessly hurtful message to someone after her death. Some consider it intrinsically *pro tanto* wrong to break this promise.[11] I myself do not. But I concluded in chapter 9 that even if deviating breaks a promise, the judge's reason to keep it is undermined in suboptimal-result cases.

In the next three subsections I shall consider three different theories, any one of which would allow us to hold an agent morally accountable for a state of affairs to which she makes no perceptible contribution: *imperceptible harms*, *triggering risks*, and *complicity*.

13.4.1 Imperceptible Harms

First, one could embrace the existence and moral significance of *imperceptible harms*. The classic hypothetical that motivates belief in the moral significance of imperceptible harms involves 100 bandits, who steal 100 beans from hungry villagers. Each bandit steals 1 bean from each villager. No villager can detect the difference any given bandit makes to his lunch, yet we still think the bandits act immorally. One way to explain this is to claim that each bandit causes imperceptible harm and that doing so is wrong.[12]

Analogously, one could argue that a deviant decision inflicts imperceptible harm on the legal system. True, it is rare for a single deviant decision to cause any posterior judge to weaken her subjective reasons to adhere, causing her to deviate in an optimal-result case. This is to say that the decision inflicts no *perceptible* harm. Nonetheless, one could insist that the deviating judge inflicts harm by contributing, albeit imperceptibly, to a "culture of judicial lawlessness" in which deviation is more likely in optimal-result cases.

However, some have argued that assigning moral significance to imperceptible harms entails various *repugnant conclusions*.[13] I am not sure that these objections to the moral significance of imperceptible harms are conclusive, but they worry me enough to motivate me to continue my search for reasons for a judge to adhere even when deviating causes no perceptible harm.

---

11. And to make it in the first place, if one has no intention of keeping it.

12. See Jonathan Glover, "It Makes No Difference Whether or Not I Do It," in *Applied Ethics*, ed. Peter Singer (Oxford: Oxford University Press, 1990).

13. Derek Parfit, *Reasons and Persons* (Oxford: Clarendon Press, 1984), pp. 381–90. See also Michael J. Almeida, ed., *Imperceptible Harms and Benefits* (Dordrecht: Kluwer, 2000); Larry S. Temkin, "Rethinking the Good, Moral Ideals and the Nature of Practical Reasons," in *Reading Parfit*, ed. Jonathan Dancy (Oxford: Blackwell, 1997).

13.4.2 Triggering Risks

Here is a second way of supporting the idea that an action that causes no perceptible harm to anyone—nor any deception, nor any infidelity, et cetera—can still be objectively wrong. One could treat each deviant decision as imposing a small *risk* of causing perceptible harm and hold agents objectively responsible for exposing others to such risks.[14] Unlikely as it may be in any given case, there could in principle be a deviant decision in a suboptimal-result case that directly causes one or more deviant decisions in posterior optimal-result cases. Judge Karl reads or otherwise learns about a deviant decision by Judge Rita. Thereafter, Karl has to decide a case that he erroneously believes to be a suboptimal-result case. Remembering Rita's deviant decision or subconsciously aware of it, Karl is now encouraged to deviate and does so. Perhaps Rita's decision reduces Karl's sense of how "unprofessional" deviation is, just to the point at which he summons his resolve to deviate. Whatever the causal mechanism, the fact is that if Rita had adhered, then so would have Karl. Rita's deviation is decisive for Karl: it is a *trigger*. She has "provoked" him to deviate. So she has an objective *pro tanto* reason to adhere that competes with any *pro tanto* reason she might have to deviate. If Karl's decision is more suboptimal than an adherent decision by Rita would be, then she has an objective all-things-considered reason to adhere. If she deviates, then she runs a risk of acting against her objective, all-things-considered reasons. Some would claim that she has an objective reason not to take such risks.

Any deviant decision could potentially have a triggering effect. But how great is the risk? Of course, virtually every ruling, deviant or not, adversely affects the losing party, his family, and others in virtue of its content. But only in extraordinary cases does anyone exist whose interests are perceptibly affected for the worse *by the fact that a decision is deviant*. In realistic, stable legal systems very few deviant decisions directly cause subsequent deviation in optimal-result cases. Any given deviant decision runs only a *miniscule* risk of triggering.

The question, then, is whether people have a right not to be exposed to miniscule risks of undeserved harm. If they do, then judges have objective, *pro tanto* moral reasons to adhere, despite the fact that deviation rarely has harmful effects. In this section I ask how we should evaluate actions that impose miniscule risks of harm.

---

14. See, e.g., Frank Jackson and Michael Smith, "Absolutist Ethical Theories and Uncertainty," *Journal of Philosophy* 103 (2006): 267–283; David McCarthy, "Rights, Explanation, and Risks," *Ethics* 107 (1997): 205–25; Dennis McKerlie, "Rights and Risk," *Canadian Journal of Philosophy* 16 (1986): 239–51; Judith Jarvis Thomson, *Rights, Restitution, and Risk* (Cambridge: Harvard University Press, 1986); Peter Railton, "Locke, Stock, and Peril: Natural Property Rights, Pollution, and Risk," in *To Breathe Freely*, ed. Mary Gibson (Totowa, N.J.: Rowman & Littlefield, 1985).

Dan pops a hole in a bag of pretzels on a supermarket shelf and inserts a peanut, creating a small chance that someone with a severe peanut allergy will eat it and die. If this happens, then Dan's act is an unjustifiable homicide. Objectively, it is extremely immoral. Nevertheless, Dan might not be guilty of criminal homicide. Reckless homicide requires risks to be substantial, whereas the risk Dan runs may be insubstantial.[15]

If no allergic person eats the peanut, then Dan's act has no *effects* that make it objectively very immoral.[16] But it might have aspects other than its effects that make it objectively very immoral. Dan exposes allergic consumers to a risk of severe harm. It is, however, a miniscule risk. One might suggest that agents should simply ignore risks below a certain probability, however severe the harm risked. One could claim that below a certain level of risk, agents who knowingly take a risk of doing something objectively wrong (even extremely wrong) are not *pro tanto* blameworthy. If a fully informed agent is not *pro tanto* blameworthy for an action, then he has no objective *pro tanto* moral reason not to perform it. So Dan has no objective *pro tanto* moral reason to refrain from hiding the peanut on this view. Again, the criminal law has something in common with this position. Dan is probably not guilty of reckless endangerment, either, given the low level of risk.

At the other extreme, one could maintain that individuals have an absolute right not to have others expose them to even miniscule risks of harm. This entails that Dan violates the rights of allergic individuals and has an objective all-things-considered moral reason not to hide the peanut. This view, however, is highly restrictive. It entails that pedestrians have an absolute right to keep cars off the road.

There is a moderate view that is less restrictive than the former, but more restrictive than the criminal law. This is the view that individuals have a right not to have others expose them to *unjustifiable* risks of harm— even miniscule risks.[17] This is a nonabsolute right against risks because some risks are justifiable. This view entails that Dan has an objective *pro tanto* moral reason not to hide the peanut, which becomes an all-things-considered reason because he has no justification for doing so. This is a theory that we could use to analyze a judge's decision to deviate. If deviating creates a risk of provoking deviation in optimal-result cases, then the judge has an objective *pro tanto* reason to adhere, even if that risk is miniscule (as it probably is). Unlike Dan, however, the judge also has *pro tanto* reasons to deviate in suboptimal-result cases.

---

15. *Model Penal Code* § 2.02(2)(c) (reckless actors consciously disregard a substantial and unjustifiable risk).

16. Popping holes in pretzel bags at the market and inserting peanuts is also wrong in itself, as destruction and adulteration of groceries, but these are petty wrongs that I shall disregard.

17. See, e.g., Larry Alexander and Kimberly Kessler Ferzan, *Crime and Culpability: A Theory of Criminal Law* (Cambridge: Cambridge University Press, 2009).

13.4.3 Complicity

Now for a third way of supporting the idea that an action that causes no perceptible harm to anyone can be objectively wrong. Some philosophers have recently argued that a contributing agent is accountable for the cumulative effects of the actions of the members of a group to which she belongs. Christopher Kutz's complicity principle holds an agent accountable for what others do when she "intentionally participates" in the wrong they do or the harm they cause, independently of the actual difference she makes.[18] The complicity principle holds individuals accountable for such actions as driving a car that emits greenhouse gases in quantities too small to register on the global scale.[19] It holds accountable each of the Allied pilots who participated in the firebombing of Dresden civilians during World War II, whether or not any particular pilot caused any particular injury.[20] It also condemns anyone who indifferently provides tools to criminals, even if the tools are widely available elsewhere.[21] These actions make no perceptible difference to outcomes but the complicity principle holds the agents accountable nonetheless.

Assuming that the citizenry as a group acts wrongly by failing to provide public goods through taxpaying, the complicity principle could support the claim that anyone who reroutes her tax payment intentionally participates in the group wrongdoing. Under the complicity principle she acts wrongly herself, even though her act makes no perceptible difference. The goods will not be provided whatever she does. Assume that all other citizens are rerouting their payments to charity, so public goods are not provided whatever the citizen does. This constitutes a great misfortune for everyone. Any citizen who reroutes his payment under these conditions intentionally participates in causing this misfortune, although he makes no difference to the outcome. Therefore, under the complicity principle each is morally accountable for the general pattern of nonpayment. Each has a *pro tanto* reason to pay even though no one else is paying.

Returning to the judicial case, we have noted that the systemic effects of a single deviant decision are usually imperceptible. However, the cumulative systemic effects of a set of deviant decisions can still give a judge a reason to adhere. The complicity principle links deviant decisions to the systemic effects of deviation patterns. Each agent is objectively responsible for the effects (intended or not) of her actions *and* for the effects (intended or not) of any joint intentional activity in which she participates.[22] A pattern of deviant decisions in suboptimal-result cases by Group

---

18. Christopher Kutz, *Complicity: Ethics and Law for a Collective Age* (Cambridge: Cambridge University Press, 2000), p. 122.
19. Ibid., pp. 171–77.
20. Ibid., pp. 117–20.
21. Ibid., pp. 168–70.
22. See §13.4.3.

O provokes posterior judges to deviate in a larger number of optimal-result cases than the number in which they would have otherwise deviated. Because of mimetic failure, a widespread practice of deviation, even if limited to suboptimal-result cases, indirectly encourages deviation in optimal-result cases. Judges who deviate in optimal-result cases often use unjustified force. They also violate their judicial oaths and frustrate parties' reasonable expectations. The complicity principle holds each judge in Group O responsible for the collective actions of Group O that provoke posterior judges (outside Group O) to engage in this behavior.

This section (13.4) has described three different ways to conceptualize the *pro tanto* wrong of deviation in suboptimal-result cases when other members of Group O deviate excessively. We can understand deviation under these conditions as inflicting imperceptible systemic effects, or as running a risk of triggering perceptible systemic effects, or as participating in a wrongful enterprise that causes perceptible systemic effects. Each of these theories is controversial, and I shall not attempt to defend any of them. Any of the three supports the claim that systemic effects give judges *pro tanto* reasons to adhere in suboptimal-result cases. Recall that my argument in part II addresses those who believe that judges are morally forbidden to make a practice of deviating in every suboptimal-result case. Anyone who believes this must hope that one of these theories, or another that does the same work, is correct.

If any of the principles associated with these theories has normative authority, then agents have more natural reasons than I originally identified.[23] They still have *pro tanto* natural reasons to use justified force and not to use unjustified force.[24] But they also have *pro tanto* natural reasons to join enterprises with participants who use justified force and enterprises that cause nonparticipants to use justified force. They have *pro tanto* natural reasons not to participate in enterprises with participants who use unjustified force or fail to use justified force. And they have *pro tanto* natural reasons not to participate in enterprises that cause nonparticipants to use unjustified force or to fail to use justified force.

We can now address the case of general deviation in suboptimal-result cases with the following argument:

Clean Hands Argument
1. If a group has an all-things-considered group reason to Φ, but does not Φ, then its members have individual *pro tanto* reasons to Φ so as not to contribute to the failure of the group to Φ.
2. Group O has an all-things-considered group reason to obey group restriction (by the group adherence argument).

---

23. See §2.5.
24. By *force*, as usual, I mean force, threat of force, or other coercion.

3. If Group O disobeys group restriction, then adhering at no less than the optimal average rate is the only way for a judge in Group O to avoid contributing to the group's disobedience of group restriction.

4. Therefore, if Group O disobeys group restriction, then each member of Group O has an individual *pro tanto* reason to adhere at no less than the optimal average rate.

13.5 THE COMPARATIVE WEAKNESS OF ADHERENCE REASONS

I pause in this section to forestall a potential misunderstanding. Theories of imperceptible effects, triggering risks, and complicity can be used to support strict principles of abstention: the bandit must not take the single bean; Dan must not hide the peanut; the pilot must not firebomb Dresden. One might infer that if one of these theories is correct, then judges in Group O must *never* deviate if the deviation rate of Group O is excessive.

This conclusion does not follow because a judge is not similarly situated to the agents in the aforementioned scenarios. The agents in these scenarios have no moral reasons whatsoever to act as they do. The bandit has no moral reason to take the villager's bean. Nor has Dan any moral reason to hide the peanut in the pretzel bag. Nor has the pilot any (adequate) moral reason to bomb Dresden. The puzzles arise because, even so, theories that incorporate a causal limitation cannot easily explain the evident immorality of these actions. Embracing the moral significance of imperceptible harm, or responsibility for imposing miniscule risks, or the complicity principle at least allows one to condemn the bandits, Dan, and the Dresden bombers, respectively. These agents lack even *pro tanto* moral reasons for their actions.

By contrast, judges in suboptimal-result cases have strong *pro tanto* moral reasons to deviate. Theories based on imperceptible harms, triggering risks, or complicity provide competing *pro tanto* reasons to adhere, but these reasons do not necessarily prevail in the competition. Administering a vaccination subjects the patient to a minute risk of death. This risk gives the doctor a *pro tanto* reason not to administer the vaccine, but it is a weak reason. Of course if the vaccine serves no medical purpose, then this weak reason becomes an all-things-considered reason. But if the vaccine will prevent disease, then the doctor has a *pro tanto* reason to administer it that overrides the opposing *pro tanto* reason and generates an all-things-considered reason to do so.

Similarly, imagine that each bandit is a "Robin Hood" who steals a bean from one of a hundred wealthy villagers in order to contribute it to a food bank that saves much hungrier people in the next town from starvation. In that case the imperceptible harm that he inflicts may be outweighed by benefits to others.[25]

---

25. Depending, of course, upon the correct theory of distributive justice.

The point is that small disadvantages and risks of harm may be justified as unavoidable side effects of permissible means to permissible ends. The negative effects of adherence, on the losing party and others, are often direct and substantial in suboptimal-result cases. However, the systemic effects of a single decision to deviate rarely constitute adherence reasons that are strong enough to override a judge's natural duties and sustain an all-things-considered reason to adhere. Because deviation either imposes a triggering risk of systemic effects, or inflicts imperceptible systemic effects, or constitutes complicity in a harmful enterprise, judges have *pro tanto* reasons to adhere. However, these reasons may not be strong enough to defeat the judge's *pro tanto* reasons to deviate in all suboptimal-result cases. Running the risk of provoking deviation by Judge Karl in an optimal-result case is an unavoidable side effect of Judge Rita's choice to deviate in a suboptimal-result case. So the risk gives Rita a *pro tanto* reason to adhere, but may not provide an all-things-considered reason, depending on the deviation density of the system at the time.

13.6 DEVIATION RATE ABOVE THE OPTIMUM

We can now address the scenario in which Group O's average deviation rate is above the optimum. What is Judge Juan permitted to do under those conditions? He may not deviate above the optimal average rate. Otherwise he participates in the ongoing deviation enterprise that is causing excessive mimetic failure. If some members deviate at or below the optimal average rate, then he has an additional reason not to deviate above the optimal average rate. Otherwise he rides free on the members who deviate less often than he.

So Juan is forbidden to deviate above the optimal average rate. Beyond that there are two possibilities that make some intuitive sense. The first is that Juan is permitted to deviate at the optimal average rate. In doing so he does not ride free on anyone. He inflicts *pro tanto* unjustified harm on legally disfavored parties in the suboptimal-result cases in which he adheres, but some adherence is necessary lest he participate in a deviation enterprise that causes mimetic failure. If some members of Group O deviate at or below the optimal average rate, then Juan must not exceed the optimal average rate either, in order to avoid free riding. If everyone else deviates above the optimal average rate, then Juan could, without riding free on anyone, deviate as often as the one who deviates least frequently. But he would still participate in an enterprise of excessive deviation by deviating that often, so he must deviate at or below the optimal rate.

If Group O's average deviation rate is above the optimum, then deviating at the optimal average rate is sufficient to avoid free riding. However, one might wonder whether deviating at the optimal average rate is sufficient to avoid participation in the enterprise of excessive deviation. It might seem that Juan participates in this enterprise if he deviates *at all*. This is the second of the two, intuitively sensible possibilities mentioned in the previous paragraph.

I think this suggestion about Juan is false. The fact that other judges are deviating above the optimal average rate does not obligate Juan to keep his deviation rate *below* the optimal average rate. He is not obligated to compensate for the excessive deviation of other members of Group O.[26] More to the point, the legally disfavored parties whom Juan could protect by deviating should not have to suffer on account of excessive deviation by other members of Group O. Juan does not participate in an enterprise of deviating above the optimal average rate unless *he* deviates above that rate. I suggest the following rule:

Third Individual Restriction
If Group O deviates more often than group restriction permits, then do not deviate at a rate higher than the optimal average deviation rate.

I have proposed three individual restrictions that I now incorporate into the following:

Combined Restriction
1. If Group O deviates as often as, or more often than, group restriction permits, then deviate at no higher than the optimal average deviation rate.
2. Where n is the maximum number of cases in which group restriction permits Group O to deviate during a certain time period and m is the number of cases in which Group O actually deviates during that period, if $m < n$, then do not deviate in more than $n - m$ cases during that period.

13.7 ADAPTATION EFFECTS REVISITED

Earlier I distinguished adaptation effects from mimetic effects.[27] Adaptation effects result when nonjudicial actors adapt to patterns of deviation by Group O. Mimetic effects result when judges outside Group O unsuccessfully attempt to imitate Group O's deviation. Since drawing this distinction I have neglected adaptation effects, using only mimetic effects in my arguments. I can now explain why we should not substitute adaptation effects for mimetic effects in these arguments.

The problem is simple: depending on the law adaptation effects can be bad, as in cases like Yasmin's, but they can also be good, from the moral standpoint of anterior judges. Consider judges who are persuaded by economic arguments against rent-control statutes. Assume that a widespread practice of judicial deviation from such statutes would have

---

26. I see parallels with arguments in Garrett Cullity, *The Moral Demands of Affluence* (Oxford: Oxford University Press, 2004), but I cannot explore them here.
27. See §§11.2–11.3.

adaptation effects. Do these effects give prior judges a reason to adhere to such statutes? From the moral standpoint of the anterior judges these effects are likely to be *positive*. At least, the effects are likely to be positive if lawyers and their clients can discern a pattern of judicial deviation. From the moral standpoint of judges who disapprove of rent-control statutes, this pattern of otherwise optimal deviation will have negative adaptation effects only if no pattern becomes apparent to other actors.

We can, in theory, imagine legal actors reacting to a pattern of judicial deviation from rent-control statutes by arriving at the hysterical conclusion that judges have become less willing to enforce all rental contracts or even contracts in general. In that case the prior pattern would discourage beneficial economic activity. More likely, however, lawyers will figure out that judges are deviating from rent-control statutes because the judges think them economically inefficient. Lawyers will not, therefore, advise their clients to refrain from other economically efficient transactions involving real estate. Private parties who are broadly self-interested have powerful incentives to obtain accurate predictions of judicial behavior. Inaccurate predictions lead to lost opportunities and poor investments. There is no economic reward for paranoia. Suppose judges are regularly nullifying rent-control statutes. Lawyers respond by advising prospective tenants not to assume that rent control will be enforced in the future. But lawyers will not interpret the trend as evidence that courts will also deviate from economically *efficient* laws that favor landlords. Lawyers will not, for example, advise their clients not to sign leases as a general matter, regardless of whether the building has rent control. The point is that adaptation effects provide reasons to adhere in some cases but not others depending upon the content of the controlling law. In fact, adaptation effects provide reasons to *deviate* in some cases. They provide no general reason to obey a nonpermissive rule.

Now we can see why mimetic failure is a better candidate for a general reason to obey a nonpermissive rule. Compared with the incentives for legal subjects to predict judicial decisions accurately, the incentives are weak for judges to imitate one another accurately when deviating. Although a judge has various incentives to adhere to the law,[28] on those occasions when she chooses to deviate she has little incentive to do so in accordance with anyone's values but her own. When Judge Dave the Democrat deviates from a statute providing mandatory minimum sentences for felons, he may inspire Judge Ruth the Republican to deviate from a statute extending civil rights to lesbians and gay men—a statute that Dan favors. The symmetrical possibility exists if Ruth's decision precedes Dan's. Dave sees Ruth's decision as suboptimal, as she sees his, no matter who goes first.

---

28. See §§3.2, 4.6.

Adaptation effects can provide *pro tanto* reasons for a group of judges to adhere in certain suboptimal-result cases, but these reasons vary with the content of the laws in question. Adaptation effects do not provide content-independent reasons to adhere in suboptimal-result cases unless lawyers and their clients are very bad at predicting judicial behavior—worse, I think, than they are in realistic modern legal systems. By contrast, mimetic failure provides content-independent *pro tanto* reasons for the group to adhere in suboptimal-result cases under a much weaker condition: that a substantial plurality of their fellow judges will respond to the group's deviation pattern by deviating in optimal-result cases. This is so if other judges attempt to imitate the group by deviating, but either reject or misunderstand the group's classification of suboptimal-result cases. Given the range of moral opinions and the variations in moral perceptiveness on the bench in modern legal systems, this condition plausibly holds. This is why mimetic failure could, perhaps, provide content-independent *pro tanto* reasons for judges to adhere in suboptimal-result cases.

13.8 COHERENCE AND COMMON SENSE

Many people believe that judges in reasonably just legal systems have an all-things-considered moral obligation to adhere to the law in all cases—to obey restrictive rule. Given current circumstances as I understand them, my arguments thus far do not support this conclusion. My conclusion thus far appears to conflict with a common belief about the ethical obligations of modern judges. I have admitted that I cannot demonstrate that judges have no obligation to obey restrictive rule. I have simply considered arguments for the opposite conclusion and found them wanting. Therefore, we must choose between (1) denying that judges must obey restrictive rule, because we have found no sound argument for that conclusion, and (2) accepting as a foundational principle, requiring no argument, that judges must obey restrictive rule.

One reason to prefer the first position is that the second seems to impute to the law certain unexplained, primitive justificatory powers: the law always overrides moral reasons to deviate in reasonably just legal systems, we are told, but we are not told why. A defender of the second position might respond that popular support for obeying restrictive rule is so pervasive that we should simply accept it on faith. But this argument ignores a crucial variable. The two positions also differ in their levels of *coherence* with the rest of common morality and practical philosophy. I think the first position dominates the second on this dimension. This is not to say that the second position is less *consistent* than the first with common morality and modern practical philosophy. The positions might be comparably consistent in this respect. But consistency is only one element of coherence.[29] Another is the extent to which beliefs form mutually supportive, justificatory connections with one another. The second position has few justificatory connections to the rest of common morality and practical philosophy. We are not told how any of our other beliefs connects with the principle that judges must obey restrictive rule. By contrast, the first position connects adjudication to a range of plausible moral judgments and principles. I have offered arguments for the conclusion that judges in reasonably just legal systems have *pro tanto* reasons to adhere in all cases and all-things-considered reasons to adhere in most. The arguments of part II depend on premises that, although controversial, have not been refuted. It is not unreasonable to accept them. The first position contradicts common sense to some extent, but I think its revisionism is more than compensated by its advantages in linking adjudication theory to the rest of common morality and practical philosophy. I think the real choice we face is between (1) a theory that conflicts with one popular belief about judicial duties, but makes more mutually supportive connections to the rest of common morality and practical philosophy, and (2) a theory that matches one popular belief, but makes fewer such connections. I have tried to persuade you that the first position is at least as reasonable as the second. Perhaps you will even come to prefer the first, as I do.

29. See, e.g., Norman Daniels, *Justice and Justification: Reflective Equilibrium in Theory and Practice* (Cambridge: Cambridge University Press, 1996); Michael R. DePaul, *Balance and Refinement: Beyond Coherence Methods of Moral Inquiry* (New York: Routledge, 1993).

14

Guidance Rules

The previous chapter culminated with support for the following:

Combined Restriction
1. If Group O deviates as often as, or more often than, group restriction permits, then deviate at no higher than the optimal average deviation rate.
2. Where n is the maximum number of cases in which group restriction permits Group O to deviate during a certain time period and m is the number of cases in which Group O actually deviates during that period, if $m < n$, then do not deviate in more than $n - m$ cases during that period.

Combined restriction simply imposes some constraints on deviation. Many possible adherence rules are consistent with combined restriction. We can now conjoin combined restriction with the imperative embodied in the basic intention shared by Group O: to avoid suboptimal results. The result is as follows:

Individual Policy
Deviating in suboptimal-result cases is permissible, subject to combined restriction.

14.1 APPRAISAL AND GUIDANCE

Individual policy specifies criteria for the objective appraisal of decisions made by a judge in Group O. It is designed for use by an outside observer who wants to determine whether a member of Group O has produced a decision sequence over the course of her career that is objectively permissible, all things considered. If a judge makes decisions that conform to individual policy, then her behavior is objectively permissible. This is not to say anything about her conscious deliberation processes. Nor is it to comment on her character: to say that she necessarily deserves praise. Perhaps she made all her decisions randomly and they coincidentally happen to conform to individual policy. Such a judge would deserve blame for her irresponsible methods despite having performed objectively permissible actions.

I think a good case can be made for individual policy as an objective appraisal standard. It is a moderate rule, an intermediate position between permissive rule and restrictive rule, and superior to both. But major questions remain. Could judges in realistic legal systems actually implement individual policy? What guidance rules might they use?

Alan Goldman rejects the whole idea of trying to maintain the "optimal level of deviation." He concludes that every taxpayer must simply pay his taxes and every judge must simply adhere to the law. I shall pause at intervals to consider Goldman's objections to optimizing. His first is epistemic: "[I]ndividuals will not have a way of knowing how many other individuals are reasoning in the same way in justifying deviation, how close to the threshold of excessive deviation they may be. They will not be able to coordinate their decisions to achieve the optimal level of deviation."[1] Analogously, he thinks, each judge suffers "an inability . . . to identify the optimal pattern or to know how close to the threshold of damage to the legal system he might be in not enforcing the law."[2]

This objection might apply to taxpayers, who do not communicate to one another their plans to reroute tax payments and cannot do so without risking criminal penalties. But the decisions of judges are matters of public record, extensively indexed and available for research. Judges can, in theory, learn how many other judges are deviating. To some extent their job even requires them to stay informed about these facts. They could develop a sense of how close to threshold their system is. Goldman's epistemic argument succeeds only if one of the following two assumptions holds:

1. Judges decide under conditions of *uncertainty*. They do not know even the probability that their system is at its threshold; or
2. Judges decide under conditions of *risk*: they do not know whether their system is at its threshold, but they know that the probability is relatively high.

However, Goldman's epistemic argument fails if

3. Judges decide under conditions of *risk*: they do not know whether their system is at its threshold, but they know that the probability is relatively low.

I submit that the third assumption describes realistic legal systems more accurately than the first two. Goldman briefly considers this possibility. His response consists of two assertions. The first is that "the negative consequences of crossing [the threshold] are enormous."[3] I shall consider this assertion before turning to the second. The consequences of crossing

---

1. Alan H. Goldman, *Practical Rules: When We Need Them and When We Don't* (Cambridge: Cambridge University Press, 2002), p. 44.
2. Ibid.
3. Ibid., pp. 44–45.

threshold are, by definition, bad. But attempting to optimize is rational, nevertheless, if they are not too bad and if the risk of crossing threshold is low enough. The negative consequences of crossing threshold are "enormous" only if two conditions hold: first, crossing threshold dramatically increases the number and/or severity of suboptimal results; second, having crossed threshold, the system takes too long to return to subthreshold equilibrium, or maybe never returns. If these two conditions obtain, then crossing threshold is like falling off a cliff: we should stay far from the edge. Whether these conditions obtain depends upon the shape of the curve relating deviation density to mimetic failure. We can assume that it slopes monotonically upward, but what else can we say about it?

If it is fairly straight and shallow, then there is no dramatic difference between the system at one level of deviation density and at a slightly higher level, even when the incremental increase pushes the system over threshold. If Group O accidentally pushes the system over threshold, then it can return to subthreshold equilibrium by slightly reducing its own deviation rate.

Imagine, instead, that the curve is roughly shaped like a backward L: its slope is shallow for awhile and then suddenly becomes steep. Imagine, also, that threshold is located very close to the sharp upward turn. If these conditions hold, then crossing threshold triggers a cascade of deviation, including much deviation in optimal-result cases. Once the fact that judges are deviating so often becomes common knowledge, it is difficult to persuade judges to return to a more adherent pattern. Even if Group O reduces its own deviation rate to previous levels, it takes too long to restore subthreshold equilibrium. The system has fallen off the cliff.[4]

If the curve has a backward-L shape, then the argument for restrictive rule is strengthened. I have no empirical data about the shape of the curve, but there is potentially relevant social science: a body of research documenting "informational cascades" and other forms of "herd behavior" and "bandwagon effects" in various settings.[5] Under certain conditions even otherwise rational actors who "know better" will adopt the beliefs of others and imitate their behavior. General convergence in the population

---

4. See the literature on the provision of collective *step goods*. Ramzi Suleiman, "Provision of Step-Level Public Goods under Uncertainty," *Rationality and Society* 9 (1997): 163–87; Jean Hampton, "Free-Rider Problems in the Production of Collective Goods," *Economics and Philosophy* 3 (1987): 245–73.

5. See, e.g., Timur Kuran and Cass R. Sunstein, "Availability Cascades and Risk Regulation," *Stanford Law Review* 51 (1999): 683–768; Sushil Bikhchandani, David Hirshleifer, and Ivo Welch, "Learning from the Behavior of Others: Conformity, Fads, and Informational Cascades," *Journal of Economic Perspectives* 12 (1998): 151–70; Lisa R. Anderson and Charles A. Holt, "Information Cascades in the Laboratory," *American Economic Review* 87 (1997): 847–62; Abhijit Banerjee, "A Simple Model of Herd Behavior," *Quarterly Journal of Economics* 107 (1992): 797–818; Sushil Bikhchandani, David Hirshleifer and Ivo Welch, "A Theory of Fads, Fashion, Custom and Cultural Change as Informational Cascades," *Journal of Political Economy* 100 (1992): 992–1026.

can occur rapidly, like a stampede. A few scholars have applied cascade theory to judicial behavior, but they have concentrated on precedent, not mimesis.[6] The backward-L hypothesis remains speculative, but it could be true. If so, then judges who attempt to optimize risk falling off the cliff. I shall assume *arguendo* that this risk is real.

I note, however, that Goldman provides no reason to assume that threshold falls close to the point at which the curve begins its sharp upward slope. I shall assume *arguendo* that it does—that crossing threshold runs an unacceptably high risk of destroying the rule of law indefinitely. If this assumption proves false, then my argument for moderate rules becomes more compelling.

This brings me to Goldman's second objection to optimizing: "a judge can assume that, in the absence of a rule, she or one of her colleagues will [cross the threshold]."[7] If the judges in Group O deviate in all suboptimal-result cases, with no regard for threshold, then it is probable that the judiciary will eventually cross threshold. If that is what "absence of a rule" means, then Goldman is correct. But he treats restrictive rule as the only alternative to no rule at all. Judges can guard against falling off the cliff by obeying moderate rules.[8] If the members of Group O conform to individual policy, then they deviate in some but not all suboptimal-result cases. No one crosses threshold. I conclude that Goldman's objection to optimizing does not reach judges who conform to individual policy. Even if crossing threshold destroys the rule of law, indefinitely, judges who conform to individual policy do not push their system over that cliff.

My argument in this section has assumed that judges internalize individual policy—they use it as their guidance rule. Real judges could, in theory, do this. In practice, however, it may be a terrible prescription, for reasons that mirror the well-known shortcomings of act utilitarianism as a decision procedure.[9] Much as utility may not be maximized if every individual attempts to maximize utility, so the goals of individual policy may be achieved less effectively if judges try to apply it directly than if they follow another guidance rule. Accurately applying individual policy requires extensive gathering of information and deliberating. It requires each judge to determine how often other judges are deviating relative to the maximum rate permitted by group restriction. It requires judges to calculate the proximity of current deviation density to threshold, to ascertain what standards their colleagues have adopted to regulate their own deviation, and to determine in which deviation enterprises they would

---

6. Cass R. Sunstein, *Why Societies Need Dissent* (Cambridge, Mass.: Harvard University Press, 2003), pp. 59–60; Eric Talley, "Precedential Cascades: An Appraisal," *Southern California Law Review* 73 (1999): 87–137.

7. Goldman, *Practical Rules*, pp. 44–45.

8. Goldman rejects moderate rules for moral reasons that I shall discuss in chapter 15.

9. See, e.g., J. L. Mackie, *Ethics: Inventing Right and Wrong* (Harmondsworth: Penguin Books, 1977), p. 129.

participate were they to deviate in a given case. Judges who attempt to follow individual policy as a guidance rule will rarely succeed in approximating the optimal decision pattern. This observation does not assume that the judges to whom guidance rules are addressed are imperfect identifiers of suboptimal-result cases. I am still discussing the judges in Group O. My reservations about individual policy merely assume that directly determining the location of threshold and the current level of deviation density are extremely difficult and time-consuming tasks. The research takes time, effort, and resources that judges should not be expected to expend. If we asked judges to use individual policy as a guidance rule, then we could not blame them for failing to approximate the ideal decision pattern because reasonably competent agents with their beliefs and information would perform no better. Thus, individual policy makes a poor guidance rule and I would not urge judges to adopt it. I merely maintain that individual policy is the objectively correct appraisal policy for patterns of judicial decision. The best guidance rules are those that most closely approximate the patterns approved by individual policy. These rules I have yet to identify.

14.2 SIMPLER GUIDANCE RULES

We can formulate simpler guidance rules for implementing individual policy. Consider two old friends: restrictive rule and permissive rule. Neither assigns any relevance to deviation density. Although I have argued that neither succeeds as an appraisal rule, I have not yet considered their potential as guidance rules.

Permissive rule fares no better as a guidance rule than it did as an appraisal rule. In real legal systems, deviating in all suboptimal-result cases probably exceeds threshold. Restrictive rule, by contrast, forbids all deviation. It has some definite advantages over individual policy as a guidance rule: it is simple, easy to learn, and relatively easy to follow.[10] Obeying restrictive rule guarantees that the two conditions of individual policy are met. It keeps the system below threshold, so it is at least a candidate for a viable guidance rule. However, restrictive rule also has substantial moral disadvantages, discussed earlier,[11] that carry over to its employment as a guidance rule. Restrictive rule forbids judges to attain the optimal decision pattern in any legal system in which the optimal average deviation rate is greater than zero, which is all realistic legal systems. Restrictive rule requires judges to use *pro tanto* unjustified force, or threats thereof, in an unnecessarily large number of suboptimal-result cases. The higher the optimal average deviation rate in the system, the greater becomes the

---

10. I am not sure whether restrictive rule is easier to follow than permissive rule or vice versa, but I need not address that question.

11. See §§8.4–8.6.

divergence between the optimal pattern and the best patterns permitted by restrictive rule.

14.3 BETTER GUIDANCE RULES

I shall now evaluate candidates for a guidance rule better than restrictive rule—one that allows judges to deviate at closer to the optimal rate. Consider a rule slightly more permissive than restrictive rule:

> *First Moderate Rule*: Over the course of your judicial career, deviate in no more than 1 percent of suboptimal-result cases.

First moderate rule is more difficult to apply than restrictive rule, but still manageable. It is much easier to apply than individual policy. First moderate rule relieves judges of the burden of monitoring the deviation rate of other judges. Instead, it merely requires each judge to monitor *her own* deviation rate over the course of his career. It makes the permissibility of deviation in a given case by a certain judge partly depend upon the number of other cases in which she has already deviated, or anticipates deviating. First moderate rule seems like an improvement on restrictive rule, at least for legal systems that are well below threshold. Deviating in 1 percent of suboptimal-result cases will not push any such system above threshold.

First moderate rule answers Goldman's epistemic objection. Interestingly, with respect to prudential reasoning by individuals in their private lives, Goldman supports a position similar to first moderate rule. He observes that

> we can more easily solve the coordination problem over time for our own actions than we can coordinate with the actions of others in the relevant moral contexts. This ability to coordinate actions over time allows the adoption of strategies to optimize instead of settling for the second-best strategy of strict rules. We can have the occasional snack or martini.[12]

Goldman's reference to the "occasional snack or martini" shows that he accepts a prudential, intrapersonal counterpart to first moderate rule. However, he sees moral and epistemic problems in the interpersonal case that do not arise in the intrapersonal case. I shall argue that these problems are not fatal in the interpersonal case, either.

An obvious objection is that first moderate rule provides no *basis* for selecting the 1 percent. It seems to invite judges to use arbitrary criteria. This is a good objection. When allocating a scarce, indivisible privilege to one of several deserving beneficiaries, the allocator is not necessarily permitted to choose arbitrarily if the beneficiaries differ on morally relevant criteria. For example, if every potential beneficiary deserves or needs the

---

12. Goldman, *Practical Rules*, p. 6.

privilege, but one is *more* deserving or needy than the others, then the allocator may be morally obligated to favor the most deserving or needy, as in emergencies calling for medical triage. First moderate rule allows judges to violate this principle. Fortunately, we can revise first moderate rule to correct this problem:

> *Rebuttable Presumption*: Adhere in suboptimal-result cases, unless the law requires an extremely suboptimal result.

In realistic legal systems, extreme suboptimal-result cases are relatively rare, comprising less than 1 percent of suboptimal-result cases (my estimate). In such systems, the members of Group O can obey rebuttable presumption without pushing the system above threshold. As does first moderate rule, rebuttable presumption allows for occasional deviation, but unlike first moderate rule, it provides a nonarbitrary criterion for selecting cases for deviation. Rebuttable presumption requires judges to choose their "1 percent" on a morally appropriate basis.

Rebuttable presumption captures a familiar idea.[13] I have mentioned that even writers who deny that it is ethically permissible for a judge to deviate from the law *simpliciter* often make exceptions for extremely suboptimal results.[14] Faced with cases involving slavery laws in the American South, anti-Semitic laws in Nazi Germany, the laws of the Taliban in Afghanistan, or the laws sustaining South African apartheid, all but the most committed supporters of restrictive rule tend to admit that they really favor only something like rebuttable presumption. A judge is morally permitted to deviate from a Nazi law that forbids harboring Jews, even if his fellow judges uphold it faithfully. By deviating, he rides free on his fellow judges, but he is justified in doing so because the law requires an extremely unjust result. Goldman actually implies, occasionally, that judges should obey rebuttable presumption, not restrictive rule.[15]

Rebuttable presumption will remind some readers of the Radbruch formula, which denies legal validity to extremely unjust positive laws.[16] Both the Radbruch formula and rebuttable presumption entail that judges are not morally obligated to adhere to extremely unjust laws. However, rebuttable presumption does not impugn the legal validity of extremely unjust laws, as does the Radbruch formula. Also, although rebuttable

---

13. "[I]n a flourishing legal system the fact of law provides a case for coercion that must stand unless some exceptional counterargument is available." Ronald Dworkin, *Law's Empire* (Cambridge, Mass.: Harvard University Press, 1986), p. 110. See also Gerald J. Postema, *Bentham and the Common Law Tradition* (Oxford: Oxford University Press, 1986), ch. 12.

14. See §8.4.

15. He states that judges "can ignore recognized legal requirements only in the direst of circumstances" (p. 148) and that they should not treat like cases differently "except in the direst of circumstances that would call the validity of the legal system itself into question" (p. 46). Goldman, *Practical Rules*.

16. See §8.4.

presumption applies to both suboptimal-rule cases and negative-gap cases, the Radbruch formula might not apply to the latter.

One might doubt whether rebuttable presumption even constitutes a serious rule, because applying it seems to require moral judgment concerning whether a certain result is extremely suboptimal. But it could work as a serious rule if there were sufficient consensus regarding which results are extremely suboptimal. Ex hypothesi such consensus prevails in Group O. However, obeying rebuttable presumption as a serious rule is equivalent to treating *restrictive rule* as something less than a serious rule. It is equivalent to acting as a "rule-sensitive particularist" with respect to restrictive rule. Another variation of rebuttable presumption would be akin to taking a "presumptive positivist" approach to restrictive rule,[17] directing judges to obey restrictive rule, unless they just happen to perceive especially strong reasons to deviate.

As I mentioned, rebuttable presumption makes sense in reasonably just systems: it is a permissible implementation of individual policy. However, there are conceivable legal systems so unjust that rebuttable presumption permits too much deviation in them. Imagine a horribly unjust system in which the law requires so many extremely suboptimal results that if Group O deviates in all of them, then it pushes the system past threshold. In such systems, rebuttable presumption is the wrong adherence rule.[18] In more just legal systems, by contrast, rebuttable presumption is acceptable. In such systems Group O can safely obey rebuttable presumption without pushing the system past threshold.

Applying rebuttable presumption requires some sense of what makes a result *extremely suboptimal* as opposed to just *moderately suboptimal*. This assumes that some results are more suboptimal than others and that people can distinguish between extremely and moderately suboptimal. Returning a slave to his master, for example, is an extremely suboptimal result. Someone who believes this might also believe that preventing a university from giving preferential admission to African-Americans, although a suboptimal result, is not extremely suboptimal. I have been assuming that the extension of *extremely suboptimal* is fixed independently of facts about threshold or the types of cases heard in any particular system. A result is extremely suboptimal if and only if it involves a degree of injustice, unfairness, or undeserved misfortune that is very high, in absolute terms. Because such cases are very rare in reasonably just systems, rebuttable presumption happens to be an acceptable implementation of individual policy in such systems. But rebuttable presumption is not specifically calibrated to any particular system. Therefore, rebuttable presumption is not the best implementation of individual policy in all legal

---

17. Frederick Schauer, *Playing by the Rules: A Philosophical Examination of Rule-Based Decision-Making in Law and in Life* (Oxford: Oxford University Press, 1991), pp. 196–206.

18. Unless, of course, the system is so unjust that the rule of law should, morally speaking, be destroyed there.

systems. Some systems are sufficiently just that Group O can deviate in *more* cases than rebuttable presumption permits, without exceeding threshold. It remains an open question whether modern legal systems meet this condition. If they do, then rebuttable presumption is needlessly restrictive for those systems. It would be desirable to formulate a more precisely tailored rule than rebuttable presumption—one that allows judges to approach threshold more closely without going over. In the next section, I present an analogy meant to illustrate the irrational restrictiveness of rebuttable presumption in reasonably just systems.

14.4 EMISSIONS TRADING ANALOGY

Think of a deviant decision as analogous to an act that releases into the environment a very small quantity of a toxin that, in much larger quantities, unjustifiably harms identifiable individuals to a perceptible extent.[19] This is like mimetic failure. Suppose the toxin is released as the undesired byproduct of a process that itself prevents societal harm (e.g., the manufacture of safety devices or beneficial pharmaceuticals). Now picture two different environmental policies. Both are versions of *cap-and-trade* environmental regulations. These policies efficiently limit the aggregate level of pollution by allocating *pollution credits* to firms and allowing firms that pollute less to trade their credits to firms that pollute more.

Standard cap-and-trade policies allow firms to purchase any quantity of credits and spend them as they wish, either gradually or all at once. Call this a *no-minimum* policy. It does not attempt to ensure that each firm expels even approximately the same quantity of pollution. The state does not monitor whether any given firm is profitable, either. Rather, the state creates market incentives that induce firms to respond rationally to the overall level of pollution. As the overall level of pollution increases, credits are spent and the remaining credits command commensurately higher prices in trade. It makes little difference if one firm buys most of the credits and pollutes extensively or if the credits are spread across many

---

19. Stephen Burton draws a similar analogy:

The political common ground is like an economic commons that benefits the community only as long as everyone acts with self-restraint. Any one person, however, can be made better off by acting opportunistically in his or her individual or subgroup self-interest if everyone does not do so and thereby bring down the cooperative scheme altogether. So some people will try in any case quietly to take a piece of the common ground for themselves while continuing to benefit from the general scheme of order and justice that prevails nonetheless. When too many get away with it the common ground may give way to a repellent kind of politics that will strike most as a degeneration of the society.

Stephen J. Burton, *Judging in Good Faith* (Cambridge: Cambridge University Press, 1992), p. 258.

firms, each of which pollutes modestly. Overall pollution levels matter; the identities of the polluting firms do not.

This is the way real cap-and-trade policies work.[20] However, we can imagine a bizarre alternative policy that requires firms to choose between (1) buying no credits and (2) buying and spending a large minimum number of credits all at once. Call this a *minimum-purchase* policy. A minimum-purchase policy might be acceptable in a society given the following scenario. Most of the time, most of the many firms in this society have no opportunity to prevent even small degrees of harm (thereby earning profits) by engaging in harm-preventing but polluting processes. Therefore, they have no reason to pollute. They buy no pollution credits. On rare occasions, however, one of these firms or another has the opportunity to prevent great harm, thereby earning large profits, although doing so will produce high levels of pollution all at once. When a firm finds itself in this rare position, it purchases the prescribed minimum credits and spends them all at once.

Although a minimum-purchase policy is acceptable in such a society, it is excessively restrictive for one in which opportunities to prevent small quantities of harm, by means of moderately polluting processes, are distributed widely across the firms. In such a society the no-minimum policy is superior. It allows firms to purchase credits in a continuous range of quantities. Each firm can tailor its purchases to its individual needs and opportunities.

Now apply the analogy back to the legal system. A market in which a single firm buys a large bundle of credits and spends them all at once is analogous to a legal system in which a single judge deviates from a law that requires an extremely suboptimal result, but she thereby causes substantial mimetic failure. For some reason her decision leads many other judges to deviate in optimal-result cases. By contrast, a market in which the same credits are spread more evenly across many firms is analogous to a legal system in which many judges deviate at various times from laws that require moderately suboptimal results, each contributing modestly to an overall degree of mimetic failure.

Rebuttable presumption is analogous to the minimum-purchase policy. It permits a judge to deviate from the law only if she must in order to avoid an extremely suboptimal result. This rule may be appropriate to very unjust legal systems in which a single deviant decision can prevent an extreme injustice. The prerogative is useless, however, to a judge in a reasonably just legal system who may never hear an extreme suboptimal-result case in her entire career. Rather, she will hear hundreds of cases in which the law requires *moderately* suboptimal results. Preventing the

---

20. These policies, as implemented in the real world, invite objections from distributive justice and expressive meaning that I shall not address. See Mark Sagoff, "Controlling Global Climate: The Debate over Pollution Trading," in *Philosophical Dimensions of Public Policy*, ed. Verna V. Gehring (New Brunswick, N.J.: Transaction, 2002).

same "amount" of injustice as the judge in the highly unjust system prevented with a single decision would require her to deviate in many of these moderate cases. She could do so without contributing to any enterprise that will push her system past threshold. Unfortunately, rebuttable presumption forbids her from doing so. As a result, she reaches many moderately suboptimal results that she could have avoided without undermining the rule of law had she obeyed a better adherence rule.

14.5 IMPROVING UPON THE REBUTTABLE PRESUMPTION

Is there an alternative to rebuttable presumption that allows judges in reasonably just systems more closely to approximate individual policy? The problem with rebuttable presumption is that it is not calibrated to the system's optimal deviation rate. We need a rule that is properly calibrated while still feasible to apply. Suppose we determine a value for n that is the optimal average rate of deviation in suboptimal-result cases for all judges in Group O. Then we can formulate the following:

> *Final Moderate Rule*: Over the course of your judicial career, deviate in no more than n percent of suboptimal-result cases.

Final moderate rule improves upon rebuttable presumption. I think a good implementation of individual policy will incorporate final moderate rule. By itself, however, it has the same flaw as first moderate rule. A typical judge in an actual legal system might decide a much larger number of suboptimal-result cases than the total number in which final moderate rule permits deviation. Final moderate rule provides no criteria for selecting which cases will comprise the n percent. So judges need additional standards for deciding between two suboptimal-result cases when final moderate rule permits deviation in only one of them. These standards could take the form of *priority rules*. Our first priority rule recalls rebuttable presumption, in that it assigns relevance to degrees of suboptimality:

> *First Priority Rule*: If final moderate rule permits you to deviate in only one of two suboptimal-result cases, then deviate in the one in which the legally required result is more suboptimal.

First priority rule ensures that the n percent will comprise the more serious of the suboptimal-result cases that arise in the system. Notice that this is not the same as limiting deviation to "extreme" suboptimal-result cases as rebuttable presumption does. First priority rule specifies no absolute level of suboptimality as a floor. The maximum percentage of suboptimal-result cases in which moderate rule permits deviation is determined by n. The value of n varies directly with the overall level of justice that prevails in the legal system. In an extremely just system there are only a few suboptimal-result cases and the legally required results are only slightly suboptimal, yet first priority rule permits judges to deviate in most of them. At the limit there are no suboptimal-result cases and $n = 100$.[21]

First priority rule instructs judges to give higher priority to avoiding a result, the more suboptimal it is. Ignoring for the moment the objection that judges should not deviate in the first place, this is an intuitive idea. The opposite instruction would give priority to avoiding *less* suboptimal results. At the limit it would instruct judges to deviate in *optimal-result* cases. This view makes no sense. Somewhat more defensible is the view that judges should give no priority based on degrees of suboptimality. On this view judges should not treat the fact that the law requires a more suboptimal result in one case than in another as a reason to deviate in the first case rather than the second. Perhaps some people accept this view, but it is hard to defend. The argument would appear to rest upon the assumption that the systemic effects of deviating, which vary from one case to another, fluctuate directly with the suboptimality of the legally required result. The idea would be that deviating in order to avoid a more suboptimal result causes more systemic damage than does deviating in order to avoid a less suboptimal result. If that were true, then the relatively greater benefits of deviating in a more extreme suboptimal-result case would be cancelled out by the relatively greater systemic damage. However, there is no reason to believe in a direct correlation between suboptimality and systemic effects. This is not to claim that the systemic effects of deviation are constant across all cases. Some cases naturally receive more attention than others and provoke more mimetic failure. But there is no reason to think that these are necessarily cases in which the avoided result was more suboptimal, or more suboptimal than the judge believed it to be. If anything, one might predict that deviating causes more mimetic failure the *less* suboptimal the avoided result is perceived to be: the more subtle the argument for deviation, the more easily is it misconstrued by posterior judges.

14.6 TYPE-SELECTIVE DEVIATION

I suggested that judges in Group O can move their system toward threshold, without going over, by obeying first priority rule in addition to final moderate rule. First priority rule provides some basis for choosing in which suboptimal-result cases to deviate. But first priority rule does not entirely solve the arbitrariness problem. First priority rule permits judges to deviate in n percent of suboptimal-result cases and to give priority to more serious suboptimal-result cases, but it does not require a judge who

---

21. Obviously, in that scenario there are no suboptimal-result cases in which to deviate. One hundred percent of zero is zero.

deviates in one case to deviate in every other case at the same level of suboptimality. The following story illustrates.

Your friend, Rita, is a federal district judge. Once a month you visit her courtroom. In July she hears a free speech challenge to a statute making it a misdemeanor to engage in certain kinds of bias-motivated speech. A higher court has ruled that a similar statute violates the Free Speech Clause.[22] The defendant moves for dismissal for that reason, but Judge Rita ignores the precedent and applies the statute. You ask her privately if she believes that the precedent did not apply to the facts of the case. Was there some legally relevant difference between the statute challenged and the statute that was invalidated by the higher court? Rita confides in you that she sees no such difference. The precedent clearly applies to the recent case, but she fundamentally disagrees with the higher court's decision. She believes that hate speech should be subject to such regulations. That is why she ignored the precedent.

You return to the courtroom in August to find Judge Rita hearing another free speech challenge, this one to a statute that makes it a misdemeanor to engage in nude dancing. The higher court has ruled that a similar statute violates the Free Speech Clause.[23] Rita cites this precedent as authority and rules the statute unconstitutional.

You privately question the judge. Did the second free speech precedent actually control her reasoning, as the language in her opinion suggests, or did she invalidate the nude dancing statute because she disapproves of it? She replies that the precedent controlled her reasoning, although she disagrees with it. She believes that nude dancing should be subject to regulation. She approves of the challenged statute and believes it to be consistent with a proper reading of the First Amendment.

So why did she follow precedent in the second case but not the first? Does she find nude dancing intrinsically *less* eligible for regulation than hate speech? No, she replies, she finds the two practices equally eligible for regulation. So what was her reasoning?

Rita explains that, in a certain sense, she invalidated the nude dancing statute *because* she upheld the hate speech statute. She followed precedent in the second case because she disregarded it in the first. In a world without systemic effects, she gladly would have upheld both statutes. But every month she hears cases in which higher-court precedent requires her to reach results that she considers suboptimal. If judges such as she were to disregard too many precedents with which they disagree, then less "wise" judges would begin disregarding precedents with which *they* disagree and many of these would be *good* precedents. Therefore judges (wise or not) must limit themselves to deviating in a certain percentage of cases

---

22. Compare *R.A.V. v. City of St. Paul*, 505 U.S. 377 (1992).

23. As if the opposite result had been reached in *Barnes v. Glen Theatre, Inc.*, 501 U.S. 560 (1991).

and no more. Rita limits herself to deviating in no more than 15 percent of the cases in which the law requires her to reach a result that is (in her opinion) suboptimal.

First priority rule permits judges to practice *type-selective deviation*—deviating in some, but not all, suboptimal-result cases at a certain level of suboptimality. This is the basis for a major objection to first priority rule and a defense of restrictive rule: the objection from comparative justice or "treating like cases alike." I think the comparative justice objection to type-selective deviation can be answered. As I shall explain, individual policy permits judges, in principle, to practice an even more surprising kind of selectivity: *token-selective deviation*. The comparative justice argument has its greatest force against this kind of selectivity. I shall challenge the argument even as an objection to token-selective deviation. If it fails there, then it fails a fortiori with respect to type-selective deviation.[24]

14.7 SUBOPTIMAL-RULE CASES

Assume that $n = 15$, and picture Judge Rita hearing a series of 100 suboptimal-result cases. Fifteen of these are cases in which the law requires an extremely suboptimal result: *high-level* cases. In remaining 85, the law requires moderately suboptimal results: these are *low-level* cases. Judge Rita can deviate in all 15 of the high-level cases and adhere in the remaining low-level cases. This result conforms to final moderate rule and first priority rule. It does not require her to choose arbitrarily.

However, first priority rule tolerates a different kind of arbitrariness that is almost as troubling. Other judges have not deviated and will not deviate in every high-level case. In fact, they have adhered and will adhere in case tokens very similar to those in which Rita deviates. Rita can point to no features of the tokens in which she deviates that justify deviating in them but not in other tokens of the same type, nor in suboptimal-result cases of a different type at the same level of suboptimality.[25]

Furthermore, Rita got lucky. She heard exactly the right number of high-level cases. What if she hears fewer? We can depict the case tokens in a legal system as a layered pyramid. Each layer represents a set of cases at the same level of suboptimality. The top layer represents the most extreme suboptimal-result cases. The area of each layer represents the number of cases at that level. Picture a system represented by a pyramid with only two layers: a tiny top layer and a large bottom layer. In this system, 5 of the suboptimal-result cases are high-level cases, while the remaining 95 are low-level cases. None of the low-level cases is noticeably

---

24. See §15.2.
25. C. S. Peirce first used the terms *type* and *token* to mark such distinctions. Charles S. Peirce, *Collected Papers of Charles Sanders Peirce*, eds. Charles Hartshorne and Paul Weiss (Cambridge, Mass.: Harvard University Press, 1932), §4.537.

more or less suboptimal than the other low-level cases. That is why they are represented by a single layer.

Rita can still deviate in the 5 high-level cases, but beyond that she faces a conundrum. If she deviates in all 95 of the low-level cases, then she violates first priority rule, because $n = 15$. First priority rule permits her to adhere in all 10 of the low-level cases that she hears, but if she does so then she reaches 10 unnecessary suboptimal results. Alternatively, first priority rule permits her to deviate in 10 of the low-level cases, adhering in the rest. But first priority rule provides no reason to choose any particular 10 from the 95. The arbitrariness problem recurs.

It would be desirable to find further criteria for choosing between suboptimal-result cases at the same level. I think there are such criteria. In this section I entertain the idea that judges should give some deviation priority to suboptimal-rule cases over gap cases, assuming equally suboptimal results. The limits of this priority are decision patterns involving deviation only in suboptimal-rule cases but never in gap cases. One might interpret the claim of the natural law tradition that "unjust laws do not bind in conscience" as requiring such a pattern.[26]

Consider two criminal statutes: one criminalizes fornication, whereas the other imposes strict liability for possessing 500 grams of heroin. Each carries a $500 fine. Assume that fornication is not so immoral as to merit this fine and that the fornication law serves no other adequate public purpose. Therefore, virtually all convictions under that law are suboptimal results. Assume, also, that heroin possessors usually deserve to be convicted, so that only a few convictions under the heroin law are suboptimal, as in the rare case when a defendant receives a box containing heroin, unbeknownst to him.[27] However, a conviction in that gap case is just as suboptimal as is the typical conviction under the fornication law.

Do judges have a stronger reason to deviate in a suboptimal-rule case, such as one brought under the fornication law, than in a gap case under the heroin law? The reason to deviate in a suboptimal-rule case is not intrinsically stronger than the reason to deviate in a gap case if the law in the latter requires a comparably suboptimal result. However, imagine a judge who must choose between (1) deviating in m gap cases, each under different suboptimal rules, and (2) deviating in m cases under one suboptimal rule. I think she has reasons to choose to deviate in the cases falling under the single rule. This idea is captured by the following:

Second Priority Rule: If final moderate rule and first priority rule permit deviation in only one of two sets, each composed of the same number of cases, where the members of the first set fall under more than one rule and the

---

26. Thomas Aquinas, *Summa Theologiae*, trans. Fathers of the English Dominican Province (London: Washbourne, 1915), Question 96.
27. This defendant could still be convicted under a strict liability statute.

members of the second set fall under a single rule, and are otherwise as apt for deviation as are the members of the first set (regarding suboptimality, etc.), then deviate in the second set.

Second priority rule is consistent with some deviation priority for suboptimal-rule cases. It does not, however, entail that judges must never deviate in negative-gap cases. Recall Rita's conundrum. It is statistically likely that fewer than 10 of the remaining high-level cases are suboptimal-rule cases under the same rule. If Rita does not hear as many suboptimal-rule cases as the overall number in which second priority rule permits her to deviate, then she is permitted to deviate in *some* negative-gap cases until she reaches her permitted deviation allotment, whatever that may be.

Second priority rule instructs judges to give deviation priority to suboptimal-rule cases over gap cases. This is an intuitive idea. By definition a suboptimal rule can be improved. By deviating from a suboptimal rule, a judge paves the way for improvements, judicial or legislative. This is obvious in cases in which the judge has legal authority to improve the rule, but it is true even in cases in which the rule could be improved although the judge lacks legal authority to improve it, as when a superior court has already ruled out the improvement. A judge who improves the rule by departing from vertical precedent deviates from the law, but she points the way to a more coherent and optimal set of legal standards from which deviation will be less often necessary.

By contrast, a judge who deviates in a gap case does not point the way to a more coherent and optimal set of legal standards. In a gap case, by definition, the controlling legal standards cannot be improved as a practical matter, yet they still dictate suboptimal results in some cases. A judge who deviates in a gap case does not suggest any superior legal standard. He does not propose a new exception that should be appended to existing standards. He simply deviates in order to avoid a suboptimal result. This can be morally permissible if my argument is correct. It protects the legally disfavored party from unjustified disadvantages and it might inspire posterior judges to deviate in other suboptimal-result cases. But it does nothing to improve legal standards themselves. By contrast, deviating properly in a suboptimal-rule case benefits the legally disfavored party and also makes a potential contribution to an improvement in legal standards, possibly benefiting future parties in this additional way. Ceteris paribus, judges should give priority to suboptimal-rule cases over gap cases.

Consider cases that arise under the following conditions. Under existing law, each of a class of persons is suffering or will suffer a suboptimal result. Changing the law would protect these persons. However, if the law were changed to protect everyone in the class, then this would have negative effects on balance. The law would not have these negative effects if it were changed to protect some but not all members of the class, but

Guidance Rules

there are no politically feasible criteria for the law to use to select the beneficiaries.

I classify such cases as gap cases even though, in theory, a better rule is possible. A judge who hears such a case should not attempt to change the law because such attempts are futile. Ex hypothesi there are no politically feasible criteria for selecting the beneficiaries. If he announces a new legal rule that selects the right number of beneficiaries, then his decision will be reversed by a higher court, overridden by the political branches, or simply ignored by other judges. He will fail to change the law. The most he can realistically hope to accomplish is an optimal result in the case at bar. So the difference between a suboptimal-rule case and a gap case is that a judge who deviates and announces a new rule in a suboptimal-rule case has a better chance of improving the law than a judge who does the same in a gap case.

14.8 BLAME AND WARRANT

I have defended guidance rules that permit deviation in some suboptimal-result cases. I have stipulated that the judges in Group O always accurately identify suboptimal-result cases. By obeying my proposed rules, they can be very confident that their decisions are objectively permissible, given that they accurately identify suboptimal-result cases. However, they probably want to avoid subjectively impermissible actions—blameworthy actions—as well as impermissible ones. Even if a judge is objectively permitted to deviate, she is blameworthy if she deviates without having adequate evidence that the deviant result is at least not normatively inferior to the legally required result. She is like a motorist who drives with severely impaired vision, but gets lucky and hits no one.

Judges know that reasonable citizens in pluralistic societies disagree about many moral issues. They know that even competent judges reach some morally mistaken conclusions. Therefore, before she knowingly deviates for the first time, any judge who wishes to avoid blameworthy decisions will want to know how strong her evidence of suboptimality must be if she is to remain blameless.[28] The following argument elaborates:

1. An agent is blameworthy if she knowingly performs an action that she does not reasonably believe to have a probability below y of being objectively wrong.
2. Judges cannot reasonably deny that reaching suboptimal results is objectively wrong.

---

28. I am referring to the concern that blame would be justified, not that some actual observer will blame her.

3. Therefore, a judge is blameworthy if she knowingly deviates in order to avoid a result that she believes to be suboptimal and she does not reasonably believe that the probability is below y that she is mistaken.

What is the value of y? In other words, how subjectively confident in her judgments of suboptimality must a judge be before she deviates?[29] How confident should we require a judge to be before she can deviate without risking our condemnation? These are difficult questions. Fortunately, legal systems deal constantly with questions of probability and confidence in judgment. A judge who concludes that a result is suboptimal can always ask himself whether his level of confidence satisfies a specified evidentiary standard. In Anglo-American law the most familiar standards are preponderance of the evidence, clear and convincing evidence, and reasonable doubt. Judges could use one of these standards, or something similar, to determine whether they are sufficiently confident that a result is suboptimal.

First consider a reasonable-doubt standard. Some might argue that judges who used this standard in reasonably just legal systems would never deviate in socially controversial cases, because they could not have sufficient confidence in the suboptimality of any result in such cases. Consider controversies about economic justice, environmental policy, affirmative action, capital punishment, abortion, assisted suicide, prostitution, recreational drugs, et cetera. If, as philosophers often suggest, "reasonable people" disagree about such issues, then one might claim that no one can ever believe "beyond a reasonable doubt" that his own position is correct. If so, and if the proper evidentiary standard is reasonable doubt, then judges who deviate in such cases are always blameworthy even when their decisions are objectively correct as a moral matter. Therefore, they should never deviate in such cases.

I dispute the major premise of this argument: that if reasonable people disagree about an issue, then one cannot have confidence beyond a reasonable doubt in one's own position. Judge John T. Noonan, Jr., a federal appellate judge, believes that abortion is as objectively immoral as infanticide, ceteris paribus. He believes that criminalizing it is morally obligatory and that the right to abort is not protected by the U.S. Constitution, properly understood.[30] He knows that reasonable people disagree with

---

29. See the discussion of the *epistemic threshold* in Douglas E. Edlin, *Judges and Unjust Laws: Common Law Constitutionalism and the Foundations of Judicial Review* (Ann Arbor: University of Michigan Press, 2008), pp. 139–49. See also Stephen R. Perry, "Second-Order Reasons, Uncertainty, and Legal Theory," *Southern California Law Review* 62 (1989): 913–94, p. 967.

30. John T. Noonan, Jr., *Persons and Masks of the Law: Cardozo, Holmes, Jefferson, Holmes, and Wythe as Makers of the Masks* (New York: Farrar, Straus & Giroux, 1976).

him, but their general reasonableness does not make their views *on this topic* reasonable. I think Judge Noonan could consistently claim that he is confident beyond a reasonable doubt that abortion should be criminalized, knowing that many reasonable people disagree with him.[31] This is not, of course, to imply that the esteemed Judge Noonan would actually deviate from the law. Nor is my point that pro-life judges have better reasons than pro-choice judges to claim that they have no reasonable doubts about the correctness of their respective positions. Justice Ruth Bader Ginsburg may be just as confident that abortion should not be criminalized. I happen to disagree with Judge Noonan about abortion. I have simply used him as an example of a judge whose subjective level of confidence in one of his moral judgments would seem to satisfy even a reasonable-doubt standard.[32] I conclude that even a standard as stringent as reasonable doubt could allow judges to deviate in socially controversial cases on the basis of their own moral convictions.

I have made no argument in favor of any particular evidentiary standard. Different standards might be equally compatible with the guidance rules proposed. However, the stringency of the chosen standard has a direct impact on n: the maximum permissible deviation rate in final moderate rule. Fewer cases satisfy more stringent standards, so judges who use a more stringent standard can permissibly deviate in a greater percentage of the cases that satisfy it. However, more cases satisfy less stringent standards, so judges who use such standards must deviate in a smaller percentage of those cases.

Judges should not assign lexical priority to the cases in which they are most confident that the legally required result is suboptimal. Picture a judge who hears two cases on the same day. In both cases he is sufficiently confident that the legally required result is suboptimal, so deviation is permitted according to his chosen evidentiary standard. However, he is more confident in the first case than in the second. Furthermore, in the first case an adverse judgment will not greatly disadvantage the legally disfavored party: the amount in controversy is small and the party is well-off. The stakes are much higher in the second case: the law requires prison time. Assuming that he has not exceeded his deviation limit and that he

---

31. Referring to the late Justice William Brennan, also Catholic, Noonan writes, "I have not understood how a Catholic or any judge who was guided by the terms of the Constitution could conscientiously [join the majority in *Roe v. Wade*]. But obviously Catholic consciences differ. Brennan in *Roe* showed that they can differ on abortion. It is not, I think, the business of anyone to judge the conscience of another." John T. Noonan, Jr., "The Religion of the Justice: Does It Affect Constitutional Decision Making?" *Tulsa Law Review* 42 (2007): 761–70, p. 763.

32. Concerning results that impose undeserved disadvantages or infringe rights, it is often the case that the greater the magnitude of the disadvantage or infringement, the higher our level of confidence in our judgments of suboptimality. Forcing a suspect to take a forensic blood test is a lesser infringement than forcing him to undergo abdominal surgery for forensic purposes, so I am more confident that the latter is unjust. But we can also be extremely confident that a trivial infringement, such as shoplifting a magazine without justification, is wrong.

must choose between these cases, he is morally permitted to deviate in the second case rather than the first.

Judges probably have as many mistaken moral opinions as anyone else. Judges may disagree about morality as often as anyone else. Moderate rules do not presuppose judicial infallibility or judicial consensus. They merely assume that judges can apply evidentiary standards to their judgments of suboptimality, much as they apply these standards when they arrive at legal judgments. Using a standard as stringent as reasonable doubt may not be necessary in order to avoid engaging in blameworthy deviation, but even a reasonable-doubt standard would seem to permit some deviation in reasonably just legal systems. There is, of course, much more to be said about this topic, but I must leave it there.

15

Treating Like Cases Alike

15.1 AN ILLUSTRATION

After obeying second priority rule, judges will still find that many suboptimal-result cases are tied for deviation priority. Now we face what may be the most counterintuitive implication of individual policy. Individual policy does not, as a matter of principle, forbid judges to practice *token-selective deviation*—deviating in some, but not all, tokens of a single case type. Such deviation invites the objection from comparative justice in its strongest form. The time has come to consider this objection in detail. The following scenarios illustrate token-selective deviation.

Once a month you visit the courtroom of Susan, a state trial judge. In February, Judge Susan hears the case of Fred, a teenager who has shoplifted jewelry from Walmart, a large, corporate retail store. Fred has returned the jewelry. The statute classifies shoplifting as a Class A misdemeanor, minimum. Fred will lose his college scholarship if he is convicted of a Class A misdemeanor, whereas he can keep it if he is convicted of a lesser Class B. The Class A conviction will ruin Fred's promising future. Let us also stipulate that the Class A conviction will not benefit anyone, including Walmart (more than negligibly).[1]

You return to the courtroom in March and watch Susan hear the case of George, another teenager who has shoplifted jewelry from Walmart. There are no morally or legally relevant distinctions between the cases: George has returned the jewelry, the Class A conviction will cost him his scholarship, et cetera.

Assuming all these facts, how should Susan decide the two cases? First, she has a *pro tanto* moral reason not to convict either Fred or George of a Class A misdemeanor. Many would argue that the law gives her a stronger reason to convict both defendants of Class A misdemeanors. I rejected some of these arguments in part I. However, I have also defended final moderate rule, which entails that Susan could have an all-things-considered reason not to deviate in both Fred's and George's cases.

---

1. The judge and I are ignoring the likelihood that losing his scholarship might teach Fred a "valuable lesson" and thereby benefit him in some broader sense.

Final moderate rule forbids judges to deviate in more than n percent of cases. It is heuristically useful to think of each judge as being allocated a corresponding number of "deviation credits." I put the term in scare quotes because these credits are fictional—no one literally allocates them to judges in actual legal systems. Nevertheless, judges could consciously or subconsciously regulate their own decisional conduct *as if* they had a finite supply of deviation credits to "spend" in a given period of time. When Susan deviates in Fred's case, she spends some of her finite allocation. At some point she has no credits left. Whether she rations her credits over the course of her career or spends them all at the beginning, she will hear many suboptimal-result cases in which final moderate rule forbids her to deviate. If she spends her credits early, then these cases will all arise in the latter portion of her career. If she rations her credits, then these cases will arise at the end of each rationing period, however that period is defined. Therefore, it is possible that Susan will deviate in a case, at some point, only to be assigned thereafter a token of the same type with her credits now exhausted. In such situations, final moderate rule forbids Susan to deviate.

To your surprise, Susan convicts Fred of a Class B misdemeanor, but proceeds to convict George of a Class A. You privately question her. Did she forget Fred's case? Was she privy to distinguishing facts of which you were unaware? Susan assures you that there were no distinguishing facts and that she remembers Fred's case. In fact, she explains, in a sense she was hard on George *because* she was easy on Fred. She would have liked to have given George the Class B as well: the Class A conviction benefited no one and greatly harmed George. But she "spent her last available deviation credit" on Fred. It would be wrong for her to deviate in George's case, having deviated in Fred's.

If my arguments so far are sound, and Susan has only one deviation credit left when she hears Fred's case, then she must not deviate in both Fred's and George's cases. Her only remaining choices are adhering in both or deviating selectively. Could she have all-things-considered reasons to deviate in one case but not the other?

15.2 COMPARATIVE JUSTICE

Comparative justice now takes the stage, supporting the claim that Susan has all-things-considered reasons to adhere in both cases. Goldman thinks comparative justice provides a decisive objection to token-selective deviation. He advocates what he calls the *Kantian constraint*: "We must not judge two cases differently without being able to cite a relevant difference between them, where relevance is relative to domain of discourse (e.g., moral or legal)."[2] He also argues that judges "ought to distinguish cases only on legally recognized grounds."[3] He applies the Kantian constraint to courts as follows, referencing his hypothetical of the impoverished widow:

> If some impoverished people were allowed to keep their homes while others were evicted, these egregious violations of the fundamental principle not to treat like cases differently without morally relevant differences between them would be as damaging to the legal system as would crossing the original threshold. The optimal pattern from a purely consequentialist viewpoint would soon be upset as citizens reacted to these considerations of (comparative) fairness.[4]

Goldman's argument appears to be as follows:

1. Judges have a *pro tanto* reason not to follow a policy of deviating in every token of case type, t.
2. Judges have a *pro tanto* reason to treat tokens of the same case type alike.
3. Therefore, judges have a *pro tanto* reason to adhere in every token of t.

This argument is sound. The first premise follows from a systemic-effects argument, such as the one described in chapter 11. But the argument supports only a *pro tanto* reason to adhere. In order to support an all-things-considered reason to adhere consistently, Goldman must argue that the reason mentioned in the second premise is always strong enough to outweigh any reasons to deviate. In order to evaluate this claim, we must examine the second premise more closely. The rest of this section seeks a conception of comparative justice that makes this premise plausible.

The comparative justice principle goes by many names: *justice, fairness, equality, formal justice, formal equality*, et cetera. It is often stated in Aristotelian terms, as requiring adjudicators to "treat like cases alike."[5] It receives great attention and deference, under many descriptions, in Anglo-American

---

2. Alan H. Goldman, *Practical Rules: When We Need Them and When We Don't* (Cambridge: Cambridge University Press, 2002), p. 2, also pp. 3, 9, 22, 41, 79, 138–40, 143–44, 159, 161, 167.

3. Ibid., p. 139.

4. Ibid., p. 45.

5. See, e.g., Michael Bayles, *Procedural Justice: Allocating to Individuals* (Dordrecht: Kluwer Academic, 1989); Neil MacCormick, *Legal Reasoning and Legal Theory* (Oxford: Clarendon Press, 1978), ch. 4; Joel Feinberg, "Noncomparative Justice," *Philosophical Review* 83 (1974): 297–338; James I. MacAdam, "The Precepts of Justice," *Mind* 77 (1968): 360–71; S. I. Benn and R. S. Peters, *The Principles of Political Thought* (New York: Free Press, 1965), pp. 127–28; William K. Frankena, "The Concept of Social Justice," in *Social Justice*, ed. Richard Brandt (Englewood Cliffs, N.J.: Prentice-Hall, 1962), pp. 9–13.

jurisprudence.[6] To say that one case is "like" another is to say that the two cases are tokens of one case type. Only a miniscule fraction of the features of a case are features upon which judges should base their decisions. Most are legally and morally irrelevant: the day of the week on which the case is filed, the number of letters in the names of the parties, the mass of the defendant's kidneys, et cetera. The fact that Fred's case was heard on a Tuesday is a property of Fred's case, as is the fact that Fred's name begins with a consonant and the fact that he enjoys opera. But none of these is a *case-type-specific* feature of Fred's case. None determines the legal or moral type to which his case belongs. If such factors determined case types, then every case type would be a singleton. Every case token differs from all others in *some* respect. No two cases would be "alike" so it would be impossible to infringe comparative justice.

If we define case types so inclusively, then the suggestion that a judge has a good reason to deviate in one token of a type but not another becomes logically incoherent. If the judge really has such a reason, then the tokens must differ in some respect. And they always do. Two case tokens cannot be identical in both intrinsic and extrinsic attributes. A case filed on Tuesday could, in principle, be intrinsically identical to a case filed on Wednesday, but the cases are extrinsically distinct, nevertheless: one was filed on Tuesday, the other on Wednesday. The day of the week on which a case is filed is an extrinsic attribute. It is generally irrelevant to the disposition of the case (unless, of course, the law makes Tuesday a filing deadline or something). On pain of trivializing the concept of a case type, we must understand each case type as supervening exclusively on what lawyers call the *fact pattern* of the case. I call the elements of the fact pattern the *intrinsic* features of the case type or its *case-type-specific* features.

The *legal* type to which a case belongs supervenes on intrinsic features of the case. Many of these features are mentioned in legal standards. Legal standards assign legal consequences to specified combinations of actions, mental states, and circumstances. These standards are always relevant to

---

6. See, e.g., Timothy A. O. Endicott, "The Impossibility of the Rule of Law," *Oxford Journal of Legal Studies* 19 (1999): 1–18, p. 3 ("Government is arbitrary if it does not treat like cases alike—if it does not treat people consistently"); H. L. A. Hart, *The Concept of Law*, 2nd ed. (Oxford: Oxford University Press, 1994), p. 157 (noting the "peculiarly intimate connection" between justice and law); David Lyons, "On Formal Justice," in *Moral Aspects of Legal Theory* (Cambridge: Cambridge University Press, 1993); Peter Westen, *Speaking of Equality: An Analysis of the Rhetorical Force of "Equality" in Moral and Legal Discourse* (Princeton, N.J.: Princeton University Press, 1990); William Van Alstyne, "Notes on a Bicentennial Constitution: Part II, Antinomial Choices and the Role of the Supreme Court," *Iowa Law Review* 72 (1987): 1281–99 (advocating a consistency criterion of judicial good faith); Ronald Dworkin, *Law's Empire* (Cambridge, Mass.: Harvard University Press, 1986), p. 183; Peter Ingram, "Maintaining the Rule of Law," *Philosophical Quarterly* 35 (1985): 359–81, p. 361 ("To follow a rule, or more universally, to be committed to a system of rules as operative for guiding behavior, is to accept the principle that like cases should be treated alike").

judicial decisions.[7] The central version of comparative justice in legal discourse is *legal comparative justice*.[8] Legal comparative justice requires judges to give identical treatment to each token of a given legal case type. Fred's and George's cases are tokens of a single legal case type. If Susan deviates in Fred's case but not in George's, then she infringes legal comparative justice.

Most legal writers assume that legal comparative justice has some moral weight. There are several reasons for this. The first is that someone may suffer emotional distress if he believes that a court has treated him less favorably than someone in a legally indistinguishable situation. He may feel resentment, frustration, envy, et cetera. He may lose respect for, or question the legitimacy of, the legal system, the judiciary, the state, or his entire society. At the least, the value of preventing these feelings and their consequences gives courts a *pro tanto* reason to create the *impression* that they follow legal comparative justice. Actually following legal comparative justice is one way to create this impression. If courts have a *pro tanto* duty of candor,[9] then they have a *pro tanto* reason not to create the false impression of following legal comparative justice—hence a reason to actually follow it.

These reasons to follow legal comparative justice might be weak if the aforementioned feelings usually resulted from irrationality or misinformation, but they do not. Violations of legal comparative justice correlate, albeit imperfectly, with other wrongs and injustices. A judge violates legal comparative justice when she adheres to the law in one case but deviates in another with indistinguishable facts presented. If these are optimal-result cases, then her deviation in the second case is morally unjustified. Because many cases are optimal-result cases, decisions that violate legal comparative justice are often morally unjustified. However, the second decision is independently *pro tanto* unjustified, legal comparative justice notwithstanding, because of this conjunction: it deviates from the law *and*

---

7. But a legal case type is not limited to facts mentioned in preexisting legal standards. Judges often decide on the basis of other facts: sociological, economic, historical, et cetera. When judges create new legal standards or revise old ones, especially in common law cases, they often advert to new social conditions concerning the economy, technology, social mores, demographics, crime, et cetera. We can regard the social conditions in which a case arises as part of its legal case type. It is consistent for a judge in an industrial society to announce that he is modifying a doctrine because it no longer makes sense in a post-agrarian economy. Economic facts about his society are part of the legal case type to which the cases he hears belong. The judge would consider revising any similarly obsolete doctrine. Social conditions can also be relevant when a judge decides to deviate from the law without revising the applicable legal standards. See, e.g., Morton J. Horwitz, *The Transformation of American Law: 1780–1860* (Cambridge, Mass.: Harvard University Press, 1979).

8. See, e.g., Andrei Marmor, "Should Like Cases Be Treated Alike?" *Legal Theory* 11 (2005): 27–38; Ken Winston, "On Treating Like Cases Alike," *California Law Review* 62 (1974): 1–39; Lyons, "On Formal Justice."

9. See §16.1 on judicial candor.

it generates a suboptimal result. It would be *pro tanto* unjustified even if the judge had also deviated in the first case. The injustice of deviating in the second case might be overdetermined, but we have yet to find a reason to believe that violations of legal comparative justice are intrinsically wrong.

There are other arguments for legal comparative justice. Judges who follow legal comparative justice are more likely to apply general rules when this is possible and general rules have some virtues. Also, judges who anticipate that violations of legal comparative justice will receive extra scrutiny will be less likely to allow bias, partiality, or prejudice to compromise their decisions when that would lead them to violate legal comparative justice. But these, too, are instrumental defenses of legal comparative justice. I confess that I do not believe that violations of legal comparative justice are intrinsically wrong, although they are extrinsically wrong, *pro tanto*, in realistic legal systems. Despite this belief of mine, my next arguments are compatible with the proposition that violations of legal comparative justice are intrinsically wrong.

Recall the second premise of the argument attributed to Goldman: that judges have a *pro tanto* reason to treat tokens of the same case type alike. I shall now explain why this premise is implausible if we use legal comparative justice as our conception of comparative justice. Consider two tokens of the same legal case type that differ from one another in morally relevant ways. If the law grants the judge who hears both cases discretion to take these differences into account, then she is morally permitted to treat the tokens differently, rather than reaching a suboptimal result. Judges are morally permitted to infringe legal comparative justice in order to avoid sufficiently suboptimal results. Alternatively, we might say that two tokens do not actually belong to the same legal case type if the law grants the judge discretion to treat them differently.

So Goldman's objection to token-selective deviation cannot simply appeal to legal comparative justice. It must appeal to another version of comparative justice. One such version is *conditional legal comparative justice*, which states that judges have a *pro tanto* moral reason to treat two cases alike if the law requires it. The law requires Judge Susan to treat Fred's and George's cases alike so conditional legal comparative justice entails that she has a *pro tanto* reason to do so.

However, in suboptimal-result cases judges also have a *pro tanto* moral reason to deviate. That reason will often outweigh the *pro tanto* reason specified by conditional legal comparative justice. Conditional legal comparative justice does not preclude token-selective deviation in moderate suboptimal-result cases unless deviating from the law is worse, morally speaking, than reaching all but the most suboptimal results. I disputed this claim in part I.

Therefore, Goldman's second premise needs yet a different version of comparative justice. Consider *moral comparative justice*: judges have a *pro tanto* moral duty to treat alike cases that share all morally relevant case-type-specific features. Moral comparative justice is somewhat plausible, but the reasons it provides must be extremely weak. The fact that the law requires a certain result in a case is not itself a case-type-specific feature of the case. Courts infringe moral comparative justice whenever laws change. Sue parks on the street at 5 P.M. on July 10 and again on July 17. She is ticketed on both occasions. On July 10, however, parking at 5 P.M. was legal. The parking officer mistakenly believed that the city council had banned street parking during rush hour. The ban did not actually take effect until July 11. Sue contests both tickets. The court nullifies the July 10 ticket but upholds the July 17 ticket. The morally relevant intrinsic features of the two cases are identical. Perhaps the court has a *pro tanto* moral reason to treat these cases alike, but it must be a very weak reason.

Any change in the law can make the same point. When Oregon passed the Death with Dignity Act in 1997 certain acts of assisted suicide that had been criminal became legal.[10] Moral comparative justice entails that Oregon courts have a *pro tanto* moral reason to continue convicting defendants for actions that are no longer criminal. Perhaps they do, but it must be a very weak reason. This is significant because the argument I attributed to Goldman does not support the conclusion that judges have an all-things-considered reason to adhere consistently unless moral comparative justice always provides reasons that are strong enough to outweigh their reasons to deviate. If this is ever so it is only in the most trivial of suboptimal-result cases.

That leaves us with the narrower comparative justice principle of *formal equality*: judges have a *pro tanto* moral duty to treat alike cases that share all morally relevant features, local or nonlocal. Formal equality provides a very strong reason when it applies, but it applies only to certain kinds of cases, such as those involving judicial discretion. Judge Jack hears the case of *State v. Adams*. The law gives him discretion to impose upon Adams a prison sentence between one and twelve months. Let us suppose that no penal purposes, such as retribution, uniquely determine a sentence within this range. As are many important concepts, desert is vague. Although we can say that Adams deserves more than one week in prison and less than three years, there is no fact of the matter as to whether he deserves four, five, or six months. Jack arbitrarily chooses a five-month sentence. We can agree that this is an optimal sentence based on what Adams deserves (and all other penal purposes), but it is no more optimal than a sentence of four months or six. Jack needs no reason to choose five months over four or six.

Jack then hears the case of *State v. Bonn*, which shares all morally relevant features with *Adams*. Given Adams's sentence, formal equality

---

10. *Or. Rev. Stat. Ann.* §§ 127.800–127.897 (2006).

gives Jack a *pro tanto* reason also to sentence Bonn to five months in prison. Whereas Jack needed no reason to give Adams six months, formal equality entails that he needs a reason to give Bonn six months. Formal equality requires judges to treat like cases alike when the first decision was one of a number of equally permissible decisions. Formal equality requires a judge to make the same decision in the second case, unless he has a good reason to do otherwise. It forbids deciding differently for *arbitrary* reasons or *bad* reasons or *morally irrelevant* reasons. That is the function of formal equality.[11]

The story continues. Upon subsequent reflection, Jack concludes that he was mistaken, that in fact Adams and Bonn really deserved six-month sentences. He then hears the case of *State v. Carlo*, which shares all morally relevant features with *Adams* and *Bonn*. A fortiori Carlo deserves a six-month sentence and Jack has a *pro tanto* reason to impose it. But formal equality entails that Jack also has a *pro tanto* reason to give Carlo the same five months that Adams and Bonn received. This is a suboptimal result ex hypothesi, but it is only slightly suboptimal. There is only one month of difference. So Jack's reason to give Carlo six months is weak. It could be weaker than Jack's formal-equality reason to give him five months, although I need not explore this.

Adams, *Bonn*, and *Carlo* differ in many ways. The defendants have different names and birthdays. They committed their crimes on different days at different locations. But none of these cases has a *morally relevant* feature, intrinsic or extrinsic, that distinguishes it from the other two. Having given Adams and Bonn five months each, Jack has a reason to give Carlo five months. But Jack also has a reason to give Carlo six months. Without knowing more, we cannot say whether either sentence would be wrong, all things considered. Either might be morally permitted. It would, however, be wrong for Jack to treat the fact that he dislikes Carlo's haircut, or that Carlo's ex-wife has bribed him, as reasons to give Carlo six months, rather than five. These are morally irrelevant factors.

Formal equality applies to *Adams*, *Bonn*, and *Carlo* because they are optimal-result cases in which the judge has some discretion. By contrast, Fred's and George's are suboptimal-result cases. The law gives Judge Susan no discretion to reach optimal results in these cases. Two suboptimal-result cases can have different, morally relevant, nonlocal features even if they share all local features. Fred's and George's cases have different, morally relevant, nonlocal features. Specifically, Fred's case comes before Judge Susan when she has deviation credits left, whereas George's case arises when she has no credits left. So Susan has a good, nonarbitrary reason to

---

11. Judges are, in fact, disciplined for "abuse of discretion" when they act within their discretion, but do so on an arbitrary or inappropriate basis. See, e.g., *In re Brown*, 662 N.W.2d 773 (Mich. 2003) (awarding temporary custody of children during Christmas to father on basis of coin flip).

adhere in George's case. Deviation credits are a scarce resource. Susan must spend them if she is to advance the impartially defensible enterprise of minimizing suboptimal results. As she spends them, she must allocate them fairly. But these credits are finitely divisible. She faces a binary choice between Class A and Class B misdemeanors. She cannot give Fred and George each "half of a Class A and half of a Class B," Solomonic as this might sound. Under these conditions, her choice to give Fred a Class B and George a Class A is arbitrary but not unfair. It is not as though Susan decides to disfavor George because she dislikes his red hair, or because his ex-girlfriend bribes her. Choosing on those bases would be arbitrary and unfair. Biased decisions do not further the enterprise of minimizing suboptimal results. But deviating in Fred's case but not George's for the reasons I have specified is not biased. Nor does it infringe formal equality.

I concede that there are versions of comparative justice that Susan infringes if she deviates in Fred's case but not in George's: legal comparative justice (conditional or unconditional) and moral comparative justice. But I have argued that these versions provide extremely weak reasons to adhere. There is also a version that provides very strong reasons to adhere: formal equality. However, Susan does not infringe formal equality if she deviates in Fred's case, but not George's, in order to conserve deviation credits.

No argument can change the fact that token-selective deviation is an unfamiliar and probably unsettling idea. I must emphasize that this section serves primarily philosophical purposes. True, individual policy does not forbid token-selective deviation as a matter of principle. But I do not believe that we have any reason to oppose it as a matter of principle. Nor can I easily predict how often real judges will have an all-things-considered reason to engage in token-selective deviation according to individual policy. But token-selective deviation often goes unnoticed. I have deliberately concocted stark and artificial juxtapositions of identical cases for the purpose of explaining what token-selective decisions are. If individual policy entailed frequent episodes of token selectivity as conspicuous as those I have described, then that might give cause for alarm. In the real world, however, the type identity of cases is often camouflaged behind distinguishing features that seem, at least to some people, to have practical relevance.[12] Much token selectivity takes place "under the radar."

I mentioned earlier that first priority rule permits judges to practice type-selective deviation—deviating in some but not all suboptimal-result cases at a certain level of suboptimality.[13] I also mentioned that there is a comparative justice argument against this practice but I declined to present it. Now you can see why. If two suboptimal-result cases are tokens of the same type, then the legally required results are equally suboptimal in both.

---

12. See the discussion of legal mirages in §16.9.
13. See §14.5.

All instances of token-selective deviation are also instances of type-selective deviation. If an argument condemns type-selective deviation, then it condemns token-selective deviation. I have attempted to refute comparative justice objections to token-selective deviation. My arguments, if successful, refute parallel objections to type-selective deviation.

15.3 INTEGRITY

As I have noted, judges following individual policy in real legal systems rarely have reason to make a conspicuous display of token-selective deviation. But I am willing to bite this particular bullet and admit that individual policy presents no principled objection to token-selective deviation, and that engaging in it inconspicuously can be justified under certain conditions. In this respect, my position appears to conflict with *integrity*—the central value of Dworkin's jurisprudence. Dworkin opposes deviation, selective or not.[14] But integrity seems to provide a further reason to oppose token-selective deviation, in particular, with special vehemence. To what extent can my position reconcile with Dworkin's?

Dworkin argues that integrity, in his special sense, is a basic value that everyone accepts.[15] He illustrates this by having us imagine legislatures that respond to electoral disagreement about moral issues by enacting legislative schemes in which "each body of opinion is represented, to a degree that matches its numbers, in the final result."[16] He gives three examples of such *checkerboard laws*:[17]

> Do the people of North Dakota disagree whether justice requires compensation for product defects that manufacturers could not reasonably have prevented? Then why should their legislature not impose this "strict" liability on manufacturers of automobiles but not on manufacturers of washing machines? Do the people of Alabama disagree about the morality of racial discrimination? Why should their legislature not forbid racial discrimination on buses but permit it in restaurants? Do the British divide on the morality of abortion? Why should Parliament not make abortion criminal for pregnant women who were born in even years but not for those born in odd years?[18]

Dworkin argues convincingly that checkerboards offend neither justice, nor fairness, nor expedience. But he insists that everyone nonetheless condemns checkerboard solutions. The best explanation for our condemnation, he infers, is that integrity—a value distinct from justice, fairness, and

---

14. Except, perhaps, to avoid extreme injustices. See §1.2.
15. Dworkin, *Law's Empire*, pp. 182–83.
16. Ibid., p. 178.
17. Ibid., p. 179.
18. Ibid., p. 178.

expedience—is basic to our political morality.[19] The checkerboard state lacks integrity because it is unprincipled: "it must endorse principles to justify part of what it has done that it must reject to justify the rest."[20]

Now imagine a checkerboard statute requiring judges to convict shoplifters of Class A misdemeanors in odd months but allowing them to convict shoplifters of Class B misdemeanors in even months. Dworkin would surely oppose such statutes so he would probably oppose how Judge Susan decides Fred's and George's cases (beyond the fact that she deviates). However, I shall argue that Dworkin provides no reason to embrace a conception of integrity that actually condemns Susan's selectivity.

Dworkin would point out that because Fred's and George's cases are tokens of the same type, no case-type-specific principle could justify deciding them differently. In this respect, Susan's policy resembles legislation that criminalizes abortion only for women born in even years. In the abortion case, however, Parliament also has the option of enacting a better law (whatever that is). By contrast, Judge Susan's alternatives to selectivity are *worse*. If she adheres in both cases, then she inflicts more undeserved disadvantages. If she deviates in both, then she rides free on her fellow judges or participates in an excessive-deviation enterprise. Susan simply lacks the ability to prevent mimetic failure. She cannot control the decisions of future judges who hold erroneous moral opinions. So it is unreasonable to expect her to eschew token selectivity but reasonable to demand that Parliament eschew checkerboard legislation.[21]

Interestingly, Dworkin even permits some forms of token selectivity. He admits that "arbitrarily" choosing to rescue some prisoners of tyranny from torture, when one cannot rescue them all, makes good sense and is morally permissible.[22] Susan, similarly, chooses to "rescue" one of the two shoplifters from an unjustified fate when she cannot rescue both.

Dworkin also supports token selectivity in the guise of prosecutorial discretion: "If a prosecutor's reason for not prosecuting one person lies in policy—if the prosecution would be too expensive, for example, or would for some reason not contribute effectively to deterrence—integrity offers no reason why someone else should not be prosecuted when these reasons of policy are absent or reversed."[23] Susan's reason for deviating selectively is, likewise, a reason of policy, rather than principle. If principle alone mattered, then Susan would deviate in both cases. But deviating in too

---

19. Ibid., pp. 179–83.
20. Ibid., p. 184.
21. On a related point see Frank Easterbrook, "Ways of Criticizing the Court," *Harvard Law Review* 95 (1982): 802–32 (concluding that we may reasonably expect each justice of the Supreme Court to develop a consistent, principled jurisprudence, but we must not ask the Court as whole to do so).
22. Dworkin, *Law's Empire*, pp. 181, 184.
23. Ibid., p. 224.

many cases will cause too much mimetic failure. Dworkin gives us no reason to reject Susan's reasoning.

Dworkin mentions, however, that some kinds of selectivity cannot be justified by reasons of policy: "Obviously integrity would also condemn prosecutors' decisions that discriminate, even for reasons of ostensible policy, on grounds that violate rights otherwise recognized, as if our prosecutors saved expense by prosecuting only blacks for a kind of crime that was particularly prevalent in mainly black communities."[24] Similarly, he asserts that "[a]n American legislature could not decide that no Catholic farmer should receive subsidies even if, incredibly, there were sound reasons of policy for this discrimination."[25] Dworkin does not tell us why he singles out racial and religious categories in these passages, but it matters not. Presumably he objects to laws that relegate a "discrete and insular minority" to second-class status. But Susan's reason for favoring Fred over George is not racial, or religious, or anything remotely similar. I can agree that she should not decide on such grounds. In the next section I shall argue that deciding randomly in such situations may be appropriate, in theory.

15.4 RANDOMIZING

The previous sections illustrate that formal equality permits Judge Susan, in principle, to engage in token-selective deviation. But individual policy provides her no reason to decide among the suboptimal-result cases that second priority rule classifies as equally eligible for deviation. How should she decide? One possible method involves a simple randomizing device. This is what game theorists call a *mixed strategy*.[26]

Randomizing becomes appropriate only when all nonarbitrary selection criteria are exhausted. As mentioned, judges should give priority to the more suboptimal of the suboptimal-result cases and to suboptimal-rule cases over gap cases. Whenever possible, Susan should group together gap-case tokens of a single type and deviate in all of them, rather than deviating in some tokens of a type but not others. But this is rarely possible. Usually Susan will find herself choosing between (1) leaving some of her deviation allotment unused and (2) spending her remaining allotment on a set of case tokens that includes some but not all of the tokens of the type. After these priorities have been applied an argument can be made for a randomizing strategy. From the set of all case tokens that are equally eligible for deviation, Susan could randomly choose a subset to fill out her deviation allotment. She could opt for the following:

---

24. Ibid.
25. Ibid., p. 223.
26. See, e.g., R. Duncan Luce and Howard Raiffa, *Games and Decisions* (New York: Dover, 1989), p. 70.

Default Rule: If final moderate rule permits deviation in only one of two suboptimal-result case-tokens, which cannot be distinguished under first and second priority rules, then choose between the cases on the basis of any morally permissible criteria, including random choice.

Although the optimizing power of mixed strategies has been understood for decades, few philosophers have entertained the possibility of using them as solutions to moral-moral prisoner's dilemmas. Goldman comes close. He briefly entertains the idea of using "some randomizing procedure" to optimize, but he promptly rejects the idea as facing "insuperable" problems.[27] He "take[s] it as obvious that designing and implementing such a procedure would be neither feasible nor acceptable to the majority of citizens." In a subsequent paper he states that randomizing would not be feasible because "it would be too difficult to check whether the individuals allowed not to comply with the rule were donating their money to moral projects."[28]

Consider Goldman's claim that it would be too difficult to monitor individual compliance. Regarding taxpayers, he may be correct. Taxpayers have powerful incentives to reroute tax funds to their own selfish purposes rather than moral purposes. Monitoring them would be imperative, but there are millions of taxpayers. Tracking their activities is costly and infringes on their privacy. Perhaps this is what Goldman means when he writes that a randomizing procedure would not be "acceptable to the majority of citizens." Monitoring would be too invasive and costly, but without it citizens would not trust that their peers were using the exemption for moral purposes. For these reasons taxpayers would also have difficulty coordinating their behavior, as Goldman suggests. A taxpayer has little information about what his fellow taxpayers are doing, and he knows that others have little information about him.

Judges, by contrast, are relatively few and easy to monitor. They can obtain information about one another, as can others. Although their deliberations are private, their rulings and opinions are matters of public record in which they have no privacy interest whatsoever. Moreover, a judge cannot benefit himself in any direct way by deviating from the law if checks on judicial corruption and self-dealing are vigorously enforced. If anything, he has reputational incentives to adhere even when he believes that deviation is morally warranted. Anyone who wants to know how often a certain judge deviates from the law can examine his judicial record. We must also remember Posner's claim that judges *enjoy* adhering to the law.[29]

Goldman also states that "considerations of fairness tell against allowing some individuals, but not others, to make their own decisions in this

---

27. Goldman, *Practical Rules*, p. 44.
28. Alan H. Goldman, "The Rationality of Complying with Rules: Paradox Resolved," *Ethics* 116 (2006): 453–70," p. 456.
29. See §4.6.

regard." He concludes that all citizens should simply pay their taxes rather than rerouting to charity. He takes a parallel position regarding judicial deviation: all judges should simply adhere to the law.[30] But Goldman's envisioned randomizing procedure has an unnecessary feature that diminishes its appeal. His procedure arbitrarily divides the population into two castes: those who may deviate and those who may not. There are, of course, unfair ways of distributing scarce privileges. Consider a system that allowed only Protestants or only right-handed citizens to redirect their tax payments to charities. Creating this hierarchy may be wrong in itself. It is likely to foster resentment between the castes and suspicion that the sorting was based on morally irrelevant attributes even if it was not. Moreover, if the activity of defecting exhibits diminishing marginal utility for defectors, then Goldman's way of allocating the privilege is still unfair as well as Pareto-inferior. Rather than allowing some to reroute all while others reroute none, it would be fairer, and Pareto-superior, to allow everyone (or the largest possible randomly selected subpopulation) to reroute *some fraction* of his tax payment to charity. That is the proper analog to a randomizing procedure that permits each judge to deviate in some percentage of his suboptimal-result cases.

Nevertheless, the mere fact that default rule authorizes judges to decide randomly under certain conditions will alarm some readers, so I must explain what it does and does not mean. Judges are blameworthy for making decisions randomly if they disregard relevant legal or moral considerations. Decision by coin flip "obviously constitutes a complete abdication of the judicial function, which is . . . the duty to make reasoned decisions according to law."[31] Judges have been censured for deciding cases by flipping coins,[32] for arbitrarily dismissing criminal charges,[33] and for deciding based on the odor of a defendant's hair.[34] These judges acted unethically, and default rule does not come to their defense. Default rule should be understood in light of other special contexts in which we allow random factors to influence legal outcomes. Consider some familiar examples. The complaints filed with a court are assigned randomly to sitting judges. Different judges apply the law differently and exercise discretion differently, so these random assignments affect outcomes. The same is true, of course, of jury selection, another random process. The military draft in the United States operates by lottery. From a set of income

---

30. Goldman, *Practical Rules*, pp. 147–48.
31. Steven Lubet, "Judicial Discipline and Judicial Independence," *Law and Contemporary Problems* 61 (1998): 59–74, p. 74.
32. *In re Daniels*, 340 So.2d 301 (La. 1976); *In re Brown*. Another judge was sanctioned for giving the *appearance* of having decided on the basis of a coin flip. *Turco*, Stipulation (Washington Commission on Judicial Conduct, Oct. 2, 1992).
33. *In re DeRose*, 1980 Annual Report 181 (New York State Commission on Judicial Conduct, Nov. 13, 1979).
34. *Aaron* (California Commission on Judicial Performance, July 8, 2002).

tax returns with equally significant indicators, the Internal Revenue Service randomly chooses some for tax audits. Highway patrol officers perform random traffic stops. Indeed, whether someone is arrested and prosecuted for any crime depends substantially on random factors such as the proximity of law enforcement, the availability of witnesses, and the caliber of detective work.

Scholars, too, have defended random decision in various settings, including some legal ones.[35] Deciding randomly between two or more options is not unjust absent a moral basis for choice. Default rule authorizes random decision only under those conditions. It permits judges to appeal to random factors for the purpose of deciding in which of two suboptimal-result case tokens to deviate when final moderate rule permits deviation in only one of them and they cannot be distinguished under first and second priority rules.

I can now state the entire scheme of guidance rules that I call *selective optimization*:

Final Moderate Rule: Over the course of your judicial career, deviate in no more than n percent of suboptimal-result cases.

First Priority Rule: If final moderate rule permits you to deviate in only one of two suboptimal-result cases, then deviate in the one in which the legally required result is more suboptimal.

Second Priority Rule: If final moderate rule and first priority rule permit deviation in only one of two sets, each composed of the same number of cases, where the members of the first set fall under more than one rule and the members of the second set fall under a single rule, and are otherwise as apt for deviation as are the members of the first set (regarding suboptimality, etc.), then deviate in the second set.

Default Rule: If final moderate rule permits deviation in only one of two suboptimal-result case tokens, which cannot be distinguished under first and second priority rules, then choose between the cases on the basis of any morally permissible criteria, including random choice.

Final moderate rule is lexically prior to first priority rule, which is prior to second priority rule, which is prior to default rule.

---

35. The most thorough, sympathetic treatment of randomization in the law is Neil Duxbury, *Random Justice: On Lotteries and Legal Decision-Making* (Oxford: Clarendon Press, 1999). See also Barbara Goodwin, *Justice by Lottery* (Hemel Hempstead: Harvester Wheatsheaf, 1992); David Lewis, "The Punishment that Leaves Something to Chance, " *Philosophy and Public Affairs* 18 (1989): 53–67; John Harris, *Violence and Responsibility* (London: Routledge & Kegan Paul, 1980), pp. 66–84.

15.5 BLAMEWORTHY ADHERENCE

I have suggested using evidentiary standards similar to those used in law in order to determine whether a judge has sufficient evidence of suboptimality to warrant blameless deviation in a given case, pursuant to selective optimization.[36] Observers could use these standards to evaluate judges. Judges could use them to evaluate themselves. But what about a judge who adheres more often than selective optimization requires, obeying restrictive rule or a moderate rule more restrictive than selective optimization? Is he blameworthy for reaching suboptimal results that selective optimization permits him to avoid?

Wrongdoers can sometimes avoid blame by demonstrating that they lack the requisite mental state. However, this moral defense is unavailable to judges. A judge knows that his decision threatens the losing party with undeserved force.[37] If he adheres in what he believes to be an optimal-result case, then he believes that the threat is morally justified and that it would be justified even if the law did not require it. If his beliefs are reasonable, then he is blameless. However, if he adheres in what he believes to be a suboptimal-result case, then he believes that the threat would not be morally justified if the law did not require it. Because he knows that his decision threatens force under these conditions, he cannot claim to be merely reckless or negligent. His mens rea is, at least, "knowledge."

Agents who knowingly act wrongly can sometimes avoid blame if they act under duress. Again, this defense rarely applies to judges. If someone credibly threatens to maim the judge if she deviates, then she can claim duress.[38] However, deviation in the United States carries no risk of criminal or civil penalties and minimal risk of formal sanctions.[39] Realistically speaking, a judge who deviates runs some reputational risks at most. He may lose some esteem in the eyes of professional colleagues, commentators, and the general public.[40] How should we morally evaluate a judge who adheres to the law in a suboptimal-result case in order to avoid reputational risks? I suggest that his desire to avoid damaging his reputation does not undermine his subjective moral reasons to deviate. It does not subjectively justify adhering. One's reputation is precious, to be sure, but I cannot think of another situation in which protecting one's reputation

---

36. See §14.8.
37. Notwithstanding the possibilities of reversal on appeal, legislative intervention, defiance by subordinate officials, executive pardon, et cetera. See the discussion of "institutions of amelioration" in Kent Greenawalt, *Conflicts of Law and Morality* (New York: Oxford University Press, 1987), pp. 271–376.
38. Lyons discusses such an example in David Lyons, "Derivability, Defensibility, and the Justification of Judicial Decisions," in *Moral Aspects of Legal Theory* (Cambridge: Cambridge University Press, 1993) p. 138.
39. See §4.3.
40. See §4.6.

undermines a moral reason against using force. A teenager has an all-things-considered moral reason not to vandalize windows, even if his friends will ostracize him for refusing. At most, we might mitigate his blameworthiness, blaming him somewhat less than we would blame a solitary, thrill-seeking vandal. Analogously, perhaps a judge who adheres in a suboptimal-result case in order to protect his reputation is less blameworthy than a judge with no reputational concerns—one who adheres in the case simply because he enjoys enforcing the law. But reputational concerns cannot eliminate blame.

Nevertheless, judges who knowingly adhere in suboptimal-result cases are frequently blameless. In reasonably just legal systems many suboptimal-result cases are ones about which reasonable people could disagree. Therefore a judge may be sincerely and reasonably uncertain that the instant case is, in fact, a suboptimal-result case. He is blameless for adhering in such a case. Many cases in modern legal systems will fall in this category.

Even if a judge is confident that a case is a suboptimal-result case, he may be blameless for adhering. Selective optimization *requires* judges not to deviate in more than n percent of their suboptimal-result cases. They must adhere in the remainder. A judge is blameless if she reasonably adheres in a suboptimal-result case in order to conserve deviation credits. She adheres because she aims to contribute to the enterprise of minimizing suboptimal results.

One can, however, imagine special situations in which conserving credits would be unreasonable. If a judge knows that his judicial career is almost over and that he has deviation credits left and he is sufficiently confident that the case before him is a suboptimal-result case, then adhering could be blameworthy even if he adheres in order to conserve credits. Even before the end of his career a judge might become blameworthy if he deviates too infrequently in cases that he confidently believes to be suboptimal-result cases. But an observer will rarely be in a position to blame a judge for any particular adherent decision if the judge reasonably adheres in order to conserve credits. Blame for adhering becomes warranted only if two conditions are met. First, the judge exhibits a long-term pattern of adhering in cases that he does not reasonably believe to be optimal-result cases. Second, the judge does not reasonably believe that selective optimization requires adhering as often as he does. I do not know how often these conditions are satisfied.

16

Implementation

Does selective optimization have anything to do with the real world? Perhaps. Judges may already be using various elements of selective optimization, although I shall not test that hypothesis. Instead, I shall address the prospects for implementing selective optimization. Lawmakers could, in theory, codify it in legislation or codes of judicial conduct. However, no lawmaker today would want to be associated with the claim that deviation is sometimes permissible. Therefore, I shall concentrate on the feasibility of selective optimization serving as a set of uncodified guidance rules: rules not formally enacted or announced by lawmakers. Although not backed by formal sanctions, they can still guide action and serve as the basis for instruction, criticism, praise, and blame.[1] They can function as social norms for particular groups,[2] as do rules of etiquette, or as personal policies for particular individuals.

In this chapter I address two basic questions about implementing selective optimization: (1) to what extent should judges disclose or conceal the fact that they selectively optimize (§§16.1–16.6), and (2) are judges psychologically capable of internalizing selective optimization (§§16.7–16.9)?

16.1 CANDOR

Deviation involves either advancing fallacious legal arguments or reaching results for which no sound legal argument can be given. When judges deviate knowingly, not mistakenly, they almost never express in advance their intention to deviate or admit it when they do so. Instead they make

---

1. Larry Alexander and Emily Sherwin, *The Rule of Rules* (Durham, N.C.: Duke University Press, 2001), p. 39 (positive rules need not be written); Frederick Schauer, *Playing by the Rules: A Philosophical Examination of Rule-Based Decision-Making in Law and in Life* (Oxford: Oxford University Press, 1991), p. 71 (rules can exist without "canonically inscribed formulations").
2. See, e.g., Eric Posner, *Law and Social Norms* (Cambridge, Mass.: Harvard University Press, 2000).

legal assertions—in filed opinions or statements from the bench—that they do not believe to be true. They deliberately foster the impression of adherence. Such *surreptitious deviation* raises ethical questions because judges have a *pro tanto* moral duty to be candid about the law in their public statements.[3] Published opinions are supposed to persuade readers that any applicable law has been applied correctly and to inform readers of the state of the law (which may or may not have changed). If a judge does not believe a certain legal proposition to be true, then she has a *pro tanto* duty not to assert it publicly.[4] In this section I argue that, nevertheless, judges who knowingly deviate have reasons to do so surreptitiously—reasons that compete with and sometimes outweigh their reasons to be candid.

A judge who plans to selectively optimize could, in theory, announce his intention to do so or announce it whenever he deviates. However, such announcements hurt the judge's career in realistic societies. An elected judge who makes such an announcement lowers his chance of reelection. An unelected judge increases his chance of impeachment, removal, or non-promotion. So a judge has prudential reasons not to announce his deviation. However, prudential reasons do not typically outweigh moral reasons.

Consider, instead, the fact that a candid judge might be replaced by—or passed over in favor of—a judge who reaches suboptimal results more often than he would. If his announcement has that effect, then it actually increases the number of suboptimal results reached, thereby defeating the purpose of selective optimization. Candor also exacerbates mimetic failure, of course, encouraging subpar judges to deviate in optimal-result cases. The chance of any given judge's announcement having this effect is probably small, but it still provides a *pro tanto* reason against making the announcement.

For the reasons given, selective optimization comprises *esoteric* rules for the members of Group O in realistic societies: the rules fail to achieve their purpose if it is generally known that they are followed.[5] Judges who choose to selectively optimize have prudential reasons not to announce that they plan to do so and not to announce when they actually deviate, at

---

3. See, e.g., Scott C. Idleman, "A Prudential Theory of Judicial Candor," *Texas Law Review* 73 (1995): 1307–417; Deborah Hellman, "The Importance of Appearing Principled," *Arizona Law Review* 37 (1995): 1108–51; David Shapiro, "In Defense of Judicial Candor," *Harvard Law Review* 100 (1995): 731–50; *Phototron Corp. v. Eastman Kodak Co.*, 687 F. Supp. 1061 (N.D. Tex. 1988) ("The requirement that the judiciary be candid is perhaps absolute . . .").

4. She probably also has a duty to volunteer reasons for her decisions and a duty to avoid actions that could lead reasonable people to infer that she believes false propositions.

5. On esoteric theories see Ben Eggleston, "Self-Defeat, Publicity, and Incoherence: Three Criteria for Consequentialist Theories," Ph.D. diss., University of Pittsburgh, 2001; Derek Parfit, *Reasons and Persons* (Oxford: Clarendon Press, 1984), p. 40–43; Peter Railton, "Alienation, Consequentialism, and the Demands of Morality," *Philosophy and Public Affairs* 13 (1984): 134–71; Henry Sidgwick, *The Methods of Ethics*, 7th ed. (Indianapolis, Ind.: Hackett, 1981).

least until deviation gains broader acceptance (which may never happen). Judges in Group O also have moral reasons not to be candid about their deviation.[6]

Some readers will be suspicious of esoteric rules. Rules that could be publicized seem preferable, ceteris paribus. Some philosophers even treat publicity as a "formal constraint" on principles of right.[7] They categorically reject esoteric rules. However, the total package of rules that I support is not esoteric in the sense contemplated by the publicity condition. The publicity condition rules out principles that could not be publicized to everyone. It does not require that principles be safely capable of publicity under all nonideal conditions. No principle passes that test. The only reason that the members of Group O should not publicly admit that they are deviating is that many judges in realistic societies hold incorrect opinions about which results are optimal. Under these conditions mimetic failure remains a danger. The larger Group O becomes, the more openly can its members optimize. At some point the danger of mimetic failure disappears and total candor—total publicity—becomes feasible. Total candor is unjustified, however, if it might encourage someone to deviate in an optimal-result case. Group O must interact with many such individuals in realistic societies.

Therefore, judges have moral reasons to persuade readers that they have adhered, whether or not they have. Imagine that Justice Douglas had written the following opinion for the Court in *Griswold v. Connecticut*,[8] without offering any additional reasoning: "Because we find §53–32 of the General Statutes of Connecticut to be an uncommonly silly law, appellants' convictions are hereby reversed."[9] Such an opinion might, in fact, represent accurately why the majority wished to invalidate the law. But even lawyers who believe that Connecticut's contraception laws were profoundly unjust and unconstitutional will agree that this argument represents fallacious legal reasoning. Not just any argument for an optimal result is a sound legal argument. Even Panglossians know this. The justices have no legal authority to invalidate a statute simply because they think it "uncommonly silly." The hypothetical opinion is deviant. More important, it fails

---

6. Compare Meir Dan-Cohen's argument that legal systems maintain "acoustic separation" between decision rules and conduct rules in criminal law and that this is often appropriate. Meir Dan-Cohen, "Decision Rules and Conduct Rules: On Acoustic Separation in Criminal Law," *Harvard Law Review* 97 (1984): 625–77.

7. See, e.g., Bernard Williams, *Ethics and the Limits of Philosophy* (Cambridge, Mass.: Harvard University Press, 1985), pp. 101–2, 108–9; John Rawls, *A Theory of Justice* (Cambridge, Mass.: Harvard University Press, 1971), p. 130. I actually reject publicity as a formal constraint, for reasons advanced by Brink and others, but I set aside my general objection here. See David O. Brink, *Moral Realism and the Foundations of Ethics* (New York: Cambridge University Press, 1989), p. 428; Eggleston, "Self-Defeat, Publicity, and Incoherence: Three Criteria for Consequentialist Theories."

8. Introduced in §6.1.

9. *Griswold v. Connecticut*, 381 U.S. 479, 527 (1965) (Stewart, J., dissenting) (Connecticut's law "uncommonly silly").

to disguise its deviance well.[10] It runs a greater risk of causing mimetic failure than would an opinion containing more persuasive legal reasoning in support of the result, or an opinion at least appearing to reflect a good-faith effort to adhere. A judge who deviates has a *pro tanto* moral reason to write an opinion that causes minimal mimetic failure. Assume *arguendo* that Justice Douglas actually agreed with the critics of *Griswold* that his argument was fallacious. On that assumption, one can plausibly infer that he wrote the opinion as he did—dutifully citing the Bill of Rights and precedent—in order to disguise its deviance as best he could. This was, apparently, the best legal argument he could devise for declaring Connecticut's statute unconstitutional as applied to married couples.

On these assumptions, restrictive rule entails that it was morally impermissible for Justice Douglas to file the *Griswold* opinion. However, if selective optimization is true and surreptitious deviation is permissible, then a judge is morally permitted to advance a fallacious legal argument in order to avoid a suboptimal result, if he cannot find a sound legal argument for avoiding it and his system is below threshold. Therefore, the *Griswold* Court was morally permitted to advance a fallacious argument if the following three conditions obtained in 1965: the Court could not find a sound legal argument for reversing Griswold's conviction; upholding her conviction was a suboptimal result; and the U.S. legal system was below threshold.

Although surreptitious deviation attracts less attention than overt deviation, it is still risky. Disingenuous opinions never persuade everyone that the judge has adhered. Observers may infer that she is incompetent or corrupt. Even if they reach a less derogatory conclusion—that she is using consistent adherence rules that permit some deviation—they may conclude that these rules are indefensible. Someone who reaches negative conclusions about too many judges loses faith in the judiciary and the rule of law. If too many people lose faith, then the system fails. Therefore, judges have *pro tanto* moral reasons not to engage in such ruses,[11] but in some cases they may be justified in doing so.[12]

---

10. I am not sure whether other public officials would even defer to such opinions if the Court were crazy enough to file them. Perhaps justices who filed such opinions would be impeached and removed from office.

11. See Charles Fried, "Impudence," *Supreme Court Review* 1992 (1992): 155–94 (distinguishing between open judicial "defiance" of the law and covert "impudence," vehemently condemning the latter).

12. Dworkin envisions situations in which a judge believes himself to have a moral duty to advance fallacious legal arguments: "If the judge decides that the reasons supplied by background moral rights are so strong that he has a moral duty to do what he can to support these rights, then it may be that he must lie, because he cannot be of any help unless he is understood as saying, in his official role, that the legal rights are different from what he believes they are." Ronald Dworkin, "A Reply to Critics," in *Taking Rights Seriously* (Cambridge, Mass.: Harvard University Press, 1978), p. 327. See also Paul Butler, "When Judges Lie (and When They Should)," *Minnesota Law Review* 91 (2007): 1785–828; Martin Shapiro, "Judges as Liars," *Harvard Journal of Law and Public Policy* 17 (1994): 155–56, p. 156 (because judges "must always deny their authority to make law, even when they are making law. . . . [c]ourts and judges always lie").

I hope it is obvious that selective optimization by itself does not entail that invalidating Connecticut's law was permissible. It merely entails that, *if* banning contraceptives is unjust and the system is below threshold, then courts may be morally permitted to invalidate such bans even if the Constitution does not authorize them to do so. This particular result will please opponents of such bans. However, selective optimization does not entail that upholding Connecticut's law would necessarily have been impermissible, either. On the contrary, it entails that *if* allowing married couples to use contraceptives was a suboptimal result and the system was below threshold, then the Court was morally permitted to uphold such bans even if constitutional law actually *required* invalidation. In fact, selective optimization does not entail that a court today is morally obligated to invalidate such bans. Imagine that a state today criminalizes contraceptive use. A woman convicted under the new law challenges her conviction, citing the *Griswold* line of cases. The trial judge, however, believes that there are strong reasons of morality and public policy to ban contraceptives. He affirms the conviction, writing a fallacious opinion that purports to distinguish the new law from those overturned in *Griswold* and its progeny. Nonetheless, selective optimization entails that he has acted permissibly if he is correct that acquittal is a suboptimal result and his system is below threshold.

The preceding conclusion may disappoint those seeking an unconditional defense of birth control rights, but they cannot have it both ways. If one agrees that the *Griswold* Court deviated, but rejects that fact as a reason to disapprove of the decision, then one cannot consistently treat deviation itself as a reason to disapprove of other decisions. Conversely, if the optimality of the *Griswold* holding justified deviation, then the (ostensible) optimality of the contrary result could justify deviation in the opposite direction. Of course, I am not questioning the overwhelming moral and policy arguments against banning birth control. I merely demand consistent criteria for permissible deviation. Because selective optimization incorporates no one's opinions about optimal results—neither yours nor mine—we cannot expect it to permit and forbid deviation in just the cases in which you or I would deviate or adhere, respectively. If the general enabling conditions for deviation are met, but you would prefer the court to adhere, then your only honest arguments for adherence are nonlegal. You could argue that the legally required result is, in fact, optimal—using moral or policy considerations that have not yet been incorporated into the law. Or you could argue that the judge is likely to hear many other cases in which the legally required results are more suboptimal than in this case, such that spending deviation credits now would be foolish. According to selective optimization, the fact that the law requires a certain result constitutes a disjunctive reason: a reason either to reach that result or to "debit one's deviation account."

Consider, in light of the previous discussion, two landmark cases concerning sexual orientation. In *Romer v. Evans* a 6–3 majority of the Supreme

Court used the Equal Protection Clause to strike down a provision of the Colorado Constitution that permanently banned legislation making sexual orientation into a civil rights category.[13] In *Lawrence v. Texas* a 5–4 majority held that a criminal prohibition on same-sex sodomy, along with most state sodomy laws,[14] deprived individuals of liberty under the Due Process Clause of the Fourteenth Amendment.[15] Justice Antonin Scalia dissented vigorously in both cases. He believes that *Romer* and *Lawrence* were incorrectly decided as matters of constitutional law. If I understand him, then this is what he thinks happened. The *Romer* and *Lawrence* majorities believed the challenged laws to be unjust and were determined to invalidate them. They did their best to write opinions supporting invalidation using accepted forms of legal argument.[16] This was impossible: there was no way to support invalidation with accepted legal arguments. So the majorities deviated, knowingly or not. Believing that judges must always adhere, Scalia concludes that the majorities acted impermissibly, all things considered.

The most direct response to Scalia is to defend *Romer* and *Lawrence* as legally sound opinions. This is the standard response of liberal lawyers who believe that criminalizing sodomy is unjust and that sexual orientation should be a proscribed classification under civil rights laws.[17] But those of us who hold these moral opinions must be especially careful when evaluating *Romer* and *Lawrence*. Moral convictions can make fallacious legal arguments seem sound even to good lawyers. Socially conservative lawyers object that the arguments in *Lawrence* and *Romer* tacitly rest upon premises that they reject and that are not part of the law: (1) the premise that gay men and lesbians have a moral right to greater sexual liberty (*Lawrence*) or greater social equality (*Romer*) than they currently enjoy, and (2) the premise that the state should vindicate these rights under law.

In response to this objection, liberals have three options: first, deny that the arguments actually rely upon these premises; second, argue that these premises are, in fact, part of the law; third, offer different arguments for the holdings. Perhaps one of these options will yet succeed, but selective optimization offers a fourth alternative. It allows one to defend *Lawrence* and *Romer* as justifiable, all things considered, while admitting—at least to oneself—that they were quite possibly deviant[18] decisions: maybe

---

13. *Romer v. Evans*, 517 U.S. 620 (1996).
14. Whether or not they singled out same-sex sodomy.
15. *Lawrence v. Texas*, 539 U.S. 558, 578 (2003). This case explicitly overruled *Bowers v. Hardwick*, 478 U.S. 186 (1986).
16. See, e.g., Philip Bobbitt, *Constitutional Interpretation* (Oxford: Basil Blackwell, 1991), pp. 12–13.
17. Or at least that state constitutions should not permanently proscribe such legislation.
18. Le mot juste.

there was no sound constitutional argument for invalidating these laws. If surreptitious deviation is permissible, then one can even defend *Lawrence* and *Romer* on the assumption that the majorities *knowingly* deviated. In order to minimize the impression of deviation, they wrote opinions in the style of constitutional argument. These arguments were flawed, but the justices did their best.

However, announcing that *Lawrence* and *Romer* are "legal mistakes" could confuse people, for the following reason. Treating restrictive rule as true is a widely accepted social norm governing public discourse about the law. Restrictive rule states that reaching legally incorrect results is morally impermissible in reasonably just societies, so people reasonably assume that anyone who publicly calls *Lawrence* a "legal mistake" also believes that the decision was morally impermissible, all things considered. They will severely misunderstand anyone who makes this statement unless they realize that she also rejects restrictive rule, which they will not understand unless it is carefully explained to them. Therefore, I am not suggesting that it makes political sense for liberals to stop defending *Lawrence* and *Romer* as legally sound.

16.2 SELECTIVITY

Scalia underscores his objection to *Lawrence* and *Romer* by suggesting that his brethren do not really endorse the broad constitutional principles from which they claim to reason. In his *Lawrence* dissent he argues as follows:

> State laws against bigamy, same-sex marriage, adult incest, prostitution, masturbation, adultery, fornication, bestiality, and obscenity are . . . sustainable only in light of *Bowers'* validation of laws based on moral choices. Every single one of these laws is called into question by today's decision; the Court makes no effort to cabin the scope of its decision to exclude them from its holding. . . . The impossibility of distinguishing homosexuality from other traditional "morals" offenses is precisely why *Bowers* rejected the rational-basis challenge.[19]

Scalia makes a similar point in *Romer*:

> The constitutions of [five states] *to this day* contain provisions stating that polygamy is "forever prohibited." . . . Polygamists, and those who have a polygamous "orientation," have been "singled out" by these provisions for much more severe treatment than merely denial of favored status. . . . The Court's disposition today suggests that these provisions are unconstitutional, and that polygamy must be permitted in these States . . . unless, of course, polygamists for some reason have fewer constitutional rights than homosexuals.[20]

---

19. *Lawrence v. Texas* at 586 (Scalia, J. dissenting).
20. *Romer v. Evans* at 648 (Scalia, J. dissenting).

Acknowledging Scalia's sarcasm, we can reconstruct his argument in these dissents as the following reductio ad absurdum:

1. If the Texas sodomy statute and Amendment 2 of the Colorado Constitution are unconstitutional, then at least some other morals laws are unconstitutional.[21]
2. The Texas sodomy statute and Amendment 2 of the Colorado Constitution are unconstitutional.
3. Therefore, at least some other morals laws are unconstitutional.

Scalia rejects the third proposition, intending his argument as a reductio of the second premise.[22] The majorities draft their opinions in ways that suggest that they, too, reject the third proposition. One could, of course, take a libertarian position against all morals laws, but the *Lawrence* and *Romer* majorities do not. They do not mention other morals laws. Nor do they mention, much less reverse, any precedents upholding such laws. Nor do they attempt to distinguish the Texas and Colorado laws. Scalia concludes that the second premise is false and that *Romer* and *Lawrence* are, accordingly, constitutional mistakes, even in terms of the majority justices' own commitments.

The following hypothetical—similar to ones in the literature—reinforces Scalia's point.[23] It is 2004, the year after *Lawrence* was decided. An adult brother and sister are involved in a long-term romantic relationship that includes consensual sexual intercourse.[24] The sister has had a hysterectomy, so there is no danger of pregnancy. They are convicted of criminal incest and challenge the constitutionality of the state law, citing *Lawrence*. Could the court distinguish the incest case from *Lawrence*? As Scalia emphasizes, *Lawrence* does not contain any argument, much less a sound one, for distinguishing such cases.[25] Yet the majorities do not even suggest that other morals laws are unconstitutional or that any prior cases[26] are inconsistent with *Lawrence*.

---

21. Morals laws encompass, inter alia, state laws against sodomy, bigamy, same-sex marriage, consensual adult incest, prostitution, adultery, fornication, bestiality, and obscenity.

22. This argument should not be confused with Scalia's more familiar opposition to nonoriginalist modes of constitutional deliberation and the notion of a "living constitution." Cf. Antonin Scalia, "Originalism: The Lesser Evil," *University of Cincinnati Law Review* 57 (1989): 849–65.

23. Such hypotheticals are discussed in John Corvino, "Homosexuality and the PIB Argument," *Ethics* 115 (2005): 501–34.

24. See Arthur P. Wolf and William H. Durham, eds., *Inbreeding, Incest, and the Incest Taboo: The State of Knowledge at the Turn of the Century* (Stanford, Calif.: Stanford University Press, 2005). A sexual relationship between half-siblings is the dramatic subject of Sam Shepard, *Fool for Love* (New York: Dramatists Play Service, 1984).

25. *Lawrence v. Texas* at 590, 599 (Scalia, J., dissenting); *Romer v. Evans* at 636 (Scalia, J. dissenting).

26. Other than *Bowers v. Hardwick*, of course.

Liberals who do not wish to challenge incest laws could look for constitutionally relevant distinctions between the incest hypothetical and the facts of *Lawrence*.[27] The cases differ in two basic respects. The brother and sister are siblings; John Lawrence and his partner were unrelated by blood. The siblings engaged in sexual intercourse; Lawrence and his partner engaged in sodomy. However, it is hard to see any constitutional significance in these distinctions. Incest has long been criminalized in all states, but sodomy was once criminalized in all states and was still criminalized in many as of 2003. Incest is widely regarded as immoral, but so was sodomy. Certainly, sodomy is enjoyed by millions and plays a vital role in millions of intimate relationships, whereas adult incest is probably rarer by several orders of magnitude. But why should that matter? If sodomy loses popularity, will banning it become constitutional again? Siblings who copulate may have serious psychological problems, for all I know, but will banning sodomy become constitutional again if sodomy starts causing such problems?

Perhaps incest between two infertile adults has more negative effects on *other* people than sodomy has. The parents of incestuous adult siblings usually experience emotional distress, for example, if they learn of the relationship. But so do parents who learn that their son is gay, in many cases. So do parents whose offspring marry outside their faith or race. This cannot be the issue.

This is not the place to analyze Justice Kennedy's majority argument in *Lawrence*. If you believe that it is legally sound, then I suggest the following thought experiment: imagine that you consider decriminalizing incest between infertile adults to be an important matter of social justice—as important as you now consider decriminalizing sodomy to be. I submit that you would not, under those conditions, find a parallel legal argument for invalidating incest laws (as applied to infertile adults) notably weaker than you presently find the *Lawrence* argument.[28] The only reason I can see why someone might want to uphold the incestuous siblings' conviction while reversing Lawrence's is if she accepts a certain comparative moral judgment: that the moral right of any two unrelated adults to practice sodomy is more compelling than the right of any two adult siblings to copulate. I cannot formulate a sound constitutional argument for

---

27. Writing before *Lawrence* was decided, Cass Sunstein tried to distinguish between Amendment 2 and antipolygamy laws by emphasizing that Amendment 2 is based on status, not conduct. Cass R. Sunstein, "The Supreme Court 1995 Term: Foreword: Leaving Things Undecided," *Harvard Law Review* 110 (1996): 6–101, p. 63. But "being polygamous" is no less a status than is "being gay." In any case, Sunstein's distinction is useless in *Lawrence*, in which the challenged statute proscribes conduct and makes no reference to status.

28. In reality, very few consider decriminalizing incest between infertile adults to be a high political priority, and those who do are politically disorganized. If the day comes when enough intelligent, informed people agree with them, then courts will probably invalidate incest statutes, so applied.

invalidating sodomy laws but not incest laws (as applied to infertile adults) without simply assuming that the comparative moral judgment is true and legally dispositive. Perhaps someone will produce a legal argument that does not tacitly make this assumption, but I am pessimistic.

My point is that supporters of the *Lawrence* and *Romer* holdings who favor other morals laws need not challenge the major premise of Scalia's reductio: that some other morals laws would be unconstitutional if the Texas and Colorado laws were. Only if they accept restrictive rule do they bear a burden to challenge Scalia's premise. If, instead, they favor selective optimization, then they can defend *Lawrence* and *Romer* as morally permissible (albeit deviant) decisions without challenging Scalia's premise. They can concede that the majorities never explain how the Texas and Colorado laws differ from other morals laws that they do not wish to invalidate. They can admit that there may be no constitutional argument for invalidating the Texas and Colorado laws without also invalidating some other morals laws.

The *Romer* and *Lawrence* majorities could have confessed their inability to draw a constitutional distinction between sodomy laws and incest laws, while declaring their intention to uphold the latter and invalidate the former. However, such confessions draw undesirable attention to the fact that the court has deviated. Scalia's dissents already drew attention to that fact. Once a judge on a panel realizes that a majority of his brethren are going to endorse a fallacious legal argument, despite his efforts to persuade them otherwise, he has a moral reason to avoid drawing attention to their deviation, as doing so may provoke mimetic failure. Judges have reasons to keep quiet about deviation—their own and that of other judges. Of course, they may also have reasons to point out deviation—judicial candor is, after all, a virtue, and pointing out deviation keeps judges "honest." These reasons may sometimes be strong enough to justify announcing that someone has deviated. Scalia apparently believed that his reasons for candor in *Romer* and *Lawrence* were strong enough.

16.4 FINAL MODERATE RULE AND DEFAULT RULE

I have argued that judges who deviate should not usually announce it, partly because deviation is widely condemned. Two other aspects of selective optimization would also encounter resistance from lawyers and the general public: final moderate rule and default rule. These rules make the disposition of a case sometimes depend on factors that are not case-type-specific. In final moderate rule the relevant factor is the number of other cases in which the judge has deviated or anticipates deviating. Default rule makes the outcome sometimes depend on random factors. Both rules have an alarming implication—the outcome of a case could depend on factors over which the parties have no control. No one likes the idea that his fate depends on such factors. A crucial function of the rule of law is to reduce the dependence of fate on circumstances beyond our control. I can easily imagine what an outraged party might say upon learning that the judge assigned to his case obeyed final moderate rule and default rule:

> Each case should be judged on its merits and nothing else. The fact that my judge has already bent the rules for other folks doesn't make *my* case any weaker. He shouldn't punish me for my position in the "line." If anything, the fact that the judge has bent the rules for other people entitles me to have them bent in my case, too. And a coin flip certainly shouldn't have any bearing on the outcome of my case!

Understandable as this reaction is, no one who has fully internalized selective optimization would react in this way. It *is* usually unfair when someone's fate is affected by forces beyond his control, but so is it usually unfair to the losing party when the judge adheres in a suboptimal-result case. The first source of unfairness does not always outweigh the second. Selective optimization takes both sources into account and strives to minimize the aggregate level of unfairness in the system. The outraged party quoted above fails to appreciate that selective optimization could also benefit him—in suboptimal-result cases in which the law disfavors him. Perhaps he never expects to find himself on the losing end of a suboptimal-result case.

I think selective optimization comprises a fair set of guidance rules. My point in this chapter so far is that until enough people agree with me, acquiring a reputation for selectively optimizing will only hurt a judge's career and increase the relative influence of other judges. For the foreseeable future, therefore, judges should not publicize selective optimization.

16.5 PRECEDENT

I have made the unorthodox suggestion that judges who deviate should sometimes file fallacious opinions. How should other courts treat such opinions, given the doctrine of stare decisis?[29] Before answering this question I must distinguish between deviation from the law and judicial revision of legal doctrine. Consider cases in which the judge has legal authority to revise legal rules created by lower courts or courts of coordinate jurisdiction. Although judges in such cases have the legal authority to revise rules that dictate suboptimal results, they should not always do so. First, the rule might be an optimal rule, the present result notwithstanding. In gap cases, by definition, rule revision is unjustified: the judge should either adhere or deviate.

---

29. See Barbara B. Levenbook, "The Meaning of a Precedent," *Legal Theory* 6 (2000): 185–240; Larry Alexander, "Constrained by Precedent," *Southern California Law Review* 63 (1989): 1–64; Frederick Schauer, "Precedent," *Stanford Law Review* 29 (1987): 571–605.

Second, even if the rule should be revised, a decision to revise it has systemic effects. Revising rules—optimal or suboptimal—can encourage other judges to revise optimal rules. This is a form of mimetic failure. A judge who revises rules bears some moral responsibility for it, just as she bears responsibility for mimetic failure when she deviates. The norm of stare decisis discourages an excessive rate of rule revision.[30]

When a judge in a common-law jurisdiction announces a new rule of law or revises an existing rule, she intends to set precedent. She intends for inferior judges to follow the new rule. She probably also intends to follow it herself and to have courts of coordinate jurisdiction follow it. However, she need not intend anyone—including herself—to follow the new rule in *every* case. If she is moderately rational and informed, then she believes that her new rule will dictate some suboptimal results. Gap cases can arise under any legal rule. She may not even believe that her new rule is the optimal rule—the one with the fewest gap cases of all those possible. She probably just believes that her new rule dictates fewer suboptimal results than the old rule. Otherwise, why would she have revised it? So she intends to follow the new rule *at least as often* as she would have followed the old rule, and she intends other judges to do likewise. This, I suggest, is what it ordinarily means to set a precedent—a *standard precedent*.

By contrast, a judge who deviates does not intend to change the rule from which she deviates. She need not be committed to deviating in all similar cases, even those that are factually type identical to the case at bar. Nor, a fortiori, does she intend that other judges should deviate in every type-identical case. Selective optimization forbids judges to follow a policy of deviating in every token of this case type if too many such tokens arise.

Therefore, a rational judge never intends to set a standard precedent by deviating. However, she might intend to set a weaker kind of precedent. She might intend to deviate in some similar cases and to increase the probability that other judges will deviate in some similar cases. After all, many similar cases will be, for the same kinds of reasons, suboptimal-result cases—cases in which posterior judges have *pro tanto* moral reasons to deviate that are just as strong as the anterior judge's reasons. The anterior judge will want posterior judges to heed those reasons and to deviate as well, unless the system is at threshold. These intentions do not entail an intention to deviate in every similar case or to have others do so.

Picture an appellate court announcing a new interpretation of a statute or constitutional provision. The judges intend that other judges at their level and below should follow the new interpretation. The new interpretation will still generate gap cases, so rational judges do not intend that

---

30. There is, we might say, a "revision density threshold" akin to the deviation density threshold. With any luck, the norm of stare decisis prevents courts from crossing the revision density threshold.

others should always follow it. In fact, they may even anticipate that their new interpretation will generate *more* gap cases than the old. They may have aimed for an accurate reading of text or legislative purpose rather than aiming to minimize gap cases with their interpretation. But the judges intend to follow their interpretation at least as often as they follow comparable precedents: precedents of similar age that generate a similar number of suboptimal-result cases (adjusted, perhaps, for the severity of the suboptimal results). They intend for others to do likewise.

By contrast, when an appellate court deviates in a suboptimal-result case, the judges cannot rationally intend to set a standard precedent. Rational judges cannot intend that posterior judges should deviate in similar suboptimal-result cases as often as they follow other precedents. The judges can rationally want posterior judges to deviate in similar suboptimal-result cases, but to do so subject to selective optimization. The judges might also intend to increase the probability of such warranted deviation.

What sort of precedent did the *Griswold* majority intend to set, a standard one or a weak one? The tempting answer is: a standard one. I think the tempting answer is mistaken, but I must first explain why it is tempting. The *Griswold* majority certainly intended courts at every level to treat the opinion as controlling with respect to similarly situated parties and other state bans on the use of contraceptives as applied to married couples. The decision was not limited to Estelle Griswold or the State of Connecticut. As to similar bans on the use of contraceptives by married couples, the majority intended to set a typical precedent and did so.

The important question, however, is whether the *Griswold* majority could have rationally intended other courts to consistently apply their *reasoning*. Suppose judges in Group O were to imitate *Griswold* consistently: for any challenged state law, if they can find a legal argument for invalidation as strong as the *Griswold* argument, then they invalidate the law, using the corresponding argument in their opinion. Being Group O, they reach only optimal results. However, using too many fallacious arguments encourages judges outside Group O to use them. Eventually an idiosyncratic outsider (inspired by judges who were inspired by judges who were inspired by Group O) would use a fallacious argument to reach a suboptimal result: perhaps invalidating laws against animal cruelty, counterfeiting, or criminal solicitation when committed privately in the home. That is why selective optimization does not support a policy of deviating in every suboptimal-result case. The *Griswold* majority could not rationally intend its reasoning to serve as a standard precedent, even for Group O. Selective optimization permits only occasional forays into fallacious legal reasoning.

The same goes for the *Romer* and *Lawrence* Courts. Perhaps they did not intend for other courts to adopt their reasoning. They merely intended to invalidate statutes criminalizing sodomy between adults and state constitutional amendments banning the recognition of sexual orientation as a civil rights category, leaving other morals legislation undisturbed.

Selective optimization does not forbid such selectivity in principle and actually provides a principled rationale for it.

16.6 MINIMALISM

Selective optimization entails that judges are morally permitted to offer fallacious legal arguments for optimal results when they cannot formulate sound arguments, provided they exercise moderation. Selective optimization also provides reasons for courts sometimes to write what Cass Sunstein calls "minimalist" opinions. These reasons are distinct from Sunstein's own. First, I shall explain minimalism and review one of Sunstein's arguments for it.

Sunstein draws two distinctions: between *narrow* and *broad* opinions and between *shallow* and *deep* opinions. A broad opinion announces a general legal rule that could be applied to different cases. A narrow one does not. A deep opinion articulates, as the bases for the holding, an underlying principle that could be applied to different cases. A shallow one does not. Courts often must choose between multiple arguments in support of a given result. They could write a broad opinion or a narrow one, a deep opinion or a shallow one.

Reasonable people can sometimes agree on a holding while disagreeing about the correct principle upon which the decision should rest or the best statement of the applicable rule of law. Similarly, a judge may find that she is confident about a holding but less so about the underlying principle or the best rule to announce. Judges should not have great confidence in their own moral insights in difficult cases that raise novel issues, Sunstein insists. He argues that in such cases, the Court should render decisions that are narrow and shallow rather than wide and deep.[31] An ambitious opinion that offers wide and deep reasoning can do great good as a precedent or great harm. A less ambitious opinion affords a greater margin for error and revision in future generations.[32] The opinion should offer just enough reasoning to support the holding, but no more. It need not offer deep rationales or explain how to distinguish similar cases.[33]

Sunstein's judge intends to reach a result that she believes the law permits and to write an opinion that reflects the actual state of the law or announces a new rule. She faces a choice between minimalist and non-minimalist opinions, but she believes that both opinions contain sound legal arguments. Sunstein believes that judges write minimalist opinions when they lack confidence in the underlying moral judgments. He suggests that the *Romer* majority declined to articulate the differences

---

31. Cass R. Sunstein, *One Case at a Time: Judicial Minimalism on the Supreme Court* (Cambridge, Mass.: Harvard University Press, 1999), pp. 10–14.
32. Ibid., ch. 3.
33. Ibid., chs. 1–4.

between Amendment 2 and other morals legislation—such as the entrenched antipolygamy provisions of several state constitutions—because although they agreed that relevant differences existed, they could not agree on what those differences were.[34] He could explain *Lawrence* in the same way.[35]

However, these explanations would not satisfy Scalia, nor do they satisfy me. The justices could have authored separate opinions, as they often do, each explaining how he or she distinguishes between the invalidated law and other morals laws. No justice did so. So I still think it reasonable to infer that they did not know how to draw a constitutional distinction between sodomy laws and, for example, laws banning adult incest. Sunstein neglects the possibility that *Romer* and *Lawrence* were suboptimal-result cases. I cannot tell whether he believes that judges should ever deviate in suboptimal-result cases. In any event, I shall argue that suboptimal-result cases provide another reason for judges to write minimalist opinions. Although courts should always offer the best legal arguments they can find for their conclusions, there are no sound arguments—minimalist or otherwise—for the optimal result in suboptimal-result cases. A judge who chooses to deviate in such a case could, in theory, present no argument whatsoever, as I imagined the *Griswold* Court doing earlier, but this approach draws unwanted attention to her deviation. On the other hand, if she writes a nonminimalist opinion, then she propagates fallacious legal reasoning. Less enlightened judges may try to imitate this reasoning and be led to suboptimal results.

A minimalist opinion could represent a happy compromise between these unattractive extremes. Of course the argument will still be fallacious—ex hypothesi, no sound argument for the holding exists. But a well-written minimalist opinion, even a fallacious one, has at least the superficial appearance of legal reasoning. It disguises its own fallaciousness. But precisely because its reasoning is so shallow and narrow, it gives other judges less material with which to work and thus makes them less likely to treat it as a standard precedent. Therefore, minimalist arguments may be the best kind for a judge to use if she wants to reach an optimal result in a suboptimal-result case. Perhaps the justices joined minimalist opinions in *Lawrence* and *Romer* because they could not think of any sound arguments for the holdings.

Sunstein does not condone courts making fallacious legal arguments, minimalist or otherwise. He advocates minimalist opinions that contain "just enough" reasoning to support the holding. But lawyers disagree about how much reasoning is enough. Critics of the opinions praised by Sunstein could object that these opinions do not, in fact, contain enough

---

34. Ibid., ch. 7.
35. In fact, he appeals primarily to the infrequency of enforcement of sodomy laws in Texas. Cass R. Sunstein, "What Did Lawrence Hold? Of Autonomy, Desuetude, Sexuality, and Marriage," *Supreme Court Review* 2003 (2003): 27–74.

reasoning to support the holdings. I shall not ask whether Sunstein or his critics have the stronger argument with respect to any particular case. My point is that there are two situations in which a judge might want to use minimalism. In the situation described by Sunstein, the judge is confident that his intended result is legally permissible but not confident about any given argument. In my situation, by contrast, the judge is not confident that his intended result is legally permissible. He may even be confident that it is not. In that situation he may want to avoid raising similar doubts in other people and to minimize the quantity of fallacious legal reasoning that he introduces into the jurisprudential corpus. That is a different reason to write a minimalist opinion.

Opponents of minimalism believe that a sound, nonminimalist argument for a legally defensible conclusion is always possible and should be used instead of minimalist arguments. They accuse judges of using minimalism to reach results for which no strong legal arguments exist. I suggest that even if these critics are correct, we should not conclude that judges act impermissibly if they write minimalist opinions to reach deviant results: if they use minimalism pursuant to selective optimization, then their actions may be permissible.

In addition to writing minimalist opinions, judges who plan to selectively optimize might consider filing *unpublished* opinions—ones not intended for citation by other courts—or publishing only selected parts of certain opinions. These techniques could be especially useful in gap cases, in which the court wants to avoid suboptimal results without changing optimal rules. There are notable arguments against filing unpublished opinions, but doing so could facilitate selective optimization and may be worth contemplating.[36]

16.7 COGNITIVE AND PSYCHOLOGICAL BURDENS

I turn now to the second question of this chapter: are judges psychologically capable of internalizing selective optimization? Insofar as selective optimization allows judges to deviate more frequently than does restrictive rule, it seems to impose fewer demands. However, it also imposes greater cognitive and psychological burdens on judges. Restrictive rule merely requires judges to find and apply the law. Of course this can be challenging if the law is complicated or unclear, and if the law explicitly

---

36. See, e.g., Arthur J. Jacobson, "Publishing Dissent," *Washington and Lee Law Review* 62 (2005): 1607–36; Elizabeth M. Horton, "Selective Publication and the Authority of Precedent in the United States Courts of Appeals," *UCLA Law Review* 42 (1995): 1691–778; William L. Reynolds and William M. Richman, "The Non-Precedential Precedent—Limited Publication and No-Citation Rules in the United States Courts of Appeals," *Columbia Law Review* 78 (1978): 1167–208.

grants the judge discretion, as it usually does in criminal sentencing, for example, then she faces some additional work after she finds the law. But once she finds it, restrictive rule does not invite her to consider deviating. In that respect it is easier to obey than selective optimization. Selective optimization also requires the judge to find the law when there is law to find, but it assigns her some additional jobs. She must determine the best result notwithstanding the law. She must monitor her own deviation rate and decide when to deviate. These tasks may be intellectually demanding.

Furthermore, a judge who consciously optimizes lives with some unsettling self-knowledge. He knows that he sometimes deviates from the law and that some of his filed opinions misrepresent his actual reasoning—he publishes *lies*. He knows that his decision patterns are type selective, maybe even token selective. They may even involve random decision. For all these reasons some judges will find that consciously following selective optimization would lower their self-esteem or cause them mental distress. Some will be unable to reflectively endorse selective optimization for these reasons.

These tasks and this self-knowledge will weigh more heavily upon some judges than others, according to variations in psychological profile. Bearing these burdens requires a combination of self-confidence, humility, intelligence, initiative, and willingness to risk one's reputation for the sake of others. There may be judges who, because of their individual psychologies, will reach decisions that approximate selective optimization less closely if they try to optimize than if they use some other method. Perhaps the cognitive and psychological demands overwhelm them: they make too many mistakes or become too distressed or frustrated to function. For them, selective optimization may be a *self-effacing* method: one that cannot serve its purpose if they consciously attempt to follow it.[37] Such judges should not consciously obey selective optimization. Not everyone is cut out to be a double agent, or a Marine officer, or a surgeon, or a criminal defense attorney, either. To demand that judges self-consciously optimize may be asking too much. I am not confident that judges are blameworthy if they shrink from the demands of optimization. I contend only that they are morally permitted to optimize and are rarely blameworthy for doing so if they use selective optimization. I believe that judges with the right psychological profile should consciously try to optimize, perhaps surreptitiously, and to rationalize their deviation and selectivity as best they can in their opinions.

16.8 MAINTAINING EQUILIBRIUM

A critic of selective optimization might object that even if typical judges have the cognitive skills to consciously pursue it, we cannot count on

37. This usage of *self-effacing* originates in Parfit, *Reasons and Persons*, pp. 23–24.

them to do so. Suppose publication of this book leads judges to weaken their commitment to restrictive rule. If they decide to selectively optimize instead, then my critic's objection fails. But the objection succeeds if the book misfires: if its effect is that many judges become less committed to restrictive rule, but they also snub my critique of permissive rule and my arguments for selective optimization. They proceed to "overindulge" in deviation, damaging the rule of law. Maybe judicial commitment to restrictive rule is like a fence that keeps the herd from heading for the edge of the cliff. Even if the fence seems needlessly far from the edge, removing it would be disastrous if no other fence lies beyond it and the herd is ready to stampede.

The preceding objection makes an empirical claim that may be correct, for all I know. I shall merely offer some reasons for skepticism. My first reason is that judicial behavior already reflects less than perfect compliance with restrictive rule. Everyone agrees that there have been some deviant rulings over the years, despite disagreement about which ones were deviant. So far judges in the United States have not destroyed the rule of law with their deviation, although they may have damaged it.[38] Most judges claim allegiance to restrictive rule, but even those who endorse it sometimes deviate in practice. At least some of the deviation in U.S. history has surely been self-conscious, even ignoring the extremely rare cases of candid deviation. No one can read a judge's mind, but the more intelligent and experienced the judge and the more obvious her deviation, the more confident one can be that she knew she was deviating, even without a signed confession. Perfect compliance with restrictive rule has never existed and is not necessary for the rule of law to survive.[39]

My critic could revise her objection. She need not make the hyperbolic claim that anything less than perfect compliance with restrictive rule destroys the rule of law. Rather, she could argue that reducing current levels of commitment to restrictive rule *as a social norm* will destroy the rule of law. At least some judges would prefer to deviate more often than they do in suboptimal-result cases. Incentives surely provide at least part of the explanation for their relative self-restraint. Formal sanctions for deviation hardly exist, but judges have several other incentives to adhere, as discussed in chapter 4. Researchers have only recently begun creating testable models of the incentive mechanisms that bear on judicial behavior, using resources from economics, game theory, and the theory of social norms. Little research has studied adherence incentives in general, as opposed to stare decisis, in particular.

---

38. See generally Brian Z. Tamanaha, *Law as a Means to an End: Threat to the Rule of Law* (New York: Cambridge University Press, 2006).

39. See Margaret Jane Radin, "Reconsidering the Rule of Law," *Boston University Law Review* 69 (1992): 781–819 (discussing how the rule of law survives without "formalism").

Most judges want to maintain good reputations. Lower court judges may also want to avoid reversal and to be promoted. Each of these incentives depends on social norms condemning deviation. Reputational incentives do not exist unless judges believe that they are more likely to suffer reputational losses if they deviate. The other incentives do not exist unless lower court judges believe that they are more likely to be reversed or to lose potential promotions if they deviate. As the social norm of restrictive rule weakens, tolerance for deviation increases, with a commensurate drop in the associated risk of reversal and cost to one's reputation and career. Judges who adhere mainly for prudential reasons begin deviating more often, eventually pushing the system over threshold.

Again, it is an empirical question whether wider rejection of restrictive rule as a social norm would have these effects. It is possible. But it is also possible that judges will still have incentives to adhere. There is no reason to anticipate that incentive mechanisms will disappear as restrictive rule becomes less popular. At least, there is no reason to predict this outcome provided that enough morally motivated people embrace selective optimization instead. Just as those who accept restrictive rule currently criticize judges who deviate, so will those who adopt selective optimization criticize judges who deviate more often, or more conspicuously, than the theory allows. Appellate courts that accept selective optimization will freely reverse deviant decisions by such judges. Observers who accept selective optimization will think less highly of such judges and will promote them less often. For these reasons, approximate conformity to selective optimization could emerge as a stable equilibrium, even for judges whose motivations are entirely prudential and who reject selective optimization themselves.

However, there is a substantial difference between restrictive rule and selective optimization. Determining whether someone has violated selective optimization is more difficult than determining whether she has violated restrictive rule. For that reason alone, the fraction of judges who violate selective optimization and meet with criticism, if selective optimization is widely accepted, will probably be smaller than the fraction of judges who violate restrictive rule and meet with criticism, if restrictive rule is widely accepted. Perhaps there will be so little criticism of judges who violate selective optimization that adherence incentives will diminish too much and the system will cross threshold.

I admit that this is a conceptual possibility. The publication of my book could, in theory, push our legal system over the cliff. But this seems unlikely. The scenario just described occurs only if some special conditions obtain. The only dangerous individual, as I see it, rejects restrictive rule because of my book, but never adequately internalizes selective optimization. He is too lazy or cognitively impaired. He criticizes deviation less often than selective optimization prescribes. If he is a judge, then he is also too unresponsive to adherence incentives. He deviates more often than selective optimization permits. If there were too many people like that—judges, lawyers, scholars, commentators, and politicians—then my book could send them over the cliff.

I see no reason to believe, however, that many people fit this profile. I argued that judges have no moral or legal obligation to obey restrictive rule. No judge who would choose to slog through this book could be obtuse enough to conclude that I had shown his adherence *incentives* to be weaker than he had believed them to be. Similarly, any observer of the courts who rejects restrictive rule because of this book probably has the cognitive skills to use selective optimization criteria for praise and blame.

The only type of person who worries me is a critic of the bench who rejects restrictive rule because of this book, but is lazy and simply stops criticizing judges for deviating in suboptimal-result cases, even when they deviate more often than selective optimization permits. I hope there are few such people, but they might exist.

16.9 CONFORMING UNREFLECTIVELY TO DEFAULT RULE

I recognize that some judges—perhaps most—lack a psychological profile that facilitates conscious optimization. If too many reject restrictive rule without adopting selective optimization, then the rule of law could be destroyed. Therefore, a judge should not consciously reject restrictive rule if the cognitive and psychological burdens of selective optimization seem too great for him.

However, I am curious about mechanisms for enabling judges to inch closer to conformity with selective optimization without consciously following it. Consider a set of cases heard by Judge Janet during her career. In each of these cases the law requires results that Janet believes to be suboptimal and equally so. If Janet recognizes this fact, then she will face a conundrum. She believes herself to have a *pro tanto* reason, and an equally strong one, to reach the optimal result in each case. If she recognizes that the law forbids this, then she will conclude that she has an equally strong *pro tanto* reason to deviate in each case. However, she also believes (correctly) that it would be wrong to deviate in so many cases and that doing so would ruin her reputation. In such situations, default rule recommends randomly choosing a permissible fraction of the cases for deviation.[40] However, Janet believes that random deviation is wrong as a matter of principle. She believes that judges should not "dice" with justice.

I have argued that random deviation is not wrong as a matter of principle. I still believe that, but because Janet disagrees with me, I want to know if she can decide correctly without consciously violating any of her own principles. I think she can. She can achieve the same results as random

---

40. See §15.4.

deviation without having to consciously randomize. She can do so by acquiring the false belief that the law permits her to reach optimal results in a certain fraction of her suboptimal-result cases. This is psychologically possible because the fact patterns of the cases differ from one another in various ways. If we stipulate a set of suboptimal-result cases, then none of these differences actually justifies reaching the optimal result, by definition. But Janet might easily reach the mistaken conclusion that some are optimal-result cases. She might perceive a *legal mirage*: the appearance of legally relevant factors where none actually exists. Judicial perception of legal mirages can serve as a proxy for conscious randomizing. In some fraction of the cases, the judge perceives some "special features" that seem to her to justify reaching the optimal result as a matter of law. Recall the statutes that banned hate speech and nude dancing, respectively.[41] When deciding these cases, Judge Janet might find that hate speech "seems" similar to certain other speech, the banning of which has been previously upheld, whereas nude dancing "seems" less similar to her, although she may not be able to put the perceived difference into perspicuous language.

Some people believe that experienced lawyers possess special capacities that enable them to ascertain with confidence that an answer to a legal question is legally correct or legally superior to the alternatives when equally intelligent individuals, who have access to the same source materials but lack comparable training and experience, reach the opposite conclusions, or reach their conclusions with less confidence. These capacities are sometimes described in perceptual or visual terms ("seeing the right answer"), sometimes in cognitive terms ("thinking like a lawyer"). They are sometimes said to be irreducible to propositional knowledge. In this respect, the experienced lawyer's putative capacities invite comparison to certain forms of "knowledge how," or aspect seeing,[42] or gestalt perception.[43]

Believing that one possesses these capacities enables one to conform to default rule without consciously obeying it. Imagine a judge who is committed to avoiding suboptimal results and to deciding cases only on the basis of case-type-specific factors. A judge with these commitments will experience psychological pressure to conclude that she never hears suboptimal-result cases. There are two logical ways for her to reach this conclusion. First, she could conclude that the legally required result is not,

---

41. See §14.6.
42. Malcolm Budd, "Wittgenstein on Seeing Aspects," *Mind* 96 (1987): 1–17.
43. See, e.g., Scott Brewer, "Exemplary Reasoning: Semantics, Pragmatics, and the Rational Force of Legal Argument by Analogy," *Harvard Law Review* 109 (1996): 923–1028; Brian Leiter, "Heidegger and the Theory of Adjudication," *Yale Law Journal* 106 (1996): 253–82; Anthony Kronman, *The Lost Lawyer: Failing Ideals of the Legal Profession* (Cambridge, Mass.: Belknap, 1993), pp. 170–85; Charles Fried, "The Artificial Reason of the Law Or: What Lawyers Know," *Texas Law Review* 60 (1981): 35–58.

in fact, suboptimal. Alternatively, she could conclude that there are legally relevant features of the case type that justify the optimal result.

A judge who thinks she possesses the aforementioned capacities is more likely to perceive legal mirages in one or both case tokens that help her to justify *to herself* her decision to deviate in one token but not the other. These mirages emerge from intrinsic features of the case token. We should not assume that the judge's belief in her special capacities is insincere. On the contrary, the more sincerely held the belief, the more effectively can it ameliorate cognitive dissonance for judges who believe that adjudication should ignore features that are not case-type specific, but who also want to avoid suboptimal results. Legal mirages provide judges with resources for rationalizing selective deviation, even token-selective deviation, in suboptimal-result cases, thereby facilitating conformity to selective optimization without consciously obeying it. Judges who make proper "use" of the mirages they see can achieve these goals without suffering the cognitive dissonance associated with consciously adopting default rule. A judge who uses mirages believes that she sees legally relevant, intrinsic factors that distinguish the case tokens. This belief enables her to conclude that she has both adhered to the law *and* reached a morally optimal result. In fact, she has done only the latter, but she may sleep more soundly if she believes otherwise.[44]

With these regrettably speculative remarks, I must leave the topic of implementation.

---

44. Compare Henry S. Richardson, discussing the "evicted widow" case: "Theoretically, an optimal intermediate solution may exist that would evict only a certain percentage of such widows—either on the basis of an arbitrary randomizing device or (more likely within the law) on the basis of a more finely specified principle." Henry S. Richardson, "Review of Alan H. Goldman, *Practical Rules*," *Notre Dame Philosophical Reviews* (2002).

17

Theoretical Implications

17.1 FORMALISM

Several scholars have recently defended the view that judges should treat legal rules as "serious rules." This means applying the rule without looking behind it to the reasons that support it or, a fortiori, to other reasons. Frederick Schauer calls his version of this view *presumptive positivism*, which assigns presumptive priority to the most "local" rule.[1] He characterizes positivism as entailing "systemic isolation" and claims that a positivist system is the systemic analog of a rule.[2] Alexander and Sherwin defend a related view, *formalism*.[3] Unlike these three theorists, Alan Goldman does not believe that judges should treat legal rules as serious rules, but he argues that judges should treat as a serious rule what he calls the "fundamental rule of the legal system," which is what I call restrictive rule.

My primary objection to Schauer's position is that he assumes that authority to deviate includes authority *to define what constitutes deviation*. On this assumption, deviation invades the jurisdiction of the rule maker, just as Schauer concludes. But I think judges can deviate without transferring jurisdiction from the rule-maker to the judge. They can do this if they obey selective optimization and the rule-maker retains jurisdiction to define what constitutes deviation in the first place. The judge has no jurisdiction to make *that* decision and that decision is still binding on the judge, albeit in an indirect way.

I mentioned earlier that obeying rebuttable presumption is equivalent to taking a rule-sensitive particularist or presumptive positivist approach to restrictive rule.[4] Since then I have defended selective optimization. Selective optimization is like permissive rule and unlike restrictive rule in

---

1. Frederick Schauer, *Playing by the Rules: A Philosophical Examination of Rule-Based Decision-Making in Law and in Life* (Oxford: Oxford University Press, 1991), p. 191.
2. Ibid., p. 199.
3. See also Antonin Scalia, "The Rule of Law as a Law of Rules," *University of Chicago Law Review* 56 (1989): 1175–88 (connecting formalism to textualism and the rule of law); Frank Easterbrook, "Ways of Criticizing the Court," *Harvard Law Review* 95 (1982): 802–32.
4. See §14.3.

that it allows judges to deviate in some suboptimal-result cases. But it is also rule-sensitive, unlike permissive rule and like restrictive rule, in that it aims to preserve the rule of law and thus does not allow judges to follow a policy of deviating in all suboptimal-result cases. The question remains whether objections that others have raised against rule-sensitive particularism and presumptive positivism apply to selective optimization. As a quasi-particularist view, does selective optimization inherit the flaws of rule-sensitive particularism?

Discussions of rule-sensitive particularism in the literature have tended to address only the crudest possible version of the view, which I call *causal rule-sensitive particularism*. This is what Goldman, Schauer, Alexander, and Sherwin criticize.[5] Alexander and Sherwin conclude that rule-sensitive particularism is self-defeating if publicized (i.e., it is esoteric):

> [R]ule-sensitive particularism in regard to coordination rules narrows the gap only when most people avoid particularism and treat legal rules as serious rules. . . . [R]ule-sensitive particularism cannot be publicized as the correct approach to rules. It can only be effective when rules are presented, and generally accepted, as serious rules.[6]

They argue that rules can only serve their "settlement function" if we obey them blindly, without consulting the moral reasons behind them in each case. Therefore, they conclude that legal rules must be treated as serious rules, which entails obeying restrictive rule.

Alexander and Sherwin seem to have in mind an alternative to restrictive rule that instructs each judge to take into account the value of having rules and the harm that deviating will cause to that value. Call this *causal moderate rule*. Causal moderate rule permits judges to deviate whenever the net benefits to the parties outweigh the marginal systemic effects. Alexander and Sherwin's position entails that judges should not obey causal moderate rule and that it should not be publicized as the correct adherence rule. I agree. Causal moderate rule licenses so much deviation that it would be collectively self-defeating for the judges in Group O to obey it. A larger number of suboptimal results will be reached if they obey causal moderate rule than if they obey restrictive rule. Causal moderate rule fails because the only reason to adhere that it recognizes is harm *actually caused* by a deviant decision. This is a defect because the morally relevant relationship between a deviant decision and the systemic effects of deviation is not so direct. A viable adherence rule must assign relevance to the overall systemic effects of the pattern to which a deviant decision contributes. Causal moderate rule fails to do so.

---

5. Alan H. Goldman, *Practical Rules: When We Need Them and When We Don't* (Cambridge: Cambridge University Press, 2002); Schauer, *Playing by the Rules*; Larry Alexander and Emily Sherwin, *The Rule of Rules* (Durham, N.C.: Duke University Press, 2001).

6. Alexander and Sherwin, *The Rule of Rules*, p. 67.

Alexander and Sherwin might also conclude that just as "most people" must avoid particularism and treat legal rules as serious rules, so must "most judges" obey restrictive rule. But their reasoning does not support this conclusion. It supports only the conclusion that most judicial *decisions* in a given system must follow legal standards. One way to maintain this pattern is for most judges to obey restrictive rule, perhaps knowing that there will always be a few particularist judges in their midst—the "irresponsible renegades." But other divisions of labor could maintain the same pattern. An alternative division has everyone following the same rule: *usually* adhere to legal standards, but not always. This is what selective optimization prescribes.

We should distinguish the idea that judges must obey serious rules, which is a sensible idea, from the idea that judges must treat *first-order legal rules* as serious rules, which I have called into question. Alexander and Sherwin's claim that judges must obey restrictive rule conflates these ideas. I contend that judges should treat selective optimization as a serious rule. They should never disobey selective optimization even if it requires them to reach suboptimal results in some cases.[7] Unlike permissive rule, selective optimization does not guarantee that a judge who obeys it will never knowingly reach suboptimal results. Selective optimization merely attempts to minimize the number of suboptimal results that the system as a whole produces. However, selective optimization does not require judges to treat first-order legal rules as serious rules. It permits judges to deviate from such rules on some occasions.

I should reiterate that lawmakers may have conclusive reasons to codify and promulgate restrictive rule rather than selective optimization. But judges do not necessarily have an all-things-considered reason to *obey* restrictive rule rather than an uncodified rule such as selective optimization. Judges should treat selective optimization as a set of serious rules.

17.2 CONSTRAINTS AND DECISIONS

In this section, I shall consider an objection to selective optimization based on Scott Shapiro's work on the nature of rule following. Shapiro distinguishes between the *decision model* of rule following and the *constraint model*, defending the latter. He argues that when a judge genuinely commits herself to the law, she makes subsequent deviation "infeasible." Shapiro does not intend *infeasible* as a metaphor. He means that it is literally impossible for a judge who is committed to the law to deviate *for a reason*. One who deviates for a reason is not, ipso facto, committed to the law.[8]

---

7. Obeying selective optimization as a serious rule is extensionally equivalent to "obeying" restrictive rule and defining *obedience* in terms of a noncausal version of rule-sensitive particularism.

8. Scott J. Shapiro, "Judicial Can't," *Noûs* 35, Supp. 1 (2001): 530–57.

Theoretical Implications

Shapiro suggests two mechanisms by which commitment to the law renders deviation infeasible. First, adopting a rule activates the psychological mechanism of *repression*. The judge becomes "unaware of reasons for breaking the rule," rendering her "unable to break the rule for a reason." Second, even a judge who remains "aware of important reasons for breaking the rule" becomes "unable to withstand certain emotional pressures, such as guilt and shame," after she adopts the rule.[9]

The following implication appears to follow from the constraint model: if a judge commits herself to the law, then she has no choice but to obey restrictive rule. Breaking restrictive rule becomes infeasible for her. "By committing to the legal system's rule of recognition," Shapiro writes, "a judge will thus be constraining her future self to implement the rules that share these authoritative features."[10] He makes other similar remarks:

> It is rational for the committed judge to apply the law in any given instance because that is the only option available. . . . [I]f judges are constrained to apply the law, they must apply it regardless of its consequences.[11]

> If the Constraint Model of rules is correct, then judges cannot be morally obligated to decide individual cases according to the balance of reasons. Nor can they be legally obligated to do so.[12]

I am not yet prepared to endorse the constraint model, but it has some plausibility. Regardless, I do not believe that the constraint model entails that judges who commit themselves to the law have no choice but to obey restrictive rule. The constraint model is a generic model of rule guidance. It does not entail any particular adherence rule such as restrictive rule. Suppose the constraint model and selective optimization are both true. If so, then a judge who commits himself to the law has no choice but to obey selective optimization. Disobeying selective optimization becomes infeasible for him, but selective optimization does not forbid all deviation in suboptimal-result cases as restrictive rule does.

Now Shapiro could object that the constraint model entails that selective optimization cannot guide judges. According to his model, rules guide by two mechanisms: repression and the disabling of normal inhibitions. Shapiro could claim that selective optimization is incompatible with these mechanisms. Selective optimization, unlike restrictive rule, sometimes permits judges to consider the full range of reasons to deviate. Selective optimization also requires each judge to monitor his own deviation record, but if he has deviation credits remaining, then selective optimization permits him to act on reasons to deviate. In other words, selective optimization does not always require judges to *repress* these reasons from their consciousness. Deviating for reasons remains a *feasible* option.

9. Ibid., pp. 552–55.
10. Ibid., p. 550.
11. Ibid., p. 551.
12. Ibid., p. 555.

Similarly, the constraint model entails that rules can guide only if the agent's "normal psychological inhibitions" are disabled and she anticipates too much guilt or shame to consider breaking the rule. By contrast, selective optimization sometimes allows the judge's normal psychological inhibitions against mistreating other human beings to remain active and to override any guilt or shame that might be associated with being a "lawless judge." Again, deviating for reasons remains feasible. Shapiro's claim would be that selective optimization cannot guide judges because the content of selective optimization interferes with the only two mechanisms by which rules can guide agents.

It is true that a judge does not make deviating infeasible for himself by committing to selective optimization. That would defeat the purpose of selective optimization. But this commitment could make it infeasible for him to treat, *as all-things-considered reasons to deviate*, certain facts that would otherwise constitute such reasons. For a judge who is committed only to permissive rule, the fact that Yasmin does not deserve to be evicted constitutes an all-things-considered reason not to evict her. However, for one who is committed to selective optimization this fact constitutes a conditional reason: a reason that must be enabled by certain conditions. It is a reason for Judge Lucas not to evict Yasmin if selective optimization permits him to act upon that reason—if he has deviation credits left, et cetera. I can accept Shapiro's theory of rule guidance and assert that committing oneself to selective optimization makes it infeasible to treat facts about Yasmin's situation as all-things-considered reasons to deviate in her favor.

Now Shapiro might reply that this is psychologically untenable. If, as I stipulate, Judge Lucas is sufficiently aware of Yasmin's plight to treat it as a conditional reason to deviate, then how can he be unaware of it as an all-things-considered reason to deviate? My reply is that this is precisely what selective optimization entails, and that Shapiro's own constraint model cannot achieve what he wants unless judges ordinarily sustain similar psychological compartmentalization. Shapiro cannot, and need not, claim that a judge who adheres to the law in Yasmin's case is, in every sense, *unaware* of the facts that favor ruling for her. Imagine that we ask Judge Lucas, "Does Yasmin deserve to be evicted as a moral matter?" If he is committed to the law, then what honest responses are available to him, according to the constraint model? Here are some possible responses:

> "I have no idea whether she deserves to be evicted as a moral matter. All I know is what the law tells me: she must be evicted."
>
> "I think I have an opinion about whether she deserves to be evicted as a moral matter, but I can't presently remember what my opinion is."
>
> "I'm deciding her case, so I can't think about that right now. Ask me later."

Each of these responses comports with the constraint model, but none is necessary. This is fortunate, because none is especially realistic as a matter of human psychology. Here is a more realistic reply:

"No, she doesn't deserve eviction morally speaking. I know that perfectly well, but as a judge I can't treat it as a dispositive reason to rule in her favor. Therefore, I refuse to think about it when I deliberate in chambers."[13]

That sounds like a more honest answer to me. But if the constraint model allows the judge to offer this reply, then I think it also allows him to offer a reply that reflects a commitment to selective optimization:

"No, she doesn't deserve eviction, morally speaking. I know that perfectly well. But I've bent the law an awful lot this month. As a judge, I can't treat Yasmin's plight as a reason to rule in her favor if I've been deviating too often recently. So I refuse to think about her plight when I deliberate in chambers."

It is commonly assumed that a judge who deviates in a suboptimal-result case does so because he has treated the suboptimality of the legally required result as a self-sufficient reason to deviate. Only if this is true does the constraint model entail restrictive rule. But it is not necessarily true. A judge can treat suboptimality as one of several individually insufficient but jointly sufficient conditions on deviation. Suboptimality may require enablers before it constitutes a reason to deviate. It is only partly accurate to say that a judge who obeys selective optimization deviates "because the law requires a suboptimal result." A more accurate statement is that he deviates "because the law requires a suboptimal result *and he has deviation credits left.*" The latter phrase denotes what Jonathan Dancy calls a combination of a "favorer" and an "enabler."[14]

17.3 THE PRACTICAL DIFFERENCE THESIS

The question then arises whether, according to selective optimization, first-order legal standards can actually guide judges. Consider Shapiro's conception of rule guidance: "An agent is being 'guided' by a rule when that agent takes the fact that the rule is applicable as a *conclusive reason* to follow it" (emphasis in original).[15] Elsewhere Shapiro asserts that "A legal rule R guides a person P to do A only if P might not have done A if he had not appealed to R as a legal rule."[16]

---

13. "[J]udges may adhere to precedent without introspective analysis of the effects of the instant case as a means of avoiding distress and guilt over issuing difficult holdings." Eric Talley, "Precedential Cascades: An Appraisal," *Southern California Law Review* 73 (1999): 87–137," p. 109. See also Scott Altman, "Beyond Candor," *Michigan Law Review* 89 (1990): 296–351, p. 305.

14. Jonathan Dancy, *Ethics without Principles* (Oxford: Oxford University Press, 2004), pp. 38–43. Roger Crisp calls these combinations "ultimate reasons." Roger Crisp, "Particularizing Particularism," in *Moral Particularism*, eds. Brad Hooker and Margaret Olivia Little (Oxford: Oxford University Press, 2000), p. 37.

15. Shapiro, "Judicial Can't," p. 535.

16. Scott J. Shapiro, "On Hart's Way Out," in *Hart's Postscript*, ed. Jules Coleman (Oxford: Oxford University Press, 2000).

This conception of rule guidance undergirds Shapiro's defense of the *practical difference thesis*, which states, "Legal rules must in principle be capable of securing conformity by making a difference to an agent's practical reasoning."[17] Shapiro claims that many positivists, notably H. L. A. Hart, are committed to both the practical difference thesis and the *conventionality thesis*—the view that the master rule of the legal system is a conventional rule.[18] Shapiro argues that one cannot consistently endorse inclusive positivism, the practical difference thesis, and the conventionality thesis. Although Shapiro does not claim that all versions of inclusive positivism are indefensible, he favors retaining the practical difference thesis and conventionality and abandoning inclusive for exclusive positivism.[19]

Even those who reject the practical difference thesis recognize that legal rules *sometimes* secure conformity by making a difference to an agent's practical reasoning. So regardless of whether one accepts the practical difference thesis, it is important to get clear what sort of practical difference legal rules make when, as often, they make one.

Here is an illustration of rule guidance as Shapiro conceives it. Imagine a master rule that specifies the following: "All statutes enacted by the Virginia General Assembly are valid." The assembly enacts a statute criminalizing the purchase of beer on Sundays. Meg, a Virginia resident, is guided by this provision of Virginia's master rule and she is aware of the statute. As a result she refrains from buying beer on Sunday. However, it was physically possible for the state legislature not to enact (or to repeal) the beer statute. In that case, even though Meg was guided by the master rule she would not have appealed to the statute as a legal rule, for the simple reason that the statute would not have *been* a legal rule in that case. She might in that case have bought beer on Sunday. Therefore, the statute *guides* Meg not to buy beer.

If Shapiro means "all-things-considered reason" by "conclusive reason" in his statement of the practical difference thesis, then selective optimization entails that the fact that a legal standard is applicable is not always a conclusive reason for a judge to apply it. If a standard requires a suboptimal result and the judge has deviation credits left, then she could have a stronger

---

17. Ibid., p. 129.
18. See, e.g., Jules Coleman, *The Practice of Principle* (Oxford: Oxford University Press, 2001), p. 68.
19. Inclusive positivists have offered several responses to Shapiro's arguments. Some have disavowed the practical difference thesis. See Ibid., pp. 137–48; Matthew Kramer, "How Moral Principles Can Enter into the Law," *Legal Theory* 6 (2000): 83–108. Others retain some version of the thesis but argue, against Shapiro, that inclusive positivism is consistent with the practical difference thesis, properly understood. See, e.g., Kenneth Einar Himma, "Judicial Discretion and the Concept of Law," *Oxford Journal of Legal Studies* 19 (1999): 71–82; W. J. Waluchow, "Authority and the Practical Difference Thesis," *Legal Theory* 6 (2000): 45–81. Shapiro has responded imaginatively to many of these criticisms. Scott J. Shapiro, "Law, Morality, and the Guidance of Conduct," *Legal Theory* 6 (2000): 127–70.

Theoretical Implications

reason to deviate than to adhere. On this reading of Shapiro, selective optimization entails that first-order legal rules and other legal standards do not, in his sense, *guide* judges. However, I shall argue that selective optimization allows first-order legal rules to guide judges in a different way.

Shapiro believes that an agent is guided by law only if she obeys legally pedigreed rules. This belief entails that judges who deviate from pedigreed rules are not guided by the law. This is correct if one accepts Shapiro's conception of rule guidance. As Shapiro defines rule guidance, a rule guides an agent to Φ only if she might not have Φ-ed had *she herself* not appealed to that rule. This is a familiar and straightforward way for rules to influence agents. But it is not the only way. When we think of a rule guiding an agent we naturally think of cases that are regulated by the rule, as Meg's decision to refrain from purchasing beer is regulated by the statute. In regulated cases the rule guides by discounting certain reasons that would otherwise apply. *Unconditional discounting reasons* are second-order reasons to treat specified first-order reasons as having less force than they otherwise would. Discounting reasons can themselves be discounted. When an agent defers to a conflicting rule, she discounts the discounting reasons supplied by the first rule, thereby allowing the first-order reasons again to play their usual role.

Shapiro concentrates on cases of unconditional discounting. But rules can also discount conditionally. A *conditional discounting reason* is a second-order reason to accept a conditional according to which, if some condition is met, then one will treat specified first-order reasons as having less force than they otherwise would. The specified condition could concern virtually anything, including the conformity of oneself or other agents to other rules.

The following scenario illustrates all the previous points at once. It shows how a rule can guide an agent, in a case not regulated by that rule, by providing conditional discounting reasons, where the specified condition concerns the conformity of another agent to another rule. Cordelia and Goneril are teenage sisters. Goneril, the elder sister, has an 11 P.M. curfew, whereas Cordelia's curfew is earlier. Goneril sits at home at 10:30 P.M. one night. She wants to attend a late-night concert that would require her to violate her 11 P.M. curfew. She is considering leaving the house when she notices Cordelia coming home. Goneril does not know whether Cordelia has missed her curfew, however, because Goneril cannot remember if her parents have changed Cordelia's curfew from 10 P.M. to 10:30 P.M. Goneril has special reason to care about Cordelia's curfew because Goneril is eagerly anticipating a family vacation and she knows from experience that her parents will cancel the vacation if *both* sisters violate their respective curfews, but not if only one of them does so. If Cordelia has missed her curfew then Goneril must stay home, or lose the vacation. If, however, Cordelia's curfew has been moved to 10:30 P.M., then Goneril has the option to attend the concert, thereby violating her own curfew without jeopardizing the vacation.

Goneril's own curfew remains 11 P.M., regardless of whether Cordelia's has changed. Goneril could decide to guide her conduct exclusively on the basis of her *own* curfew rule and take no account of Cordelia's rule or behavior. We can analogize Goneril's situation to that of a judge deliberating in a suboptimal-result case. Much as Goneril could decide to consult only her own curfew rule, so the judge could decide to consult only pedigreed legal standards. But Shapiro does not just claim that judges *could* decide to consult only pedigreed legal standards. He denies that judges who ignore such standards are guided by the law. Presumably Shapiro would also deny that Cordelia's rule guides Goneril, which is true in one sense but false in another. Cordelia's curfew rule influences Goneril's deliberations in an obvious way. Although Goneril could decide to ignore Cordelia's rule and behavior, she could also decide to respond strategically to Cordelia. Suppose Goneril takes the strategic route. In that case Cordelia's curfew rule provides Goneril with a conditional discounting reason, which is a second-order reason to accept the following conditional: if Cordelia comes home later than the hour specified in Cordelia's curfew rule, then Goneril shall discount her reasons to attend the concert. Cordelia's rule addresses Cordelia directly, but it also addresses Goneril indirectly, by providing conditional discounting reasons. If Goneril is trying to obey the rules that apply to her, then as the content of Cordelia's rule fluctuates so does Goneril's behavior in response. I take this to suggest that Cordelia's rule is guiding Goneril, albeit indirectly. So a rule can indirectly guide an agent even in a case that is not regulated by that rule.

Shapiro, however, assumes that a rule cannot guide an agent unless it provides her with unconditional discounting reasons. In one sense, this is correct. If r is a legal rule, then there could, in principle, exist an agent for whom r provides unconditional discounting reasons. However, Shapiro's argument depends on a stronger condition. His argument presupposes that r cannot constitute a legal rule for a certain agent unless r provides unconditional discounting reasons *for that very agent*. This is not so. Indeed, no agent for whom r provides unconditional discounting reasons must actually exist in order for r to constitute a legal rule for other agents, by providing them with conditional discounting reasons.

This last point becomes clearer if we modify our scenario. Suppose Cordelia and Goneril are twins, each with an 11 P.M. curfew. They encounter one another downtown at 10:45 P.M. Still assuming their parents' vacation rule to be in effect, Cordelia's rule provides Goneril with a conditional reason and Goneril's provides Cordelia with a conditional reason. Cordelia's rule guides Goneril and Goneril's rule guides Cordelia—indirectly in both cases. Neither rule provides either teenager with an unconditional discounting reason. Yet the curfew rules clearly play as important a role as ever in their deliberation. The parents have effectively issued this command: "Girls, you mustn't *both* break curfew!"

I suggest that what Shapiro describes as rule guidance is really a special case of a more general phenomenon, *generalized rule guidance*:

Theoretical Implications

A legal rule r guides (in the generalized sense) a person p to Φ only if p might not have done Φ if a person q had not appealed to r as a legal rule (where q might or might not be the same person as p and q actually does appeal to r as a legal rule).

In terms of my condition on generalized rule guidance, Shapiro describes the special case in which q is the same person as p. I call this *direct rule guidance*, in contrast to *indirect rule guidance*, where q and p are different persons. It is true that Cordelia's curfew rule cannot guide Goneril directly. Shapiro's position, again in my terms, is that a legal rule cannot make a practical difference for a certain agent unless it guides her *directly*.

Someone might object that what guides Goneril is not Cordelia's rule *simpliciter* but rather the conjunction of Cordelia's rule and the parents' vacation-canceling rule. True, Cordelia's rule guides Goneril only if the vacation rule is also in force. But if the vacation rule is in force, then Cordelia's rule does, indeed, guide Goneril. The vacation rule simply makes it the case that Cordelia's rule guides Goneril. It does not supplant Cordelia's rule, but rather extends to Goneril that rule's capacity to guide.

Alternatively, Shapiro could object that Cordelia's rule does not guide Goneril because Goneril does not appeal to it *as an authoritative rule*. Indeed, Goneril does not "follow" Cordelia's rule. If Cordelia's curfew is 10 P.M., that fact will not motivate Goneril to get home by 10 P.M. Nevertheless, Goneril appeals to Cordelia's rule as a rule that is directly authoritative for Cordelia and indirectly authoritative for Goneril. Compare Goneril's attitude toward a rule announced by her little brother (who has no authority over Cordelia): "Cordelia must return by 8 P.M.!" Goneril does not appeal to this rule as authoritative, whereas she does appeal to Cordelia's rule as authoritative.

Now consider how my generalized conception of rule guidance applies to the judiciary. Some exclusive positivists portray legal rules as supplying judges with unconditional discounting reasons. These reasons, moreover, are supposed to reference only case-type-specific facts. I contest both points. First, I suggest that we need not understand legal rules as providing real judges with anything more than conditional discounting reasons. Second, I suggest that the conditions can reference facts that are not case-type-specific, such as the judge's own deviation record, or even (in principle) the proximity of the legal system to its threshold.

Shapiro believes that judges who deviate from pedigreed rules are not guided by law. He might be correct that they are not guided directly and unconditionally. But I disagree if he also means that judges who deviate from pedigreed rules are not guided by the law in any way. Suppose Goneril takes the strategic route. She decides to understand her parents as having established a violation threshold: two curfew violations will cancel the vacation. In that case, Goneril would understand Cordelia's rule as providing her with a special kind of conditional discounting reason, one that references the violation threshold. Here is the parallel strategy in the judicial case. According to selective optimization, valid legal rules provide judges with conditional discounting reasons that reference the judge's own deviation rate. Much as Goneril has reason both to attend the concert and to protect the vacation, so our judge has reason to deviate, thus avoiding a suboptimal result in the case at bar without violating selective optimization. On my view a valid legal rule gives judges reasons of two kinds in cases regulated thereby: first, an unconditional reason to discount private reasons to deviate; and second, a conditional reason to discount moral reasons to deviate when required by selective optimization. However, if selective optimization permits deviation in a certain suboptimal-result case, then the suboptimality of the legally required result discounts the reason to adhere that is provided by the legal rule. This parallels the case in which Cordelia has not actually violated her own curfew. In that case, given Cordelia's conduct and her curfew rule, the condition specified in the parents' vacation rule is not met. Therefore, Goneril's own curfew rule gets discounted. Rather than providing Goneril with a second-order reason to discount her first-order reasons to attend the concert, Goneril's curfew rule gives her, at most, an ordinary first-order reason to stay home that must compete with her reasons to attend the concert. I conclude that legal standards can indirectly guide judges who deviate in suboptimal-result cases.

I agree with exclusive positivists that there is an important difference between deviating from pedigreed rules and adhering to them. Deviation contributes to an enterprise that could, in excess, weaken the rule of law. Adherence does not. But exclusive positivists are incorrect if they also believe that deviating from a particular legal standard must involve a failure to be guided by the law as a whole. Legal standards can guide and constrain the judiciary in more ways than that.

17.4 EQUITY

Readers familiar with the concept of equity in legal history will rightly wonder if selective optimization should be understood as a form of equitable decision making. A comparison with various historical conceptions of equity would be fascinating but must await another occasion.[20] Here

20. *Equity* has multiple meanings in legal history that I shall not bother to differentiate. See, e.g., John F. Manning, "Textualism and the Equity of the Statute," *Columbia Law Review* 101 (2001): 1–127; John R. Kroger, "Supreme Court Equity, 1789–1835, and the History of American Judging," *Houston Law Review* 34 (1998): 1425–86; John J. Farley, III, "Robin Hood Jurisprudence: The Triumph of Equity in American Tort Law," *St. John's Law Review* 65 (1991): 997–1021 (conceding that equitable notions still exist in American tort law); Peter Charles Hoffer, "Principled Discretion: Concealment, Conscience, and Chancellors," *Yale Journal of Law and the Humanities* 3 (1991): 53–82 (analysis of American equity jurisdiction); Calvin Woodard, "Joseph Story and American Equity," *Washington and Lee Law Review* 45 (1988): 623–44; Gary McDowell, *Equity and the Constitution: The Supreme Court, Equitable Relief, and Public Policy* (Chicago: University of Chicago Press, 1982); Walter Wheeler Cook, *Cases and Other Authorities on Equity* (St. Paul: West, 1923).

I limit myself to a prominent contemporary treatment. Lawrence Solum defines equity as "the practice of doing particularized justice, when the just result is not required by, or is contrary to, the result required by the set of applicable legal rules."[21] Solum's equity differs from all moderate rules, including selective optimization, in several respects. First, Solum's equity applies only to negative-gap cases:

> Equity tailors the law to the requirements of the particular case. Understanding equity as a particularized practice allows us to distinguish it from other practices that involve a departure from legal rules. For example, equity is not identical to the resolution of conflicts between law and morality in favor of the latter. Judges might nullify a statute that legalized the practice of slavery on the ground that slavery is always morally wrong. This is not an example of the practice of equity, because such a decision would not involve a departure from the rule on the basis of the facts of the *particular* case. Rather the decision would be based on a general moral principle—for example, that wicked or immoral statutes should not be enforced.[22]

By contrast, moderate rules apply to all suboptimal-result cases, including both negative-gap cases and suboptimal-rule cases.

Second, Solum's equity involves doing particularized justice. Solum permits deviation from legal rules only when necessary to avoid *unjust* results, whereas moderate rules permit deviation to avoid the broader category of suboptimal results. All unjust results are suboptimal, but not all suboptimal results are unjust.

Third, moderate rules allow deviation from the law *simpliciter*, whereas Solum's equity, as described, allows deviation only from legal rules. It is not clear whether Solum also allows deviation from the law *simpliciter*. Perhaps he regards equitable decisions as legally correct and believes that deviation from the law *simpliciter* is never necessary or justified.[23]

Despite these differences between moderate rules and Solum's equity, Solum's view remains a relative of selective optimization and serves as an instructive foil for it. Selective optimization can even be seen as a generalization of Solum's equity with some added safeguards and qualifications.

In addition to these generic contrasts between Solum's equity and any moderate rule, there are two additional differences between Solum's equity and selective optimization, specifically. First, Solum appears to accept a strong comparative justice principle that rules out token-selective deviation.

---

21. Lawrence B. Solum, "Equity and the Rule of Law," in *The Rule of Law*, ed. Ian Shapiro (New York: New York University Press, 1994), p. 123. See also Gerald J. Postema, *Bentham and the Common Law Tradition* (Oxford: Oxford University Press, 1986), pp. 200, 407–8, 416–17, 429.

22. Solum, "Equity and the Rule of Law," p. 124.

23. The idea that equitable deviation from legal rules does not constitute deviation from the law, *simpliciter*, is reinforced by assertions such as this: "An adjudicator with judicial integrity cares about the coherence of the law and is motivated to ensure that her departure from the letter of the rules accords with their *spirit*." Ibid., p. 136 (emphasis added).

Although he notes that equity can involve treating differently two case tokens that the legal rules classify as identical,[24] thereby infringing legal comparative justice, the differential treatment must be itself justified by differences between the factual case types. The "particulars" of the case to which Solum demands judicial sensitivity are particulars of the *moral* case type.[25] Cases apt for equitable treatment are those in which the particular fact pattern was not anticipated by the lawmaker, contracting party, testator, et cetera. For Solum, if the particular facts entail that the result required by a generally good legal rule is unjust, then the judge should deviate. Otherwise, she should adhere. These facts are both necessary and sufficient to warrant deviation, so there is no possibility of deviation being appropriate in one case token but inappropriate in another token of the same type. Selective optimization could, in principle, permit this.

Solum's theory is indifferent to systemic factors, including deviation density, which brings me to the second contrast with selective optimization. Chapter 11 demonstrates that indifference to deviation density is acceptable only if suboptimal-result cases are very rare.[26] This is true in modern legal systems only on certain conceptions of justice—those according to which it is very rare for the good laws of such systems to dictate unjust results. Perhaps Solum accepts such a conception of justice. In that case his position would be coherent, but his theory of equity would then depend upon his conception of justice. I am trying to construct a theory of permissible deviation that is compatible with a wider range of conceptions of justice—those that classify many cases in modern legal systems as suboptimal-result cases, as well as those that place fewer cases in that category. Therefore, selective optimization conditions the permissibility of deviation on the proximity of the system to threshold. Solum's theory has no counterpart to this condition.

17.5 LEGAL PRAGMATISM

Profitable as it would be to compare selective optimization with various incarnations of legal pragmatism, a brief note will have to suffice. Judge Richard Posner, the preeminent legal pragmatist of our time, believes that when judges have the authority to formulate legal rules they should craft rules that they predict will produce the best consequences. They should use the best available social science for that purpose, as well as common sense, and they should explain their use of these sources in their opinions. Departing from bad horizontal precedent is permissible, Posner thinks, although judges should give it some weight, recognizing the values of

---

24. Ibid., p. 125.
25. "A judge doing equity will give reasons for his decision that are based on the facts of the particular dispute. . . ." Ibid., p. 126.
26. See §11.9.

Theoretical Implications

stability, predictability, and reliance. He appears to believe that judges have the legal and moral authority to choose optimal rules more often than mainstream legal scholars think they have it.[27] So Posner and the selective optimizer both believe that judges are morally permitted to reach the optimal result more often than some scholars consider permissible.

None of Posner's prescriptions seems to conflict with selective optimization. However, the two positions address different types of cases. In the cases that interest Posner, judges have legal authority to choose or modify rules. Posner expresses opinions about how they should decide such cases, what sources they should use, and how they should justify their choices in print. By contrast, I have considered cases in which binding legal standards apply: the text is unambiguous or vertical precedent controls. Judges have no legal authority to deviate in such cases. I cannot tell if Posner believes that judges must always adhere in such cases. But I think he could consistently endorse restrictive rule without retracting his forward-looking criteria for the best rules, his recommendation that judges write empirical evidence into their opinions, or his belief that they should often reverse horizontal precedents with bad consequences. To this extent, Posner's pragmatism and selective optimization complement each other, but their distinctive features do not substantially overlap.

17.6 POLITICAL NEUTRALITY

Finally, I return to the issue of political neutrality in adjudication theory, first raised in chapter 1.[28] Commentators of all political persuasions complain about judges who ignore the law, but American conservatives have been more likely than liberals to make such complaints, at least for the past few decades. The correlation has loosened somewhat as the federal bench has become more conservative. Of course, most liberals do not openly advocate ignoring the law, but it remains reasonable to infer that a writer in the early twenty-first century who advocates ignoring the law is probably not conservative. I do not claim that political conservatives should welcome my conclusions in this book. No interesting prescription concerning adjudication will, at a particular moment in history, be equally appealing to everyone in complex pluralistic societies. If political neutrality requires pleasing everyone, then adjudication theory should not aspire to such neutrality.

There is, however, another sort of political neutrality toward which we should aspire. It is rational for conservatives to assume, upon encountering an argument for deviation, not just that its author is liberal, but that it

---

27. Richard A. Posner, *The Problematics of Moral and Legal Theory* (Cambridge, Mass.: Belknap, 1999), pp. 240–52.

28. See §1.8.

rests upon liberal premises. Close scrutiny by clever conservatives usually reveals these premises, depriving the argument of any persuasive force for conservative readers who reject those assumptions. Some writers on adjudication acknowledge that their arguments proceed from politically controversial premises. They assume, for example, that their reader is a fellow liberal, and they advocate a particular theory of adjudication that enables them to defend various rulings and legal arguments favored by liberals. I do not oppose this kind of scholarship. I would be happy to discover a coherent theory of adjudication that enabled judges to implement all of my political views, while preventing them from implementing anyone else's. I have not found such a theory, nor did I formulate selective optimization with that goal in mind. Instead, I have tried to avoid any premises that are closely identified with the political left or right. Part I uses widely accepted normative premises with no distinctive political associations. Part II uses premises that remain controversial in academic philosophy, but they are not distinctively creatures of the political right or left, either. I hope I have offered arguments for selective optimization that people with a wide range of political opinions can accept.

Nevertheless, I must make a confession: I believe that legalizing contraception was morally correct and that Justice Douglas acted permissibly in *Griswold*, even if there was no sound legal argument for his ruling, as many lawyers believe. Selective optimization is consistent with these beliefs, but not because my arguments for it depend on my political convictions. Selective optimization authorizes judges to deviate only if the legally required result is actually suboptimal. If I am wrong about the injustice of birth control bans and no sound legal argument existed for the *Griswold* holding, then selective optimization entails that Justice Douglas acted impermissibly. Selective optimization cannot guarantee that anyone is, in fact, morally enlightened. It merely assures me that morally enlightened judges are sometimes morally permitted to apply their wisdom, even when the law disagrees. It gives precisely the same assurance to those who reject my politics. In fact, I offer an uncomfortable prediction: if judges in the United States today were faithfully to obey selective optimization, then they would reach *fewer* results that I favor as a political citizen than if they were to obey restrictive rule. This prediction disappoints me as a political citizen, but it strangely reassures me as a theorist. It provides some circumstantial evidence that my arguments do not presuppose my idiosyncratic opinions about justice and public policy.

At the same time, if selective optimization is correct, then we must reexamine popular attacks on lawless judging. Commentators often state that a court has "misread," "misstated," "misinterpreted," or "ignored" the law. The literal content of such statements is theoretical, not practical: the judge has made a legally incorrect assertion. A professor could make exactly the same theoretical criticism of a legal assertion in a paper submitted by a law student. However, when a commentator makes such a statement about a judicial decision, he usually intends to imply much more than a theoretical criticism. He intends to imply practical claims such as one or more of the following conversational *implicatures*:[29]

1. The judge had an all-things-considered reason to decide differently.
2. If the judge knowingly did what the commentator claims she did (i.e., deviate from the law), then she is blameworthy.
3. The judge acted unethically, at least if she deviated knowingly, and perhaps even if she deviated unknowingly.

If selective optimization is true, then such implicatures are usually false. If judges have an all-things-considered duty to obey restrictive rule, then it is not especially important to distinguish between the theoretical claim that a judge has deviated and practical claims such as the three above. If restrictive rule is correct, then the theoretical claim implies at least some of these practical claims. However, if selective optimization (or any moderate or permissive rule) is correct, then we must carefully distinguish between the theoretical claim and the practical claims because the former does not imply the latter. Selective optimization entails that if a judge deviates in more than a certain fraction of his cases, then he creates an impermissible decision pattern. But selective optimization also entails that very few, if any, of these decisions is morally impermissible in itself if it avoids a suboptimal result.

---

29. For an introduction to conversational implicature see Paul Grice, "Logic and Conversation," in *Studies in the Way of Words* (Cambridge, Mass.: Harvard University Press, 1989).

18

Conclusion

I have called into question three adjudication principles that many knowledgeable people accept, uncritically:

1. Judges in reasonably just legal systems are morally obligated to apply the law correctly in all cases in which the law requires a certain result or range of results.
2. Judges are morally permitted to deviate from the law only, if ever, when the legally required result is extremely unjust.
3. Only the fact pattern of the case is relevant to the moral permissibility of deviation from the law.

Popular as these principles are, they are rarely defended. I considered and rejected various arguments for them. Whereas most discussions of judicial deviation concentrate on its political legitimacy, I asked whether it is reasonable for society to ask judges, as autonomous moral agents, to refrain from deviation in suboptimal-result cases as often as the conventional wisdom demands. I considered not just the legitimacy of the judicial role, but the moral rights of the individuals who occupy it. I shall now review my lengthy argument and offer some concluding reflections about the implications of selective optimization.

My investigation began with an account of judicial authority based on the natural rights and duties of judges. In a state of nature, individuals have duties of nonmaleficence, samaritan rights, and rights of justice. In civil society they retain their duties of nonmaleficence and their samaritan rights, but their rights of justice are partially undermined as the state largely takes over the function of pursuing justice. Judges are agents of the state. When they decide cases they create, withdraw, or block threats of force. They have legal authority to do so. They are also morally permitted to use force in certain situations in which the law authorizes them to use it.

Some people appear to accept the undermining principle, which states that if the law requires a public official to use force in a given situation, then he has no moral reason not to use it. The undermining principle has implications for adjudication in suboptimal-result cases: those in which the law, properly understood, requires a result that the judge would have an all-things-considered reason to avoid if the law permitted her to avoid

Conclusion

it. If the undermining principle is true, then judges never have moral reasons to deviate from the law. I considered many arguments for the undermining principle, including arguments from legal positivism, ordinary discourse, role morality, formal legality, political legitimacy, legal authority, intention, and means. I found none of these arguments to be sound. In the absence of a sound argument for the undermining principle, I concluded that judges have *pro tanto* moral reasons to deviate from the law in suboptimal-result cases.

I then turned to the topic of adherence rules, which require judges to adhere to the law. I distinguished between restrictive, moderate, and permissive rules. I noted the centrality of adherence rules to the rule of law and considered various reasons for lawmakers to promulgate restrictive rule. These included reasons of settlement, predictability, coordination, reliance, efficiency, error, stability, legitimacy, autonomy, respect, and fairness. I concluded that most of these are good reasons to promulgate restrictive rule.

My next question was whether judges have reasons to obey adherence rules. After concluding that judges have excellent *pro tanto* moral reasons to obey at least permissive rule, I asked whether they have moral reasons to obey restrictive rule. I found that the arguments for promulgating restrictive rule do not support obeying it in suboptimal-result cases. Neither do consequentialist or contractualist arguments. In fact, these arguments fail to support a moral duty to obey anything stronger than permissive rule. Chapter 9 evaluated and rejected the claim that judges must adhere to the law in suboptimal-result cases because they swore a solemn oath of office to uphold the law. Chapter 10 evaluated and rejected the claim that judges have a moral duty to adhere because they are legally obligated to do so. I considered how several familiar arguments for a duty to obey the law apply to the issue of judicial obligation: arguments from consent, fair play, natural duty, gratitude, and samaritanism. I also argued that judges are morally permitted to decide suboptimal-result cases rather than self-recusing.

Part I reached three main conclusions. First, we have no reason to accept the undermining principle. Second, lawmakers have good reasons, perhaps all-things-considered reasons, to promulgate restrictive rule. Third, the obvious arguments for the claim that judges have moral reasons to obey nonpermissive rules are fallacious. If that were the end of the story, then we would be left with the unpopular conclusion that judges have no moral reason to obey anything but permissive rule.

Part II described the normative structure that one must, I think, endorse if one wishes to maintain that judges have a moral reason to obey a nonpermissive rule. The needed normative structure is intricate and contains some philosophically controversial elements. I did not thoroughly defend all of these elements. I simply showed why they are necessary and how they fit together. I invite the reader to investigate the literatures defending these elements and to decide if she is prepared to accept them as the price of believing that judges have an all-things-considered moral reason to obey a nonpermissive rule.

The argument of part II proceeds from the premise that the judges who possess good moral judgment constitute a group—Group O—the members of which share two collective intentions: to minimize suboptimal results throughout their legal system and to avoid reaching suboptimal results themselves. They can fulfill the second intention by deviating from the law in suboptimal-result cases, but a pattern of deviating from the law, even in suboptimal-result cases, causes mimetic failure—other judges will imitate Group O and deviate in optimal-result cases, thereby reaching suboptimal results. At some point the rate of deviation by Group O could encourage so much deviation by other judges that the suboptimal results reached by those judges would outweigh the suboptimal results avoided by Group O. That point is what I call the deviation density *threshold*.

However, as I discussed in chapter 12, there are four agent-relative principles that, if true, entail that mimetic failure does not give Group O any reason to adhere to the law in suboptimal-result cases, even if additional deviation will transgress threshold. The principles that entail this result are ones that assign moral significance to intention, means, proximity, and agential mediation. I argued that we must abandon, qualify, or demote all of these principles if we wish to support the principle that judges have moral reasons to obey a nonpermissive rule. Adjudication theory should be foundationally agent-neutral.

The next question was whether the members of Group O have individual reasons to contribute to the group's efforts by adhering in at least some suboptimal-result cases. I argued that if enough of them are actually contributing, then they all have moral reasons to contribute in order to avoid riding free on one another. If too few of them are contributing, however, then the case for contributing becomes more difficult to make. I suggested three possible moral principles, any one of which would support contributing under conditions of general defection. The first principle holds individuals responsible for the imperceptible effects of their actions. The second holds them responsible for subjecting others to minimal, but unjustified, risks of harm. The third holds them responsible for participating in harmful or wrongful actions even when they cause no harm and otherwise do no wrong. Each of these principles is controversial. But if one or more of them is true, then we can argue that judges have reasons to adhere in at least some suboptimal-result cases, even when most other judges are deviating too frequently. This discussion culminated in the defense of individual policy, which specifies permissible deviation rates for judges based in part on how often other judges deviate.

In chapters 14, 15, and 16, I asked how judges might actually implement the rules defended in the previous chapters of part II (i.e., combined restriction). The discussion shifted from objective appraisal rules to subjective guidance rules. I responded to Alan Goldman's objections to rules that permit judges sometimes to deviate in suboptimal-result cases.

Conclusion

I defended guidance rules that permit each judge to deviate in a certain percentage of the suboptimal-result cases that she decides over the course of her career. I defended two priority rules for judges. The first rule assigns deviation priority to cases based on how suboptimal the legally required results are. The second rule assigns priority to suboptimal-rule cases over gap cases. I also defended a default rule that permits judges, after they obey the priority rules, to use any morally permissible criteria as the basis for their selection of suboptimal-result cases for deviation. I made the surprising claim that even random selection is not ruled out as a matter of principle. I defended this claim against arguments from comparative justice and Dworkinian integrity. The emerging theory is selective optimization.

In chapter 16, I examined some basic concerns about implementing selective optimization. I considered some familiar court cases and showed how selective optimization allows one coherently to make a claim that sounds paradoxical: that the judges were justified, all things considered, in reaching results that could not be defended as legally correct. I argued that judges are often in such a position, even in reasonably just legal systems.

In chapter 17, I examined more restrictive theories of rule guidance, including those of some exclusive positivists and legal formalists. I showed that their arguments do not impugn selective optimization. I also briefly contrasted selective optimization with pragmatism and equity.

I now offer some concluding reflections. Much judicial rhetoric is legalistic: it expresses the principle that judges have an all-things-considered moral obligation to obey restrictive rule while they remain on the bench. When a judge says "the law requires result x," you can be sure that he is going to reach x. However, "the law requires result x" can express at least two distinct propositions. One is that reaching a result inconsistent with x would violate the conventions of legal argument. Another is that judges have an ethical duty to reach x. When someone asserts "the law requires result x," without qualification, he usually means to assert both propositions and it is reasonable to infer as much. The absence of this distinction in legal discourse is understandable, given the traditional commitment to restrictive rule. If judges must obey restrictive rule, then the distinction serves no practical purpose. But equating "what the law requires" with "what judges must do" makes it impossible even to state selective optimization.

I do not know how many judges actually believe that they are morally obligated to obey restrictive rule, but I assume that many of them do. A morally conscientious judge who sincerely believes this will make one of two opposing mistakes. First, her desire to avoid suboptimal results may turn her into a kind of Panglossian. She desperately wants to believe that the law permits every result that she considers optimal and she is prepared to warp her theory of law in whatever direction enables her to embrace that harmonious conclusion. She distorts her perception of the law until it no longer functions in her mind as a set of standards that can dictate determinate results. Alternatively, if she avoids the Panglossian trap, then her desire to be moral will lead her to reach an unnecessarily large number of suboptimal results.

In realistic legal systems it is impossible to guarantee, a priori, that a judge will never hear a case in which he has an all-things-considered moral obligation to reach a suboptimal result. A judge in such a case faces an uncomfortable dilemma (ignoring the recusal option): he must either reach a suboptimal result or deviate. The only way to preclude such dilemmas, a priori, is to loosen the conventions of legal argument to such a degree that the law always permits reaching optimal results. That would sacrifice the advantages of a legal system over a system of unguided judicial discretion. Judges are fated to face some of these dilemmas even if my defense of selective optimization is successful. However, they face *more* such dilemmas if they obey restrictive rule than if they selectively optimize.

The rhetoric of lawyers is legalistic, too. An essential part of a litigator's job is to persuade the judge that the law at least permits a ruling in favor of her client. Even when a litigator presents arguments from justice or policy, she presents them as arguments about what the law says or should say. She encourages the judge to *understand* existing law in a certain way or to develop the law in a certain direction. She knows that judges sometimes deviate and she will encourage deviation if the law disfavors her client, but she will do so by persuading the judge to believe, or at least to assert, that the law permits what it actually forbids. Urging a judge to deviate in so many words is a rare act of desperation. If judges actually have an all-things-considered moral obligation to obey restrictive rule, then encouraging them—whether explicitly or implicitly—to deviate is probably unethical, too, even in suboptimal-result cases. By contrast, if selective optimization is permissible, then encouraging judges to deviate in suboptimal-result cases is not unethical.

Selective optimization also has implications for critics of lawless judging. It entails that, in realistic legal systems, the mere fact that a decision is deviant never provides a reason to conclude that the judge has acted immorally. The *result* may be suboptimal, but that is a separate matter. The only way to determine whether a judge has behaved unethically in virtue of having deviated is to assess her entire record for a pattern of excessive deviation as defined by selective optimization. The fact that a judge has deviated is not, in itself, a reason for censure, impeachment, removal, or any form of retaliation against her. It is not even a reason to vote against a judge when she runs for reelection, or a reason for a senator to vote against confirming a presidential nominee to the federal bench. Only a pattern of excessive deviation provides such reasons. Nor should judges generally face consequences for reaching suboptimal results that are required by law. Whether judges should face consequences for reaching suboptimal results not required by law is a larger issue that I cannot address here.

Of course, avoiding criticism and disciplinary action is an important incentive for many judges. If everyone stopped criticizing deviation, then judges would deviate more often, perhaps eventually crossing threshold. Such criticism should continue, in order to guard against that possibility. However, critics of the bench should heed the distinction between the proposition that a judge has deviated and the judgment that he has acted wrongly. They should recognize that calling a decision "lawless" is generally understood to express both. Until the linguistic conventions of legal discourse change, commentators should seek creative ways to convey the difference between these propositions and to avoid being misunderstood. At least, they should draw the distinction in their own minds. Perhaps they have been privately drawing it all along and I am not telling them anything new. If they have been drawing this distinction, however, then they have been hiding it very well.

Although selective optimization challenges the ideal of judicial adherence to the law, it is not skeptical or nihilistic about legal discourse. It is entirely compatible with the claim that some legal questions, or even all of them, have legally correct answers, although it does not entail this claim. Selective optimization does not call into question the objectivity of legal reasoning or the autonomy of legal reasoning from other kinds of discourse. Neither does it affirm legal objectivity and autonomy. It provides a principled alternative to the largely discredited, radical indeterminacy claims commonly ascribed to critical legal studies. Whereas radical indeterminacy implies that legal standards never preclude reaching morally optimal results, selective optimization avoids this indefensible claim.

Selective optimization entails, nevertheless, that evaluating the work of judges involves more than asking whether their legal reasoning is correct, however broadly we understand legal reasoning. It provides an ethical justification for reaching the morally optimal result, even when the law precludes it, in at least some cases. The rule of law cannot survive if judges deviate from the law too frequently, thereby violating selective optimization. However, traditional conceptions of judicial duty and the rule of law constrain adjudication to an extent that cannot be easily justified.

List of Authorities

Aaron, California Commission on Judicial Performance (July 8, 2002)
Albrecht v. Herald Co., 390 U.S. 145 (1968)
Alden, United States v., 141 Fed. Appx. 562 (9th Cir. 2005)
Ashcroft v. Free Speech Coalition, 535 U.S. 234 (2002)
Barnes v. Glen Theatre, Inc., 501 U.S. 560 (1991)
Bayless, United States v., 913 F. Supp. 232 (S.D.N.Y. 1996)
Bayless, United States v., 921 F. Supp. 211 (S.D.N.Y. 1996)
Bennis v. Michigan, 116 S. Ct. 994 (1996)
Bethlehem Steel Co. v. New York State Labor Relations Bd., 330 U.S. 767 (1947)
Bittaker v. Enomoto, 587 F.2d 400 (9th Cir. 1978)
Boumediene v. United States, 128 S. Ct. 2229 (2008)
Bowers v. Hardwick, 478 U.S. 186 (1986)
Boy Scouts of America v. Dale, 530 U.S. 640 (2000)
Bracy v. Gramley, 520 U.S. 899 (1997)
Bradley v. Fisher, 80 U.S. 335 (1872)
Bradley v. Richmond School Board, 416 U.S. 696 (1974)
Brignoni-Ponce, United States v., 422 U.S. 873 (1975)
Broadman v. Commission on Judicial Performance, 959 P.2d 715 (Cal. 1998)
Brown v. Board of Education, 347 U.S. 483 (1954)
Bush v. Gore, 531 U.S. 98 (2000)
Callender, United States v., 25 F. Cas. 239 (C.C.D. Va. 1800)
Chickasaw Nation v. United States, 534 U.S. 84 (2001)
Connecticut National Bank v. Germain, 503 U.S. 249 (1992)
District of Columbia v. Heller, 128 S. Ct. 2783 (2008)
Dred Scott v. Sandford, 60 U.S. 393 (1857)
Ekwunoh, United States v., 888 F. Supp. 369 (E.D.N.Y. 1994)
Elk Grove Unified School District v. Newdow, 542 U.S. 1 (2004)
Everson v. Board of Education, 330 U.S. 1 (1947)
Florida v. Rodriguez, 469 U.S. 1 (1984)
Furman v. Georgia, 408 U.S. 238 (1972)
Glassroth v. Moore, 335 F.3d 1282 (11th Cir. 2003)
Gonzales v. Carhart, 550 U.S. 124 (2007)
Gonzales v. Raich, 545 U.S. 1 (2005)
Griswold v. Connecticut, 381 U.S. 479 (1965)
Harrod v. Illinois Courts Commission, 372 N.E.2d 53 (Ill. 1977)
Henchey v. City of Chicago, 41 Ill. 136 (1866)
Henningsen v. Bloomfield Motors, 32 N.J. 358 (1960)
Hutto v. Davis, 454 U.S. 370 (1982)

Illinois v. Wardlow, 528 U.S. 119 (2000)
In Re Benoit, 487 A.2d 1158 (Me. 1985)
In Re Brown, 662 N.W.2d 773 (Mich. 2003)
In Re Cargill, 66 F.3d 1256 (1st Cir. 1995)
In Re Cooks, 694 So.2d 892 (La. 1997)
In Re Curda, 49 P.3d 255 (Alaska 2002)
In Re Daniels, 340 So.2d 301 (La. 1976)
In Re Derose, 1980 Annual Report 181 (New York State Commission on Judicial Conduct, Nov. 13, 1979)
In Re Duckman, 699 N.E.2d 872 (N.Y. 1998)
In Re Friess, 1984 Annual Report 84 (New York State Commission on Judicial Conduct, Mar. 30, 1983)
In Re Friess, 1984 Annual Report 84 (New York State Commission on Judicial Conduct, Mar. 30, 1983)
In Re King, 568 N.E.2d 588 (Mass. 1991)
In Re Labelle, 591 N.E.2d 1156 (N.Y. 1992)
In Re Mattera, 168 A.2d 38 (N.J. 1961)
In Re Mckinney, 478 S.E.2d 51 (S.C. 1996)
In Re Quirk, 705 So.2d 172 (La. 1997)
In Re Spencer, 798 N.E.2d 175 (Ind. 2003)
Inquiry Concerning a Judge No. 52 (Hampton) (Texas Commission on Judicial Conduct, 1989)
Isgro, United States v., 974 F.2d 1091 (9th Cir. 1992)
Jackson v. Lykes Bros. S.S. Co., No. 575, 386 U.S. 731 (1967)
Kelo v. City of New London, 545 U.S. 469 (2005)
Khan v. State Oil Co., 93 F.3d 1358 (7th Cir. 1996)
Kloepfer v. Commission on Judicial Conduct, 782 P.2d 239 (Cal. 1989)
Lawrence v. Texas, 539 U.S. 558 (2003)
Lewis v. Green, 629 F. Supp. 546 (DC Dist. Col. 1986)
Lockyer v. Andrade, 538 U.S. 63 (2003)
Lopez, United States v., 514 U.S. 549 (1995)
Marbury v. Madison, 5 U.S. 137 (1803)
Maryland St. Dept. Of Educ., Div. Of Rehabilitation Servs. v. United States Dept. Of Veterans Affairs, 98 F.3d 165 (4th Cir. 1997)
McCartney v. Commission on Judicial Quality, 526 P.2d 268 (Cal. 1974)
McCulloch v. Maryland, 17 U.S. 316 (1819)
McCullough v. Commission on Judicial Performance, 776 P.2d 259 (Cal. 1989)
Mirsky, United States v., 17 F.2d 275 (S.D.N.Y. 1926)
Model Code of Judicial Conduct (1990, 2007)
Morrison, United States v., 529 U.S. 598 (2000)
Morrow v. Hood Communications, Inc., 69 Cal. Rptr. 2d 489 (Cal. Ct. App. 1997)
Mosley, United States v., 965 F.2d 906 (10th Cir. 1992)
Murtagh v. Maglio, 9 A.D.2d 515 (N.Y. 1960)
Neary v. Regents of the University of California, 834 P.2d 119 (Cal. 1992)
Newdow v. U.S. Congress, 292 F.2d 597 (9th Cir. 2002)
Newdow v. U.S. Congress, 328 F.3d 466 (9th Cir. 2003)
Oberholzer v. Commission on Judicial Performance, 975 P.2d 663 (Cal. 1999)
Oregon Waste Systems, Inc. v. Department of Environmental Quality, 511 U.S. 93 (1994)

List of Authorities

Orjuela, United States v., 809 F. Supp 193 (E.D.N.Y. 1992)
Payne v. Tennessee, 501 U.S. 808 (1991)
People ex rel. Harrod v. Illinois Courts Commission, 372 N.E.2d 53 (Ill. 1977)
People v. Zaring, 10 Cal. Rptr. 2d 263 (5th Dist. 1992)
Phototron Corp. v. Eastman Kodak Co., 687 F. Supp. 1061 (N.D. Tex. 1988)
Planned Parenthood v. Casey, 505 U.S. 833 (1992)
Prima Paint Corp. v. Flood & Conklin Mfg. Co., 388 U.S. 395 (1967)
R.A.V. v. City of St. Paul, 505 U.S. 377 (1992)
Restatement First of Contracts (1932)
Riggs v. Palmer, 115 N.Y. 506 (1889)
Rogers v. Tennessee, 532 U.S. 451 (2001)
Romer v. Evans, 517 U.S. 620 (1996)
Roper v. Simmons, 543 U.S. 551 (2005)
San Antonio v. Rodriguez, 411 U.S. 1 (1973)
Santa Fe Independent School District v. Doe, 530 U.S. 290 (2000)
Shonubi, United States v., 895 F. Supp. 460 (E.D.N.Y. 1995)
Sokolow, United States v., 490 U.S. 1 (1989)
Sparf v. United States, 156 U.S. 51 (1895)
State Oil Co. v. Khan, 118 S. Ct. 275 (1997)
States v. Schooner Peggy, 1 Cranch 103 (1801)
Stump v. Sparkman, 435 U.S. 349 (1978)
Troen, State v., 786 P.2d 751 (Or. Ct. App. 1990)
Tropiano, United States v., 898 F. Supp. 90 (E.D.N.Y. 1995)
Turco, Stipulation (Washington Commission on Judicial Conduct, Oct. 2, 1992)
Weber v. Kaiser Aluminum & Chemical Corp., 611 F.2d 132 (5th Cir. 1980)
Williams, United States v., 504 U.S. 36 (1992)
Wilson v. State, 279 Ga. App. 459 (Ga. Ct. App. 2006)

Bibliography

Abramson, Leslie W. "Appearance of Impropriety: Deciding When a Judge's Impartiality 'Might Reasonably Be Questioned.'" *Georgetown Journal of Legal Ethics.* 14 (2000): 55–102.

Ackerman, Bruce. "Anatomy of a Constitutional Coup." *London Review of Books*, Feb. 8, 2001.

———. *We the People: Foundations*. Cambridge, Mass.: Belknap, 1991.

Alexander, Larry. "Constrained by Precedent." *Southern California Law Review* 63 (1989): 1–64.

———. "Deontology at the Threshold." *San Diego Law Review* 37 (2000): 893–912.

———. "The Gap." *Harvard Journal of Law and Public Policy* 14 (1991): 695–701.

———. "Law and Exclusionary Reasons." *Philosophical Topics* 18 (1990): 5–22.

———. "'With Me, It's All Er Nuthin': Formalism in Law and Morality." *University of Chicago Law Review* 66 (1999): 530–65.

Alexander, Larry, and Kimberly Kessler Ferzan. *Crime and Culpability: A Theory of Criminal Law*. Cambridge: Cambridge University Press, 2009.

Alexander, Larry, and Ken Kress. "Against Legal Principles." *Law and Interpretation: Essays in Legal Philosophy*. Ed. Andrei Marmor. Oxford: Clarendon, 1995. 279–327.

Alexander, Larry, and Emily Sherwin. *The Rule of Rules*. Durham, N.C.: Duke University Press, 2001.

Alexy, Robert. "A Defence of Radbruch's Formula." *Recrafting the Rule of Law: The Limits of Legal Order*. Ed. David Dyzenhaus. Oxford: Hart, 1999.

Alfini, James J., et al. *Judicial Conduct and Ethics*. 4th ed. Newark, N.J.: LexisNexis, 2007.

Almeida, Michael J., ed. *Imperceptible Harms and Benefits*. Dordrecht: Kluwer, 2000.

Alstyne, William Van. "Notes on a Bicentennial Constitution: Part II, Antinomial Choices and the Role of the Supreme Court." *Iowa Law Review* 72 (1987): 1281–99.

Altman, Andrew. *Critical Legal Studies: A Liberal Critique*. Princeton, N.J.: Princeton University Press, 1990.

———. "Legal Realism, Critical Legal Studies, and Dworkin." *Philosophy and Public Affairs* 15 (1986): 205–35.

Altman, Scott. "Beyond Candor." *Michigan Law Review* 89 (1990): 296–351.

Anderson, Lisa R., and Charles A. Holt. "Information Cascades in the Laboratory." *American Economic Review* 87 (1997): 847–62.

Applbaum, Arthur Isak. *Ethics for Adversaries: The Morality of Roles in Public and Professional Life*. Princeton, N.J.: Princeton University Press, 1999.

Aquinas, Thomas. *Summa Theologiae*. Trans. Fathers of the English Dominican Province. London: Washbourne, 1915.
Aristotle. *Nicomachean Ethics*. Trans. W. D. Ross. Oxford: Oxford University Press, 1980.
Atiyah, P. S. *Promises, Morals, and Law*. Oxford: Clarendon, 1981.
Austin, J. L. "A Plea for Excuses." *Proceedings of the Aristotelian Society* 57 (1956–57): 1–30.
Austin, John. *The Province of Jurisprudence Determined*. Ed. Wilfrid E. Rumble. New York: Cambridge University Press, 1995.
Baier, Kurt. "The Justification of Governmental Authority." *Journal of Philosophy* 69 (1972): 700–16.
Bales, R. E. "Act Utilitarianism: Account of Right-Making Characteristics or Decision-Making Procedure." *American Philosophical Quarterly* 8 (1971): 257–65.
Balkin, J. M., ed. *What Roe v. Wade Should Have Said*. New York: New York University Press, 2005.
Balkin, J. M., and Bruce A. Ackerman, eds. *What Brown v. Board of Education Should Have Said*. New York: New York University Press, 2001.
Balkin, Jack M. "*Bush v. Gore* and the Boundary between Law and Politics." *Yale Law Journal* 110 (2001): 1407–58.
Banerjee, Abhijit. "A Simple Model of Herd Behavior." *Quarterly Journal of Economics* 107 (1992): 797–818.
Barak, Aharon. *Judicial Discretion*. Trans. Yadin Kaufmann. New Haven, Conn.: Yale University Press, 1989.
Baron, Marcia, Philip Pettit, and Michael A. Slote. *Three Methods of Ethics*. Oxford: Wiley-Blackwell, 1997.
Bassett, Debra Lyn. "Judicial Disqualification in the Federal Courts." *Iowa Law Review* 87 (2002): 1213–56.
———. "Recusal and the Supreme Court." *Hastings Law Journal* 56 (2005): 657–98.
Bauer, Joseph P. "Addressing the Incoherency of the Preemption Provision of the Copyright Act of 1976." *Vanderbilt Journal of Entertainment & Technology Law* 10 (2007): 1–119.
Bayles, Michael. *Procedural Justice: Allocating to Individuals*. Dordrecht: Kluwer Academic, 1989.
Benn, S. I., and R. S. Peters. *The Principles of Political Thought*. New York: Free Press, 1965.
Bennett, Jonathan. *The Act Itself*. Oxford: Oxford University Press, 1995.
Bentham, Jeremy. *A Fragment on Government*. Eds. J. H. Burns and H. L. A. Hart. Cambridge: Cambridge University Press, 1988.
Berger, Raoul. *Government by Judiciary: The Transformation of the Fourteenth Amendment*. Cambridge, Mass.: Harvard University Press, 1977.
Bikhchandani, Sushil, David Hirshleifer, and Ivo Welch. "Learning from the Behavior of Others: Conformity, Fads, and Informational Cascades." *Journal of Economic Perspectives* 12 (1998): 151–70.
———. "A Theory of Fads, Fashion, Custom and Cultural Change as Informational Cascades." *Journal of Political Economy* 100 (1992): 992–1026.
Bix, Brian. *Law, Language, and Legal Determinacy*. Oxford: Clarendon, 1993.
Black, Hugo L. *A Constitutional Faith*. New York: Knopf, 1968.
Bloom, Frederic M. "State Courts Unbound." *Cornell Law Review* 93 (2008): 501–54.
Bobbitt, Philip. *Constitutional Interpretation*. Oxford: Basil Blackwell, 1991.

Bonfield, Arthur E. "The Abrogation of Penal Statutes by Nonenforcement." *Iowa Law Review* 49 (1964): 389–440.
Bork, Robert H. *The Tempting of America*. New York: Simon & Schuster, 1990.
Bradley, Gerard V. "Plea Bargaining and the Criminal Defendant's Obligation to Plead Guilty." *South Texas Law Review* 40 (1999): 65–82.
Brand-Ballard, Jeffrey. "Contractualism and Deontic Restrictions." *Ethics* 114 (2004): 269–300.
———. "Innocents Lost: Proportional Sentencing and the Paradox of Collateral Damage." *Legal Theory* 15 (2009): 65–105.
Bratman, Michael E. "I Intend That We J." *Contemporary Action Theory*. Eds. Ghita Holmström-Hintikka and Raimo Tuomela. Vol. 2. Dordrecht: Kluwer, 1997, 49–63.
———. "Shared Intention." *Ethics* 104 (1993): 97–113.
———. "What Is the Accordion Effect?" *Journal of Ethics* 10 (2006): 5–19.
Brennan, Samantha. "Thresholds for Rights." *Southern Journal of Philosophy* 33 (1995): 143–68.
Brewer, Scott. "Exemplary Reasoning: Semantics, Pragmatics, and the Rational Force of Legal Argument by Analogy." *Harvard Law Review* 109 (1996): 923–1028.
Bright, Stephen B. "Let's Try Brian Nichols Properly the First Time." *Atlanta Journal-Constitution*, Nov. 7, 2007, 19A.
Brink, David O. "Legal Positivism and Natural Law Reconsidered." *Monist* 68 (1985): 364–87.
———. *Moral Realism and the Foundations of Ethics*. New York: Cambridge University Press, 1989.
Brown, Darryl K. "Jury Nullification within the Rule of Law." *Minnesota Law Review* 81 (1997): 1149–200.
Budd, Malcolm. "Wittgenstein on Seeing Aspects." *Mind* 96 (1987): 1–17.
Burton, Stephen J. *Judging in Good Faith*. Cambridge: Cambridge University Press, 1992.
———. "Law as Practical Reason." *Southern California Law Review* 62 (1989): 747–93.
Bushnell, Eleanore. *Crimes, Follies and Misfortunes: The Federal Impeachment Trials*. Urbana: University of Illinois Press, 1992.
Butler, Paul. "When Judges Lie (and When They Should)." *Minnesota Law Review* 91 (2007): 1785–828.
Calabresi, Guido. *A Common Law for the Age of Statutes*. Cambridge, Mass.: Harvard University Press, 1982.
Caminker, Evan H. "Why Must Inferior Courts Obey Superior Court Precedents?" *Stanford Law Review* 46 (1994): 817–73.
Cardozo, Benjamin N. "Jurisprudence." *Selected Writings of Benjamin Nathan Cardozo*. Ed. Margaret E. Hall. New York: Fallon, 1947.
———. *The Nature of the Judicial Process*. New Haven, Conn.: Yale University Press, 1921.
Carter, Stephen L. "The Religiously Devout Judge." *Notre Dame Law Review* 64 (1989): 932–44.
Christopher, Russell L. "Deterring Retributivism: The Injustice of 'Just' Punishment." *Northwestern University Law Review* 96 (2002): 843–976.
Cohen, Mark A. "The Motives of Judges: Empirical Evidence from Antitrust Sentencing." *International Review of Law and Economics* 12 (1992): 13–30.

Colby, Paul L. "Two Views of the Legitimacy of Nonacquiescence in Judicial Opinions." *Tulane Law Review* 61 (1987): 1041–69.
Coleman, Jules. *The Practice of Principle*. Oxford: Oxford University Press, 2001.
Coleman, Jules L., and Brian Leiter. "Determinacy, Objectivity, and Authority." *University of Pennsylvania Law Review* 142 (1993): 549–637.
Conkle, Daniel O. "Religiously Devout Judges: Issues of Personal Integrity and Public Benefit." *Marquette Law Review* 81 (1998): 523–32.
Cook, Walter Wheeler. *Cases and Other Authorities on Equity*. St. Paul, Minn.: West, 1923.
Cooter, Robert D. "The Objectives of Private and Public Judges." *Public Choice* 41 (1983): 107–32.
Copp, David. "Introduction: Metaethics and Normative Ethics." *Oxford Handbook of Ethical Theory*. Ed. David Copp. New York: Oxford University Press, 2006.
Corvino, John. "Homosexuality and the PIB Argument." *Ethics* 115 (2005): 501–34.
Cover, Robert M. *Justice Accused: Antislavery and the Judicial Process*. New Haven, Conn.: Yale University Press, 1975.
———. "Violence and the Word." *Yale Law Journal* 95 (1986): 1601–29.
Crisp, Roger. "Particularizing Particularism." *Moral Particularism*. Eds. Brad Hooker and Margaret Olivia Little. Oxford: Oxford University Press, 2000.
Cullity, Garrett. *The Moral Demands of Affluence*. Oxford: Oxford University Press, 2004.
———. "Moral Free Riding." *Philosophy and Public Affairs* 24 (1995): 3–34.
D'Amato, Anthony. "Aspects of Deconstruction: Refuting Indeterminacy with One Bold Thought." *Northwestern University Law Review* 85 (1990): 113–27.
Dagger, Richard. "Playing Fair with Punishment." *Ethics* 103 (1993): 473–88.
Damasio, Antonio R. *Descartes' Error: Emotion, Reason, and the Human Brain*. New York: Harper & Row, 1995.
Dan-Cohen, Meir. "Decision Rules and Conduct Rules: On Acoustic Separation in Criminal Law." *Harvard Law Review* 97 (1984): 625–77.
———. "In Defense of Defiance." *Philosophy and Public Affairs* 23 (1994): 24–51.
Dancy, Jonathan. *Ethics without Principles*. Oxford: Oxford University Press, 2004.
Daniels, Norman. *Justice and Justification: Reflective Equilibrium in Theory and Practice*. Cambridge: Cambridge University Press, 1996.
Darwall, Stephen L. "Agent-Centered Restrictions from the Inside Out." *Philosophical Studies* 50 (1986): 291–319.
DePaul, Michael R. *Balance and Refinement: Beyond Coherence Methods of Moral Inquiry*. New York: Routledge, 1993.
Dershowitz, Alan M. *Supreme Injustice: How the High Court Hijacked Election 2000*. Oxford: Oxford University Press, 2001.
De Sousa, Ronald. *The Rationality of Emotion*. Cambridge, Mass.: MIT Press, 1987.
Dobbs, Dan B. *The Law of Torts*. Vol. 2. St. Paul, Minn.: West, 2001.
Drahos, Peter, and Stephen Parker. "Rule Following, Rule Scepticism and Indeterminacy in Law: A Conventional Account." *Ratio Juris* 5 (1992): 109–19.
Dressler, Joshua. *Understanding Criminal Law*. 3rd ed. New York: Lexis, 2001.
Dubber, Markus Dirk. "The Pain of Punishment." *Buffalo Law Review* 44 (1996): 545–611.

Duncan, William C. "*Goodridge* and the Rule of Law Same-Sex Marriage in Massachusetts [*sic*]: The Meaning and Implications of *Goodridge v. Department of Public Health*." *Boston University Public Interest Law Journal* 14 (2004): 42–55.

Duxbury, Neil. "Faith in Reason: The Process Tradition in American Jurisprudence." *Cardozo Law Review* 15 (1993): 601–705.

———. *Random Justice: On Lotteries and Legal Decision-Making*. Oxford: Clarendon, 1999.

Dworkin, Ronald. "A Badly Flawed Election." *New York Review of Books*, Feb. 8, 2001, 1.

———. *Freedom's Law: The Moral Reading of the American Constitution*. Cambridge, Mass.: Harvard University Press, 1996.

———. "Hard Cases." *Taking Rights Seriously*. Cambridge, Mass.: Harvard University Press, 1977. 81–130.

———. *Law's Empire*. Cambridge, Mass.: Harvard University Press, 1986.

———. *Life's Dominion: An Argument about Abortion, Euthanasia, and Individual Freedom*. New York: Knopf, 1993.

———. *A Matter of Principle*. Cambridge, Mass.: Harvard University Press, 1985.

———. "The Model of Rules I." *Taking Rights Seriously*. Cambridge, Mass.: Harvard University Press, 1977. 14–45.

———. "The Model of Rules II." *Taking Rights Seriously*. Cambridge, Mass.: Harvard University Press, 1977.

———. "A Reply to Critics." *Taking Rights Seriously*. Cambridge, Mass.: Harvard University Press, 1978. 291–368.

———. *Sovereign Virtue: The Theory and Practice of Equality*. Cambridge, Mass.: Harvard University Press, 2000.

———. *Taking Rights Seriously*. Cambridge, Mass.: Harvard University Press, 1977.

Dyzenhaus, David. *Hard Cases in Wicked Legal Systems: South African Law in the Perspective of Legal Philosophy*. Oxford: Clarendon, 1991.

———. "Positivism's Stagnant Research Programme." *Oxford Journal of Legal Studies* 20 (2000): 703–22.

Easterbrook, Frank. "Ways of Criticizing the Court." *Harvard Law Review* 95 (1982): 802–32.

Edlin, Douglas E. *Judges and Unjust Laws: Common Law Constitutionalism and the Foundations of Judicial Review*. Ann Arbor: University of Michigan Press, 2008.

Edmundson, William A. "State of the Art: The Duty to Obey the Law." *Legal Theory* 10 (2004): 215–59.

———. *Three Anarchical Fallacies*. Cambridge: Cambridge University Press, 1998.

Edwards, Harry T. "To Err Is Human, but Not Always Harmless: When Should Legal Error Be Tolerated?" *New York University Law Review* 70 (1995): 1167–213.

Eggleston, Ben. "Self-Defeat, Publicity, and Incoherence: Three Criteria for Consequentialist Theories." Ph.D. diss., University of Pittsburgh, 2001.

Eisenberg, Melvin Aron. *An Introduction to Agency, Partnerships, and LLCs*. 3rd ed. New York: Foundation, 2000.

Ellis, Anthony. "Deontology, Incommensurability and the Arbitrary." *Philosophy and Phenomenological Research* 52 (1992): 855–75.

Ely, John Hart. "The Wages of Crying Wolf: A Comment on *Roe v. Wade*." *Yale Law Journal* 82 (1973): 920–49.

Endicott, Timothy A. O. "The Impossibility of the Rule of Law." *Oxford Journal of Legal Studies* 19 (1999): 1–18.
Enoch, David. "Intending, Foreseeing, and the State." *Legal Theory* 13 (2007): 69–99.
Epstein, Richard A. "Blind Justices: The Scandal of Kelo v. New London." *Wall Street Journal*, July 3, 2005.
Eskridge, William N., Jr. *Dynamic Statutory Interpretation*. Cambridge, Mass.: Harvard University Press, 1994.
Estreicher, Samuel. "Judicial Nullification: Guido Calabresi's Uncommon Common Law for a Statutory Age." *New York University Law Review* 57 (1982): 1126–73.
Estreicher, Samuel, and Richard L. Revesz. "Nonacquiescence by Federal Administrative Agencies." *Yale Law Journal* 98 (1989): 679–772.
Fallon, Richard H., Jr. "'The Rule of Law' as a Concept in Constitutional Discourse." *Columbia Law Review* 97 (1997): 1–56.
Farley, John J., III. "Robin Hood Jurisprudence: The Triumph of Equity in American Tort Law." *St. John's Law Review* 65 (1991): 997–1021.
Farnsworth, Ward. "'To Do a Great Right, Do a Little Wrong': A User's Guide to Judicial Lawlessness." *Minnesota Law Review* 86 (2001): 227–66.
Farrell, Daniel M. "Punishment without the State." *Noûs* 22 (1988): 437–53.
Feinberg, Joel. "Causing Voluntary Actions." *Metaphysics and Explanation*. Eds. W. H. Capitan and D. D. Merrill. Pittsburgh: University of Pittsburgh Press, 1966.
———. "Collective Responsibility." *Doing and Deserving*. Princeton, N.J.: Princeton University Press, 1970.
———. "Noncomparative Justice." *Philosophical Review* 83 (1974): 297–338.
Fisher, William W., III, Morton J. Horwitz, and Thomas Reed, eds. *American Legal Realism*. Oxford: Oxford University Press, 1993.
Fitzpatrick, William J. "The Intend/Foresee Distinction and the Problem of 'Closeness.'" *Philosophical Studies* 128 (2006): 585–617.
Fletcher, George P. "Domination in the Theory of Justification and Excuse." *University of Pittsburgh Law Review* 57 (1996): 553–78.
Flikschuh, Katrin. "Reason, Right, and Revolution: Kant and Locke." *Philosophy and Public Affairs* 36 (2008): 375–404.
Forer, Lois. "Justice by Numbers." *Washington Monthly*, April 1992.
Frankena, William K. "The Concept of Social Justice." *Social Justice*. Ed. Richard Brandt. Englewood Cliffs, N.J.: Prentice-Hall, 1962.
Fraser, David. "'This Is Not Like Any Other Legal Question': A Brief History of Nazi Law before U.K. and U.S. Courts." *Connecticut Journal of International Law* 19 (2003): 59–125.
Fried, Charles. "The Artificial Reason of the Law Or: What Lawyers Know." *Texas Law Review* 60 (1981): 35–58.
———. "Impudence." *Supreme Court Review* 1992 (1992): 155–94.
———. "Scholars and Judges: Reason and Power." *Harvard Journal of Law and Public Policy* 23 (2000): 807–32.
Friedman, Barry. "The Cycles of Constitutional Theory." *Law and Contemporary Problems* 67 (2004): 149–74.
Fuller, Lon L. *The Morality of Law*. 2nd rev. ed. New Haven, Conn.: Yale University Press, 1969.
———. "Positivism and Fidelity to Law: A Reply to Professor Hart." *Harvard Law Review* 71 (1958): 630–72.
Gandhi, M. K. *Selected Writings of Mahatma Gandhi*. Boston: Beacon, 1951.

Gardner, John. "Concerning Permissive Sources and Gaps." *Oxford Journal of Legal Studies* 8 (1988): 457–61.
Garner, Bryan A., ed. *Black's Law Dictionary*. 8th ed. St. Paul, Minn.: Thomson/West, 2004.
Garvey, John H., and Amy V. Coney. "Catholic Judges in Capital Cases." *Marquette Law Review* 81 (1998): 303–50.
Gert, Bernard. *Morality: Its Nature and Justification*. New York: Oxford University Press, 1998.
Gettier, Edmund L. "Is Justified True Belief Knowledge?" *Analysis* 23 (1963): 121–23.
Geyh, Charles Gardner. "Informal Methods of Judicial Discipline." *University of Pennsylvania Law Review* 142 (1993): 243–331.
Gilbert, Margaret. "Group Membership and Political Obligation." *The Monist* 76 (1993): 119–31.
———. *Living Together: Rationality, Sociality, and Obligation*. Lanham, Md.: Rowman & Littlefield, 1996.
———. *On Social Facts*. Princeton, N.J.: Princeton University Press, 1989.
———. "Reconsidering the 'Actual Contract' Theory of Political Obligation." *Ethics* 109 (1999): 236–60.
———. *Sociality and Responsibility: New Essays in Plural Subject Theory*. Lanham, Md.: Rowman & Littlefield, 2000.
Glover, Jonathan. "It Makes No Difference Whether or Not I Do It." *Applied Ethics*. Ed. Peter Singer. Oxford: Oxford University Press, 1990, 125–44.
Goldman, Alan H. *The Moral Foundations of Professional Ethics*. Totowa, N.J.: Rowman & Littlefield, 1980.
———. *Practical Rules: When We Need Them and When We Don't*. Cambridge: Cambridge University Press, 2002.
———. "The Rationality of Complying with Rules: Paradox Resolved." *Ethics* 116 (2006): 453–70.
Goodin, Robert E. *Utilitarianism as a Public Philosophy*. New York: Cambridge University Press, 1995.
Goodwin, Barbara. *Justice by Lottery*. Hemel Hempstead, U.K.: Harvester Wheatsheaf, 1992.
Graber, Mark A. *Dred Scott and the Problem of Constitutional Evil*. Cambridge: Cambridge University Press, 2006.
Graves, Rachel. "The Terri Schiavo Case; Schiavo Dies, but Debate Lives; Delay Insists Judges Must 'Answer for Their Behavior.'" *Houston Chronicle*, April 1, 2005, A1.
Gray, Cynthia. "The Line between Legal Error and Judicial Misconduct: Balancing Judicial Independence and Accountability." *Hofstra Law Review* 32 (2004): 1245–80.
Green, Leslie. *The Authority of the State*. Oxford: Clarendon, 1988.
Greenawalt, Kent. *Conflicts of Law and Morality*. New York: Oxford University Press, 1987.
———. "Discretion and Judicial Decision: The Elusive Quest for the Fetters that Bind Judges." *Columbia Law Review* 75 (1975): 359–99.
———. *Law and Objectivity*. Oxford: Oxford University Press, 1992.
———. "The Perplexing Borders of Justification and Excuse." *Columbia Law Review* 84 (1984): 1897–927.
Greenberg, Mark. "How Facts Make Law." *Legal Theory* 10 (2004): 157–98.

Grice, Paul. "Logic and Conversation." *Studies in the Way of Words*. Cambridge, Mass.: Harvard University Press, 1989.
Griffen, Wendell L. "The Case for Religious Values in Judicial Decision-Making." *Marquette Law Review* 81 (1998): 513–21.
Grimes, Warren S. "Hundred-Ton-Gun Control: Preserving Impeachment as the Exclusive Removal Mechanism for Federal Judges." *UCLA Law Review* 38 (1991): 1209–55.
Gunther, Gerald. *Learned Hand: The Man and the Judge*. Cambridge, Mass.: Harvard University Press, 1998.
Haley, John O. "The Civil, Criminal and Disciplinary Liability of Judges." *American Journal of Comparative Law* 54 (2006): 281–91.
Hall, Jerome. *General Principles of Criminal Law*. 2nd ed. Indianapolis, Ind.: Bobbs-Merrill, 1960.
Hamburger, Philip. "Law and Judicial Duty." *George Washington Law Review* 72 (2003): 1–41.
Hampton, Jean. "Free-Rider Problems in the Production of Collective Goods." *Economics and Philosophy* 3 (1987): 245–73.
Hand, Learned. *The Bill of Rights*. Cambridge, Mass.: Harvard University Press, 1958.
Hardimon, Michael O. "Role Obligations." *Journal of Philosophy* 91 (1994): 333–63.
Harris, John. *Violence and Responsibility*. London: Routledge & Kegan Paul, 1980.
Hart, H. L. A. "Are There Any Natural Rights?" *Philosophical Review* 64 (1955): 175–91.
———. "Commands and Authoritative Legal Reasons." *Essays on Bentham*. Oxford: Oxford University Press, 1982.
———. *The Concept of Law*. 2nd ed. Oxford: Oxford University Press, 1994. First published 1961.
———. "Positivism and the Separation of Law and Morals." *Harvard Law Review* 71 (1958): 593–629.
Hart, H. L. A., and Tony Honoré. *Causation in the Law*. Oxford: Clarendon, 1959.
Hasnas, John. "The Myth of the Rule of Law." *Wisconsin Law Review* 1995 (1995): 199–233.
Hatch, Orrin, and Sam Brownback. "'Extreme' Judicial Activism." *Washington Times*, Feb. 10, 2005, A19.
Hawkins, Keith, ed. *The Uses of Discretion*. Oxford: Oxford University Press, 1992.
Hellman, Deborah. "The Importance of Appearing Principled." *Arizona Law Review* 37 (1995): 1108–51.
Henderson, Lynne. "Authoritarianism and the Rule of Law." *Indiana Law Journal* 66 (1991): 379–456.
Henkin, Louis. "Privacy and Autonomy." *Columbia Law Review* 74 (1974): 1410–33.
Heyd, David. *Supererogation*. Cambridge: Cambridge University Press, 1982.
Higgins, Richard S., and Paul H. Rubin. "Judicial Discretion." *Journal of Legal Studies* 9 (1980): 129–38.
Himma, Kenneth Einar. "Judicial Discretion and the Concept of Law." *Oxford Journal of Legal Studies* 19 (1999): 71–82.
Hodges, Ann C. "Protecting Unionized Employees against Discrimination: The Fourth Circuit's Misinterpretation of Supreme Court Precedent." *Employee Rights and Employment Policy Journal* 2 (1998): 123–74.

Hoffer, Peter Charles. "Principled Discretion: Concealment, Conscience, and Chancellors." *Yale Journal of Law and the Humanities* 3 (1991): 53–82.
Hohfeld, Wesley Newcomb. *Fundamental Legal Conceptions*. New Haven, Conn.: Yale University Press, 1919.
Honoré, Tony. "Must We Obey? Necessity as a Ground of Obligation." *Virginia Law Review* 67 (1981): 39–61.
Hooker, Brad. *Ideal Code, Real World: A Rule-Consequentialist Theory of Morality*. Oxford: Oxford University Press, 2000.
Horton, Elizabeth M. "Selective Publication and the Authority of Precedent in the United States Courts of Appeals." *UCLA Law Review* 42 (1995): 1691–778.
Horwitz, Morton J. "The Rule of Law: An Unqualified Human Good?" *Yale Law Journal* 86 (1977): 561–66.
———. *The Transformation of American Law: 1780–1860*. Cambridge, Mass.: Harvard University Press, 1979.
Hulse, Carl. "Lawmakers Vow to Fight Judges' Ruling on the Pledge." *New York Times*, June 27, 2002, A20.
Hurd, Heidi M. "Justifiably Punishing the Justified." *Michigan Law Review* 90 (1992): 2203–324.
———. *Moral Combat*. Cambridge: Cambridge University Press, 1999.
Hurley, Paul. "Agent-Centered Restrictions: Clearing the Air of Paradox." *Ethics* 108 (1997): 120–46.
Hurley, Susan. *Natural Reasons*. Oxford: Oxford University Press, 1989.
Husak, Douglas. *Overcriminalization: The Limits of the Criminal Law*. New York: Oxford University Press, 2008.
Hutchinson, Allan C. *Dwelling on the Threshold: Critical Essays on Modern Legal Thought*. Toronto: Carswell, 1988.
Idleman, Scott C. "A Prudential Theory of Judicial Candor." *Texas Law Review* 73 (1995): 1307–417.
———. "The Role of Religious Values in Judicial Decision Making." *Indiana Law Journal* 68 (1993): 433–87.
Igneski, Violetta. "Distance, Determinacy and the Duty to Aid: A Reply to Kamm." *Law and Philosophy* 20 (2001): 605–16.
Ingram, Peter. "Maintaining the Rule of Law." *Philosophical Quarterly* 35 (1985): 359–81.
Isaacs, Tracy. "Collective Moral Responsibility and Collective Intention." *Midwest Studies in Philosophy* 30 (2006): 59–73.
Jackson, Frank, and Michael Smith. "Absolutist Ethical Theories and Uncertainty." *Journal of Philosophy* 103 (2006): 267–83.
Jacobson, Arthur J. "Publishing Dissent." *Washington and Lee Law Review* 62 (2005): 1607–36.
Johnston, David, and Neil A. Lewis. "Ending Raids of Dispensers of Marijuana for Patients." *New York Times*, March 19, 2009, A20.
Kadish, Mortimer R., and Sanford H. Kadish. *Discretion to Disobey: A Study of Lawful Departures from Legal Rules*. Stanford, Calif.: Stanford University Press, 1973.
Kagan, Shelly. *The Limits of Morality*. Oxford: Oxford University Press, 1989.
Kamm, F. M. *Intricate Ethics: Rights, Responsibilities and Permissible Harm*. New York: Oxford University Press, 2007.
———. *Morality, Mortality: Rights, Duties, and Status*. Vol. 2. New York: Oxford University Press, 1996.

Kaplow, Louis. "Rules versus Standards: An Economic Analysis." *Duke Law Journal* 42 (1992): 557–629.

Kaplow, Louis, and Steven Shavell. *Fairness versus Welfare*. Cambridge, Mass.: Harvard University Press, 2001.

Karlan, Pamela S. "Two Concepts of Judicial Independence." *Southern California Law Review* 72 (1999): 535–58.

Katz, Leo. "Incommensurable Choices and the Problem of Moral Ignorance." *University of Pennsylvania Law Review* 146 (1998): 1465–85.

Kauper, Paul G. "Penumbras, Peripheries, Emanations, Things Fundamental and Things Forgotten: The *Griswold* Case." *Michigan Law Review* 64 (1965): 235–58.

Keith, Darrell L. "The Court's Charge in Texas Medical Malpractice Cases." *Baylor Law Review* 48 (1996): 675–814.

Kelsen, Hans. "On the Theory of Interpretation." *Legal Studies* 10 (1990): 127–35.

Kennedy, Duncan. *A Critique of Adjudication (Fin De Siècle)*. Cambridge, Mass.: Harvard University Press, 1997.

———. "Form and Substance in Private Law Adjudication." *Harvard Law Review* 89 (1976): 1685–778.

———. "Freedom and Constraint in Adjudication: A Critical Phenomenology." *Journal of Legal Education* 36 (1986): 518–62.

Klarman, Michael J. "*Bush v. Gore* through the Lens of Constitutional History." *California Law Review* 89 (2001): 1721–65.

Klosko, George. "Parfit's Moral Arithmetic and the Obligation to Obey the Law." *Canadian Journal of Philosophy* 20 (1990): 191–214.

———. "Presumptive Benefit, Fairness, and Political Obligation." *The Duty to Obey the Law: Selected Philosophical Readings*. Ed. William A. Edmundson. Lanham, Md.: Rowman & Littlefield, 1999.

———. *The Principle of Fairness and Political Obligation*. Lanham, Md.: Rowman & Littlefield, 1992.

Kmiec, Keenan D. "The Origin and Current Meanings of 'Judicial Activism.'" *California Law Review* 92 (2004): 1441–77.

Kohlberg, Lawrence. *Essays on Moral Development: The Philosophy of Moral Development*. Vol. 1. New York: Harper & Row, 1981.

Kornhauser, Lewis A. "Adjudication by a Resource-Constrained Team: Hierarchy and Precedent in a Judicial System." *Southern California Law Review* 68 (1995): 1605–29.

———. "Modeling Collegial Courts I: Path Dependence." *International Review of Law and Economics* 12 (1992): 169–85.

———. "Modeling Collegial Courts II: Legal Doctrine." *Journal of Law, Economics, and Organization* 8 (1992): 441–70.

Korsgaard, Christine M. "Skepticism about Practical Reason." *Journal of Philosophy* 83 (1986): 5–25.

Kramer, Larry D. *The People Themselves: Popular Constitutionalism and Judicial Review*. Oxford: Oxford University Press, 2004.

Kramer, Matthew. "How Moral Principles Can Enter into the Law." *Legal Theory* 6 (2000): 83–108.

Kress, Ken. "Legal Indeterminacy." *California Law Review* 77 (1989): 283–337.

———. "Why No Judge Should Be a Dworkinian Coherentist." *Texas Law Review* 77 (1999): 1375–427.

Kretzmann, Norman. "Lex Iniusta Non Est Lex: Laws on Trial in Aquinas' Court of Conscience." *American Journal of Jurisprudence* 33 (1988): 99–122.

Kroger, John R. "Supreme Court Equity, 1789–1835, and the History of American Judging." *Houston Law Review* 34 (1998): 1425–86.
Kronman, Anthony. *The Lost Lawyer: Failing Ideals of the Legal Profession*. Cambridge, Mass.: Belknap, 1993.
Kuran, Timur, and Cass R. Sunstein. "Availability Cascades and Risk Regulation." *Stanford Law Review* 51 (1999): 683–768.
Kutz, Christopher. *Complicity: Ethics and Law for a Collective Age*. Cambridge: Cambridge University Press, 2000.
———. "The Judicial Community." *Philosophical Issues* 11 (2001): 442–69.
Lamond, Grant. "The Coerciveness of Law." *Oxford Journal of Legal Studies* 20 (2000): 39–62.
Landers, Scott. "Wittgenstein, Realism, and CLS: Undermining Rule Scepticism." *Law and Philosophy* 9 (1990): 177–203.
Landes, William M., and Richard A. Posner. "Legal Precedent: A Theoretical and Empirical Analysis." *Journal of Law and Economics* 19 (1976): 249–307.
Lefkowitz, David. "A Contractualist Defense of Democratic Authority." *Ratio Juris* 18 (2005): 346–64.
Leiter, Brian. "Heidegger and the Theory of Adjudication." *Yale Law Journal* 106 (1996): 253–82.
———. "Legal Realism and Legal Positivism Reconsidered." *Ethics* 111 (2001): 278–301.
Levenbook, Barbara B. "The Meaning of a Precedent." *Legal Theory* 6 (2000): 185–240.
Levinson, Sanford. "The Confrontation of Religious Faith and Civil Religion: Catholics Becoming Justices." *DePaul Law Review* 39 (1990): 1047–81.
Lewis, David. *Convention*. Cambridge, Mass.: Harvard University Press, 1969.
———. "The Punishment That Leaves Something to Chance." *Philosophy and Public Affairs* 18 (1989): 53–67.
Li, Xiaorong. "License to Coerce: Violence against Women, State Responsibility, and Legal Failures in China's Family-Planning Program." *Yale Journal of Law and Feminism* 8 (1996): 145–91.
Lightman, David. "Lawmakers Stand up to Court; Bipartisan Coalition Hopes to Dilute Impact of Eminent Domain Ruling." *Hartford Courant*, July 1, 2005, A1.
Locke, John. *Second Treatise of Government*. Ed. C. B. McPherson. Indianapolis: Hackett, 1980.
Lode, Eric. "Slippery Slope Arguments and Legal Reasoning." *California Law Review* 87 (1999): 1469–543.
Luban, David. *Lawyers and Justice: An Ethical Study*. Princeton, N.J.: Princeton University Press, 1988.
Lubet, Steven. "Judicial Discipline and Judicial Independence." *Law and Contemporary Problems* 61 (1998): 59–74.
Luce, R. Duncan, and Howard Raiffa. *Games and Decisions*. New York: Dover, 1989.
Lyons, David. "The Correlativity of Rights and Duties " *Noûs* 4 (1970): 45–55.
———. "Derivability, Defensibility, and the Justification of Judicial Decisions." *Moral Aspects of Legal Theory*. Cambridge: Cambridge University Press, 1993.
———. *Forms and Limits of Utilitarianism*. Oxford: Clarendon, 1965.
———. "On Formal Justice." *Moral Aspects of Legal Theory*. Cambridge: Cambridge University Press, 1993.

MacAdam, James I. "The Precepts of Justice." *Mind* 77 (1968): 360–71.
Macchiarola, Frank J. "Why the Decision in *Zelman* Makes So Much Sense." *N.Y.U. Annual Survey of American Law* 59 (2003): 459–67.
MacCormick, Neil. *Legal Reasoning and Legal Theory*. Oxford: Clarendon, 1978.
———. "Voluntary Obligations and Normative Powers I." *Proceedings of the Aristotelian Society* 46 (1972): 59–78.
Macey, Jonathan R. "The Internal and External Costs and Benefits of Stare Decisis." *Chicago-Kent Law Review* 65 (1989): 93–112.
Mackie, J. L. "Clauses and Conditions." *American Philosophical Quarterly* 2 (1965): 245–64.
———. *Ethics: Inventing Right and Wrong*. Harmondsworth, U.K.: Penguin, 1977.
———. "Morality and the Retributive Emotions." *Persons and Values*. Oxford: Clarendon, 1985.
———. "Obligations to Obey the Law." *Virginia Law Review* 67 (1981): 143–58.
Manning, John F. "The Absurdity Doctrine." *Harvard Law Review* 116 (2003): 2387–486.
———. "Textualism and the Equity of the Statute." *Columbia Law Review* 101 (2001): 1–127.
Marmor, Andrei. "The Rule of Law and Its Limits." *Law and Philosophy* 23 (2004): 1–43.
———. "Should Like Cases Be Treated Alike?" *Legal Theory* 11 (2005): 27–38.
Mason, Elinor. "We Make No Promises." *Philosophical Studies* 123 (2005): 33–46.
McCarthy, David. "Rights, Explanation, and Risks." *Ethics* 107 (1997): 205–25.
McCarthy, Nancy. "Judge Faces Discipline: Commission Charge Unleashes Protest in Legal Community." *California State Bar Journal*, August 1998, 1–3.
McDermott, Daniel. "The Permissibility of Punishment." *Law and Philosophy* 20 (2001): 403–32.
McDowell, Gary. *Equity and the Constitution: The Supreme Court, Equitable Relief, and Public Policy*. Chicago: University of Chicago Press, 1982.
McIntyre, Alison. "Doing Away with Double Effect." *Ethics* 111 (2001): 219–55.
McKeever, Sean, and Michael Ridge. *Principled Ethics: Generalism as a Regulative Ideal*. Oxford: Oxford University Press, 2006.
McKerlie, Dennis. "Rights and Risk." *Canadian Journal of Philosophy* 16 (1986): 239–51.
McMahan, Jeff. "Self-Defense and the Problem of the Innocent Attacker." *Ethics* 104 (1994): 252–90.
McMahon, Christopher. *Collective Rationality and Collective Reasoning*. Cambridge: Cambridge University Press, 2001.
Mian, Emran. "The Curious Case of Exclusionary Reasons." *Canadian Journal of Law and Jurisprudence* 15 (2002): 99–124.
Miceli, Thomas J., and Metin M. Cogel. "Reputation and Judicial Decision-Making." *Journal of Economic Behavior and Organization* 23 (1994): 31–51.
Miller, Arthur R. "The Pretrial Rush to Judgment: Are the 'Litigation Explosion,' 'Liability Crisis,' and Efficiency Cliches Eroding Our Day in Court and Jury Trial Commitments?" *New York University Law Review* 78 (2003): 982–1134.
Miller, David. *On Nationality*. Oxford: Oxford University Press, 1995.
Miller, Richard W. "Beneficence, Duty and Distance." *Philosophy and Public Affairs* 32 (2004): 357–83.
Miller, William Ian. *Bloodtaking and Peacemaking: Feud, Law, and Society in Saga Iceland*. Chicago: University of Chicago Press, 1990.

Mintz, Howard. "Disciplinary Case against Judge Raises Legal Uproar." *San Jose Mercury News* July 11, 1998, 1A.

Mitchell, Allison. "Clinton Pressing Judge to Relent." *New York Times*, March 22, 1996, A1.

Modak-Truran, Mark C. "Reenchanting the Law: The Religious Dimension of Judicial Decision Making." *Catholic University Law Review* 53 (2004): 709–816.

Moore, Michael. "Law as a Functional Kind." *Natural Law Theory: Contemporary Essays.* Ed. Robert P. George. Oxford: Oxford University Press, 1992.

Moore, Michael S. "Authority, Law, and Razian Reasons." *Southern California Law Review* 62 (1989): 827–96.

———. "The Metaphysics of Causal Intervention." *California Law Review* 88 (2000): 827–77.

———. *Placing Blame*. Oxford: Clarendon, 1997.

Murphy, Liam B. *Moral Demands in Nonideal Theory*. Oxford: Oxford University Press, 2000.

Murphy, Mark C. "Natural Law Jurisprudence." *Legal Theory* 9 (2003): 241–67.

———. "Natural Law, Consent, and Political Obligation." *Social Philosophy and Policy* 18 (2001): 70–92.

Nagel, Thomas. *The View from Nowhere*. Oxford: Oxford University Press, 1986.

———. "War and Massacre." *Mortal Questions*. Cambridge: Cambridge University Press, 1979.

Newman, Jon O. "The Judge Baer Controversy." *Judicature* 80 (1997): 156–64.

Nichols, Shaun. *Sentimental Rules: On the Natural Foundations of Moral Judgment*. Oxford: Oxford University Press, 2004.

Noonan, John T., Jr. *Persons and Masks of the Law: Cardozo, Holmes, Jefferson, Holmes, and Wythe as Makers of the Masks*. New York: Farrar, Straus & Giroux, 1976.

———. "The Religion of the Justice: Does It Affect Constitutional Decision Making?" *Tulsa Law Review* 42 (2007): 761–70.

Nozick, Robert. *Anarchy, State, and Utopia*. New York: Basic Books, 1974.

Nussbaum, Martha C. "Emotion in the Language of Judging." *St. John's Law Review* 70 (1996): 23–30.

O'Hara, Erin. "Social Constraint or Implicit Collusion? Toward a Game Theoretic Analysis of Stare Decisis." *Seton Hall Law Review* 24 (1993): 736–78.

Olowofoyeku, Abimbola A. *Suing Judges: A Study of Judicial Immunity*. Oxford: Clarendon, 1993.

Orsi, Francesco. "Obligations of Nearness." *Journal of Value Inquiry* 42 (2008): 1–21.

Osborn, Rebekah L. "Beliefs on the Bench: Recusal for Religious Reasons and the Model Code of Judicial Conduct." *Georgetown Journal of Legal Ethics* 19 (2006): 895–905.

Otsuka, Michael. "The Paradox of Group Beneficence." *Philosophy and Public Affairs* 20 (1991): 132–49.

Parfit, Derek. *Reasons and Persons*. Oxford: Clarendon, 1984.

Parker, Tom. "Alabama Justices Surrender to Judicial Activism." *Birmingham (Ala.) News*, January 1, 2005, 4B.

Paulsen, Michael Stokes. "Accusing Justice: Some Variations on the Themes of Robert M. Cover's *Justice Accused*." *Journal of Law and Religion* 7 (1989): 33–97.

Peirce, Charles S. *Collected Papers of Charles Sanders Peirce*. Eds. Charles Hartshorne and Paul Weiss. Cambridge, Mass.: Harvard University Press, 1932.

Penzell, Abigail. "Note: Apology in the Context of Wrongful Conviction: Why the System Should Say It's Sorry." *Cardozo Journal of Conflict Resolution* 9 (2007): 145–61.
Perry, Stephen R. "Second-Order Reasons, Uncertainty, and Legal Theory." *Southern California Law Review* 62 (1989): 913–94.
Pettit, Philip. *The Common Mind: An Essay on Psychology, Society, and Politics*. Oxford: Oxford University Press, 1993.
———. "The Consequentialist Can Recognise Rights." *Philosophical Quarterly* 38 (1988): 42–55.
———. "Responsibility Incorporated." *Ethics* 117 (2007): 171–201.
———. "Universality without Utilitarianism." *Mind* 72 (1987): 74–82.
Plato. *Crito*. Trans. Hugh Tredennick. Baltimore, Md.: Penguin, 1959.
Posner, Eric. *Law and Social Norms*. Cambridge, Mass.: Harvard University Press, 2000.
Posner, Richard A. *Economic Analysis of Law*. 4th ed. Boston: Little, Brown, 1992.
———. *The Problematics of Moral and Legal Theory*. Cambridge, Mass.: Belknap, 1999.
———. "What Do Judges and Justices Maximize? (the Same Thing Everybody Else Does)." *Supreme Court Economic Review* 3 (1993): 1–41.
Postema, Gerald J. *Bentham and the Common Law Tradition*. Oxford: Oxford University Press, 1986.
———. "Moral Responsibility in Professional Ethics." *New York University Law Review* 55 (1980): 63–89.
Prichard, H. A. "The Obligation to Keep a Promise." *Moral Obligation*. Oxford: Clarendon, 1949.
Prosser, William Lloyd, et al. *Prosser and Keeton on the Law of Torts*. 5th ed. St. Paul, Minn.: West, 1984.
Pryor, William H., Jr. "The Religious Faith and Judicial Duty of an American Catholic Judge." *Yale Law and Policy Review* 24 (2006): 347–62.
Quinn, Warren. "Actions, Intentions, and Consequences: The Doctrine of Double Effect." *Philosophy and Public Affairs* 18 (1989): 334–51.
———. "The Right to Threaten and the Right to Punish." *Philosophy and Public Affairs* 14 (1985): 327–73.
Rabin, Edward H. "Symposium: The Revolution in Residential Landlord-Tenant Law: Causes and Consequences." *Cornell Law Review* 69 (1984): 517–84.
Radbruch, Gustav. "Gesetzliches Unrecht Und Übergesetzliches Recht." *Süddeutsche Juristen-Zeitung* 1 (1946): 105–8. Translated as "Statutory Lawlessness and Supra-Statutory Law (1946)." Trans. Bonnie Litschewski Paulson and Stanley L. Paulson. *Oxford Journal of Legal Studies* 26 (2006): 1–11.
Radin, Margaret Jane. "Reconsidering the Rule of Law." *Boston University Law Review* 69 (1992): 781–819.
Raftery, William E. "The Legislatures, the Ballot Boxes, and the Courts." *Court Review* 43 (2006): 102–7.
Railton, Peter. "Alienation, Consequentialism, and the Demands of Morality." *Philosophy and Public Affairs* 13 (1984): 134–71.
———. "Locke, Stock, and Peril: Natural Property Rights, Pollution, and Risk." *To Breathe Freely*. Ed. Mary Gibson. Totowa, N.J.: Rowman & Littlefield, 1985.
Rawls, John. "The Idea of Public Reason Revisited." *University of Chicago Law Review* 64 (1997): 765–807.

———. "Legal Obligation and the Duty of Fair Play." *Law and Philosophy: A Symposium.* Ed. Sidney Hook. New York: New York University Press, 1964.
———. *Political Liberalism.* New York: Columbia University Press, 1993.
———. *A Theory of Justice.* Cambridge, Mass.: Harvard University Press, 1971.
Rawls, Phillip. "Parker 'Attack' Irks Fellow State Justice." *Huntsville Times (Alabama)*, January 16, 2006, 2B.
Raz, Joseph. *The Authority of Law.* Oxford: Clarendon, 1979.
———. "Law and Value in Adjudication." *The Authority of Law.* Oxford: Clarendon, 1979.
———. "Legal Positivism and the Sources of Law." *The Authority of Law.* Oxford: Clarendon, 1979.
———. "Legal Reasons, Sources, and Gaps." *The Authority of Law: Essays in Law and Morality.* Oxford: Clarendon, 1979.
———. *The Morality of Freedom.* Oxford: Clarendon, 1986.
———. "The Obligation to Obey: Revision and Tradition." *Ethics in the Public Domain.* Rev. ed. Oxford: Clarendon, 1994.
———. *Practical Reason and Norms.* 1970. 2nd ed. New York: Oxford University Press, 1990.
———. "Promises in Morality and Law." Rev. of P. S. Atiyah, *Promises, Morals, and Law. Harvard Law Review* 95 (1982): 916–38.
———. "The Rule of Law and Its Virtue." *The Authority of Law.* Oxford: Clarendon, 1979.
Regan, Donald H. "Authority and Value: Reflections on Raz's *Morality of Freedom*." *Southern California Law Review* 62 (1989): 995–1095.
Reibetanz (now Moreau), Sophia. "A Problem for the Doctrine of Double Effect." *Proceedings of the Aristotelian Society* 98 (1998): 217–23.
Reynolds, William L., and William M. Richman. "The Non-Precedential Precedent—Limited Publication and No-Citation Rules in the United States Courts of Appeals." *Columbia Law Review* 78 (1978): 1167–208.
Richardson, Henry S. "Review of Alan H. Goldman, *Practical Rules*." *Notre Dame Philosophical Reviews*, 2002.
———. "Specifying Norms as a Way to Resolve Concrete Ethical Problems." *Philosophy and Public Affairs* 19 (1990): 279–310.
Ridge, Michael. "Reasons for Action: Agent-Neutral vs. Agent-Relative." *Stanford Encyclopedia of Philosophy*, August 11, 2005. Retrieved July 21, 2009, from http://plato.stanford.edu/entries/reasons-agent/.
Ring, Wilson. "Vt. Judge Criticized for Molester Sentence." *Associated Press Online*, January 10, 2006.
Rizzo, Mario J., and Douglas Glen Whitman. "The Camel's Nose Is under the Tent: Rules, Theories, and Slippery Slopes." *UCLA Law Review* 51 (2003): 539–92.
Roberts, Thomas E. "Facial Takings Claims under Agins-Nectow: A Procedural Loose End." *Hawaii Law Review* 24 (2002): 623–55.
Robinson, Paul H. "The A.L.I.'s Proposed Distributive Principle of 'Limiting Retributivism': Does It Mean in Practice Anything Other than Pure Desert?" *Buffalo Criminal Law Review* 7 (2003): 3–15.
Ross, W.D. *The Right and the Good.* Oxford: Clarendon, 1930.
Roth, Abraham Sesshu. "Shared Agency and Contralateral Commitments." *Philosophical Review* 113 (2004): 359–410.
Rovane, Carol. *The Bounds of Agency.* Princeton, N.J.: Princeton University Press, 1998.

Sachs, Stephen E. "Saving Toby: Extortion, Blackmail, and the Right to Destroy." *Yale Law and Policy Review* 24 (2006): 251–61.

Sagoff, Mark. "Controlling Global Climate: The Debate over Pollution Trading." *Philosophical Dimensions of Public Policy*. Ed. Verna V. Gehring. New Brunswick, N.J.: Transaction, 2002.

Salmon, Marylynn. *Women and the Law of Property in Early America*. Chapel Hill: University of North Carolina Press, 1986.

Sankar, Sambhav N. "Disciplining the Professional Judge." *California Law Review* 88 (2000): 1233–80.

Saphire, Richard B. "Religion and Recusal." *Marquette Law Review* 81 (1998): 351–63.

Sartorius, Rolf. *Individual Conduct and Social Norms*. Encino, Calif.: Dickenson, 1975.

———. "Political Authority and Political Obligation." *Virginia Law Review* 67 (1981): 3–17.

Scalia, Antonin. *A Matter of Interpretation: Federal Courts and the Law*. Princeton, N.J.: Princeton University Press, 1997.

———. "Originalism: The Lesser Evil." *University of Cincinnati Law Review* 57 (1989): 849–65.

———. "The Rule of Law as a Law of Rules." *University of Chicago Law Review* 56 (1989): 1175–88.

Scanlon, T. M. *What We Owe to Each Other*. Cambridge, Mass.: Belknap, 1998.

Schapiro, Tamar. "Compliance, Complicity, and the Nature of Nonideal Conditions." *Journal of Philosophy* 100 (2003): 329–55.

Schauer, Frederick. "Easy Cases." *Southern California Law Review* 58 (1985): 399–440.

———. "Incentives, Reputation, and the Inglorious Determinants of Judicial Behavior." *University of Cincinnati Law Review* 68 (1999): 615–36.

———. *Playing by the Rules: A Philosophical Examination of Rule-Based Decision-Making in Law and in Life*. Oxford: Oxford University Press, 1991.

———. "Precedent." *Stanford Law Review* 29 (1987): 571–605.

———. "Slippery Slopes." *Harvard Law Review* 99 (1985): 361–83.

Scheffler, Samuel. *The Rejection of Consequentialism*. 1982. Revised ed. Oxford: Oxford University Press, 1994.

Schmidtz, David. "Islands in a Sea of Obligation: Limits of the Duty to Rescue." *Law and Philosophy* 19 (2000): 683–705.

Searle, John R. "Collective Intentions and Intentional Actions." *Intentions in Communication*. Eds. Philip R. Cohen, Jerry Morgan, and Martha E. Pollack. Cambridge, Mass.: MIT Press, 1990.

Seelye, Katharine Q. "A Get-Tough Message at California's Death Row." *New York Times*, March 24, 1996, 29.

Shaman, Jeffrey M. "Judicial Ethics." *Georgetown Journal of Legal Ethics* 2 (1988): 1–20.

Shapiro, David. "In Defense of Judicial Candor." *Harvard Law Review* 100 (1995): 731–50.

Shapiro, Ian, ed. *The Rule of Law: Nomos XXXVI*. New York: New York University Press, 1994.

Shapiro, Martin. "Judges as Liars." *Harvard Journal of Law and Public Policy* 17 (1994): 155–56.

Shapiro, Scott J. "Judicial Can't." *Noûs* 35, Supp. 1 (2001): 530–57.

———. "Law, Morality, and the Guidance of Conduct." *Legal Theory* 6 (2000): 127–70.

———. "Law, Plans, and Practical Reason." *Legal Theory* 8 (2002): 387–441.

———. "On Hart's Way Out." *Hart's Postscript*. Ed. Jules Coleman. Oxford: Oxford University Press, 2000.

Shepard, Sam. *Fool for Love*. New York: Dramatists Play Service, 1984.

Sher, George. *Approximate Justice: Studies in Non-Ideal Theory*. Lanham, Md.: Rowman & Littlefield, 1997.

Sherrer, Hans. "The Complicity of Judges in the Generation of Wrongful Convictions." *Northern Kentucky Law Review* 30 (2003): 539–83.

Shklar, Judith N. "Political Theory and the Rule of Law." *The Rule of Law: Ideal or Ideology*. Eds. Allan C. Hutchinson and Patrick Monahan. Toronto: Carswell, 1987.

Sidgwick, Henry. *The Methods of Ethics*. 7th ed. Indianapolis: Hackett, 1981. First published 1874.

Siegel, Neil S. "The Virtue of Judicial Statesmanship." *Texas Law Review* 86 (2008): 959–1032.

———. "Why President Bush Should Not Take the 5th; Judges Who Ignore Law Are Possible Court Candidates." *Houston Chronicle*, June 17, 2005, B11.

Simmons, A. John. "Locke and the Right to Punish." *Philosophy and Public Affairs* 20 (1991): 311–49.

———. *Moral Principles and Political Obligations*. Princeton, N.J.: Princeton University Press, 1979.

Simon, Dan. "The Double-Consciousness of Judging: The Problematic Legacy of Cardozo." *Oregon Law Review* 79 (2000): 1033–80.

Simon, William H. *The Practice of Justice: A Theory of Lawyers' Ethics*. Cambridge, Mass.: Harvard University Press, 1998.

———. "Should Lawyers Obey the Law?" *William & Mary Law Review* 38 (1996): 217–53.

Singer, Peter. "Famine, Affluence, and Morality." *Philosophy and Public Affairs* 1 (1972): 229–43

Smith, M. B. E. "Do Appellate Courts Regularly Cheat?" *Criminal Justice Ethics* 16 (1997): 11–20.

———. "Is There a Prima Facie Obligation to Obey the Law?" *Yale Law Journal* 82 (1973): 950–76.

———. "May Judges Ever Nullify the Law?" *Notre Dame Law Review* 74 (1999): 1657–71.

Smith, Matthew Noah. "The Law as a Social Practice: Are Shared Activities at the Foundations of Law?" *Legal Theory* 12 (2006): 265–92.

Smith, Steven D. "Why Should Courts Obey the Law?" *Georgetown Law Journal* 77 (1988): 113–64.

Solum, Lawrence B. "Equity and the Rule of Law." *The Rule of Law*. Ed. Ian Shapiro. New York: New York University Press, 1994.

———. "Faith and Justice." *DePaul Law Review* 39 (1990): 1083–106.

———. "Indeterminacy." *A Companion to Philosophy of Law and Legal Theory*. Ed. Dennis Patterson. Oxford: Blackwell, 1996.

———. "On the Indeterminacy Crisis: Critiquing Critical Dogma." *University of Chicago Law Review* 54 (1987): 462–503.

Songer, Donald R., Martha Humphries Ginn, and Tammy A. Sarver. "Do Judges Follow the Law When There Is No Fear of Reversal?" *Justice System Journal* 24 (2003): 137–61.

Soper, Philip. *The Ethics of Deference: Learning from Law's Morals*. Cambridge: Cambridge University Press, 2002.
———. *A Theory of Law*. Cambridge, Mass.: Harvard University Press, 1984.
Sowell, Thomas. "Real Judicial Crisis Is Judges Who Ignore the Law." *The Post and Courier* (Charleston, S.C.), January 14, 1998, A11.
Stark, Cynthia A. "Decision Procedures, Standards of Rightness and Impartiality." *Noûs* 31 (1997): 478–95.
Stavropoulos, Nicos. *Objectivity in Law*. Oxford: Clarendon, 1996.
Stern, Gerald. "Is Judicial Discipline in New York State a Threat to Judicial Independence?" *Pace Law Review* 7 (1987): 291–388.
Strauss, David A. "The Common Law Genius of the Warren Court." *William & Mary Law Review* 49 (2007): 845–79.
———. "Little Rock and the Legacy of Brown." *Saint Louis Law Journal* 52 (2008): 1065–86.
Suleiman, Ramzi. "Provision of Step-Level Public Goods under Uncertainty." *Rationality and Society* 9 (1997): 163–87.
Sullivan, Kathleen M. "The Justices of Rules and Standards." *Harvard Law Review* 106 (1992): 22–123.
Sulmasy, Daniel P. "What Is an Oath and Why Should a Physician Swear One?" *Theoretical Medicine and Bioethics* 20 (1999): 329–46.
Summers, Robert S. "The Principles of the Rule of Law." *Notre Dame Law Review* 74 (1999): 1691–712.
Sunstein, Cass R. "Moral Heuristics." *Behavioral and Brain Sciences* 28 (2005): 531–73.
———. "On Academic Fads and Fashions." *Michigan Law Review* 99 (2001): 1251.
———. *One Case at a Time: Judicial Minimalism on the Supreme Court*. Cambridge, Mass.: Harvard University Press, 1999.
———. "The Supreme Court 1995 Term: Foreword: Leaving Things Undecided." *Harvard Law Review* 110 (1996): 6–101.
———. "What Did Lawrence Hold? Of Autonomy, Desuetude, Sexuality, and Marriage." *Supreme Court Review* (2003): 27–74.
———. *Why Societies Need Dissent*. Cambridge, Mass.: Harvard University Press, 2003.
Sunstein, Cass R., and Richard A. Epstein, eds. *The Vote: Bush, Gore, and the Supreme Court*. Chicago: University of Chicago Press, 2001.
Sunstein, Cass R., and Adrian Vermeule. "Deterring Murder: A Reply." *Stanford Law Review* 58 (2006): 847–57.
"Symposium: *Bush v. Gore*." *University of Chicago Law Review* 68 (2001): 613–791.
Sypnowich, Christine. "Utopia and the Rule of Law." *Recrafting the Rule of Law*. Ed. David Dyzenhaus. Oxford: Hart, 1999.
Talley, Eric. "Precedential Cascades: An Appraisal." *Southern California Law Review* 73 (1999): 87–137.
Tamanaha, Brian Z. *Law as a Means to an End: Threat to the Rule of Law*. Law in Context. New York: Cambridge University Press, 2006.
———. *On the Rule of Law: History, Politics, Theory*. Cambridge: Cambridge University Press, 2004.
Temkin, Larry S. "Rethinking the Good, Moral Ideals and the Nature of Practical Reasons." *Reading Parfit*. Ed. Jonathan Dancy. Oxford: Blackwell, 1997.

Ten, C. L. "Positive Retributivism." *Social Philosophy and Policy* 7 (1990): 194–208.
Thayer, James B. "The Origin and Scope of the American Doctrine of Constitutional Law." *Harvard Law Review* 7 (1893): 129–56.
Thomson, Judith Jarvis. *Rights, Restitution, and Risk*. Cambridge, Mass.: Harvard University Press, 1986.
———. "Self-Defense." *Philosophy and Public Affairs* 20 (1991): 283–310.
Tuomela, Raimo. *The Importance of Us*. Stanford, Calif.: Stanford University Press, 1995.
Tuomela, Raimo, and Kaarlo Miller. "We-Intentions." *Philosophical Studies* 53 (1988): 115–37.
Tushnet, Mark. *Taking the Constitution Away from the Courts*. Princeton, N.J.: Princeton University Press, 1999.
Tyler, Tom R. *Why People Obey the Law*. New Haven, Conn.: Yale University Press, 1990.
Unger, Roberto Mangabeira. *Law in Modern Society*. New York: Free Press, 1976.
———. *What Should Legal Analysis Become?* London: Verso, 1996.
Velleman, J. David. "How to Share an Intention." *Philosophy and Phenomenological Research* 57 (1997): 29–50.
———. *The Possibility of Practical Reason*. Oxford: Oxford University Press, 2000.
Vermeule, Adrian. *Judging under Uncertainty: An Institutional Theory of Legal Interpretation*. Cambridge, Mass.: Harvard University Press, 2006.
Vila, Marisa Iglesias. *Facing Judicial Discretion: Legal Knowledge and Right Answers Revisited*. Boston: Kluwer, 2001.
Volcansek, Mary L. *Judicial Impeachment: None Called for Justice*. Urbana: University of Illinois Press, 1993.
Volokh, Eugene. "The Mechanisms of the Slippery Slope." *Harvard Law Review* 116 (2003): 1026–137.
Wald, Patricia M. "The Rhetoric of Results and the Results of Rhetoric: Judicial Writings." *University of Chicago Law Review* 62 (1995): 1371–419.
———. "Violence under the Law: A Judge's Perspective." *Law's Violence*. Eds. Austin Sarat and Thomas R. Kearns. Ann Arbor: University of Michigan Press, 1992.
Waldron, Jeremy. "The Core of the Case against Judicial Review." *Yale Law Journal* 115 (2006): 1346–406.
———. "Kant's Legal Positivism." *Harvard Law Review* 109 (1996): 1535–66.
———. *Law and Disagreement*. Oxford: Oxford University Press, 1999.
———. "The Rule of Law in Contemporary Liberal Theory." *Ratio Juris* 2 (1989): 79–96.
———. "Who Is My Neighbor? Humanity and Proximity." *Monist* 86 (2003): 333–54.
Walen, Alec. "Reasonable Illegal Force: Justice and Legitimacy in a Pluralistic, Liberal Society." *Ethics* 111 (2001): 344–73.
Walker, A. D. M. "Political Obligation and the Argument from Gratitude." *Philosophy and Public Affairs* 17 (1988): 191–211.
Walton, Douglas. *Slippery Slope Arguments*. Oxford: Clarendon, 1992.
Waluchow, W. J. "Authority and the Practical Difference Thesis." *Legal Theory* 6 (2000): 45–81.
———. *Inclusive Legal Positivism*. Oxford: Clarendon, 1994.

———. "Indeterminacy." *Canadian Journal of Law and Jurisprudence* 9 (1996): 397–409.
Wasserstrom, Richard A. *The Judicial Decision: Toward a Theory of Legal Justification*. Stanford, Calif.: Stanford University Press, 1961.
———. "Lawyers as Professionals: Some Moral Issues." *Human Rights* 5 (1975): 2–15.
———. "The Obligation to Obey the Law." *UCLA Law Review* 10 (1963): 780–807.
Wechsler, Herbert. "Toward Neutral Principles of Constitutional Law." *Harvard Law Review* 73 (1959): 1–35.
Weick, Karl E. *Sensemaking in Organizations*. Thousand Oaks, Calif.: Sage, 1995.
Weinstein, Jack B. "Every Day Is a Good Day for a Judge to Lay Down His Professional Life for Justice." *Fordham Urban Law Journal* 32 (2004): 131–70.
Wellman, Christopher Heath. "Liberalism, Samaritanism, and Political Obligation." *Philosophy and Public Affairs* 25 (1996): 211–37.
Wenar, Leif. "The Nature of Rights." *Philosophy and Public Affairs* 33 (2005): 223–52.
West, Robin. "The Lawless Adjudicator." *Cardozo Law Review* 26 (2005): 2253–61.
Westen, Peter. *Speaking of Equality: An Analysis of the Rhetorical Force of "Equality" in Moral and Legal Discourse*. Princeton, N.J.: Princeton University Press, 1990.
White, David. "Parker Says He's Willing to Defy High Court." *Birmingham (Ala.) News*, May 26, 2006, 1C.
Williams, Bernard. *Ethics and the Limits of Philosophy*. Cambridge, Mass.: Harvard University Press, 1985.
———. *Moral Luck*. Cambridge: Cambridge University Press, 1981.
Winston, Ken. "On Treating Like Cases Alike." *California Law Review* 62 (1974): 1–39.
Wolf, Arthur P., and William H. Durham, eds. *Inbreeding, Incest, and the Incest Taboo: The State of Knowledge at the Turn of the Century*. Stanford, Calif.: Stanford University Press, 2005.
Wolf, Susan. "Morality and Partiality." *Philosophical Perspectives* 6 (1992): 243–59.
Wolff, Robert Paul. *In Defense of Anarchism*. New York: Harper & Row, 1970.
Woodard, Calvin. "Joseph Story and American Equity." *Washington and Lee Law Review* 45 (1988): 623–44.
Yeazell, Stephen C. "Good Judging and Good Judgment." *Court Review* 35 (1998): 8–10.
Zapf, Christian, and Eben Moglen. "Linguistic Indeterminacy and the Rule of Law: On the Perils of Misunderstanding Wittgenstein." *Georgetown Law Journal* 84 (1996): 485–520.
Zimmerman, Michael J. "Intervening Agents and Moral Responsibility." *Philosophical Quarterly* 35 (1985): 347–58.
Zipursky, Benjamin C. "The Model of Social Facts." *Hart's Postscript: Essays on the Postscript to the Concept of Law*. Ed. Jules Coleman. New York: Oxford University Press, 2001.

Index

Page numbers in boldface indicate where a term is introduced or defined.

abortion
  as controversial legal question, 18, 80, 87
  John T. Noonan's position on, 250–51
  Roman Catholic position on, 109, 175
  Ronald Dworkin's position on, 89
  as subject of checkerboard legislation, 262–63
Abrahamson, Leslie W., 59n21
absolute principles, 204
absurdity doctrine, 41
Ackerman, Bruce, 6n20, 81n23
activism, judicial, 16–17, **50–52**
adaptation, 185–86, 229–31
additive principles, 203, 208
adherence (to legal standards), **39**
affirmative action, 89, 240, 250
agency (legal concept), 28
agent neutrality, 14–15, 182, 203, 310
  agent-relative principles and, 208–11
  imperceptible effects and, 221
agent relativity, 14, 182, 204, 208, 310
aggregative principles, 209, 212
Alexander, Larry
  on coordination and efficiency, 120n35
  on criminal law, 224n17
  on defiance of rules, 39n15
  on exclusionary reasons, 113n11
  on formalism, 292–94
  on gaps, 46n48, 82n31, 83n33, 134–35
  on indeterminacy, 85n43
  on legal principles, 44n44, 89n65
  on particularism, 94n7
  on posited rules, 43n39
  on precedent, 11n45, 280n29
  on promises, 146n10
  on pure rules, 115
  on renegade officials, 47n55
  on rule-sensitive particularism, 124n7
  on serious rules, 112
  on settlement function of law, 118n
  on threshold deontology, 204n, 210n11
Alexy, Robert, 129n26
Alfini, James J., 62n38, 62n40
Altman, Andrew, 46n53, 84n37, 84n38, 84n39
Altman, Scott, 297n13
anarchism, philosophical, 15, 32, 168
Anderson, Lisa R., 235n5
antimiscegenation, 169
apartheid, 9, 169, 239
appeals (to higher court), 3, 5, 63, 70, 71, 178
Applbaum, Arthur Isak, 4n7, 20n8, 97
appraisal reasons. *See* reasons: appraisal
Aquinas, Thomas, 247n26
Aristotle, 16, 83n33, 255
Ashcroft v. Free Speech Coalition, 80n18
Atiyah, P. S., 144n6
attenuation (of reasons), 21
Augustine, 87
Austin, J. L., 33n55
Austin, John, 98n17
authority
  asymmetry of, 134n45
  judicial, 30–34
  legal, 103–4
  moral, principle of, **32**
autonomy, 121–22, 137–40

backward-L (shape of curve), 235
Baer, Harold, Jr., 7
Baier, Kurt, 146n8
Bales, R. E., 22n16
Balkin, Jack M., 6n20, 81n23, 85n41
bandwagon effects, 235
Banerjee, Abhijit, 235n5
Barak, Aharon, 46n47
Barnes v. Glen Theatre, Inc., 245n23
Baron, Marcia, 23n20
Bassett, Debra Lyn, 37n6, 59n24
battered women, 80
Bayles, Michael, 255n5
Benn, S. I., 255n5
Bennett, Jonathan, 105n40
Bennis v. Michigan, 79n11
Bentham, Jeremy, 127
Berger, Raoul, 80n21, 95n10
Bethlehem Steel Co. v. New York State Labor Relations Board, 41n19
Bikhchandani, Sushil, 235n5
birth control. *See* contraception
Bix, Brian, 84n39
Black, Hugo, 95n10
Blackmun, Harry, 82
Blackstone, William, 86
blame
 for adhering, 268–69
 for deciding randomly, 266
 for deviating, 93, 249–52
 when warranted, 21–22, 218, 224
Bloom, Frederic M., 12n47
Bobbitt, Philip, 275n16
Bork, Robert H., 80n21, 95n10
Bowers v. Hardwick, 277n26
Boy Scouts of America v. Dale, 17n61
Bradley v. Fisher, 61n33
Bradley v. Richmond School Board, 128n23
Brand-Ballard, Jeffrey, 136n52, 181n2, 211n15
Bratman, Michael, 192–93, 195–97, 207n7
Brennan, Samantha, 211n14
Brennan, William, 251n31
Brewer, Scott, 290n43
bribery, 36, 54, 116
Bright, Stephen B., 6n18
Brink, David O., 22n16, 99n25, 272n7
Broadman, Howard R., 65

Brown, Darryl K., 42n32
Brown v. Board of Education, 81, 99
Brownback, Sam, 6n18
Budd, Malcolm, 290n42
Burton, Stephen J.
 on economic commons analogy, 241n19
 on indeterminacy, 46n53, 84n39, 85n42
 on judicial duties, 57n8
 on practical reason, 19n1
 on use of extralegal considerations, 8n34
Bush v. Gore, 6, 17n61
Bushnell, Eleanore, 68n86
Butler, Paul, 273n12

Calabresi, Guido, 41n24
California Commission on Judicial Performance, 65
Caminker, Evan H., 50n63, 127n12
candor, judicial, 270–76, 286
cap-and-trade. *See* emissions trading
capital punishment
 as applied to juveniles, 12
 as controversial legal question, 79, 250
 Justice Blackmun's position on, 82
 refusing to enforce, 88
 Roman Catholic position on, 109, 175
Cardozo, Benjamin N., 13n52, 57
Carhart, Gonzales v., 17n61, 80n16
Carter, Stephen L., 109n51
cascades, 235
cases
 clear, 8–10
 easy, 39n14, 108
 gap, 46n48, 133, 134–35, 248–49, 280–82
 hard, 39n14, 90–91
 high-level, 246–48
 impermissible-result, **77–78**
 legally regulated, 77–78
 low-level, 246–48
 negative-closure, 82
 negative-gap, **82–83**, 240, 248, 303
 inevitability of, 86, 188
 John Rawls on, 165

Index

optimal-but-not-required-result, 77–78, 114–15, 144
optimal-result, 77
  agent-relative principles and, 202–7
  comparative justice and, 257, 260, 269, 271
  identifying, 133
  judicial reasons in, 96, 113–14
  mimesis and, 187–201 *passim*, 212
  optimal adherence rules and, 220–31 *passim*
  permissive rule and, 163
permissible-result, 140, 144, 154, 177
positive-closure, 82
positive-gap, 82–83
required-result, 77–78, 114–15, 144
suboptimal-but-permissible-result, 77–78, 170
suboptimal-result, 77
  assumptions underlying existence of, 83–88
  classified, 82–83
suboptimal-rule, 165, 240, **246**–49, 303
Casey, Planned Parenthood v., 80n15
Cashman, Edward, 68
Catholicism, Roman, 10, 109–10, 175–77, 251
causal limitation, 221
causal moderate rule, 293
checkerboard legislation, 262–64
Chickasaw Nation v. United States, 51n72
child molestation, 79. See also sex with minors
Christopher, Russell L., 204n2
Cicero, 86
civil disobedience, 15
claim-rights (Hohfeldian), 24n25
clean hands, 226–27
cliffs, 235–36, 287
Code of Conduct of United States Judges, 36n5, 54n86, 56n1, 58–61, 62n37, 63
Cogel, Metin M., 37n7, 72n104
cognitive dissonance, 94–95
cognitive laziness, 73

Cohen, Mark A., 37n7, 72n104
coherence, 231–32
coin flip, as basis for decision, 52n79, 260n11, 266, 280
Coleman, Jules
  on conventionality thesis, 298n18
  on definition of "positivism," 99n25, 99n26
  as inclusive positivist, 44n41, 89n63
  on indeterminacy, 84n39, 85n42
  on separability thesis, 98n17
  on social fact thesis, 98n18, 197
collective agency, 194
collective reasons. *See* reasons: collective
combined restriction, 229, 233
common morality, 23, 231–32
comparative harm functions, 208–10
comparative justice, 246, 254–62, 311
  as argument for restrictive rule, 122
  conditional legal, 258
  legal, 257, 261
  moral, 258–61
  as related to equity, 303
complicity, 225–26
concept/conception distinction, 100n30
Coney, Amy V., 109n51
conflicts of interest, 54, 116
conform/comply distinction, 159
congruence condition (of formal legality), 116–17
Conkle, Daniel O., 109n51
Connecticut National Bank v. Germain, 51n72
Connor, John, 69
conscientious objection, 15
consequentialism
  act, 147–48, 173, 221
  causal limitation and, 221
  indirect, 23, 135–36
  prospective arguments and, 182n4
  rule, 135–36
  sophisticated, 15
  status of agent-relative principles within, 210
  as theory of punishment, 173–74
conservatives, 16–18, 80, 82, 275, 305–6
constitutional theory, 17

content independence, 113–14, 118, 158–60, 231
contraception, 94–95, 272, 274, 282, 306
contractualism, 23, 136–37, 210, 216
Controlled Substances Act, 3–4, 10
conventionalism, strict, 98
conventionality thesis, 298
conversational implicature, 307
Cook, Walter Wheeler, 302n20
cooperation, 190–91, 216–17, 220
  with evil, 109–10, 175–77
coordination
  as function of shared intention, 192
  impossibility of, 234, 265
  possibility of, 238
  as reason for rules, 118–20, 126
  as requiring predictability, 130
Cooter, Robert D., 71n101
Copp, David, 190n28
Corvino, John, 277n23
Coughlin, John W., 69
Coulter, Ann, 35
counterfeiting, 76–77
courts, collegial, 35
Cover, Robert M., 5, 9, 27n37, 28
Crisp, Roger, 297n14
critical legal studies, 84–85, 313
Cuba, constitution of, 169
Cullity, Garrett, 190n27
cumulative harm. *See* harm, cumulative

Dagger, Richard, 76n7
Dalton, Clare, 84n38
Damasio, Antonio R., 37n10
D'Amato, Anthony, 84n40
Dan-Cohen, Meir, 123n4, 159n5, 272n6
Dancy, Jonathan, 21n10, 93n6, 113, 297n14
Daniels, Norman, 232n29
Darwall, Stephen L., 14n54, 210n13
Daschle, Tom, 6
De Sousa, Ronald, 37n10
death penalty. *See* capital punishment
Death with Dignity Act (Oregon), 259
decision patterns, 212
decision rules, 123–24
default rule, **265**, 267, 279–80, 311
  unreflective conformity to, 289–91

defection, 190, 220
DeLay, Tom, 6n18
deontology, 23, 204, 213
DePaul, Michael R., 232n29
deportation, 79
Dershowitz, Alan M., 6n20
desuetude, 41
determinacy, 83–85, 112. *See also* indeterminacy
deviation, 5, **39**
  contrasted with judicial activism, 50–52
  express, 53
  from the law, simpliciter, **45**
  legally unauthorized, 48
  surreptitious, 213n3, 271, 273, 276, 286
  tacit, 53
  token-selective, 246, **253–54**, 258, 261–64, 286, 291, 303
  type-selective, **244–46**, 281–82, 286
deviation credits, 254, 260–61, 269, 274, 295–98
deviation density, 198–99, 228, 235–37, 304
  mimetic failure and, 213–14, 235
deviation density threshold, **212–14**, 310
  criticism of judiciary and, 288
  deviation rate below or above, 217–20
  equity and, 304
  Griswold v. Connecticut and, 273–74
  guidance rules and, 234–41
  precedent and, 281
  rebuttable presumption and, 243–44
deviation rate, **198**, 228–29
  optimal average, 216–19, 229, 233, 237
  optimal collective, 214
disagreement, moral, 75, 118, 262. *See also* pluralism, reasonable
discipline, judicial, 52n75, 61–69
  informal, 71
discretion, 50, 69, 90
  abuse of, 63, 260n11
  contrasted with deviation, 42–43, 46–48
  in criminal sentencing, 286
  delegated, 47

Index

deviational, 42–43, 90n67
  objective, 46, 47
  optimal results and, 76, 87, 104, 153
disqualification. *See* recusal
distinguishing (cases), 12, 41–42, 48–49, 274–78, 283
divorce, 109–10, 175
Dole, Robert, 7
double effect, doctrine of, 105–6, 205
Douglas, William O., 272–73, 306
Drahos, Peter, 84n39
Dred Scott v. Sandford, 7
Dresden, bombing of, 225, 227
Dubber, Markus Dirk, 28n37
duties
  of fidelity (promise-keeping), 144–46
  of judicial office, 36, 56–57, 58–61
  natural, 23
  of nonmaleficence, **23**, 26, 308
  samaritan, 24, 147, 167
duty to obey the law, 32, 103, 157–60
  consent argument for, 161
  fair play argument for, 161–64
  gratitude argument for, 164
  natural duty argument for, 165–67
  samaritan argument for, 167
duty to rescue. *See* samaritanism
Duxbury, Neil, 46n52, 267n35
Dworkin, Ronald
  on *Bush v. Gore*, 6n20
  on checkerboard laws, 262–64
  on comparative justice, 256n6
  on concept/conception distinction, 100n30
  on controversial legal questions, 89
  on duty to obey, 158n2
  on force of law, 85–86
  on hard cases, 39n14, 91
  on integrity, 128, 311
  on judicial candor, 273n12
  on judicial discretion, 46n47
  on legal pragmatism, 115n17
  on locality, 40n18
  on nonenforcement, 8–10, 89n64, 89n66, 92, 127–28, 239n13
  on principles, 40n17, 44–45, 47
  on strict conventionalism, 98n23
  on wealth redistribution, 127–28

Dyzenhaus, David, 9, 90–91, 97–98, 128n24

Easterbrook, Frank, 263n21, 292n3
Edlin, Douglas E.
  on epistemic threshold, 250n29
  on judicial role, 141n58
  on obsolete laws, 41n24
  on unjust laws, 43n37, 43n38, 87–88
Edmundson, William A., 15n56, 103n39, 158n1, 160n6
Edwards, Harry T., 3n4
efficiency, 119–20, 131–32
Eggleston, Ben, 271n5, 272n7
Ellis, Anthony, 210n11
Ely, John Hart, 81n24
emissions trading, 241–42
emotion, 37n10, 295
enablers (of reasons), 21, 113, 154, 296–97
Endicott, Timothy A. O., 116, 256n6
Enoch, David, 211n16
entrenchment (of reasons), 115, 126
environmental policy, 250
epistemic threshold. *See* threshold, epistemic
Epstein, Richard A., 6n20, 7
equal protection, 6, 17, 81, 128, 275
equilibrium, 235, 286–89
equity, 16, 302–4
error argument, 120, 132–35
Eskridge, William N., Jr., 41n24
esoteric rules, **271–72**, 293
establishment clause, 6
Estreicher, Samuel, 5n11, 6n17, 41n25, 129n28
euthanasia, 89. *See also* suicide: assisted
evidence, exclusion of, 79
evidentiary standards, 250–52
evil, cooperation with, 109–10, 175
exclusionary reasons. *See* reasons: exclusionary
excuses, 33n55
expectations, epistemically reasonable, 151–52

fair share argument, 215–20
fairness, 122. *See also* comparative justice

Fallon, Richard H., Jr., 100n29
Farley, John J., III, 302n20
Farnsworth, Ward, 6n20
Farrell, Daniel M., 25n30
favorers (of reasons), 21, 297
Feinberg, Joel, 26n32, 207n7, 255n5
fellatio, 79
Ferzan, Kimberly Kessler, 224n17
final moderate rule, 243, 254, 267, 279–80
First Amendment, 6, 80, 245
first moderate rule, 238–39
first priority rule, **243–47**, 267
Fletcher, George P., 27n36
Flikschuh, Katrin, 24n28
force, judicial use of, 27–30, 95–96, 237, 268
Forer, Lois, 176–77
formal equality, 255, 259–61, 264
formal justice. *See* comparative justice
formal legality, 100–102, 116–18
formalism, legal, 15, 85–86, 183, 292–94, 311
fornication, 247, 276–77
Frankena, William K., 255n5
Fraser, David, 169n34
free riding, 149–50, 215–19, 228
free speech, 80, 245
Fried, Charles, 60n28, 273n11, 290n43
Friedman, Barry, 17
Fugitive Slave Act, 10, 88–89
Fuller, Lon L., 9, 52n74, 101n31
Furman v. Georgia, 82

Gandhi, Mahatma, 176–77
gaps (in the law), 46
Gardner, John, 46n50
Garvey, John H., 109n51, 110n56
gay men. *See* sexual orientation
Gee, Thomas, 176–77
genocide, 9, 93
Gert, Bernard, 144n6
Gettier, Edmund L., 83n32
Geyh, Charles Gardner, 68n88, 71n102
Gilbert, Margaret
    on collective agency, 192, 194n41, 194n42, 196n44
    on political obligation, 158n2, 161n10

Ginn, Martha Humphries, 71n100
Ginsburg, Ruth Bader, 251
Glassroth v. Moore, 80n19
Glover, Jonathan, 222n12
Goldman, Alan H., 15n57, 310
    comparative justice argument (Kantian constraint), 254–55, 258
    defense of restrictive rule, 183
    epistemic argument, 234, 238
    on error, 134
    on judges, 184, 239
    on moderate rules, 184
    on optimal decision pattern, 212, 234, 236
    on predictability, 130n35, 131n36
    on prisoner's dilemma, 190–92
    on professional ethics, 4n7
    on prudential reasoning, 238
    on randomizing, 265
    on rationality of rule compliance, 215
    on serious rules, 112n4, 292–93
    on suboptimal results, 120n35, 120n36
    on systemic effects, 182–85
Goodin, Robert E., 211n16
Goodwin, Barbara, 267n35
Graber, Mark A., 9n38
Gray, Cynthia, 63n50, 66n75, 68n84
Green, Leslie, 159
Greenawalt, Kent
    on indeterminacy, 84n39
    on institutions of amelioration, 268n37
    on judicial discretion, 90n70
    on judicial nullification, 6n17, 127, 128, 129
    on justification versus excuse, 33n55
    on political obligation, 159n5
Greenberg, Mark, 44n41
Grice, Paul, 307n29
Griffen, Wendell L., 109n51
Grimes, Warren S., 68n86, 68n87
Griswold v. Connecticut, 94–95, 272–74, 282, 284
group adherence argument, 191–92
Group O, **187**, 239–41, 310
    average deviation rate of, 228–29
    maintaining equilibrium, 235–37

Index

optimal adherence rules for, 212–17, 233
reasons to adhere, 191–92, 202–11
group obligation, 191
group restriction, 213
guidance reasons. *See* reasons: guidance
gun control, 80, 185
Gunther, Gerald, 60n28

habituated view (of official use of force), 31–34
Haley, John O., 68n89
Hamburger, Philip, 57n8
Hampton, Jean, 190n27, 235n4
Hand, Learned, 81n24, 81n28
Hardimon, Michael O., 4n7
harm, cumulative, 183
Harris, John, 267n35
Hart, H. L. A.
 on causation, 207n7
 on comparative justice, 256n6
 on content independence, 113
 on conventionality thesis, 298
 on formalism, 85–86
 on judicial discretion, 8n35, 46n47
 on political obligation, 158n2
 on rules, 98n20
 on sanctions, 61
 on secondary rules, 56n2
 on unjust laws, 9
Hasnas, John, 100n28
Hatch, Orrin, 6n18
hate speech, 245, 290
Heiple, James, 68–69
Heller, District of Columbia v., 17n61, 80n20
Hellman, Deborah, 271n3
Henchey v. City of Chicago, 90n69
Henderson, Lynn, 28n37
Henkin, Louis, 95n10
Henningsen v. Bloomfield Motors, 44
herd behavior, 235
heroin, 247
Heyd, David, 23n18
Higgins, Richard S., 71n100, 72n105
Himma, Kenneth Einar, 44n41, 46n47, 298n18
Hirshleifer, David, 235n5
Hoffer, Peter Charles, 302n20

Hohfeld, Wesley Newcomb, 24n25
Holder, Eric H., Jr., 3n1
Holt, Charles A., 235n5
homosexuality. *See* sexual orientation
Honoré, Tony, 160n7, 170n35, 207n7
Hooker, Brad, 135–36
Horton, Elizabeth M., 284n36
Horwitz, Morton J., 100n28, 257n7
Hurd, Heidi M., 83n33, 146n8
Hurley, Paul, 210n13
Hurley, Susan, 23n19
Husak, Douglas, 174n40
Hutchinson, Allan C., 100n28
Hutto v. Davis, 34n59
hypersensitivity, 190
hyposensitivity, 198
hypothetical cases
 Adams/Bonn/Carlo, State v., 259–60
 bandit and villagers, 222, 227
 bank and borrower, 185–86
 Bruce (squirrel kicker), 146, 153
 Chester (pedophile), 172–74
 churchgoing tax, 101–2
 Cordelia and Goneril (sisters), 299–302
 Dan (supermarket), 224, 227
 Fred and George (shoplifters), 253–54
 lazy assassin, 149
 Leo (sexual harasser), 151
 Marine sniper, 22
 Ned (island), 218–19
 Rachel's grandmother's terrorist boyfriend, 152
 rerouting tax payments to charity (Alan H. Goldman), 191, 215, 217, 220, 225, 234, 265–66
 Russell, Mrs. (medical marijuana), 3
 Susan, J. (nude dancing/hate speech), 245–46
 Yasmin and Rafael (landlord/tenant), **78–79**, 87, 153–54, 183, 200–201, 229, 296–97

Idelman, Scott C., 109n51, 271n3
Igneski, Violetta, 206n6
impeachment, 36, 62, 68–70, 312
 of federal judges, 68
 of state judges, 68–70
imperceptible effects, 221–22

incentives, judicial, 36, 54–55, 70–73, 92, 287
incest, 276–79
inclusive positivism. *See* positivism, legal: inclusive
independence, judicial, 59
indeterminacy, 46, 84–85, 313. *See also* determinacy
indirect consequentialism. *See* consequentialism, indirect
individual adherence argument, 188–89
individual policy, 233, 237
individual restrictions
 first, 216
 second, 219
 third, 229
influence, judicial, 37, 162
Ingram, Peter, 256n6
injustices (mandated/nonmandated), **168–70**
integrity, 262–64, 311
intend/forsee distinction, 203, 205
intensifying (of reasons), 21
intentional states, 192
intentions, 104–7, 205
 shared, 192–98
intransitivity, 199–201
INUS condition, judicial oath-taking as, 155–56
invitee/licensee distinction, 48–49
Isaacs, Tracy, 194n42

Jackson, Frank, 223n14
Jackson v. Lykes Bros. S.S. Co., No. 575, 60n27
Jacobson, Arthur J., 284n36
Japanese-Americans, internment of, 169
judges (anterior/posterior), **186**
judicial activism. *See* activism, judicial
judicial authority. *See* authority: judicial
Judicial Conference of the United States, 59
judicial misconduct. *See* misconduct, judicial
judicial nullification, 5
judicial review (of legislation), 41
jury nullification, 6n17, 42

Kadish, Mortimer R. and Sanford H. (co-authors), 42, 47, 87, 130
Kagan, Shelly, 21n9, 105n40
Kamm, F. M., 105n40, 107, 206
Kant, Immanuel, 24n28, 254
Kantian constraint, 254
Kantianism, 210
Kaplow, Louis, 101n33, 211n16
Karlan, Pamela S., 53n81
Katz, Leo, 204n2
Kauper, Paul G., 95n10
Kelo v. City of New London, 7
Kelsen, Hans, 46n51
Kennedy, Anthony, 278
Kennedy, Duncan, 84n40, 101n33, 123n5
Klarman, Michael J., 6n20
Kline, J. Anthony, 53, 64n64, 65, 65n73, 140n57
Klosko, George, 158n2, 162, 190n27
Kmiec, Keenan, 50–52
Kohlberg, Lawrence, 31n49
Kornhauser, Lewis A., 11n44, 72n106
Korsgaard, Christine M., 19n4
Kramer, Larry D., 41n22
Kramer, Matthew, 44n41, 89n63, 298n18
Kress, Ken, 44n44, 84n37, 84n38, 84n39, 89n65
Kretzmann, Norman, 129n27
Kroger, John R., 302n20
Kronman, Anthony, 290n43
Kuran, Timur, 235n5
Kutz, Christopher, 190, 197, 225

Lamond, Grant, 30n47
Landers, Scott, 84n39
Landes, William M., 37n8
landlord and tenant, law of, 26n33
law, simpliciter, 11, 40
law, theory of, 44
lawmakers, **111n2**, 270
lawmaking, judicial, 141
Lawrence v. Texas, 275–79, 284
lawsuits against judges, 62
layered pyramid, 246
Lefkowitz, David, 151n21
legal content, theory of, 44, 85–86
legal error, 3, 5, 7, 62–68, 276
 egregious, 64, 67–68

Index

legal positivism. *See* positivism, legal
legal pragmatism. *See* pragmatism, legal
legalistic justification, doctrine of, 129–30
legitimacy, 121–22, 137–40
Leiter, Brian, 38n12, 84n39, 85n42, 290n43
lesbians. *See* sexual orientation
Levenbook, Barbara B., 280n29
Levinson, Sanford, 109n51
Lewis, David, 193n35, 196n44, 267n35
lex iniusta non est lex, 87, 129
lexical priority, 251, 267
Li, Xiaorong, 169n31
liability, judicial, 62
liberals, 17–18, 80, 275, 305–6
local applicability, 40
Locke, John, 24n28, 25, 25n30
Lockyer v. Andrade, 79n10
Lode, Eric, 199n55
Lopez, United States v., 17n61
Luban, David, 4n7, 16n58, 20n8
Lubet, Steven
   on bias, 66n76
   on Circuit Judicial Councils, 60n26
   on decision by coin flip, 266n31
   on decisional conduct, 61–62
   on disciplinary complaints, 63n49
   on egregious error, 67
   on Judge Heiple case, 69n91
   on Judge Kline case, 65–66
   on patterns of error, 66n74
   on willful refusal to follow law, 66n78
Luce, R. Duncan, 264n26
Lyons, David
   on correlativity of rights and duties, 22n18
   on density, 199n54
   on deviation, 129–30
   on duty to obey the law, 159n5
   on formal justice, 256n6, 257n8
   on gap cases, 83n33
   on hard cases, 39n14
   on judicial commitment, 142n1
   on justification of coercion, 30
   on moral predicament of judges, 108
   on predictability, 119n33
   on threats against judges, 268n38

MacAdam, James I., 255n5
MacCormick, Neil, 57n9, 71, 125–26, 150n18, 255n5
Macey, Jonathan R., 37n9
Mackie, J. L., 155n26, 160n7, 160n8, 236n9
mala in se offenses. *See* offenses: mala in se
Manning, John F., 41n25, 302n20
Marbury v. Madison, 41n21
marijuana, 3–4, 34n59, 80
Marmor, Andrei, 100n29, 257n8
Marshall, Thurgood, 35
Mason, Elinor, 147n15
McCarthy, David, 223n14
McCarthy, Nancy, 65n71
McCulloch v. Maryland, 41n21
McDermott, Daniel, 25n30
McDowell, Gary, 302n20
McHugh, Kenneth R., 69
McIntyre, Alison, 105n40
McKeever, Sean, 93n6
McKerlie, Dennis, 223n14
McMahan, Jeff, 24n27
McMahon, Christopher, 190, 216
means (to an end), 106–8, 206
mediated/unmediated distinction, 204, 207
mental states, judicial, 52–54, 268
Mian, Emran, 113n11
Miceli, Thomas J., 37n7, 72n104
Miller, Arthur R., 54n87
Miller, David, 158n2
Miller, Kaarlo, 193n37
Miller, Richard W., 206n6
Miller, William Ian, 26n32
mimesis, 186–88, 213, 229–31
mimetic failure, **187**
   effect of judicial candor on, 271
   empirical assumptions about, 212
   excessive, 264
   excessive rule revision as form of, 281
   as reason to adhere, 188, 202
   vulnerability to, 198
minimalism, judicial, 283–85
minimum-purchase policy, 242

minorities, discrete and insular, 264
mirages, legal, 290
misconduct, judicial, 36, 62
misdemeanors, 253–54
mixed strategies, 264
Modak-Turan, Mark C., 109n51
Model Code of Judicial Conduct, 36n5, 54n86, 56n4, 58–61, 62–64
Model Penal Code, 224n15
   criminal solicitation, 28n41
   self-defense, 26n34
Moglen, Eben, 84n39
Montesquieu, 101n31
Moore, Michael S., 43n40, 86–87, 113n11, 204n2, 207n7
Morrison, United States v., 17n61
Morrow v. Hood Communications, Inc., 53
Mosley, United States v., 47n55
Murphy, Liam B., 181n1
Murphy, Mark C., 9n36, 86n52, 158n2, 161n10

Nagel, Thomas, 14n55, 105n41, 204n2
naive view (of official use of force), 31–34
natural executive right. *See* rights: natural executive
natural lawyers, 8–9, 15, 86, 247
Nazism, 9, 169, 239
Neary v. Regents of the University of California, 53
neutrality, political, 305–7
New Jersey, Supreme Court of, 69
Newdow v. U.S. Congress, 6
Newman, Jon O., 7n29
Nichols, Shaun, 37n10
no-minimum policy, 241–42
nonideal theory, 136, 181, 217, 272
Noonan, John T., Jr., 28n37, 250–51
novus actus interveniens, 207–8
Nozick, Robert, 25n28, 25n30, 162, 204n2
nude dancing, 245, 290
nullum crimen, nulla poena, sine lege, 171–74
Nussbaum, Martha C., 37n10

oath arguments, 143, 145, 147
oaths, **142–43**
   of federal judges, 142
   as INUS condition, 155–56
   judicial, 10, 60–62, 161, 226
   special weight of, 154–55
   of state judges, 142n4
obedience, **123**
objective reasons. *See* reasons: objective
obligation, political, 14–15, 160–61
offenses
   mala in se, **31n51**, 76, 140, 171–72
   mala prohibita, **76**, 171–72
O'Hara, Erin, 72n104
Olowofoyeku, Abimola A., 62n39
open texture (of rules), 46
opinions, unpublished, 285
optimal results, **75**
optimizing collective agents, 194–97, **195**
Oregon Waste System, Inc. v. Department of Environmental Quality, 3n2
original position (John Rawls), 166
Orsi, Francesco, 206n6
Osborn, Rebekah L., 109n51
Otsuka, Michael, 190n27

paired privileges (Hohfeldian), 24n26
Panglossians, 86–88, 272, 311–12
Pareto principle, 209–10, 266
Parfit, Derek, 14n55, 222n13, 271n5, 286n37
Parker, Stephen, 84n39
Parker, Tom, 12, 53–54
Partial Birth Abortion Ban Act, 80n16
particularism, 115n17, 115n18, 183
   causal rule-sensitive, 293
   legal, 93–94
   moral, 93–94, 183
   rule-sensitive, 124, 134n46, 240, 292–93
Paulsen, Michael Stokes, 86n49, 127n12
Paulson, Bonnie Litschewski, 129n26
Paulson, Stanley L., 129n26
Payne v. Tennessee, 41n20
Peirce, C. S., 246n25
Peller, Gary, 84n38
Pelosi, Nancy, 35
Penzell, Abigail, 33n56

Index

Perry, Stephen R., 22n15, 44n41, 113n11, 250n29
Peters, R. S., 255n5
Pettit, Philip, 14n55, 23n20, 194n41, 194n42, 210n13
Plato, 102n35, 103
pleasure (of adhering to law), 72, 265
Pledge of Allegiance, 6
pluralism, reasonable, **75n1**, 79, 249, 305
politicians, 6, 69, 93, 289
pollution, 241–42
pornography, 80
positivism, legal, 98–99
   exclusive, 85, 298, 301–2, 311
   inclusive, 43, 85, 89, 298
   presumptive, 134n46, 240, 292–93
   as theory of legal validity, 97–98
Posner, Eric, 270n2
Posner, Richard A.
   on desire to be cited, 72
   on deviation, 5n10
   on judicial incentives, 37n7, 70
   as legal pragmatist, 304–5
   opinion in *Khan v. State Oil Co.*, 93n5
   on pleasure of judging, 72, 167, 265
   on precedent, 37n8
   on reputation, 71n101
   on reversal, 71n100
Postema, Gerald J., 16n58, 83n33, 127n15, 239n13, 303n21
practical difference thesis, 297–302
practical reasons. *See* reasons: practical
pragmatism, legal, 115n17, 304–5
precedent
   disregarding, 245
   horizontal, 11–12, 48–49, 305
   judicial activism and, 50–51
   mimesis and, 186
   standard, 281
   vertical, 11–12, 48–49, 245, 305
predictability, 118–19, 130–31, 183
preemption (of state law), 3, 41–42
preponderance of the evidence, 250
presumptive positivism. *See* positivism, legal: presumptive
Prichard, H. A., 149n16
Prima Paint Corp. v. Flood & Conklin Mfg. Co., 60n27

principle of permissible harm (F. M. Kamm), 107–8, 206
principles, legal, **44**, 46, 47, 86, 89–90
priority rules
   first, 243–47, 267
   second, 247–48, 253, 264–65, 267
prisoner's dilemma, 189
   moral-moral, 190–91, 265
pro tanto reasons. *See* reasons: pro tanto
promises
   to act immorally, 146–54
   forming shared intentions, 196
   in judicial oath, 61, 105, 142–56
promissory obligation, theories of, 147–54
   act-consequentialist, 147–48
   deflationary, 147–48
   free-rider, 149–50
   nonpractice, reliance-based, 150–54
   rule-consequentialist, 148–49
prostitution, 250, 276–77
proximity principle, 206–7
Pryor, William H., Jr., 109–10, 175–77
pseudorules, 111–12
public goods, 191, 215, 220, 225
public officials, 165
   demands of law upon, 170
   reasons of, 20
   rule of recognition and, 125
   use of force by, 27–34, 96–97
public schools, funding of, 79
publicity condition, 272, 280, 293
punishment, 25–26, 102–3, 171–74

Quantum Leap (television series), 156n27
Quinn, Warren, 25n30, 105n41

Rabin, Edward H., 26n33
race discrimination, 169, 262, 264
Radbruch, Gustav, 9, 129n26
Radbruch formula, 129, 239–40
Radin, Margaret Jane, 287n39
Raich, Gonzales v., 3n3, 80n17
Raiffa, Howard, 264n26
Railton, Peter, 21n14, 223n14, 271n5
random decisions, 37
   as blameworthy, 233
   as permitted by default rule, 264–67, 279, 286, 289–91

rationality, of judges, 37n10, 281–82
R.A.V. v. City of St. Paul, 245n22
Rawls, John
    on concept/conception distinction, 100n30
    on fact of reasonable pluralism, 75
    on moral significance of consequences, 182n4
    on natural duty, 164–66, 170
    on nonideal theory, 181n1
    on political obligation, 158n2, 160n7, 162, 170
    on promising, 149n16
    on publicity condition, 272n7
Raz, Joseph
    on authority, 124–25, 132–35
    on conform/comply distinction, 159
    on definition of "positivism," 99n26
    on duty to obey the law, 103n37, 159–60
    on exclusionary reasons, 21n13, 113–15
    as exclusive positivist, 85n46
    on gaps in the law, 46n48, 46n49
    on legal duties of judges, 57n7
    on norm-applying institutions, 28n38
    on promising, 146n8
    on rule of law, 102
    on sources thesis, 98n19
realism, legal, 38
reasonable doubt, 42n32, 250–52
reasonable suspicion, 7
reasons
    all-things-considered, **21**
    appraisal, **22**, 214
    collective, 191–98
    discounting, 299–302
    exclusionary, **21**, 126, 134n46, 144, 156
        Joseph Raz on, 113–15, 117
    guidance, **22**
    impartial, **20**, 115, 119, 144
    legal, **20**, 23
    moral, **20**, 126–41
    natural, **23**, 78, 104, 182, 226
    objective, **21**, 185, 215, 221, 223
    of partiality, **20**, 119
    practical, **19**, 197
    preferential, **19–20**
    prima facie, 21n9
    private, **19–20**, 144–45, 166–67, 177
        to deviate, 54–55, 115
    pro tanto, **21**
    prudential, **19–20**, 125–26, 271, 288
    residual, 154
    role, **20**
    subjective, **21–22**
    theoretical, **19**
rebuttable presumption, **239**–43, 292
recourse roles, **42**–43
recusal
    to avoid difficult cases, 36–37
    for conflict of interest, 5, 54–57
    failure as basis for discipline, 62n42
    as option, 92
    reasons against, 113, 177–78
    for religious reasons, 29n43, 110, 174–78
Regan, Donald H., 113n11
regulation (of decisions by legal standards), 39–40, 77, 92, 299–300
Reibetanz (now Moreau), Sophia, 105n40
reliance, 118–19, 123, 126, 130, 150–54
religion, free exercise of, 80
religious beliefs (as basis for deviation), 10, 35, 88, 108–10
religious persecution, 9
remote applicability, 40
remote/local distinction, 204–6
removal (from office), 36, 68–70, 271, 312
rent control, 229–30
repugnant conclusions, 222
reputation
    as incentive to adhere, 71, 106, 189, 265, 268–69, 288–89
    as incentive to perform judicial duties, 37
resignation, judicial, 57n8, 89n64, 92–93, 144, 174–78
    calls for, 7, 68
resources, decisional, 131–32
respect (for lawmakers), 137–40
restitution, 24–26, 31–32, 103–4

restrictive rule, **114**–15, 231–32, 309–12
  Alan Goldman on, 183–85, 236, 292
  as codified, 117
  constraint model and, 294–97
  formalism and, 292–94
  Griswold v. Connecticut and, 273–76
  as guidance rule, 237–40
  legal pragmatism and, 305
  promulgating, 119–22
  psychological burdens of, 285–91
  reasons to obey, 126–41, 145–78, 268
  as social norm, 287
result-oriented judging, 50–52
retributivism, 25, 78, 171–74
reversal
  of horizontal precedent, 49–50, 70–71
  as incentive to adhere, 70–72, 288
  of lower court decision.
      See appeals
  of vertical precedent, 49
Revesz, Richard L., 5n11, 129n28
Reynolds, William L., 284n36
rhetoric, judicial, 138, 311
Richardson, Henry S., 49n59, 291n44
Richman, William M., 284n36
Ridge, Michael, 14n55, 93n6
Riggs v. Palmer, 44
rights
  constitutional, 51, 94, 276
  as correlated with duties, 22
  of justice, **23**–27, 30, 32–33, 308
  legal, 26, 30, 78, 150, 153, 273
  natural, 23–25, 32–33, 308
  natural executive, 25, 31
  samaritan, **23**, 24, 26, 146–47, 308
risk, 23, 210, 223–28, 234–36, 273
Rizzo, Mario J., 199–200
role morality, 4
roles, natural, 97
Romer v. Evans, 274–79, 284
Roper v. Simmons, 12n49
Ross, W. D., 21n9
Roth, Abraham Sesshu, 194n42
Rovane, Carol, 192, 194n41
Rubin, Paul H., 71n100, 72n105
rule guidance, 295–301
rule of law, 4, 15, 43, 81

crossing threshold as destroying, 236, 243, 289, 313
formal legality as conception of, 100–102, 116–17
judicial candor and, 273
as reason to adhere, 11, 105–6, 108, 188, 206, 302
as reducing unpredictability, 280
restrictive rule and, 287
selective optimization as upholding, 293
traditional conception of, 179, 313
rule worship, 135n49
rules
  adherence
    codified, 58–61
    Group O and, 203
    promulgation of, 123–24
    as serious rules, 111–12
  adjudication, 56–57, 136–37, 143–45, 156–58, 162–64
  appraisal, 123–24, 219, 233–34, 237
  closure, 46
  conduct, 57n11, 118, 123, 132, 158, 272n6
  decision. *See* decision rules
  guidance, 123–24, 219, 233–52, 267, 311
  impure, **115**
  legal, 40, **40**
    determinacy of, 84
    deviation from, 42–45, 130
    judicial discretion and, 90
    practical difference thesis and, 297–302
    revising, 280–81
    as serious rules, 292–94
  mandatory, **57**, 85, **113**–14, 159
  moderate, **115**
  nonpermissive, **115**, 309–10
    agent-relative principles and, 205–10
    contractualism and, 136–37
    judicial oath and, 155–56
    systemic effects and, 181–92, 230
  permissive, **115**
    contrasted with selective optimization, 292–96
    as guidance rule, 237

rules (*continued*)
    in hyposensitive systems, 198
    judicial duty to obey, 163–68
    judicial oath and, 144–47
    reasons to obey, 119–26, 132–37
  pure, **115**
  restrictive. *See* restrictive rule
  serious, 111–12, 124, 131n36, 115n15, 240, 292–94
  of thumb, **124**, 131
rule-sensitive particularism.
    See particularism: rule-sensitive
Rumble, Wilfred E., 98n17
Russell, Mrs. (fictional marijuana user), 10

Sachs, Stephen E., 146n13
Sagoff, Mark, 242n20
Salmon, Marylynn, 169n32
samaritanism, 167. *See also* rights: samaritan
San Antonio v. Rodriguez, 79n9
sanctions, for deviating, 58, 61–62, 67, 70, 268, 287. *See also* discipline, judicial
Sankar, Sambhav N., 53n81, 57n9, 61n32, 64n64, 71n102
Santa Fe Independent School District v. Doe, 80n14
Saphire, Richard B., 109n51
Sarat, Austin, 28n37
Sartorius, Rolf, 83n33, 159n5
Sarver, Tammy A., 71n100
Scalia, Antonin
  on creation of new rights, 51n71
  on flogging statute, 128–29
  on formalism and textualism, 292n3
  opinions in sexual orientation cases, 275–77, 279, 284
  on wishful thinking by judges, 86
Scanlon, T. M., 23n20, 136, 143n5, 150–54, 216
Schapiro, Tamar, 181n1
Schauer, Frederick
  on arguments for rules, 119–21, 133n40
  on asymmetry of authority, 134n45
  on definition of "positivism," 99n25
  on easy cases, 39n14
  on error, 132n38
  on exclusionary reasons, 113n11, 114–15
  on gap cases, 46n49
  on judicial incentives, 37n7
  on legal standards, 44n43
  on locality, 40n18
  on mandatory rules, 57n10
  on negative-gap cases, 83n33
  on particularism, 94n7
  on precedent, 280n29
  on pressure to deviate, 179
  on presumptive positivism, 240n17, 292
  on rules, 15n57, 48, 124
  on rule-sensitive particularism, 124, 293
  on rule-worship, 135n49
  on slippery slopes, 199n55
  on unwritten rules, 270n1
Scheffler, Samuel, 14n55, 105n40
Schmidtz, David, 206n6
Searle, John, 192
segregation, racial, 99, 169
selective optimization, **267**–75, 279–307 *passim*, 311–13
  internalizing, 285–86
self help (legal concept), 24, 26–27
self-defense, 24, 27, 31, 175
self-effacing theories, 286
Sensenbrenner, F. James, Jr., 7
sentencing, mandatory minima, 47, 79, 230
separability thesis, 97
separation of powers, 10, 140–41
settlement function (of law), 118, 293
sex with minors, 172–74. *See also* child molestation
sexual orientation, 230, 274–79, 282
Shaman, Jeffrey, 61–64, 66
Shapiro, David, 271n3
Shapiro, Martin, 273n12
Shapiro, Scott J.
  adapting Michael Bratman's work, 197
  on conservatives, 82
  as exclusive positivist, 85n46
  on indeterminacy, 84n36
  on practical difference thesis, 297–302

on psychology of deviation, 71n103
  on rule following, 294–97
shared intentions. *See* intentions, shared
shared values, community of, 138
Shavell, Steven, 211n16
Sher, George, 181n1
Sherrer, Hans, 28n37
Sherwin, Emily
  on coordination and efficiency, 120n35
  on defiance of rules, 39n15
  on formalism, 292–94
  on gaps, 83 n33, 134–35
  on indeterminacy, 85 n43
  on legal principles, 89 n65
  on particularism, 94 n7
  on posited rules, 43n39
  on promises, 146 n10
  on pure rules, 115
  on renegade officials, 47n55
  on rule-sensitive particularism, 124n7
  on serious rules, 112
  on settlement function of law, 118n
  on unwritten rules, 270n1
Shklar, Judith N., 100n28, 100n29, 101n31
side-effect/aspect distinction, 107–8, 204, 206
Sidgwick, Henry, 271n5
Siegel, Neil S., 18n62
Simmons, A. John, 25n30, 32n52, 103n37, 159, 162
Simon, Dan, 13n52
Simon, William H., 16n58, 81n27
Singer, Joseph, 84n38
Singer, Peter, 206n6
single privileges (Hohfeldian), 24n26
slavery
  rulings on, 27–28, 88–89, 303
  as unjust, 9–10, 82–83, 93, 169, 239–40
slippery-slope arguments, 199–201
Slote, Michael A., 23n20
Smith, M. B. E.
  on cheating by appellate courts, 5n10, 83n34
  on duty to obey the law, 103n37, 159
  on judicial nullification, 4n9, 5n17, 127n12
Smith, Matthew Noah, 197

Smith, Michael, 223n14
Smith, Steven D., 4n9, 6n17, 127
social fact thesis, 97, 197
social norms, 214, 270, 276, 287–88
sodomy, 109, 275–79, 282, 284
Solum, Lawrence B., 84n35, 84n37, 84n39, 109n51, 303–4
Songer, Donald R., 71n100
Soper, Philip, 126, 138
sources thesis, 97
Sowell, Thomas, 6n18
stability, 120, 183
stare decisis, 127n15, 213, 280–81, 287. *See also* precedent
Stark, Cynthia A., 22n16
state of nature, 23–24, 26, 31–33, 167, 308
State Oil Co. v. Khan, 49n62
States v. Schooner Peggy, 60n27
statutory construction, 51, 111
Stavropoulos, Nicos, 44n41
step goods, 235n4
Stern, Gerald, 52n75, 63–64, 66n77
Stewart, Potter, 60n27, 95n10, 272n8
Strauss, David A., 80n22, 81n27
Stump v. Sparkman, 62n38
subjective reasons. *See* reasons: subjective
suboptimal results, **75**
  examples of, 79–80
subplans, **195n43**
suicide, 92n2
  assisted, 109, 250, 259. *See also* euthanasia
Suleiman, Ramzi, 235n4
Sullivan, Kathleen M., 101n33
Sulmasy, Daniel P., 143n5, 155n24
summary judgment, 54n87
Summers, Robert S., 43n38, 101n31, 127
Sunstein, Cass R.
  on agent-relative principles, 211n16
  on availability cascades, 235n5, 236n6
  on *Bush v. Gore*, 6n20
  on critical legal studies, 85n41
  on discrimination, 278n27
  judicial minimalism of, 283–85
  on moral heuristics, 210n12
Sypnowich, Christine, 100n28

systemic effects, **181**–85
  agent-relative principles and, 203–8
  Alan H. Goldman on, 187–93
  complicity and, 225–26
  as imperceptible, 220–21
  of rule revision, 281

Talley, Eric, 236n6, 297n13
Tamanaha, Brian Z.
  on *Brown v. Board of Education*, 81, 99
  on indeterminacy, 85, 111n2
  on rule of law, 100n28, 116–17, 287n38
Temkin, Larry S., 222n13
Ten Commandments, 80
Tennessee Senate, 69
terror bomber (in double effect debates), 106
terrorists, 22
Thayer, James B., 50n68
Thomas, Clarence, 35
Thomson, Judith Jarvis, 24n27, 27n36, 31n48, 223n14
threats, blocking of, 29–30, 95
threshold. *See* deviation density threshold
threshold, epistemic, 88, 250n29
threshold principles, 204, 208–11
treating like cases alike, 239, 246, 255–60. *See also* comparative justice
triggers, 223–24, 226–28, 235
Tuomela, Raimo, 192–94
Tushnet, Mark, 41n22, 84n38
Tyler, Tom R., 31n50
type-selective deviation. *See* deviation: type-selective
type/token distinction, 246n25

ultra vires, official actions taken, **30**, 168–69
uncertainty, 234
undermining principle, **34**, 182, 308–9
  arguments for, 96–110
Unger, Roberto Mangabeira, 85, 100n28
unjust laws
  Augustine on, 87
  deviating from, 88
  duty to obey, 9, 160, 168–70, 247
  John Rawls on, 164–66
  Radbruch formula on, 239
unjust war, 169, 175
utilitarianism, 236

Van Alstyne, William, 256n6
Velleman, J. David, 19n4, 192–94, 196
Vermeule, Adrian, 133n42, 211n16
Vila, Marisa Iglesias, 46n47
violence (of law), 28
virtue ethics, 23, 210
Volcansek, Mary L., 68n86
Volokh, Eugene, 199n55

Wald, Patricia M., 12n52, 28n37
Waldron, Jeremy
  on deviation, 127n18
  on duty to aid, 206n6
  on natural rights, 25n28
  opposition to judicial review, 41n22
  on rule of law, 102n34
Walen, Alec, 115n19
Walker, A. D. M., 158n2, 164n16
Walton, Douglas, 199n55, 200n57
Waluchow, W. J., 44n41, 84n39, 89n63, 298n18
Warren, Earl, 17, 80–81
Wasserstrom, Richard A., 16n58, 78n8, 159
Wechsler, Herbert, 81n24, 81n28
Weick, Karl E., 73n110
Weinstein, Jack B., 5n17, 60n28
Welch, Ivo, 235n5
Wellman, Christopher Heath, 158n2, 167n29
Wenar, Leif, 24n25, 24n26, 30n45
West, Robin, 127
Westen, Peter, 256n6
Whitman, Douglas Glen, 199–200
Williams, Bernard, 33n56, 272n7
Winston, Ken, 257n8
Wolf, Susan, 20n6
Wolff, Robert Paul, 159, 159n4
women, injustices against, 169
Woodard, Calvin, 302n20

Yeazell, Stephen C., 53n81

Zapf, Christian, 84n39
Zimmerman, Michael J., 207n7
Zipursky, Benjamin C., 98n18